STRUCTURING CHANGE

Effective Practice for Common Client Problems

Also Available from Lyceum Books

ADOLESCENTS IN FOSTER FAMILIES, edited by Jane Aldgate, Anthony Maluccio, and Christine Reeves

MODERN SOCIAL WORK THEORY: A CRITICAL INTRODUCTION, by Malcolm Payne, foreword by Stephen C. Anderson

WOMEN AND SOCIAL WORK: TOWARDS A WOMEN-CENTERED PRACTICE, by Jalna Hanmer and Daphne Statham, introduction by Betty Sancier

WORKING WITH CHILDREN AND THEIR FAMILIES, by Martin Herbert, introduction by Charles Zastrow

THE NEW POLITICS OF WELFARE: AN AGENDA FOR THE 1990s?, edited by Michael McCarthy, preface by Thomas Meenaghan

SCHOOL SOCIAL WORK: PRACTICE AND RESEARCH PERSPECTIVES, Second Edition, edited by Robert Constable, John P. Flynn, and Shirley McDonald

STRUCTURING CHANGE

Effective Practice for Common Client Problems

Edited by

KEVIN CORCORAN
Graduate School of Social Work
University of Houston

Once again, to G. Olivetti.
And to Beaudroux Boy-Bob Wilson, Professor
Moriarty, and the future on Pacifica Cliffs.

© Lyceum Books, Inc. 1992

Published in the United States by
LYCEUM BOOKS, INC.
59 East Van Buren, Ste. 703
Chicago, Illinois 60605

Library of Congress Cataloging-in-Publication Data

Structuring Change: Effective practice for common client problems
    Kevin Corcoran
        p.   cm.
    Includes bibliographical references.
    ISBN 0-925065-14-5
    1. Psychiatric social work—United States.   I. Corcoran, Kevin
(Kevin J.)
    [DNLM: 1. Mental Disorders—therapy.   2. Social Work, Psychiatric—
methods.   WM 30.5 S927]
HV690.U6S77   1992
362.2'0973—dc20
DNLM/DLC
for Library of Congress   91-43836
                                                               CIP

Contents

Tables and Figures

Contributors

Cobb, Norman H., PhD, Assistant Professor, Graduate School of Social Work, University of Texas, Arlington, Texas.

Corcoran, Kevin, PhD, Associate Professor, Graduate School of Social Work, University of Houston, Houston, Texas.

Fischer, Joel, DSW, Professor, School of Social Work, University of Hawaii, Honolulu, Hawaii.

Galan, Fernando J., PhD, Associate Professor, Department of Social Work, University of Texas at Pan American, Edinburgh, Texas.

Gingerich, Wallace J., PhD, Professor, Mandell School of Social Work, Case Western Reserve University, Cleveland, Ohio.

Gochros, Harvey L., DSW, Professor, School of Social Work, University of Hawaii, Honolulu, Hawaii.

Grinnell, Richard M., Jr., PhD, Professor, Faculty of Social Welfare, University of Calgary, Calgary, Alberta, Canada.

Ivanoff, André, PhD, Assistant Professor, School of Social Work, Columbia University, New York, New York.

Jordan, Catheleen, PhD, Associate Professor, Graduate School of Social Work, University of Texas, Arlington, Texas.

Keeper, Cele, MSW, CSW-ACP, Private Practitioner, Houston, Texas.

Kirk, Stuart A., DSW, Professor, School of Social Work, Columbia University, New York, New York.

LeCroy, Craig Winston, PhD, Associate Professor, School of Social Work, Arizona State University, Tempe, Arizona.

Nugent, William R., PhD, Director, Florida Network of Youth and Family Services, Tallahassee, Florida.

Smyth, Nancy J., PhD, Assistant Professor, School of Social Work, University at Buffalo, State University of New York.

Thyer, Bruce A., PhD, Professor, School of Social Work, University of Georgia, Athens, Georgia, and Department of Psychiatry and Health Behavior, Medical College of Georgia.

Van Den Bergh, Nan, PhD, Director, Staff and Faculty Service Center, University of California, Los Angeles, California.

Vandiver, Vikki, DrPh, Assistant Professor, Graduate School of Social Work, University of Texas, Arlington, Texas.

Videka-Sherman, Lynn, PhD, Dean and Associate Professor, School of Social Work, State University of New York, Albany, New York.

Wells, Richard A., MSW, Professor, School of Social Work, University of Pittsburgh, Pittsburgh, Pennsylvania.

Preface

The theme of *Structuring Change* is how to do effective clinical social work. In part one, the first two chapters review some of the current knowledge about what makes for effective intervention; namely, structure. The theme of effective practice is furthered in the third chapter by considering how to evaluate your practice. As is true throughout the book, evaluation is approached from the perspective of what you should do to set goals and monitor change in your clinical work; consequently, the emphasis is more on good social work than on good research. The goal is to show you how to do evaluation in a practical, informative manner.

The chapters in part two are organized around common client problems. Each chapter presents a specific problem, shows how you can assess the problem, and delineates how you can use an effective intervention to help your client to change. The chapters, although written by different authors, are organized around a common outline that includes how to identify and assess the problem, the relevant research, the structure of the intervention (that is, how to use it), the limitations of the intervention, and how to work with related problems. The problems, of course, do not encompass all those you will find in your professional practice of social work. Most of the areas discussed, in fact, themselves warrant entire volumes, and the coverage here is limited. It was necessary in preparing *Structuring Change* to be selective, and I have tried to include a wide range of client problems. The specific methods of intervention and problems are chosen to show you how to use a variety of techniques in your practice. Each of the chapters in part two is preceded by a brief editor's note that highlights how the principles presented in *Structuring Change* are applied in that chapter.

All of the authors hope that you will find this book useful in your efforts to do clinical social work. Clearly, we have not covered all the possible social work interventions or client problems. Those covered, we hope, will provide a good start in helping you to learn to use the interventions with specific client problems.

xiv

Acknowledgments

I would like to recognize many who influenced the completion of this book. First of all, I'd like to thank the authors of the chapters; it was delightful to work with all of them. I am also grateful to Anita Samen, managing editor of Lyceum Books, David Follmer, and Thomas M. Meenaghan for their support. I would also like to acknowledge the following events, which made the preparation of the manuscript more arduous: Allyson, the tropical storm that swelled eighteen inches of Galveston Bay into my waterfront office; and Chantel, the hurricane that six weeks later undid all the repairs and further damaged the office. After these two events, I was certain that a third impediment was unlikely. But then there was Hurricane Jerry; and all those construction workers who I feared were not going to leave until the holidays, and stay to the new year.

Kevin Corcoran
Glen Cove, Kemah,
Texas
1992

PART ONE

Effective Practice

CHAPTER 1

Defining the Structure of Change: An Introduction

Kevin Corcoran
Richard M. Grinnell, Jr.

How many times has this question been asked by clinical social work students: "What am I supposed to actually do to help my clients change?" The process of helping clients requires that someone change something. The main purpose of *Structuring Change* is to consider how to help clients change. We are using the term "change" to mean planned change—that is, change that is not accidental, change that results from your social work intervention.

THE STRUCTURE OF CHANGE

We believe that clinical social workers should structure their practices systematically in order to maximize client change. The structure of practice, as presented in this book, has six basic interrelated components: (1) setting client goals, (2) setting client objectives, (3) selecting an appropriate intervention(s), (4) structuring the intervention(s), (5) establishing a contract, and (6) monitoring and evaluating the effects of the intervention (also see Duehn, 1985).

Setting Client Goals

The first component of structuring social work practice involves goal setting, which is discussed by Corcoran and Gingerich in chapter 3. Goal setting is the process that maps where you and your client are and where you want to go. Essentially, goal setting involves asking, "What do I want to accomplish throughout and by the end of treatment?" The importance of setting clearly defined, attainable goals for clinical social work practice cannot be overemphasized. Setting vague or unreasonably high goals subjects your clients to a cruel and destructive experience in disappointment, frustration, and erosion of their confidence (Wood, 1978).

3

Three important factors should be considered before setting goals with clients (Cordon and Preston-Shoot, 1987; Locke et al., 1981):

1. Specific and challenging goals are more effective in bringing about the desired client outcomes than are vague or easy-to-achieve goals.

2. Goal setting leads to more effective results when the client is involved in goal selection rather than merely having goals assigned to him or her.

3. Goals should be realistic and attainable.

Why establish goals?   There are three main reasons to establish clear goals when working with clients (Simons and Aigner, 1985):

1. The mutuality of goal selection ensures that both you and your client are engaged in the problem-solving process with the same expectations and are pursuing the same goals.

2. The process of goal selection facilitates the development and implementation of the intervention plan. In short, when goals are specifically stated, the means to attain them become more identifiable.

3. The goal-setting process provides a basis for the eventual evaluation of your intervention plan.

In summary, client goals point all parties involved in the change process in a mutually agreed-upon direction and outcome during the treatment relationship (Anderson, 1989). Some clinical examples of goal statements are:

- To be able to cope with a dying child
- To be able to have a happy marriage
- To be able to feel good about oneself

Establishing priorities among goals.   Once the purpose of treatment has been translated into a client's goal statements, the next task is to establish an order of priority for the goals. Austin, Kopp, and Smith (1986) present three criteria that are helpful in guiding the goal selection process:

- The importance of the goal to the client
- The severity or intensity of the problem addressed by the goal
- The potential for successful goal achievement

Each of these criteria should be discussed with your client before deciding which goal to work on first, second, and so on. Once realistic goals have been established and you and the client have set priorities for them, it is important to define each goal operationally in terms of specific client objectives.

②Setting Client Objectives

The second component of structuring social work practice is setting client objectives. Although goal statements provide a general set of intervention outcomes, they lack specificity. In contrast, objective statements are specific, concrete, and measurable (Coulton and Solomon, 1977; Sheafor, Horejsi, and Horejsi, 1988). For example, with what specifically would the client be expected to cope if he or she had a dying child? What change is needed and by whom for the client to be happier in a marriage? What must change relative to the client or the social environment in order for him or her to feel good about himself or herself?

Client objectives address five questions: who, what, to what extent, where, and when?

Who? Objectives must make it clear who or what specifically is to change. Is it an individual, a family, a group, an institution, an organization, or a community? For example, as LeCroy discusses in chapter 9, is there a need for change in a troubled teenager, or is it the way in which the parents interact with their child that must change?

What? The question of "what" to change typically refers to the problem areas expressed by the client upon which you both agree to work. However, "to receive family therapy," or "to receive individual counseling" does not adequately address the question. The goal should never focus on the method of intervention, but rather on what you and your client expect to see as a result of the intervention (Howe, 1974). As Van Den Berg illustrates in chapter 6 on working with depressed women from a feminist perspective, objectives might be diverted toward the attainment of more interpersonal control, assertiveness, or political activism in oppressive situations.

Over the years, these "what" questions sometimes have been referred to as client target problems. Social work practice is always geared to changing client target problems. There are three basic types of client target problems that we try to change: behaviors, feelings, and cognitions (which include knowledge levels).

For example, clinical interventions can focus on changing client behaviors, such as school truancy, eating habits, temper tantrums, substance abuse, enuresis, compulsive fire setting, excessive smoking, and physical aggression. As illustrated by Jordan and Cobb in chapter 8, this change could be in how effectively couples can communicate and negotiate responsibility.

We can also intervene to change clients' affect; that is, the way they feel toward someone, something, or themselves, including emotions such as anger, frustration, anxiety, feelings of personal inadequacies, phobias, social rejection, depression, or self-esteem. Galan illustrates the importance of work with clients' emotions in chapter 12 by showing how to work with identity problems that developed from some Mexican-American family relations.

We also can intervene to change client cognitions, such as inappropriate self-perceptions and inadequacies in processing information about oneself. For example, Corcoran and Keeper in chapter 13 illustrate how to resolve some of the perceptions of emptiness experienced by a person with borderline personality disorder. Also on a cognitive level, we even can help clients change their knowledge levels by, for example, helping them to understand the benefits of safer sex, providing information about various public assistance programs, or educating them about sexual dysfunctions. Gochros in chapter 11 illustrates this in his discussion of the importance of the role of knowledge level when working with persons who are HIV positive.

There are, of course, times when the client change covers more than one target area. For example, in chapter 4 Thyer shows how to work with a client's anxiety (affect) in order to improve specific social behaviors (action). In chapter 15, Wells illustrates this by discussing how certain cognitive behaviors may need to be restructured for a client to develop and maintain interpersonal relations.

The important point to remember in changing clients' action, affect, or cognition (including knowledge levels), is that any change must be in a planned and desired direction (Saxton, 1979). In addition to helping clients change their target problems, we also can help them to cope with their target problems, such as by helping them to adjust to their local communities after hospitalizations. One illustration of this is provided by Vandiver and Kirk (chapter 5), who show how to do therapeutic case management with persons with schizophrenia. In short, we are always working to maintain, increase, or decrease (in the desired direction) some aspect(s) of the client's functioning relative to one or more target problems that involve some specific action, affect, or cognition.

To what extent?   The objectives that are designed to realize the broader goals should also consider the degree of change that is needed. The intent here is to provide you and the client with an idea of the magnitude of expected outcome of the intervention. Both you and the client are trying to determine, in advance of your intervention, what will constitute an acceptable level of change relative to the target problem. Will the decrease of physical abuse of one's spouse by 90 percent constitute success? Will a reduction of a child's truancy from every day to once or twice a week be considered a success? Will the reduction of the number of family arguments from every time they have dinner to only once a month constitute success? How much change, and in what, is needed for a client to be considered successful in coping with a dying child? How much change and by whom will reflect happiness in a marriage? And how much change in what about the client is necessary for him or her to feel good about himself or herself?

Where?   Many of your clients' target problems occur in specific settings or at specific times during the day. For example, Breanne may get aggressive only at school (a setting). Or, Ray may get depressed only at school (a setting). Or, Ray may get depressed only during the evening (a time). The answer to this question helps to orient you and the client as to where specifically to look for the expected outcome (Kenmore, 1987).

When?   This question establishes the time frame within which the expected outcome is supposed to occur. A realistic time frame must be established by a negotiation between you and the client. When setting specific dates for resolution of the client's target problem, the motivational levels of everyone engaged in the change process are likely to increase. Although this implies that the goals and objectives should be time limited, it does not necessarily mean that the intervention itself is short term or lacking in continuity. For example, Fischer (in chapter 10) illustrates the need for an ongoing maintenance program with recovering substance abusers, and Vandiver and Kirk (in chapter 5) assert that case management has time-limited goals but, as a social treatment, must be continuous. In contrast, certain interventions, such as Nugent's illustration of single-session mediation (chapter 14), are by design time limited. Regardless of the length of the intervention, you and your client should determine when it is reasonable to reach a goal.

Examples of objective statements.   Below are three examples of client objectives that incorporate the characteristics of the above main points:

1. Connie (who), within one month (when), will have decreased her depression (what) at home while caring for her dying child (where) by 25 points (to what extent) as measured on a standardized depression scale.
2. Mr. and Ms. Olivetti (who), within six months (when), will have increased their level of sexual satisfaction and other pleasurable leisure activities (what) at home (where) by 40 percent (to what extent) as measured on the standardized Passionate Love Scale and Index of Sexual Satisfaction.

3. Mr. Yachats's (who) emotional swings of fondness and contempt toward women (what) at work and in interpersonal settings (where) will decrease in frequency from daily mood swings to less than once per week (to what extent) within six months (when).

These types of goals and objectives are illustrated in the client target problems discussed in *Structuring Change*. The problems—and resulting goals and objectives—are typical of those encountered by social workers in a variety of clinical practice settings. The chapters in this book reflect a broad range of client problems, such as suicide, anxiety, phobia, schizophrenia, marital conflict, drug and alcohol abuse, depression, adjustment to living with HIV, disputes, social and interpersonal problems, identity problems, and troubled youth. In addition, each chapter considers a range of related client problems, allowing generalization from a specific application of an intervention to its application to other problems.

The client target problems covered in *Structuring Change* are presented in various practice settings, including hospitals, residential programs, outpatient clinics, group practices, and just about anywhere that clients are found. Frequently, each client problem is illustrated in terms of various actions, affects, or cognitions specific to the problem. By varying the problems and the settings within which they are addressed, we hope to highlight the important but subtle differences that get played out with respect to the client's specific problem. For example, Ivanoff and Smyth (in chapter 7) illustrate the different aspects of suicidal behaviors and demonstrate how to set specifically tailored goals and objectives for, e.g., suicidal ideation, para-suicidal intent, or suicidal action.

Selecting an Intervention

The third component of structuring social work practice is selecting an appropriate intervention that has been demonstrated to work on the client's target problem (Compton and Galaway, 1989). *Structuring Change* provides directives for working with a variety of different intervention strategies that are appropriate for use with several specific client target problems. The main intent is to show how to actually help clients change by using specific treatment interventions that have been demonstrated to be effective with specific problems. This does not imply that any one intervention is guaranteed to be effective. Even the most proven and apparently straightforward intervention has subtleties that can facilitate or inhibit its impact on changing a client's problem.

Because of the complexity of human behavior, the selection of an appropriate intervention strategy is extremely difficult. Moreover, because no single intervention is appropriate for every client problem, the variety of different presenting problems demands a variety of different treatment interventions. In part, this is why *Structuring Change* provides so many diverse intervention strategies.

In short, the task of the clinician is to match each client's particular target problem with the most effective and efficient intervention available. The intent is to maximize the fit between the intervention and the client's problem and avoid the temptation to redefine the problem to fit some preferred intervention (Fischer, 1978). Further, a tried-and-true intervention that is applied inappropriately to a client's problem is of little use. The interventions presented in this book are not the only effective means to bring about change in the problems that are discussed. The interventions do represent, however, a variety of structured approaches whose efficacy has been documented in the references that accompany them.

The treatment interventions presented in *Structuring Change* derived from a variety of different theoretical orientations. Several are based on a combination of theories. Admittedly, the theoretical orientation implicit in many of the accompanying chapters, or at least some of the specific techniques used in the suggested interventions, are based on social learning theory. This is because there is a lot of research literature available to support the effectiveness of interventions that are based on this theory. Additional intervention perspectives include a feminist view of treating persons with depression, conflict and conflict resolution theory, psychodynamics, gestalt, and family theories.

Whenever possible and appropriate, the treatment intervention has tried to avoid relying on a single theoretical perspective. This is important because few interventions are based on one theoretical framework. Planned short-term treatment, as illustrated by Wells in chapter 15, may be primarily a social learning approach, but it also draws on communication and interpersonal theories, a fact that speaks to its theoretical pluralism. Similarly, the discussion by Jordan and Cobb (chapter 8) concerning the role of social competency in dysfunctional relations reflects a social learning theory perspective tempered by social exchange theory. Van Den Bergh's chapter on feminist intervention with depression draws from several diverse theories and emphasizes the roles of power and politics.

It could be argued, and in fact should be argued, that all of the proposed interventions are "behaviorally grounded," in that each is designed to help clients change behaviors, whether in the form of an action, an affect, or a cognition. It is hard to imagine a clinical social work intervention that is designed to do anything other than to change at least some specific aspect of behavior, either in the client system or in some facet of the broader social environment.

Although the proposed intervention strategies apply to a particular set of social and psychological problems, each chapter also considers the application of the approach to related problems. For example, in chapter

5, Vandiver and Kirk discuss the use of case management with persons troubled by schizophrenia. Within this context, they also consider how the strategy may be adapted for use with other chronic mental disorders and why it may not be the method of choice for certain personality disorders, such as borderline or narcissistic personalities. As was discussed earlier, this discussion of related client target problems allows for generalization of the interventions to other client problems.

4 Structuring the Intervention

The fourth component of structuring social work practice refers to those identifiable elements of the intervention process that are associated with treatment effectiveness. Clearly, as discussed by Corcoran and Videka-Sherman in chapter 2, we have not identified all of the elements related to effective practice. However, there is reason to believe that by incorporating into one's own practice routine those elements that are known, there is a greater likelihood that one will help clients to change (Bloom and Fischer, 1982).

In general, the structure of effective practice refers to guidelines for using a specific intervention, well-defined and well-organized components of the intervention itself, and the appropriate fit between the intervention and the client's particular problem. Structure is not based on any one specific theory. The theoretical nature of structure, then, makes it possible to enhance the chances of helping the client regardless of the theory or theories behind the intervention.

This is not to imply that theory is inconsequential to social work practice. The theories we employ in practice guide our understanding of clients and their problems; the specific techniques that flow from them, however, can be structured in a variety of ways. For example, even the most dogmatic behaviorist needs to be empathic, and the ego-oriented practitioner uses a subtle form of the behavioral principle of exposure when working with the anxiety associated with narcissism.

We are not suggesting that all theories are equally valid or useful. We simply are asserting that the most effective treatments are based more on what is actually done, within a specific structure, relative to a client system, than on the theory one uses to understand the client. The structure of the intervention should be designed to enhance the probability of effectively helping clients to change, regardless of—and sometimes in spite of—the theory.

All the interventions in the chapters that follow are practical and are considered to be effective with the particular problem with which they are linked. They are presented in a way that will help you to apply them with a variety of clients. Some are presented in a step-by-step fashion to facilitate effective learning and accurate implementation. Interventions that are clearly specified and delineated are not only easier to learn, but also tend to be more effective because they can be implemented with more specificity.

However, not all the interventions covered in the book are highly structured. In part, this is because some techniques are simply less structured and more experiential in nature. Be that as it may, the authors have presented these interventions with specificity and guidelines for their use. When using less-structured interventions, you have to do slightly more of the work of providing the structure. This is not difficult to do and will become routine as you learn to tailor the intervention to the client problem. Even seemingly less-structured interventions can be defined clearly by delineating what specific techniques are to be used, defining the client problems and goals, and contracting with specificity. When a less-structured intervention is used, it should be designed to maximize its effectiveness by including the components that have been identified as associated with effective outcomes. By focusing on the available structure and by designing the treatment plan to maximize the structure, you should find that the intervention is not only more effective, but also easier to learn and more readily applicable to a range of social work practice situations.

The client, too, will need to participate actively in the intervention process. This includes not only goal setting, as we discussed above, but also in-session activities and outside homework assignments. The client may need to experience emotional catharsis, practice a new behavior or skill, or restructure a faulty thought process, as well as continue the efforts at change outside the session. Homework assignments are designed to help generalize what is acquired in the session to the client's natural environment. Again, the change that the client is trying to make in the psychologically safe environment of the sessions may include any action, affect, or cognition.

In summary, the treatment intervention must be appropriate for the client's target problem and the client must participate in its implementation. Even the most highly regarded and scientifically sound treatment intervention will not be effective if applied inappropriately to a client problem. For example, individual therapy is rarely effective when applied to marital problems.

Establishing a Contract

The fifth component of structuring social work practice is to formulate a treatment contract. A contract is essentially an agreement between the clinician and the client (Maluccio and Marlow, 1974; Saxton, 1979; Cordon and Preston-Shoot, 1987; Rothery, 1980). It should cover at least the following dimensions:

1. The client's target problem, toward which both the clinician and client will work.
2. The specific responsibilities of the clinician and client in terms of rights and obligations.
3. The specific treatment intervention to be used in resolving the target problem and achieving the target goals.
4. The administrative procedures and constraints involved, such as when to meet, where to meet, time, costs.

In a nutshell, a treatment contract should spell out *who, will do what, to what extent, under what conditions,* and *when.* The contract should be sufficiently explicit and detailed so that each participant understands clearly what is expected of him or her in the treatment process. The contract enhances a client's motivation to change. Notice how closely the contract relates to the establishment of treatment objectives mentioned above.

Monitoring and Evaluating

The final components of structuring social work practice are the monitoring and evaluating of progress toward the resolution of the client's target problem, as Corcoran and Gingerich discuss in chapter 3. When practice is structured to enhance effectiveness, it should include some systematic method of monitoring and evaluating whether progress is being made toward the resolution of the client's target problem (Nelsen, 1988; Howe, 1974). Monitoring and evaluating practice are integral parts of effective treatment when they facilitate the change process and assure relevant feedback within a confidential atmosphere (Grinnell, 1991; Grinnell and Williams, 1990; Bloom and Fischer, 1982).

STRUCTURING CHANGE AND CLIENT MOTIVATION

People seeking social work treatment bring with them widely varying degrees of motivation or commitment to change. Lack of motivation can be problematic with clients who are not voluntary, such as a child on probation or a husband forced into marital treatment. Even voluntary clients may need their motivation enhanced.

Often clients will ask clinicians to "change my husband; make him drink less" or to "get my parents to stop nagging me." Even the voluntary client often asks to change some antecedent condition or a consequence of a behavior, but says "don't change my behavior." It is not until the client comes to terms with the need to change some specific action, affect, or cognition that he or she is motivated.

We believe that one way to help motivate clients is to use structured interventions. This includes setting specific and realistic goals, and you might need to discuss with clients the need to focus on some behavior of theirs rather than of someone else. Moreover, structuring treatment and actively involving clients in the entire treatment process, as this chapter illustrates, will help clients to move forward to realistic change. Monitoring and evaluating, as demonstrated in chapter 3, helps clients see how they are changing. Actively participating in and knowing what is involved in the treatment process, along with seeing that things are getting better, probably influences client motivation. We think that structuring treatment results in more motivated clients.

SUMMARY

This chapter discusses some components of practice that are considered essential to maximizing client change. It is based on the assumption that the effectiveness of practice is in large part a consequence of the extent to which these components are incorporated systematically into the structure of the intervention plan.

One overriding guideline in the structure of change is specificity. An intervention is more likely to be effective if its intended purpose, the client's target problems, and the treatment protocol all are specific. The following questions provide a framework that will help to structure your intervention:

1. What are the specific client's target problems to be changed?
2. What are the specific goals to be pursued?
3. What specific treatment interventions are to be selected in relation the client's target problems?
4. How, specifically, will treatment interventions be structured? What specific homework will the client do after each session?
5. What, specifically, will the treatment contract include about who will do what, to what extent, under what conditions, and by when?
6. How will it be determined when the client's target problems have been resolved or the goals of treatment have been reached?

The client must be involved actively in answering these questions. This client involvement includes not only defining the problem and setting the goals of treatment, but also the actual process of making change within and outside the treatment setting (i.e., client homework). This active participation means that the clinician must be more than a blank screen against which the client reflects his or her feelings. To enhance effectiveness, the clinician also will need to help the client by problem solving, role modeling, confronting, reinforcing, giving advice; in essence, by actively working toward change with the client.

A Concluding Remark

There are, of course, other salient components to effectively helping clients than those discussed in *Structuring Change*. We have identified some of the most important ones. It is advisable to incorporate these components into those interventions that are less structured. Although additional components will be identified in the individual chapters that follow and by future research, we believe that interventions that are designed to include these components greatly enhance your ability to help your clients change.

CHAPTER 2

Some Things We Know about Effective Clinical Social Work

Kevin Corcoran

Lynn Videka-Sherman

INTRODUCTION

This chapter provides specifics on how you can do effective clinical social work, by which we mean what we currently think works in helping clients to resolve problems and reach goals. When you ask yourself, "What am I supposed to *do* to help this particular client change?" you are essentially asking, "What, if anything, works?" In the social work literature, these questions have been approached with both cynicism and blind faith. Recently, as we discuss later, reviews of research have been quite encouraging about the effectiveness of social work practice, as well as about which characteristics of social work practice seem to help clients.

In this chapter, we review some of the more salient conclusions about what helps clients change. There probably are thousands of research studies about various aspects of helping specific client problems; we focus here on the more practical findings about what to do to help your client change. These conclusions can help you to design your social work interventions to enhance the likelihood of effectively helping your clients change. We will consider two major sources of findings: (1) traditional literature reviews and (2) quantitative literature reviews, which statistically synthesize research findings.

Traditional literature reviews are articles that evaluate previous research studies in order to reach general or specific conclusions. Such reviews, much like the clinical observations that go into practice wisdom, are subject to extraneous influences. For example, in reviews of the effectiveness of psychological treatment, completely different conclusions have been reached from the very same research studies (see Light and Pillemer, 1984). Different conclusions also have been reached on the same studies when reviewed by social workers (Reid and Hanrahan, 1982; Fischer, 1983). Light and Pillemer (1984) observed that the conclusions of literature reviews often support the reviewer's belief, regardless of the data. Even when these limitations are taken into consideration, literature reviews provide several important conclusions for you to consider in your efforts to help your clients.

Quantitative literature reviews, the second major source considered in this chapter, are based on statistical analysis of research findings, which is called meta-analysis. The traditional review is essentially discussion, whereas meta-analysis is data based. The assertions that we make, based on these sources, about what you can do to help your clients should not be considered conclusive; they may reflect some of the application of the current research knowledge in the field, but should be used as working hypotheses of what you can do to be more effective. The suggestions in this chapter are designed to help define the structure of change; throughout your work, however, you will need to use your experiential observation of what is effective along with empirical knowledge.

TRADITIONAL LITERATURE REVIEWS

In social work literature, there are several seminal works that draw useful conclusions about practice effectiveness. These reviews vary not only in the criteria used to include and exclude studies from consideration, but also in the overall conclusions reached.

One of the earliest reviews of the research literature on the impact of social work interventions was by Mullen, Dumpson and Associates (1972). These authors discussed several studies of professional social work practice, and reached the general understanding that the research evidence was far from conclusive and does not indicate that social work intervention is either effective or ineffective.

A more definitive, and thus controversial, conclusion was argued by Fischer (1973a), who reviewed eleven studies of social casework. Fischer included only studies that used a control group (such as a no-treatment control or a control with a different type of intervention), were of casework in the United States, and were not of nonprofessional social caseworkers (unless the group was included as a control). He concluded that nine of the eleven studies showed that social caseworkers "were unable to bring about any positive, significant, measurable changes in their clients beyond those that would have occurred without the specific intervention program or that could have been induced by nonprofessionals . . ." (p. 13). Additionally, Fischer noted the lack of part of what we are calling structure; namely, the nature of the casework techniques was not adequately defined, making it difficult to determine what was being done and whether it was effective or ineffective. He speculated that this may be a result of the nature of social work theory and practice, which also lacked specific definitions. Similarly, he noted little effort to control for different types of clients in relation to differential treatment approach. He asserted that these factors do not prohibit the conclusion that social casework's "lack of effectiveness appears to be the rule rather than the exception" (p. 14).

In an update of the original review, Fischer (1976) further evaluated the research on practice effectiveness and asserted a resounding "no," casework is not effective. He speculated that this may be due, in great part, to the reliance on psychodynamic models of clinical social work. He criticized the introduction of more contemporary theories, such as role theory and systems theory, because although they allow us to understand a client, they do little to tell us how to help our clients change problems and reach goals.

Fischer stressed some of the features of effective practice by drawing from research in other fields, such as counseling and clinical psychology. Most notable are those approaches that provide reasonably clear guidelines for implementing the intervention; that is, those that provide structure to the treatment. By structure, Fischer was referring to careful planning of the intervention, introduction of certainty or specificity into the client's situation, and a commitment to action and direct influence, as well as to interventions that are systematic.

Sharpening the focus of research reviews, Wood (1978) argued that broad questions of effectiveness or ineffectiveness do not provide much practical information for the social worker. She posited specific questions, such as: What can practitioners learn from practice evaluation research? Why were interventions successful or unsuccessful? What propositions, prescriptions, or proscriptions of practice theory have been validated, refuted, or modified from research?

Wood reviewed twenty-two research studies done between 1956 and 1973 and grouped her observations into studies that are concerned with particular client groups and studies that are concerned with different modes of practice intervention. Although Wood asserted that few general conclusions could be made from the research, she noted that poorly done practice was not effective and that studies that reported positive outcomes involved better quality of practice. "Quality practice," she surmised, had the following six attributes:

- A clear definition of the problem
- An understanding of the problem, including factors that create it, maintain it, and help it change
- The setting of goals to work with the problem
- The negotiation of a contract with the client
- The planning of a strategy for the practice intervention
- The evaluation of the outcome of the intervention

We agree that these attributes comprise some of the essential characteristics of effective social work.

Similarly, Reid and Hanrahan (1982) reviewed twenty-two studies available from 1973 to 1979 and an additional six studies published by

1981. In order to discern any possible trends in practice effectiveness, an additional sixteen studies were included from the earlier reviews by Fischer (1973) and Wood (1978). Reid and Hanrahan's review advanced the understanding of what goes into effective practice by addressing more specifically the issue of structure. Reid and Hanrahan observed that many of these studies had structure, which they defined as well-explicated, well-organized interventions that often could be implemented in a step-by-step manner on specific problems or toward well-defined goals. In contrast, the earlier studies, as Fischer noted, lacked specificity and often were simply "generic" casework. Although the result of Reid and Hanrahan's review provided grounds for optimism, they were quick to caution against complacence, as few of the studies showed practical or permanent client change, as also is true of studies that do not have sufficiently long follow-up assessments. This not only points to the need for well-done follow-up evaluations, but also may suggest that what change we do know how to facilitate may be only short term; if so, it behooves practitioners to make extended follow-up evaluations of clients.

Subsequent to Reid and Hanrahan (1982), Rubin surveyed sixty-seven journalists and identified an additional twelve articles on the effectiveness of social work intervention. Rubin's observations were similar to those of Reid and Hanrahan: effective interventions had structure; they were clear and specific about what problems to resolve, the goals of treatment, and the procedures followed to reach those goals. Rubin also noted the need to match the particular circumstances of the client's problem with the appropriate intervention.

Traditional literature reviews also have considered models of practice. Focusing on four practice models (psychotherapy, marital therapy, family therapy, and behavior therapy) Thomlison (1984) evaluated several seminal reviews and reached conclusions similar to those of Reid and Hanrahan. He noted that planned and systematic efforts to produce change resulted in more positive outcomes than did either no treatment or unplanned, informal helping. He also concluded that research suggests that there are differences among the four modes of practice. For example, there are reasons to question the effectiveness of individual treatment for persons with marital and family problems. As Thomlison asserts, these differences do not necessarily point to the superiority of one method over another, but do point out the importance of appropriate fit between the intervention and the client problem or goals of treatment. In terms of practitioner characteristics, the research suggests that certain factors are more important than whether one is a social worker or a psychologist. He refers to these as "therapeutic characteristics" (p. 53), such as empathy, warmth, and genuineness.

In summary, the history of the literature of practice effectiveness has been controversial. Although there were reasons to question the effectiveness of social work practice, recent studies suggest that interventions that are well defined and well planned for a specific client problem probably are more effective than unstructured treatment. As defined earlier, structure refers to the well-defined, clearly explicated components of practice that can be replicated in some specific fashion for a particular and well-defined client problem or treatment goal. It probably is safe to say that when we structure our work with clients, regardless of our theory of practice, we are more likely to facilitate measurable change in our clients.

QUANTITATIVE LITERATURE REVIEWS

This position of the structure of change was further developed from the quantitative analysis of research results. Over the past decade, research has taken a significant step forward with the development of empirically based methods of synthesizing different studies. Traditional literature reviews, on the other hand, tend to be descriptive rather than data based. It can be challenging to write a good class paper; imagine how difficult it is to objectively review dozens of studies on such a broad topic as how to help clients. The ability to synthesize findings objectively from separate research reports allows researchers and clinicians to have more confidence in the conclusions. We can be more confident about the integrated results because personal opinions are not likely to influence the interpretation of the results.

Meta-analysis: An Overview of Data Synthesis

This new research methodology of reviewing empirical findings is known as meta-analysis (meaning analysis of analyses). Each finding is converted to a standardized score known as an effect size (ES), which reports the mean treatment effect as a deviation score in the nontreatment control distribution. In essence, an ES is derived from the difference between the treatment and control scores, divided by the standard deviation of the control group. Because the ES is a standardized score, it can be interpreted as a percentile rank reflecting the average treatment effect. Using a table of Z-scores from any statistics book, an ES of 1.0 indicates that the average person receiving an intervention had better outcomes than 84 percent of those who did not receive intervention; more conservatively, an ES of 1.0 indicates that the average person receiving intervention had better outcomes than 34 percent of the average persons receiving no intervention.

In the helping professions in general, and social work in particular, several meta-analytic studies provide conclusions that can be used to directly influence what we do in practice to help our clients.

Meta-analysis is a relatively new tool in the review of empirical literature. It includes four components:

1. Defining and locating the population of studies to be reviewed

2. Systematically surveying the studies on characteristics of interest, such as components of the intervention, implementation of the components, client or practitioner characteristics, or elements of the research design
3. Computing a quantitative estimate of the effectiveness of the intervention under study, which is known as an effect size (ES) and is a standardized score
4. Conducting analyses, including hypothesis testing, determining the association between the characteristics of interest and the effectiveness

There is an extensive literature debating the relative merits of meta-analysis versus traditional literature reviews. Cooper and Rosenthal (1980), in an experimental comparison of traditional qualitative literature reviews and meta-analysis, determined that reviewers using the meta-analysis approach found more support for the tested hypothesis in a body of studies than did reviewers using a traditional approach. Meta-analysis also has been identified as a more systematic approach to synthesizing research findings and is a useful tool in reviewing large numbers of studies (Videka-Sherman, 1990). Meta-analysis has been criticized for leading to comparisons across studies that are too different to be compared meaningfully (the ''apples and oranges'' problem), not meeting statistical assumptions made in the computation and interpretation of quantitative effect sizes, and over-weighing the findings of certain studies, such as those that are weak methodologically or have multiple dependent variables (Fischer, 1990).

Although meta-analysis never will, and probably never should, completely replace qualitative literature reviews, it makes an important contribution to synthesizing research findings. A dialogue should exist between conclusions reached from qualitative reviews and those reached from quantitative or meta-analysis reviews (Cook and Leviton, 1980). For the social work practitioner, it is important to weigh the findings of both methods of literature review and synthesize them with one's own practice experience. This approach to developing one's personal model of effective practice is consistent with the profession's current thinking about effective intervention development by practitioners (Mullen, 1985; Rothman, 1980).

Meta-analysis of psychotherapy and clinical social work. There has been an explosion of meta-analytic reviews in psychology since Smith and Glass's (1977) original meta-analysis of psychotherapy outcome studies. Re-analyses have been conducted of the original sample of the studies used by Smith and Glass (Shapiro and Shapiro, 1982; Andrews and Harvey, 1981). Analyses have been conducted on cognitive therapies compared to systematic desensitization (Berman, Miller, and Massman, 1985), marital therapies (Hazelrigg, Cooper, and Borduin, 1987), the effects of psychotherapy compared to placebo effects, and, most recently, the differential effects of relaxation techniques (Eppley, Abrams, and Shear, 1989). In social work, very few meta-analyses have been conducted. Those that have been conducted have focused on the relative effectiveness of intervention for the chronically mentally ill, prevention of substance use among adolescents, intervention for less-severe mental health problems, intervention for child abuse and neglect, and a meta-analysis of experimentally tested interventions for a variety of social problems (Tobler, 1986; Videka-Sherman, 1988, 1989).

Does treatment work? The meta-analytic findings of social work practice yield several suggestions that are consistent across different reviews. The findings particular to social work are fairly consistent with those from psychology. Meta-analyses consistently have found social work interventions to be more effective than no intervention and more effective than placebo control conditions. As Videka-Sherman (1988) reports, the average ES from the sixty-six findings of thirty controlled research studies was .51 per study, with 95 percent confidence that it ranged from .36 to .66. As a standardized score, the mean ES indicates that the average client receiving a social work intervention had a better outcome than 69 percent of those not receiving the experimental condition. In other words, the average effect moved from the fiftieth percentile to the sixtieth percentile as a consequence of the social work intervention. These findings may, in fact, actually underestimate the effectiveness of social work practice because in many of the studies the control condition was actually another form of practice.

Similar conclusions that treatment is effective are asserted in Smith and Glass's meta-analysis of psychotherapy. The authors report an average ES equivalent to the seventy-fifth percentile of the untreated control group distribution. Again, this suggests that the average person receiving psychotherapy had a better outcome than 75 percent of those not receiving treatment.

Specifying the components of effective treatment. Perhaps the most consistent finding from meta-analysis in social work applies to well-defined interventions. The most well-defined ones with developed protocols that are accurately applied are more effective than ad hoc and unstructured approaches (Videka-Sherman, 1988, 1989). Two aspects of well-defined interventions that Videka-Sherman studied were specificity and structure. Specificity of the treatment correlated .35 with the outcome effectiveness, whereas structure correlated .40. Simply stated, these findings suggest that as you use more specific interventions and apply them accurately, you will probably have more effective outcomes. In light of this, we suggest that you define your intervention as clearly and thoroughly as possible and that, if at all possible, you create a protocol of what you will do in implementing it. This conclusion is consistent with that reached in many of the qualitative literature reviews as well.

Social work meta-analysis has shown that client preparation for the intervention is correlated with effective outcomes ($r = .58$), indicating that more preparation is associated with more effective outcomes. The association between preparing your client for what you will do during the intervention and effectiveness was consistent across different social work settings, e.g., mental health settings and hospital-based settings. The different settings allow us to assume difference in client problems and severity, thus suggesting that it is important to prepare your client regardless of the setting in which you are doing your social work treatment. For example, you should educate your client about the intervention and what will be done during treatment. You might decide to invite a client to observe a group that he or she is considering joining, or to use video or audio recording to illustrate the intervention. Undoubtedly different methods of preparing your client for his or her intervention differ in effectiveness; however, it is important to keep in mind the need to induce the role of client and be certain your client is prepared to do the intervention.

Meta-analyses of social work effectiveness also have consistently found time-limited interventions to be more effective than nonlimited interventions. In outpatient mental health settings, for example, time-limited interventions correlated .43 with effectiveness; in community-based settings, they correlated .38. This finding has been consistent across different interventions for different types of problems (e.g., outpatient mental health and community-based settings); it is important, however, not to restrict the definition of time-limited intervention to short-term treatment or brief interventions. The issue is not necessarily the length of the treatment, but rather that the time frame during which treatment will be provided will be defined and limited. For example, for treating the chronically mentally ill, the most effective interventions were twelve to eighteen months in duration; for serving outpatient mental health clients, the most effective interventions were two to six months in duration (Videka-Sherman, 1988).

Fitting the method to the madness.   As was suggested by the enhanced effectiveness of behavior therapy for particular problems, meta-analysis has identified the need for different intervention models for different social problems. In outpatient mental healths settings, exploration was correlated with effectiveness ($r = .48$), as was modeling ($r = .35$), advice ($r = .22$), and the use of reinforcement ($r = .27$). In other words, higher levels of exploration, modeling, advice, and reinforcement are associated with effectiveness. These findings, then, suggest that active participation by the social worker and the client is associated with more effective outcomes. The most effective interventions with outpatient mental health clients seem to be time-limited interventions with the practitioner taking an active and directive role. Practitioner activities that help a client transfer changes made in the treatment relationship to everyday life also boost the likelihood of a successful intervention, as suggested by the correlation of therapeutic assignments with outcome ($r = .23$). Techniques that enhance this transfer of treatment gains include assigning homework tasks to the client and then following up on how well the client performed the tasks.

For the chronically mentally ill client, in addition to client preparation and time limits, effectiveness has been shown to be associated with advocacy, seeking between-session information, support, and enhanced client expectation for change. These factors clearly are components of therapeutic case management. Here the social worker must provide more concrete services, help the client to make social connections in his or her everyday community, and provide outreach to engage the client in intervention services. Enhancing clients' expectations for positive change as a result of the intervention also has been associated with successful social work with this group of clients.

In work with parents who maltreat their children, effective social workers use structured and multimodal approaches to address abusive or neglectful parents' own needs, such as learning to handle their feelings and impulses through stress management, and parenting skills training that emphasizes positive and pleasant parent-child interactions. Direct services to children, ranging from therapeutic nurseries and preschools to life skills training for school-aged children, also boost an intervention program's likelihood of success. For child abuse prevention, effective approaches include early, even prenatal, services in a nonstigmatizing environment, such as a health clinic. Engaging and maximizing the client's own social support systems, such as family and friends, is also important. In order to enhance social supports for parents at risk of maltreating their children it usually is necessary to work with them on improving their own social skills.

Does theory make a difference? When treatment seems effective, your theory of practice may make little difference. Smith and Glass (1977), for example, report that the ES for ten different types of psychotherapy (e.g., psychodynamic, client-centered, behavior) may not be significantly different, with the exception that systematic desensitization is more effective than implosive therapy. Although the average ES for the ten therapies ranged from outcomes at the sixtieth percentile to the eighty-second percentile, much of the differences tended to be due to extraneous variables, such as the difficulty of the client problem. Moreover, as a categorical variable, type of intervention accounted for only 10 percent variance in effectiveness, with another 90 percent of effectiveness being due to something else.

Similar findings are reported by Videka-Sherman (1988). Theoretical approaches do not seem to account for much difference in the effectiveness of interventions. For some problems, such as outpatient mental health or intervention for child maltreatment, behavioral approaches yielded consistent, if not statistically significant, higher effects than did other theoretical approaches. These findings seem to suggest that a practitioner's theoretical orientation does not determine effectiveness; more likely, effectiveness is determined by what he or she actually does in practice. The enhanced effectiveness of behavior interventions for certain problems, then, should not be surprising because they are more structured than many other interventions. Additionally, the added effectiveness of behavior therapy for certain problems illustrates that certain techniques are more appropriate for particular problems; this supports the argument that it is necessary for social workers to match the intervention with the particular client problem, as was discussed in the section on traditional literature reviews.

Enduring unanswered issues in research synthesis of practice effectiveness. Meta-analyses have found social work practice to be more effective than did some of the earlier (traditional) reviews (Fischer, 1976; Mullen, Dumpson and Associates, 1972). The more recent traditional reviews of social work practice effectiveness are more consistent with the meta-analytic findings that practice appears to be effective (e.g., Reid and Hanrahan, 1982; Thomlison, 1984). There also is some agreement between the two different types of reviews as to the core characteristics of effective practice, such as well-defined components, step-by-step implementation, and the use of appropriate time limits of the intervention.

Meta-analyses have revealed a number of issues that are important to social work practitioners, but are not answered by the current body of research on social work practice. One of these is that the research on social work practice seldom considers or reports descriptive characteristics of the client or the practitioners. For example, hypotheses about effective intervention with clients of different socioeconomic or educational statuses cannot be tested because very few studies report this information. Thus, although we are certain that there is a need to match the intervention with the client's problem, more information must be reported about particularities of the client for us to further understand how certain variables moderate practice effectiveness.

Another limitation of the research on social work practice is that even in the very best studies, the control conditions are largely unknown in terms of types of alternative services that the control groups receive. This is important because the usual control condition in social work practice research is "ordinary community services" rather than a no-intervention condition. Not only is "ordinary community services" rarely defined in research reports, but lack of statistical difference may be due to an improving control sample.

Another problem in most social work research studies is that samples are biased and may not represent clinical populations treated by practitioners. For example, in the empirical studies of effectiveness of treatment of child abuse and neglect, clients typically are voluntary and female. We have little empirically based knowledge about successful treatment of abusive or neglectful fathers or of those who are forced into treatment, as by court order.

A final issue that is not addressed in most of the social work practice research, but is most important in treating social work clients with such chronic problems as mental illness or situations that predispose parents to be neglectful, is that we have little empirical evidence on which to base decisions about treatment for the long-term needs of these clients. We know that time-limited interventions produce better outcomes than unlimited interventions, but we do not know how to organize coherent and coordinated episodes of services for clients over the long term.

Many of these limitations reflect the current state of research; that is, much about effective practice is unknown, and thus not available for meta-analytic synthesis. As more studies become available on the important issues of practice effectiveness, more structured intervention surely will be developed. In the meantime, we can devise tentative practical suggestions for how to help our clients change.

TOWARDS EFFECTIVE PRACTICE: STRUCTURING YOUR INTERVENTION

As is evident from this discussion, the conclusions reached by both the traditional and meta-analytic reviews of the literature have direct implications for what you should do to enhance the effectiveness of your social work practice. They suggest that you need to fit your practice to the client problem, that the client must be prepared for the intervention, and that you must specify the purpose of the intervention and provide as much prescriptive, time-limited structure as possible. For practice purposes, structure is knowing the aspects of your social work interventions and defining them as clearly and concisely as possible in order to replicate the components that facilitate client change. As Videka-Sherman noted (1985, 1988), structure includes knowing and using the sequence, or order, of an intervention's application. For example, the treatment of persons with borderline personality disorder is interpersonal in nature and uses the transference relationship between the client and the clinician. Although the intervention has discrete components, such as fixed rules with which the client must comply, that can be experienced by the client as psychologically safe (Winnecott, 1960), some components, such as transference, are not easily isolated or concisely defined. Also, currently we are not certain of precisely when in the treatment process to use these components. Such an ego-oriented approach to this type of client, then, has less structure than a form of exposure therapy used in helping an anxious client, such as an agoraphobic. By contrast, most behavioral methods not only have clear, concise definitions of the components of the intervention, they frequently even determine when to apply the techniques.

As these examples illustrate, structure varies in the degree to which it provides specific definitions of the practice methods and direction in treating the client. A highly structured intervention not only defines the components in terms that allow you to replicate them, but also may indicate when in the intervention process you are to use each component. With minimally structured interventions, you have less direction and, therefore, fewer prescriptions for actions to take to help your client; this minimal structure forces you to explore more options in your clinical decisions about what to do. Clearly, structured interventions are easier to learn because they give more specific directions for practitioner actions. Moreover, it is easier to discern whether you have used the method as it is defined and prescribed in the social work practice process. Even when the intervention lacks structure, you should define, as clearly and concisely as possible, *why* (i.e., for what purpose) you are using the intervention, and *how* and *when* you intent to use *what* techniques. We suggest that you do this with each treatment plan developed with every client.

Structure also refers to the degree of fit between the social work intervention and the client problem and treatment goals. A well-defined component of treatment will not be effective if applied to the wrong problem. Consequently, we can see the probability of enhancing our effectiveness by first making sure that our intervention is appropriate for our client's problem and the goals of treatment. Because active participation by you and your client seems to be associated with effective outcomes, we suggest that you discuss goals of treatment with your client and negotiate a contract for change.

Because effectiveness is further enhanced by determining in what order to apply the components of the intervention, you should develop a strategy for implementing your intervention that specifies *when* you will do *what*. For some of the interventions based on social learning theory, research has determined the optimal time to use a technique or a homework assignment, and you must develop a specific treatment plan in order to include the components. A fully developed treatment plan should determine in advance what activities should occur. When possible, this should be done for each session, and the more prescriptive (i.e., structured and sequential) the interventions, the easier this is to do. It is safe to generalize the benefit of such sequential structure to interventions for which research has yet to determine the optimal order. With such interventions you will be less formal in your plan, but should still map out in advance what seems to be a logical course of treatment. The duration of this intervention (long term or brief) also should be planned in advance; you and your client should negotiate the length of the intervention and set specific time limits.

You will notice that throughout this chapter we have discussed how structure enhances the likelihood of practice effectiveness. We have emphasized that no two clients are alike, even if they have the same presenting problem or goals. Additionally, each time you use an intervention it will be slightly different than before. Thus, there are few guarantees about effective practice. Structuring your intervention should, however, enhance the probability of doing effective social work.

GUIDELINES FOR STRUCTURED INTERVENTIONS

The following ten suggestions for enhancing practice effectiveness are general and comprise many important clinical skills. They are atheoretical, and can be applied regardless of your theory of social work practice. However, these suggestions do not supply the structure you need to enhance your practice effectiveness, and we anxiously await the publication of additional studies defining more components of effective practice.

1. Develop a well-defined understanding of the client problem and what behavior needs to be changed.
2. Specify the goals of treatment, including how you and your client will know when you have reached your goal.
3. Select the most appropriate and available intervention for reaching the specific goal and prepare your client for what is expected of him or her.
4. Define the intervention that you will use in well-explicated terms that provide guidelines and directions about what to actually do with your client.
5. Participate actively and directly in helping your client change.
6. Carefully and thoroughly plan a strategy for using the intervention, including what will generally occur in the sessions.
7. Develop homework assignments for your client to do between sessions in order to transfer the treatment gains.
8. Set appropriate time limits on the duration of your intervention, whether it is short term or long term.
9. Monitor your client's progress over the course of treatment and evaluate your effectiveness in reaching the goals of your intervention.
10. Engage your client in each of the above components of the intervention as part of a contract for active participation in changing a specific affect, action, or cognition.

Complying with these general guidelines will help you to design social work interventions that are more likely to effect change. Each requires, of course, knowledge and clinical skills. The social work treatment chapters that follow are designed to introduce you to some of these interventions as applied to a specific client issue. Learning these interventions and structuring all your interventions should help you to be more effective in your efforts to help clients change.

CHAPTER 3

Practice Evaluation: Setting Goals, Measuring and Assessing Change

Kevin Corcoran
Wallace J. Gingerich

This book describes a range of approaches for working with a variety of client problems and shows how you can use them in your practice. Although the approaches differ in important ways, they are all goal-oriented in the sense that they specify a particular change in the client's behavior or situation that becomes the focus of intervention. Progress toward the goal should be monitored continually throughout the intervention to determine whether the intervention is working, and to decide when services should change or are no longer needed. Thus, evaluating change is an integral process in all of the practice approaches presented in this book.

WHY EVALUATE YOUR PRACTICE?

Although social work interventions incorporate evaluation implicitly, it is important for several reasons to make evaluation an intentional and systematic part of your practice.

Probably the most important reason is that both you and your client have a stake in the client getting better, and you need reliable information on the status of the client's problem to tell you whether this is taking place. Think of your clients as consumers who need to have some way of telling whether they are getting their money's worth. Good evaluation procedures will provide accurate information on this. Knowing that things are getting better probably is an important factor in motivating clients to continue in treatment, and it is an important component of client satisfaction with social work intervention.

Systematically evaluating your practice gives you important feedback on whether your intervention is having the desired effect. If so, you will continue until the goal is reached; if not, you will need to analyze the situation and revise your intervention or perhaps modify your original goal. Reliable on-going evaluation should help you fine-tune your intervention, leading to a more efficient outcome for your client.

Another reason for evaluating your practice is that over time you will learn a great deal about which interventions work best with which clients in which situations. In other words, you are likely to become an increasingly effective social work practitioner. Practitioners report that their own practice experience is their most frequent source of knowledge about practice (Morrow-Bradley and Elliott, 1986), and systematic practice evaluation is one important source of such information.

Although we believe that evaluation will improve your practice, it is important to note that there is little or no empirical evidence to date to support this assumption (Levy, 1981; Hudson, 1987; Hayes, Nelson, and Jarrett, 1987). There is general consensus, however, that evaluation is a necessary part of practice, for reasons of professional accountability (Bloom and Fischer, 1982; Briar, 1973) as well as for improved practice. In fact, schools of social work are now required by accreditation standards to include content on practice valuation in their curriculums (Council on Social Work Education, 1988). Clearly, research is urgently needed to determine whether practice evaluation does, in fact, lead to improved outcomes.

EVALUATION VERSUS RESEARCH

What we are describing in this chapter is practice evaluation, not clinical research (Barlow, Hayes, and Nelson, 1984). Practice evaluation is a practice process used to determine whether a desired client outcome was achieved. Although practice evaluation uses research methods and procedures, its primary goals are to provide feedback about client change and enhance the client's outcome. In contrast, clinical research uses rigorous research procedures to develop scientific knowledge. Requirements regarding measurement error and design validity are much more rigorous for research than for evaluation. The distinctions between evaluation and research, then, are primarily purpose, rigor, and emphasis.

It is important to remember that evaluation is a practice activity, done to provide feedback on your work with your client. Evaluation will tell you whether your client improved, and may provide some clues as to whether your intervention was responsible for the improvement. However, because the methods used in practice evaluation are not as rigorous as those for research purposes, you will be limited in what you can conclude about the effectiveness of your intervention.

We freely admit that this version of evaluation can be criticized as weak in terms of research methodology; this weakness prevents you from proving scientifically that an independent variable (your social work intervention) caused change on a dependent variable (a client symptom). The purpose, though, is not for you to conduct research, but rather to monitor your client's change over the course of practice and facilitate your understanding of how effective you were with your clients. Other methods for evaluating your work with clients include intake assessments, family histories, diagnostic work-ups, and your ongoing experiences and clinical judgment about your client. To reiterate, practice evaluation methods are simply another source of information to use along with other data about your client and your intervention.

As the practice chapters of this volume frequently illustrate, it often is necessary and helpful to establish intermediate and instrumental goals (also see Nelsen, 1984; Rosen and Proctor, 1978). In family treatment, for example, an intermediate goal might be to resolve a particular family crisis. An instrumental goal, one that is necessary to bring about the outcome, might be to establish communication skills, which should help improve the family cohesion. In terms of practice-based evaluation, intermediate and instrumental goals provide feedback about whether you are effectively helping your client. Monitoring how you reach these goals not only serves to establish your accountability, but also has practice utility, because these goals are designed to enhance the likelihood of obtaining your final goal.

HOW TO DO PRACTICE EVALUATION

Simply stated, practice evaluation requires that you (1) specify the target behavior and set the desired goal, (2) select a suitable measure of the behavior and use it systematically throughout treatment, and (3) analyze whether change has occurred and the goal has been reached. We use the term "behavior" broadly to refer to any change that you and your client have identified as the target of intervention. This could include changes in action, affect, or cognition of your client or others.

Specify the Target Behavior and Set a Goal

As should be clear by now, practice evaluation is basically a determination of whether there has been useful improvement in the problem situation that brought the client into treatment in the first place. Accordingly, the most important part of evelution is specifying clearly the problem situation and how the client would like things to be different at the end of treatment. Note that this involves specifying both the target behavior and the amount of change that is desired.

Specifying target behaviors and setting treatment goals are integral parts of social work practice (Hepworth and Larsen, 1986). However, different treatment approaches tend to emphasize somewhat different target behaviors, reflecting their different understandings of human behavior and behavior-change interventions. The authors of the client problem chapters in part two of this book give you a good idea of the types of behaviors to focus on in their respective approaches. Therefore, we will not deal here with what behaviors you should select, but rather with how you should specify the target behavior and state the goal.

Specification of target behaviors and goals always should be based on a thorough assessment of your client's situation and the kind of changes your client desires. In other words, target behaviors and goals should reflect your client's real, practical concerns, and should flow naturally and logically from the assessment you have conducted. We emphasize this point because historically the tendency has been to select outcomes for which standardized research measures existed, instead of outcomes that seemed clinically important. With the use of individualized measures, which we will discuss shortly, this problem is less serious than it once was.

Questions to consider.   The five questions discussed below should be considered when specifying goals. They are derived from procedures described by a number of writers (Mager, 1972; Gottman and Leiblum, 1974; Bloom and Fischer, 1982; Hepworth and Larsen, 1986; deShazer, 1988). Fortunately, there is good consensus on the characteristics of good goals.

1. Who?   Be clear about whose behavior is to be the target of intervention. This is not always as obvious as it may seem. Sometimes it is the person you are seeing, as in the case of a depressed client who wants to feel happier. Sometimes your client will ask you to help bring about change in another person's behavior; for example, a mother might like her child to stop misbehaving, or a wife might like her husband to be more attentive and loving. In such cases you might help your client to specify the desired change in the other person's behavior, but you probably also would direct your client to specify changes in his or her own behavior that would facilitate or bring about the desired change in the other person's behavior (Rosen and Proctor, 1978; Nelsen, 1984).

2. Will do what?   State what the client will be doing, in observable terms, when the goal has been reached. What actual behaviors will be different? This sometimes is difficult when the client presents the problem in mental or psychological terms, such as depression, lack of trust, lack of love, and so forth. Many times, however, you can enable the client to be more specific by asking such questions as: How will things be different when the problem is solved? If you were to make a videotape, what would you see that is different? What would another family member or someone who knows you well notice? If you have ever before felt the way you hope to feel, how were things different then?

Occasionally clients are not able to specify observable behaviors or indicators of their goals, in which case you can have them make ratings on a simple scale that you construct for them. Procedures for observing behaviors and constructing self-rating scales will be discussed later in this chapter.

3. How well?   This is where you make the desired level of performance explicit. In other words, once the client has specified the target behavior, he or she decides how well or how often the behavior must occur to signify success. Usually goals can be stated along a continuum of performance. The idea here is to identify what level your client would consider satisfactory. You may need to negotiate this with your client, because some clients underestimate what they can achieve and others may be overly optimistic. In any case, discussing the range of possible performance conveys to your client that the concept of goals is negotiable, and that the outcome achieved may indeed be somewhat different than planned.

4. Is it realistic?   Treatment goals must be realistic if they are to be useful. There is no point in agreeing to goals that you or the client know are not possible. The guideline here is whether the goal you have set is viable, given your client's ability and willingness to work for change, the availability of other people necessary for the change, your ability to bring about the desired change, and the time and resources that are available.

5. Is it important?   Sometimes, in the process of making your goal specific and observable, it changes from the original complaint. Therefore, once your goal statement answers the previous four questions, you should ask yourself if indeed this is the goal that is important to your client. Assuming that your client achieves the goal, will he or she consider treatment a success? This is critical to good evaluation because we assume that attaining the goal means intervention was successful. If it turns out that the goal selected was inappropriate, achieving it would be meaningless.

Specifying the goals.   The questions discussed above for consideration when specifying behaviors and setting goals may seem more like clinical concerns than research concerns. That is because this is an area where the purposes of practice and research come together. From a practice standpoint, you want your clients to be working toward goals that are meaningful, realistic, and will make concrete differences in their lives.

And from a research standpoint, you want your indicators of change to be ones that signify real changes that were accomplished; therefore, they must be related directly to the actual goals that you and your clients are working towards with your specific social work intervention.

We have described a rather generic procedure for specifying target behaviors and setting goals. Kiresuk and associates have developed a specific technique known as goal attainment scaling (GAS) that incorporates most of these ideas and is widely used in mental health settings to set treatment goals and evaluate change (Kiresuk and Sherman, 1968; Mintz and Kiesler, 1982). We recommend GAS highly as a way to structure the goal-setting process and incorporate it into your normal clinical practice.

Goal attainment scaling is a simple procedure for observing change in relation to treatment goals (Kiresuk and Sherman, 1968). It can be used to establish goals by specifying the behavior where change is to occur and delineating outcomes, such as those reflecting the attainment of the goal or failure to meet the goal. A conventional GAS specifies in observable terms five levels of outcome: (1) the least favorable outcome, (2) a less-than-expected outcome, (3) the expected outcome if the intervention is successful, (4) a more-than-expected outcome from a successful intervention, and (5) the most favorable outcome. Each outcome should be described briefly and in such a fashion that it is observable by others, such as your client, yourself, or another relevant other (e.g., spouse or coworker).

Table 3-1 shows the five levels of outcome established for a mother and son who sought clinical social worker services because of a very conflict-ridden and occasionally combative relationship. The GAS is designed to reflect the expected outcomes from the mother's perspective, with her rating her son's behavior. The scoring system here ranges from 0 to 45, although any set of numbers can be used, provided that the same ones are used each time the GAS is completed. For example, some writers recommend using $-2 -1 0 +1 +2$, so that the less-than-expected outcome is expressed by negative numbers. You should select a numbering system that is meaningful to you and your client.

Once you have established your goal and developed the GAS, you can start rating your client's attainment of the goal. An advantage of the GAS is that the behavioral description allows for relevant others, such as a field supervisor, to interview the client and rate the goal state. In fact, the GAS was originally designed so that someone other than the social worker could conduct a follow-up interview and complete the measure. Although this is, indeed, important for research purposes, for a practice evaluation it is acceptable for you or your client to evaluate the attainment of the goal. You may decide to do this towards the end of the intervention process (see discussion below). If you have one or two intermediate goals

TABLE 3–1   Goal Attainment Scaling for Mother-Son Conflict

Outcome	Behavioral Description	Score
Most favorable	Talks almost daily. Expresses fondness toward mother.	4
More favorable	Talks several times per week. Does one fun activity each week.	3
Expected	Has at least one good talk per week. No big arguments.	2
Less than expected	Son yells at mother and verbally assaults her.	1
Least favorable	Son yells at mother, verbally and physically assaults her.	0

(such as improved communication skills, as reflected in the GAS in table 3-1) you should develop a separate GAS for each intermediate goal as well as one for final goal.

Select a Measure and Use It Systematically

The first crucial decision you must make in monitoring the progress of a client or a particular outcome is how to measure the characteristic or attribute. In technical terms, measurement is the process of assigning a number to some thing according to some rules. In social work practice, the "thing" is probably a major symptom your client is experiencing or a goal of intervention. In essence, you are observing the magnitude, intensity, or frequency of a problem or goal. The fact that the method of making the observation is standardized means that it is made the same way each time. Standardization thus means that you can be fairly certain that you are measuring pretty much the same thing each time you see it. Researchers call this "thing" the dependent variable, because it is expected to change as a consequence of an independent variable, which presumably is the social work intervention. Assigning numbers to the attribute or variable allows the use of mathematic procedures to monitor a client's progress. As we will discuss below, you can plot your observations on a graph and monitor whether the behavior changes; for example, a patient with borderline personality disorder may display a decrease in magic thinking, or a dual-career couple might show an increase in the sharing of household responsibilities as part of a fairer and more equitable relationship.

For practice-based evaluation, the basic measurement issues are deciding what measure to use and deciding where and when to make the observations.

Deciding what measure to use. We recommend that you use both individualized and standardized measures of the client problem or treatment goals. Individualized measures are tailored to the unique complaint and situation of the client (Mintz and Kiesler, 1982). These often are referred to as idiographic or tailored measures. By their nature, individualized measures usually are suitable for obtaining daily feedback on the target behavior. Standardized measures are scales that have known reliability and validity and often have been normed for clinical populations. Standardized measures usually are given only a few times during treatment (for example, before and after treatment), and are used to verify the findings obtained from the individualized measure.

Many times the target behavior is a discrete behavior or event, such as having an argument, failing to complete homework, waking up at night, having headaches, or thinking negative thoughts. In each case, the client is describing something he or she does or does not do. Even if the client's initial description of the problem or goal is not in behavioral terms, you should explore with him or her whether it can be so described. The goal-setting steps and GAS procedure outlined above are useful tools in this regard. Most client outcomes can be stated in behavioral terms, and doing so has the advantage of making them more explicit and concrete and more easily observed by social worker and client.

Individualized measures. The two individualized measurement procedures we recommend are direct observation and self-anchored rating scales (SARS). Observations made using these techniques then can be substantiated with standardized measures, such as a rapid assessment instrument (RAI).

When using direct observations, you should write out a description of the target behavior. After both you and the client have agreed on the description, it should be included in the client record. Your description should be clear, objective, and complete. *Clear* means that someone else using your description would agree with you on occurrences of the behavior. *Objective* means that the behavior is directly observable and requires little or no inference. For example, "in-seat behavior" (defined as having one's buttocks in contact with a chair) is objective, whereas "studying" is not objective. *Complete* means that your description encompasses the likely range of behaviors, and excludes those behaviors that may only be similar. For example, when describing a temper tantrum, you would exclude those times when a child cries because of a hurt finger or a bad dream.

Behaviors and discrete events can be observed and counted in a variety of ways. The most common method is a simple frequency count, in which the client (or other observer) keeps a tally of the number of times each day that the target behavior occurs. Occasionally you might be interested in the latency of a behavior; for example, the length of time it takes a child to go to bed after he or she has been asked to do so. Sometimes the duration of the behavior is of primary interest, such as how much time a couple spends talking with each other each day. There are other, more specialized observational procedures (e.g., time sampling and discriminated operants) that you may want to explore (Barlow, Hayes, and Nelson, 1984; Ciminero, Calhoun, and Adams, 1986). In any case, it is crucial that you have a clear, objective, and complete description of the behavior that can be observed and reported by the client on a regular basis, perhaps daily or weekly.

When the target problem is an internal state, such as fear, depression, or self-esteem, we recommend the use of a self-anchored rating scale (SARS). Direct observation is not appropriate in these situations because the complaint does not correspond to an observable behavior; only the client is able to observe these situations.

A SARS is so flexible and easy to use, regardless of the client situation, that it has been called the "all-purpose measurement procedure" (Bloom, 1975). To develop a SARS, establish a range of the client problem that defines the extreme ends of the problem from, say, most intense to least intense. Then determine the number of points on the scale, from say, 0 to 15 or 1 to 7, with the extreme ends of the problem reflecting the lowest and highest numbers. The number range should be based on your client's ability to discriminate the levels of the problem. With younger clients, you might use 1 to 5, or even 1 to 3. It is helpful to then define the middle range of the problem to correspond to the numbers between the lowest and highest.

The crucial point with self-anchored rating scales is to develop clear anchors. Do this by having your client imagine a recent time when she or he felt very low on the scale. Then ask him or her to describe what was happening along three dimensions: what he or she was *doing, thinking,* and *feeling.* For a client who complains of low self-esteem, reported behaviors could include procrastinating on her work, spending most of the day in the house, and turning down a request from a friend to go out. Along the second (cognitive) dimension, the client may report recurrent thoughts that she is not competent for her job, that she will not get the promotion she would like, and that her boss thinks she is not performing adequately. The third dimension, feelings, is best captured with word pictures that describe physical sensations that go along with strong emotions. For example, the client might report a "sinking" feeling or a "heavy" feeling, or perhaps simply feeling "down" or "blue" or "like the bottom is dropping out."

Once you have elicited anchors at each end of the scale and at the midpoint, ask the client to select the three or four anchors that best represent the numbers on the scale. The client then rates herself on the scale accord-

FIGURE 3–1   Self-Anchored Rating Scale of Son's Feelings toward Mother

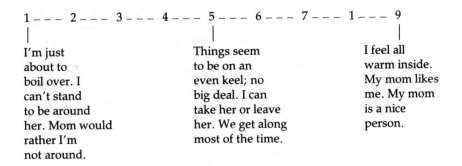

1 – – – 2 – – – 3 – – – 4 – – – 5 – – – 6 – – – 7 – – – 1 – – – 9

I'm just	Things seem	I feel all
about to	to be on an	warm inside.
boil over. I	even keel; no	My mom likes
can't stand	big deal. I can	me. My mom
to be around	take her or leave	is a nice
her. Mom would	her. We get along	person.
rather I'm	most of the time.	
not around.		

ing to whether she is experiencing those anchors or not, rather than by making a global judgement.

Figure 3.1 displays a SARS for the son in the above-mentioned mother-son conflict. Here the son is able to rate his feelings toward his mother. Because the SARS is so simple, it is possible that the client could complete the SARS daily or even several times a day at meaningful periods, such as when his mother is instructing him to do something (e.g., take out the trash, do his homework).

Standardized measures.   Direct observations and SARS, of course, have limitations when it comes to reliability and validity. This is more troublesome for research purposes than for practice evaluation purposes. However, you can minimize some of the limitations by corroborating individualized measures with a standardized measure. For clinical evaluation, we recommend that you use rapid assessment instruments (RAIs) (Levitt and Reid, 1981; Corcoran and Fischer, 1987). Because standardized scales may be time consuming, even when they are as short as twenty items, they are useful primarily to substantiate the observations made with a direction observation or a SARS.

As is illustrated in many of the chapters in this book, RAIs are available for most client problems. They can be used regardless of theoretical orientation to practice. In addition to personality traits (e.g., the Trait Anger scale [Spielberger et al., 1983] and problem states (e.g., a measure of phobia, such as the Fear Questionnaire [Marks and Mathews, 1979]), RAIs are available to observe treatment satisfaction, beliefs, and many affective and cognitive states.

Choose standardized scales that are easily administered and scored; they also should have published data on reliability and validity. Any short, easily comprehensible questionnaire has the potential to be used as a secondary measure. Several books are available that reprint scales that are appropriate for practice evaluation or that contain subscales from lengthier instruments that could be used to observe a particular characteristic of your practice (Corcoran and Fischer, 1987; Robinson and Shaver, 1973). There also are numerous books that describe various instruments, such as Sweetland and Keyser (1983), and journals that frequently publish new instruments, such as *The Journal of Personality Assessment* and *Journal of Behavioral Assessment and Psychopathology*. For a more detailed list of these books and journals, see Corcoran (1988). In addition, computerized measurement systems are available, the best of which is Hudson's Computer-Assisted Social Services (1990).

The problems and benefits of reactivity. All of the observation methods we have recommended are subject to reactivity (reactivity refers to how the process of observing something can change what is being observed). For example, if you ask a client to monitor his or her cigarette consumption, it is possible, even likely, that consumption will change as a result of self-monitoring. Consumption may go up or down, depending on a number of factors (Bloom and Fischer, 1982).

Most writers advise using procedures that reduce reactivity—so-called nonreactive measures (Webb et al., 1981). This is sound advice for research purposes, but it often is not practical in social work settings. Most nonreactive measures do not involve the client directly (for example, someone else may observe the client without his or her awareness). Helping the client to observe his or her own behavior and change it if desired usually is an important component of clinical social work. Self-observation (and hence reactivity) is an integral part of the intervention.

Because reactivity is likely to be a factor for many clients, you should use this effect to your client's advantage by designing your measurement procedure so that the anticipated effect of reactivity is to move your client closer to his or her goal. Accordingly, you should design the measurement procedure so that it heightens your client's awareness of undesired behaviors *before* he or she engages in the behavior (for example, the client could count the number of cigarettes in the pack before smoking the next one). Better yet, have him or her record the desirable counterpart of the unwanted behavior; for example, the number of times he or she had the urge to smoke but did not. Reactivity also argues for working toward positive goals, such as increasing the positive talk time between spouses. This often has the effect of drawing the spouses' attention to the positive aspects of their relationship rather than the negative.

Summary. There is a wide variety of ways to measure client problems and treatment goals. We recommend GAS, SARS, and standardized instruments. However you decide to measure the problems and goals, the measurement process should be an integral part of treatment that helps accomplish the desired change.

Deciding where and when to make the observations.   The purpose of your practice determines where and when you should make observations. If, for example, you were helping parents to manage an acting-out adolescent, it would be important to measure the problem in the family home or wherever else it occurs. On the other hand, if the problem is a more enduring characteristic of the client and does not occur in a specific situation, then you probably can make the observations at your office or some other place.

The point to keep in mind is that the observations should be made in the environment in which the problem is apparent, such as at home, school, or work. When the problem is not situation specific, you have more flexibility in terms of where the measurement should occur.

Whatever place is used to make the observation, it is important to be consistent. If, for example, your client's problem occurs only at work, he or she should complete the SARS or standardized scale while at work. The issue here is standardization. Your measurement will be more valid (that is, accurate) if done the same way and in the same circumstances each time. You and your client should decide at the beginning of your intervention where she or he will observe the problem or goal state.

In terms of how often to make the observations, we suggest daily, if feasible, for the individualized measures. The standardized scales should be completed at least three times—before, during, and after treatment— although they can be used more frequently. More frequent measures may be necessary for certain types of client problems, such as suicidal tendencies. When the practice focus is on more enduring traits, such as personality disorders or identity problems, then less frequent observations may be appropriate. It is important not to make observations too frequently or too infrequently. You should make observations at regular and meaningful intervals after the problem occurs, and in the same circumstances. In essence, the decision of when to make the observations is the basis on which you will analyze change.

Analyze Whether Change Has Occurred and the Goal Has Been Reached

Specifying the target behavior and measuring it systematically over time provide the basis for practice evaluation, but another important step is needed: deciding whether there was change, or whether the treatment goal was met, or both. These really are two different questions. The first question—was there change?— requires some notion of how the client would be if there were no change, and usually is referred to as statistical or experimental significance. The second question—was the goal reached?—compares the client's behavior at the end of treatment with the goal that was initially set. This kind of analysis is called clinical or practical significance. Each analysis requires a different basis for reaching a conclusion. Before we can analyze change, however, we must gather observations according to a systematic plan or strategy.

Strategies for collecting observations. Usually in social work treatment clients hope to achieve some change in their targeted behaviors. They want to be less depressed, more relaxed, more loving, less suspicious, more cooperative, and so forth. Usually clients expect change to occur gradually during the course of intervention. If change is going in the direction of the treatment goal, the client will be satisfied, but if there is no change or if change is in the opposite direction—that is, the client is getting worse—it is time to reevaluate the intervention.

Assessment of change requires, at a minimum, observation at two points in time using the same measurement procedure, namely, direction observation or standardized scale. If the second observation is different from the first, we say there has been change. In practice evaluation we carry this idea further to include repeated observations over time, sometimes daily, but usually at least weekly. As mentioned above, frequency depends on the client problem or treatment goal. Traditional research terminology refers to these systematic ways for observing behavior as research designs.

Designs are nothing more than the procedures by which you decide to make your observations. Although there are a variety of different designs available (see, for example, Bloom and Fischer, 1982; Jayaratne and Levy, 1979), most have two basic components: observations made when intervention is occurring and observations made when there is no intervention. Observations prior to intervention are called baseline, or A phase, and observations during intervention are referred to as the treatment phase, or B phase. In research parlance, this is referred to as the AB design. As we will discuss in the section on graphing, the purpose of collecting these systematic observations is to compare the client's performance during treatment with a time when treatment was not occurring.

One of the easiest ways to collect baseline observations is during the initial intake and assessment periods. If, for example, the client is scheduled for an intake assessment, it is a good idea to develop a SARS and start measuring the problem at that time; if the same client is scheduled to come in the next week to start work on the problem, this time also can be used for baseline observations.

To analyze change, plot the observations on a graph and compare the B phase with the A phase. This is illustrated in figure 3.2, where the base-

FIGURE 3-2 AB Design for Analyzing Change

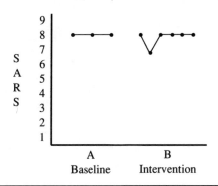

line phase is composed of three observations. By plotting the observations on a graph, you are able to monitor your client's progress by comparing the observations made during your intervention with those collected during the baseline. Failure to observe change in the A and B phases would then warrant a reconsideration of the appropriateness of your intervention. For example, if your client's SARS scores did not change, you might decide to use a different social work intervention. Your original B phase then stops and a new intervention, the C phase, begins, giving you a slightly different design, the ABC design, where the new intervention is compared to the A phase and the B phase (figure 3.3). An example appears in Corcoran (1992), where systematic communication skills training was not helping a distressed family and was then replaced with structured family therapy techniques.

Retrospective baseline observations. Sometimes clinical considerations prohibit collecting baseline observations before you must begin intervention; for example, in the case of a suicidal client. There are two solutions to this problem. One is to have your client report retrospective observations, that is, observations that your client makes based on his or her memory. Although these are less valid than observations made as the behavior is occurring, they generally are better than no baseline at all. Retrospective baseline observations usually are collected by asking your client to recall as accurately as possible the frequency of the target behavior on each day of the preceding week or two. If this is not feasible, you can ask your client to estimate the average frequency for the week prior to treatment, or perhaps for the month prior to treatment. For clear, specific,

FIGURE 3-3 ABC Design for Analyzing Change

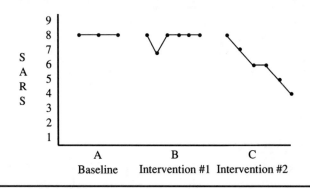

salient behaviors (such as drinking, for example), clients sometimes can provide useful information for a period of three to four weeks prior to the start of treatment. A set of retrospective observations that is particularly useful is to have the client recall the problem "last week," "in general," and "at its worst."

Postintervention retrospective baseline. A second solution to the problem of not having actual baseline observations is to collect them after the intervention has occurred. This is called a postintervention retrospective baseline (Howard, 1980), which involves asking the client, at the conclusion of treatment, to estimate the level of the behavior prior to treatment. Some kinds of client problems, such as extreme pessimism or paranoia, may affect the client's perception or judgement. In such cases, the client may give a more accurate and comparable baseline estimate after treatment than he or she could have before. There is no reported use in the social work literature of postintervention retrospective baseline, but when a prospective baseline is not possible, this may be a useful substitute.

Follow-up observations. In addition to the baseline and treatment phases, you should have your client observe the target behavior periodically after you have stopped treatment. These follow-up observations are quite valuable because they enable you to determine whether the improvement in your client's target behavior is continuing after treatment or whether it is deteriorating. It is advisable to have at least one or two follow-up contacts, either through an actual session or by telephone or mail. Giving your client a self-addressed, stamped envelope increases the likelihood that he or she will report the follow-up observations.

Intervention-only designs.   In rare instances you may not be able to collect baseline or retrospective baseline observations. When baseline of any type is not possible, it is useful nonetheless to observe and analyze the target behavior during the intervention. Observing during intervention allows you to evaluate whether the client is progressing toward the goal, and whether the goal is achieved. You can monitor your client's change in relation to the target behavior's level, magnitude, or frequency from week to week, or at the middle and end phases of practice in relation to the earlier sessions.

Many clients terminate treatment before clinicians believe that they are ready; therefore, you may not have the immediate opportunity for follow-up observations, which might leave you with an intervention-only design. Often, however, such clients will contact you when the problem again becomes distressful. The use of retrospective observations for the time between interventions enables you to develop a more accurate design to evaluate whether your intervention is indeed helping your client change.

A variation on the intervention-only design is the repeated pretest-posttest experiment proposed by Thyer and Curtis (1983). This design strategy can be used when pretreatment baseline in the usual sense is not possible, and where some of the treatment effect may be expected immediately following a therapy session, as is true in desensitization and social skill training. In this design, measures of the target behavior are taken immediately before and after each treatment session to see whether there has been change in the target behavior, presumably as a result of the intervention techniques. This strategy is repeated with each treatment session, hence the pretest-posttest designation. In essence, you do a series of pre-post observations for each session of your social work intervention.

Summary.   There are a number of strategies for observing the target behavior in order to provide a basis for analyzing change. Deciding when to make your observations sets the bases for your design. In each instance, the idea is to observe the target behavior systematically under various treatment and no-treatment conditions. With a little creative work, you will be able to develop your own variations of the above designs to monitor clients' progress.

Assessing change.   Once you have collected systematic observations of the target behavior, you will need to analyze them to decide whether they reflect real change. This is not as obvious a decision as it may seem. When the change is dramatic and consistent, there is little doubt that change has occurred. But frequently the observations do not present such a clear-cut case, and the analysis of change becomes more difficult.

There are two general approaches to analyzing change: visual analysis using graphs, and statistical analysis. We will discuss only visual analysis here, because it is the most practical approach and should always be used. Sometimes statistical analysis also can be helpful when visual analysis is inconclusive. Statistical and quasi-statistical techniques for assessing change are discussed in Bloom and Fischer (1982), Gingerich (1983), and Jayaratne (1978).

To conduct visual analysis, plot the observations on a line graph so that you can see the pattern (Jayaratne and Levy, 1979; Kazdin, 1979). The vertical axis is used to plot the target behavior, such as scores on a SARS or standardized scale; the horizontal axis is used to represent time, usually in days, sessions, or weeks (see figures 3-2 and 3-3). The observations within each phase are connected by a line, and a vertical line is drawn between phases. As the above discussion suggests, you will be comparing the treatment observations with baseline observations to see whether there is a difference.

The standard for analyzing change in visual analysis is "clearly evident and reliable"; that is, the differences in target behavior between baseline and treatment phases is unequivocal and consistent. Operationally, there are several guidelines to follow in reaching this conclusion. First, there should be little or no overlap in target behaviors between phases. This means that there should be a clear change in the level of the target behavior between baseline and treatment. Second, if the target behavior shows a trend during baseline, it should be in a direction opposite from the goal. This is because if baseline behaviors are moving toward the goal, it will be difficult to show that there is an added improvement during treatment. In fact, you may be well advised not to implement treatment at all in such cases, because the client may achieve the goal on his or her own.

Assessing goal attainment.   As noted earlier, analyzing change involves two questions: first, is the target problem any different now than it was before treatment; and second, did the client reach his or her goal? This second question is addressed here. Although change per se is not the issue, reaching the goal almost always implies that there has been some change. One exception to this is if you are working with a client to prevent further deterioration in functioning, in which case enabling the client to stay the same could be considered a worthwhile goal in comparison to further deterioration.

To assess goal attainment, plot on a line graph the level of the target behavior that you hope to achieve at the point in time that you have set. In other words, graph your goal right on the chart before intervention begins; as intervention proceeds and you graph the target behavior, you can see whether it meets or exceeds the goal.

From a graphing standpoint, assessing goal attainment is a simple matter. The critical issue is deciding upon a realistic goal. In the research literature this usually is discussed in terms of assessing clinical significance or applied significance (Gingerich, 1983). From a more practical standpoint, you might use the criteria discussed above under setting realistic treatment goals. The issue here is, how much change must there be for you and your client to conclude that treatment was a success? Unfortunately, there are no objective standards or empirical tests to tell you this. It is largely a subjective, clinical judgment, but an important one because this is in a sense the criterion for success that your client will use.

INTEGRATING EVALUATION INTO PRACTICE

For evaluation to become an integral part of your routine practice, it must be conducive to what you do as a social worker; in other words, it must have practice utility (Gingerich, 1990). Moreover, practice evaluation must be easily accomplished. With this in mind, we suggest that observation and graphing become part of your regular progress or case notes. Figure 3–4 provides an example of a practice evaluation form. The left and right axes have been left blank so that you can use any set of scores from a SARS, GAS, or standardized scale. For example, the left axis could be set from 1 to 100 in order to use one of Hudson's (1989) scales; or you might set it from 1 to 9, or whatever set of scores are appropriate for a SARS. The right axis could be set to a different scoring system on perhaps another measurement, such as a GAS. Figure 3–4 is set up for twenty-one assessment periods, which could be days, weeks, or whatever is meaningful for your client, and has space for brief notes under each observation.

Using the practice evaluation form thus enables you to chart two types of observations, such as a SARS and a GAS, on the left and right axes as well as record the date of the observations and any salient qualitative information that might facilitate your understanding of the client. If this form, or one that you develop yourself, is used as part of your standard case notes, you will find that doing practice evaluation not only is relatively easy and nonintrusive to your routine practice, but also helps you to be more thorough in observing your client's progress and evaluating your effectiveness.

SUMMARY

Practice evaluation has three primary components: (1) specifying the target behavior and setting the treatment goal; (2) selecting a measure and

FIGURE 3-4 Practice Evaluation Form

CLIENT/CONSUMER:

PROBLEMS: 1.   2.   3.

GOALS: 1.   2.   3.

TX: 1.   2.   3.

PLANNED NO.
OF SESSIONS: 1.   2.   3.

NOTES:

DATE

SCORES

1 2 3 4 5 6 7 8 9 10 11 12 13 14 15 16 17 18 19 20 21

SCORES

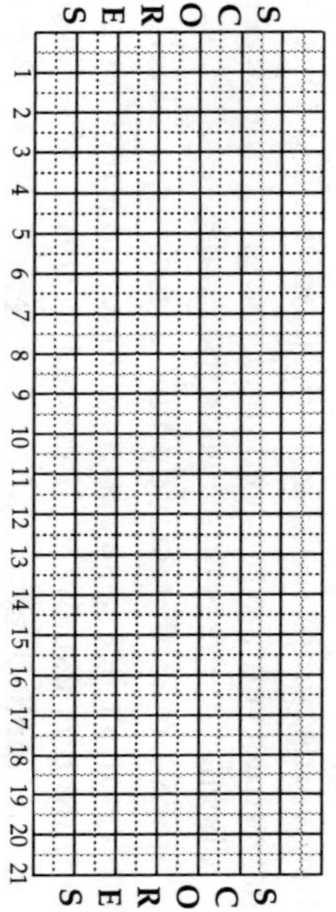

observing systematically over time; and (3) analyzing behavior change and goal attainment.

Until recently, single-case evaluation has seemed more compatible with behavior therapy than with other therapeutic approaches (Hersen and Barlow, 1986; Nelsen, 1981). This is especially true when it comes to the research purpose of asserting causality. Practice evaluation as we have described it, however, is more flexible than evaluation for the purpose of research. We hope that this discussion and the following chapters will convince you that practice evaluation is quite conducive to most social work interventions, especially because the purpose is to have more empirical bases for observing client change, as opposed to concluding a causal relationship between an independent variable and a dependent variable.

Many of the requirements of practice evaluation already are fulfilled in traditional clinical social work (Corcoran, 1985). We recommend, however, that practice evaluation become a more intentional and systematic part of your practice. We advocate more specificity in your observation of the client and more standardization—structure, if you will—in your intervention. As we discussed in the first chapter of this book, the more specific you are about what you are going to change, and the more standardized you are in how you try to change it, the more effective you will be in helping your client to change. We suggest that you use systematic measures of the target behavior and observe before, during, and after you help your client so that you can monitor client change and evaluate your effectiveness. Doing so not only will give you additional information to use in helping your client, but also will enable you to adjust your intervention according to the observations and be more effective in helping clients change.

PART TWO
Common Client Problems

CHAPTER 4

Behavior Therapies for Persons with Phobias

Bruce A. Thyer

In this chapter, Thyer discusses anxiety disorders and shows how to use exposure therapy with persons who are experiencing a simple phobia. This chapter reflects many of the components of a structured intervention, beginning with the need for an accurate assessment. The need for a well-defined problem is illustrated by showing how to make three types of assessment: observable behavior, client self-report, and physiological measures. Each of these is considered in terms of its utility in evaluating change through the treatment of the person with a phobia. Moreover, the assessments make it possible to isolate what caused the person to experience anxiety, which facilitates fitting the specific form of treatment to the client's problem. Thyer's discussion of exposure therapy also demonstrates client preparation, well-explicated components of the intervention (including homework), and how to evaluate the client's change.

INTRODUCTION

Recent developments in the fields of clinical research, experimental psychopathology, and epidemiology have highlighted the importance of the anxiety disorders in the field of mental health. The recent nationwide epidemiological study conducted by the National Institute of Mental Health has found that the anxiety disorders are the most prevalent of the so-called mental disorders, even exceeding the prevalence of depression or alcoholism (Regier et al., 1988). This suggests that mental health professionals are likely to encounter a large number of clients who suffer from a clinical anxiety disorder and indicates that current students and established practitioners should be familiar with the latest empirically based developments in the diagnosis and treatment of anxious persons.

The revised third edition of the *Diagnostic and Statistical Manual of Mental Disorders* (DSM-III-R, American Psychiatric Association, 1987) contains a number of refinements outlining a more detailed classification system for use in assessing and diagnosing persons suffering from pathological anxiety. Generally speaking, these refinements have taken the form of subdividing earlier categories into more clearly delineated and distinct diagnoses. To some extent, in keeping with the general philosophy of the DSM-III-R, these alterations in the diagnostic criteria have been made in accordance with the findings of empirical research, but a number of the criteria and diagnostic commentary continue to reflect the practice wisdom and clinical impressions of the framers of the manual.

A third significant development has been the formulation, testing, and validation of a number of behavioral therapies to help the anxious client. For most persons with an anxiety disorder, one or more clinically effective interventions are available to provide significant benefits. The remainder of this chapter will review each of the above developments, with a focus on clinical management of clients with phobias.

PROBLEM IDENTIFICATION

The accurate diagnosis of the clinically anxious client is usually not difficult for the therapist with a thorough familiarity with the DSM-III-R criteria. A brief summary of each of the currently formulated major categories of pathological anxiety appears below (all quotations from the American Psychiatric Association, 1987).

- **Simple Phobia**: ''A persistent fear of a circumscribed stimulus (object or situation). . . . Exposure to the specific phobic stimulus (or stimuli) almost invariably provokes an immediate anxiety response. . . . The object or situation is avoided, or endured with intense anxiety. . . . The fear or the avoidant behavior significantly interferes with the person's normal routine or with usual social activities or relationships with others, or there is marked distress about having the fear. . . . The person recognizes that his or her fear is excessive or unreasonable'' (pp. 244–45).

- **Social Phobia**: ''A persistent fear of one or more situations . . . in which the person is exposed to possible scrutiny by others and fears that he or she will do something or act in a way that will be humiliating or embarrassing'' (p. 243). The diagnostic criteria also note that exposure to these situations almost invariably provokes an intense anxiety response, and that these fears usually lead to avoidance, interfere with normal living, and are recognized by the person as excessive or unreasonable.

- **Obsessive Compulsive Disorder**: ''The essential feature of this disorder is recurrent obsessions or compulsions sufficiently severe to cause marked distress, be time-consuming, or significantly interfere with the person's normal routine, occupational functioning, or usual social activities or relationships with others'' (p. 245).

- **Panic Disorder**: The essential feature is ". . . recurrent panic attacks, i.e., discrete periods of intense fear or discomfort, with at least four characteristic associated symptoms. . . . The panic attacks usually last minutes or, more rarely, hours. The attacks, at least initially, are unexpected, i.e., they do not occur immediately before or on exposure . . . [to a phobic situation]" (p. 235).

- **Panic Disorder with Agoraphobia**: Meets the criteria for panic disorder and in addition suffers from a "fear of being in places or situations from which escape might be difficult (or embarrassing) or in which help might not be available in the event of a panic attack" (p. 238).

- **Generalized Anxiety Disorder**: "Unrealistic or excessive worry (apprehensive expectation) about two or more life circumstances, e.g., worry about possible misfortune to one's child (who is in no danger) and worry about finances (for no good reason), for six months or longer, during which the person has been bothered by these concerns more days than not" (p. 251).

- **Posttraumatic Stress Disorder**: "The person has experienced an event that is outside the range of usual human experience and that would be markedly distressing to almost anyone. . . . The traumatic event is persistently reexperienced [and there is] . . . [p]ersistent avoidance of stimuli associated with the trauma or numbing of general responsiveness . . . [and] persistent symptoms of increased arousal" (p. 250).

- **Organic Anxiety Disorder**: ". . . prominent, recurrent panic attacks or generalized anxiety caused by a specific organic factor" (p. 113).

It is important to note that, except in cases of anxiety attributable to an identified biological cause, such as an endocrine disorder or the use of anxiogenic drugs, the above diagnostic labels *do not* refer to disorders that persons *have*. More properly, the terms simply imply that the behavioral characteristics of the person adhere to or meet the DSM-III-R criteria for a given so-called disorder. Clinicians of all theoretical orientations, but especially behavior analysts, recognize the importance of avoiding the reification of diagnostic labels. This means not attributing reality status to any hypothesized entity (e.g., social phobia) in the absence of independent evidence of the existence of that disorder. Independent evidence refers to evidence apart from the very behaviors supposedly caused by the disorder. As yet, clinical science does not have good evidence for the existence of disease entities for most of the anxiety disorders; many are more properly viewed as a constellation of acquired behaviors attributable to the processes of respondent, operant, and observational learning (Thyer, 1987).

ASSESSMENT AND MONITORING

Arriving at an accurate diagnosis of an anxiety disorder is only the beginning of the assessment and monitoring process. Adequate behavioral treatment ideally requires the operational definition and repeated measurement of a client's problem prior to beginning treatment. This is done in order to evaluate the efficacy of treatment by comparing the client's status (signs and symptoms defining the construct of "anxiety") before treatment with his or her status during and after therapy. The above two principles, operationally defining a client's problem, and repeatedly assessing the client's status in an objective manner during treatment, have an ample historical precedent within the human services. One of the founders of the profession of social work, Mary Richmond (1917), contended that "To say that we think our client is mentally deranged is futile; to state the observations that have created this impression is a possible help" (p. 335). She further maintained that "Every treatment is an experiment" (p. 55), "there is a sense in which investigation continues as long as does treatment" (p. 363), and that "special efforts should be made to ascertain whether abnormal manifestations are *increasing* or *decreasing* in number and intensity, as this often has a practical bearing on the management of the case" (p. 435). Thus, it clearly is a mistake to contend that the above practices in any way originated with the field of behavior therapy; rather, they should be essential components of all models of practice. Developing operational definitions of anxiety disorders tailored to the unique constellation of signs and symptoms presented by a given client is a practical example of the dictum of "beginning where the client is at."

In undertaking this assessment process, the clinician has three major areas to draw upon. These three areas are the systematic assessment of *client self-reports*, the measurement of *observable behavior*, and the monitoring of any relevant *physiological parameters* (Hudson and Thyer, 1987).

Self-Report Assessment Methods

Structured self-report procedures may be used to augment information obtained through conventional clinical interviews. The value of both projective (e.g., Rorschach test, Thematic Apperception Test, sentence completion test, etc.) and generalized objective (e.g., MMPI, SCL-90, etc.) psychological tests is quite low and of little clinical utility in providing guidance in the structuring of treatment and of the client's response.

Of more clinical utility are structured rapid assessment instruments

(RAIs), which are relatively short pencil-and-paper tests that are easy to understand, administer, and score (Corcoran and Fischer, 1987). Among the more useful RAIs in working with the clinically anxious client are the Clinical Anxiety Scale (Westhuis and Thyer, 1989), the Zung Anxiety Scale (Zung, 1971) and the Social Phobia and Anxiety Scale (Beidel et al., 1989). RAIs are intended for *ipsative* use, meaning that they are to be given to a client repeatedly—say, at one- or two-week intervals—before, during, and after treatment. This is juxtaposed to the *normative* use of conventional psychological tests, which usually are given at the beginning of treatment, if at all, wherein the client's scores on a given instrument are compared to statistically obtained normative data. Thus, if a client's scores on the MMPI are similar to scores obtained from schizophrenics, that client is deemed to have certain features (e.g., psychopathology, personality, traits) similar to those seen in schizophrenia.

The client's RAI scores should be recorded in a simple graphic format. The RAI's total score may be used as an index or measure of the client's internal state or of the subjective aspects of his or her problem with clinical anxiety, and is a way to quantify affective states in a manner that lends itself to the empirical evaluation of practice.

Other self-report alternatives to RAIs include the Subjective Units of Distress Scale (SUDS) (Wolpe, 1958), and individually developed rating scales (reviewed in Hudson and Thyer, 1987). The SUDS is a simple way of asking a client to quantify his or her present affective state using a scale of 0 (completely relaxed) to 100 (absolute panic). SUDS may be used by clients to report their internal states on a moment-to-moment basis during treatment (e.g., during relaxation training), while engaged in homework exercises (e.g., undertaking fear-provoking tasks), or as an overall summary of their affective state on a daily or even weekly basis. Despite its apparent simplicity, the SUDS metric has been shown to correlate well with several physiological indices of anxiety (Thyer et al., 1984), and the approach is widely used.

Behavioral Observations

Although commonly construed as primarily a type of affective disorder, virtually all of the anxiety disorders are characterized by various behavioral impairments. These may take the form of restrictions on one's behavior, as with the agoraphobic who refuses to leave home, or the social phobic who is unable to give public talks. Alternatively, the client may suffer from a type of behavioral excess, as with the obsessive compulsive who repeatedly washes his or her hands, or the client who meets the criteria for generalized anxiety disorder who constantly displays a fine motor tremor.

A variety of methods may be used to measure behavioral aspects of an anxiety disorder. Clients themselves may be asked to keep a structured account of their activities, utilizing measures of frequency or duration, as appropriate. For example, obsessive compulsives may record the number of times per day that they wash their hands (a frequency measure); or agoraphobics may record the amount of time (a duration measure) that they spent at a shopping mall.

In some instances, behavioral observations may be recorded by the parent, caregiver, spouse, staff member, or significant other in the client's life. Using both client-recorded and other-recorded behavioral observations permits a more comprehensive assessment and monitoring than that obtained from a single perspective.

A behavioral approach test (BAT) is a more structured method of assessing various behavioral aspects of an anxiety disorder. For example, a client with a simple phobia (e.g., a fear of dogs) may be asked to confront a small dog tied to a secure leash twenty feet away, and to walk to within eighteen feet, fifteen feet, twelve feet, and so forth, until the client refuses to come any closer to the dog. As formal treatment progresses, these BATs may be repeated periodically. Any clinical improvements (i.e., a reduction in fear) should be quantitatively reflected in the client's behavior during the BAT as the client becomes able to approach the dog more closely. More sophisticated assessments may combine behavioral observations taken during BATs with concurrent assessment of client self-reports (e.g., 0–100 ratings of fear) and relevant physiological measures (e.g., measures of heart rate). Clinical examples of such procedures may be found in Curtis and Thyer (1983), Thyer and Curtis (1983), and later in this chapter.

A variation of the BAT for use with agoraphobics is a mapped walking or driving route that originates at their home. Periodically the client is asked to begin following the route and to note the point at which he or she feels compelled to turn back. Again, such quantitative measures may be used to corroborate the therapist's impressions derived from the patient's less structured self-reports obtained during clinical interviews.

Similar principles are used with a person with obsessive compulsions. For example, in the consulting room the client could be asked to "contaminate" himself or herself by touching the inside of a wastebasket. The social worker could record the length of time the client is willing to endure being contaminated before feeling compelled to wash.

Regardless of the method of collecting behavioral data, it is extremely useful to graphically portray this information. If the data are merely recorded in narrative case notes or even in a quantitative table, changes in the client's status are less readily detected than they would be in a visual presentation that is maintained separately from the narrative summary notes.

Physiological Measures

In some instances, an anxious client may present with various physiological manifestations of elevated autonomic arousal. Examples include a rapid heart rate (tachycardia), high blood pressure (hypertension), rapid breathing (hyperventilation), perspiration, and elevations in certain hormones, such as epinephrine, norepinephrine, cortisol, and growth hormone (Nesse et al., 1985). Patients with such anxiety disorders as simple phobia or social phobia may display increases in autonomic arousal only when actually confronting phobic situations. Other clients, such as those who meet the criteria for panic disorder, generalized anxiety disorder, posttraumatic stress disorder, or organic anxiety disorder, may experience chronic or frequent excessive autonomic arousal (e.g., tachycardia).

In routine clinical practice the therapist will make only rare use of measures of the above physiological conditions. An exception is the measurement of heart rate, which is readily ascertained by palpation of the radial artery or with a sports cardiotachometer, a small, inexpensive device that is attached to the wrist or finger and is available at sporting goods stores (joggers and other athletes use them). Periodic monitoring of heart rate may be useful during programmed confrontation exercises wherein phobic individuals deliberately engage in anxiety-evoking activities in a controlled and structured manner. This will be described later in this chapter.

BEHAVIOR THERAPY INTERVENTION

The treatment of choice for any anxiety disorder that involves a significant component of avoidance behavior is exposure therapy (Marks, 1987; Thyer, 1983, 1987). Literally hundreds of well-controlled experimental outcome studies, many with lengthy follow-up periods that lasted years after the completion of treatment, now exist in the clinical research literature (superlatively summarized in Marks 1987). Exposure therapy involves the careful elucidation of the exact parameters of the client's anxiety-evoking stimuli. For example, a person with a simple phobia to dogs is interviewed to determine what specifically it is about dogs that he or she fears. Is it being bitten, licked, jumped on, barked at, or contaminated by fleas, feces, urine, or germs? In what circmstances are the patient's fear responses more or less severe? Does the size, breed, or color of the dog matter? Occasionally it may be useful to answer these questions empirically by observing the client's reactions *in vivo*, in real-life exposure to dogs or to other phobic stimuli. Similar questions are asked of the social phobic with a severe fear of public speaking. Are there circumstances in which public speaking anxieties are minimized or worsened? Does the type of audience matter? What if the client were making a presentation to senior executives at work? A class of Sunday school students? Preschool-age children? Members of the opposite sex? Same sex? Once these questions have been effectively answered, formal intervention may proceed.

Client Preparation

Initially, the client education about the nature and treatment of phobic disorders takes place through one-to-one instruction in the consulting room. Clients are informed that the onset of the majority of phobic disorders is associated with one or more traumatic experiences with the animals, objects, or situations the person has come to fear. Simply put, a large proportion of dog phobics have had a frightening experience with dogs, perhaps being bitten or knocked down (see, for example, Thyer, 1981). Many driving phobics develop their fears following an automobile accident. Large-scale studies involving recall interviews with clinical phobics reveal that over half of these individuals report such a traumatic onset to their phobia (Ost and Hugdahl, 1981).

Although many phobics have had a direct traumatic experience with their anxiety-evoking stimulus that initiated the onset of their fears, another large proportion has had an indirect or vicarious traumatic experience. Examples include seeing a childhood companion being severely bitten by a dog, witnessing a car accident, or viewing a frightening movie involving snakes or insects. Role modeling on the part of parents or siblings may also play a part in the etiology of some phobias. If a child witnesses a significant other displaying fear of certain animals or objects, or when in selected situations, it is not uncommon for that child to acquire similar phobic behavior and associated emotions.

The above data are consistent with the hypothesis that a large proportion of clinical phobias are etiologically related to the processes of respondent (i.e., Pavlovian) learning. This view is corroborated by experimental laboratory-based demonstrations of the induction of conditioned fearlike reactions in humans (Malloy and Levis, 1988).

Once a conditioned fear reaction is established, a second learning process may account for the well-known persistence of phobias, that is, their resistance to apparent spontaneous remission (at least among adults). A phobic who is inadvertently or intentionally exposed to his or her anxiety-evoking stimulus (AES) generally displays a fairly consistent constellation of signs and symptoms. Efforts to escape the situation almost always occur, as do elevations in heart rate, respiration, blood pressure, and certain hormones, and the individual experiences the subjective sense of severe fear. If these efforts to escape or avoid the AES are successful, the individual's avoidance behavior is negatively reinforced, one of the fundamental learning processes associated with operant conditioning. If being in the presence of a phobic stimulus generates aversive internal states (i.e., fear, anxiety, agitation, etc.), then any action that successfully ameliorates such states (i.e., helps the person calm down) is likely to be strengthened.

You should explain to your client that, like most phobics, he or she probably has an extensive history of coming into contact with the AES, becoming frightened, and then fleeing the situation as quickly as possible. Each act of successful flight or avoidance in effect terminates the aversive situation and hence strengthens avoidance and escape behaviors. Over time, phobic escape and avoidance become more and more likely. This process probably accounts for the persistence of phobias over time. Functional equivalents to overt escape from a phobic situation may include the use of sedative drugs such as alcohol or benzodiazepines, which may account for abuse of these agents by the clinically anxious (Thyer et al., 1986). The mechanism of positive reinforcement, in which there is a significant payoff for the display of phobic behavior for some individuals, may also be at work; this, either intentionally or inadvertently, may help to maintain dysfunctional fears. For example, a phobic family member may find that his or her excessive display of fear and the corresponding demands made upon the family are useful in gaining attention and solicitous concern.

You should emphasize to your client that there is no such thing as a "phobic personality," that the existence of a phobia in no way implies the presence of deep-seated psychological problems, and that "crazy" phobias are not precursors of insanity. You may want to read selected portions of the DSM-III-R to your clients to further illustrate that the problems they are experiencing are recognized and understood. A major point to be driven home throughout all these efforts at client preparation is that phobic clients are in no way responsible or to blame for their fears and that they or their families could have done little up to this point to help them overcome their phobias.

You may wish to recommend to phobic client some of the self-help books on understanding and overcoming phobias. *Living with Fear* (Marks, 1978) is among the best. Virtually every phobic client can identify with one of the case studies in this book, which is empirically based yet packed with clinical anecdotes. Such books reinforce to clients that they are not alone in suffering from phobias, and that help in the form of behavior analysis and treatment is extremely effective in alleviating most instances of pathological fear. It is best for clients to read such materials at home, where they may be assimilated at leisure, and to jot down any questions generated by their reading for discussion with the therapist.

Client preparation continues by bringing up the subject of treatment itself, which is addressed in the self-help books. The basic principle on which virtually all effective treatments for phobias are based is therapeu =

tic exposure, or programmed confrontation. To the extent that the phobia truly is an irrational response and that there is little or no realistic element of danger involved in confronting the AES (which is by definition the case in phobias), exposure therapy is the treatment of first choice, both in terms of clinical effectiveness as demonstrated by hundreds of controlled experimental studies, and in terms of client acceptability.

Exposure therapy involves arranging for clients to gradually confront aspects of their phobic stimuli in a controlled manner. This should be undertaken in real life as much as possible, as opposed to exposure in fantasy. Most clients have had a number of episodes of unavoidable confrontation with their AES through the years, and may object that such experiences simply exacerbate the problem. Upon inquiry, however, it will almost inevitably be revealed that such exposure trials were of relatively brief duration, and that when these episodes were terminated clients were still extremely fearful. Common examples might be the speech phobic who can recall having to "tough out" a required public talk in a college class, or the flying phobic who was forced to endure a two-hour flight in order to attend a funeral. You should agree that brief periods of exposure or confrontation that terminate when the client is still agitated are not productive, but clearly differentiate such experiences from the therapeutic procedure that you propose.

In exposure therapy you and the client plan a series of potentially frightening confrontations with the client's phobic animal, object, or situation, ranging from very mildly anxiety-provoking situations to those that the client believes would be absolutely terrifying. The client is asked to take one of the more frightening situations and project what would happen if he or she were somehow forced to confront that situation. Say, for example, that a client with a dog phobia states that being in a room with a German shepherd would be one of the most awful experiences he or she could imagine. The social worker-client dialog might go like this:

Social Worker: All right, now tell me, what do you think would *really* happen if you were sitting in a room alone with a German shepherd seated three feet in front of you?

Client: Oh my God! That would be awful. I would go crazy!

Social Worker: Do you really mean that, truly insane? Or do you mean that you would be severely frightened?

Client: Well, I suppose I wouldn't actually go crazy, but I think it would be the most terrifying thing I have ever done in my life.

Social Worker: I agree, it would be terrifying, and you wouldn't go insane. But now tell me, what would you actually *do*? How would you feel?

Client: Well, my subjective anxiety would be sky high, 90 or more on that scale you talked to me about. My heart would be going a mile a minute, I'd be sweating, and looking about frantically for a means of escape.

Social Worker: Yes, that's probably a realistic description. Now tell me, suppose that the dog simply looked at you, didn't growl or bark or try to touch you. Imagine that you've been seated in this room for over an hour. Would you be as frightened after sixty minutes as you were in the very beginning?

Client: Well, probably not, but I'd still be terrified and I'm not willing to do that!

Social Worker: Of course not, and I'll not suggest that you do. I am simply trying to use an extreme case to illustrate how exposure therapy is likely to work. Would you agree that after two hours of this, as long as the dog just sat there, that your subjective anxiety would be lower than it was when you began, that your heart rate would be slower and your shaking would be diminished? How about after six hours, wouldn't you be getting a bit bored?

Client: Yes, I'd be pretty sick of the whole thing by then, I imagine.

Social Worker: Yes, and that is precisely the point. Virtually any frightening experience can be overcome if you confront it long enough to become bored, provided, of course, that the activity is not actually dangerous. That is how we will try to work together to gradually help you overcome your fear of dogs. Now I know you are not willing to enter a room containing a German shepherd, but how about one that has an eight-week-old beagle puppy on a leash tied to the opposite wall?

At some stage you will reach the point that the client will allow you to arrange a mildly anxiety-evoking confrontation with his or her phobic stimulus. You then move from the stage of client preparation to the actual conduct of exposure therapy.

Exposure Therapy

You should set up an appointment with the client at which you will recreate the appropriate anxiety-evoking situation. Then you will have to arrange the logistics. Small animals must be obtained from friends or a local pet shop or caught in the wild (e.g., bees and other "bugs"). You must locate small lockable rooms for sessions with claustrophobic patients, an automobile for use with driving phobics, and high buildings for work with clients who are afraid of heights. If the client is afraid of certain objects, a selection of these stimuli must be gathered. With living creatures, arrangements must be made to restrain them appropriately to prevent clients from coming into more intimate contact than they are willing to experience at that stage of therapy. Secure leashes or animal cages may be needed, or glass jars or a terrarium for smaller animals. In some cases only a portion of a client's AES may be acceptable for initial stages of exposure therapy. One client seen by the author had a severe fear of birds. Early treatment sessions involved the use of a series of feathers, because initially she would not tolerate an entire bird and found the touch of feathers to be very anxiety evoking.

At the actual exposure session, you should greet the client in the consulting room or other appropriate location with the AES out of view or out of the room. You should deal with any last-minute questions and provide the client once more with the following reassurances:

1. There will be no tricks or surprises during the session. You will be responsible for ensuring, for example, that the animal does not escape and in general see that the client is not exposed to greater levels of contact than he or she agrees to.
2. The client's permission will be obtained at each stage of the process prior to making any changes.
3. The client may terminate the session at any point by simply making a firm request to stop.

The next step is to get the client's permission to begin the exposure to the AES, perhaps at a specified distance away from the client. As this is done, you should observe the client carefully and ask him or her to rate his or her subjective anxiety. Give reassurance as necessary that the AES is harmless, controlled, restrained, etc. Urge the client to look carefully at the AES, to refrain from averting his or her eyes or body, and to note various features of the AES that you point out. Generally, clients initially are highly anxious, but with the passage of time, often just a few minutes, begin to calm down. With support, facilitative suggestions, the judicious use of humor, or some coaxing, they can be persuaded to approach the AES (or let you bring it closer) and eventually touch it. Periodically the client should give you a rating of subjective anxiety, and you may wish to note the client's heart rate by palpation or through use of a cardiotachometer.

Variations on this process should be used, depending upon the client's AES. A person with height phobia may accompany you to the first landing of a lengthy stairwell and look down the central well until calm. At that point, you suggest moving to the second landing, repeating the process, and so forth until the highest level is reached. You may take a person with driving phobia to a deserted shopping mall's expansive, empty parking lot, seat him or her behind the wheel, and with you seated alongside, have him or her circumnavigate the lot. Continue this until the client is calm, at which point you may seek permission to move the practice scene to a nearby residential street, and from there to a quiet business district, etc.

With social phobics, most of whom are afraid of public speaking, the unique feature of their AES may require some creative arrangements on the part of the social worker. One series of programmed confrontation exercises that the author has developed involves having the client prepare a written speech of about three minutes in length that he or she delivers to the social worker in the privacy of the consulting room over and over until he or she is comfortable making the speech. At this point permission is sought to admit a third person to the sessions (another person with a speech phobia is ideal for this purpose) and the process is repeated. Secretaries, fellow social workers, other agency staff, or friends of the client may also be used. When the client becomes comfortable with an audience of two, subsequent sessions incorporate three, four, or more additional members of the "audience." Videotaped practice with immediate feedback is also useful with clients who fear giving public talks, both to help them improve their manner of delivery and to demonstrate that although they may be feeling very shaky internally, most often an external observer cannot detect any signs of tremulousness.

A variation of this approach is to bring speech phobics to a classroom environment (the author has used graduate classes for this purpose), and arrange for most of the class to remain in the hall or nearby lounge while the client begins making the speech to an initial audience of one or two unfamiliar students. As the client becomes more comfortable, the social worker obtains permission at intervals to bring in one or two more students, until the class reaches its maximum audience size. If the client becomes distressed, members of the audience may be asked to leave. In this manner, the AES (public speaking situation) can in effect be titrated in a careful manner so as to never overwhelm the client, yet provide an appreciable challenge.

As noted earlier, a large body of empirical research has documented the value of exposure therapy in the treatment of simple and social phobias, the phobic avoidance associated with agoraphobia, panic disorder, certain cases of obsessive-compulsive disorder, and various features of posttraumatic stress disorder (Marks, 1987; Cooper and Clum, 1989; Clum, 1989; Steketee, 1987). Exposure-based techniques also seem quite helpful in ameliorating various pathological conditions dominated by private events, internal states that have been given labels such as "obsessions," hypochondriacal concerns, and morbid grief (see Himle and Thyer, 1989; Mawson et al., 1981). Exposure therapy has been found to be appropriate with a number of special populations as well, including the mentally retarded (Matson, 1981), the elderly (Thyer, 1981) and the blind (Thyer and Stocks, 1986). The following brief case description and single-subject study will further illustrate the conduct of exposure therapy in the treatment of phobias.

Case Description

Mrs. Wilkes (a pseudonym) was a fifty-six-year-old woman who was self-referred to the Anxiety Disorders Program of the Department of Psychiatry at the University of Michigan Medical Center, where the author was employed as a clinical social worker. Her presenting complaint was a severe fear of birds that resulted in significant phobic avoidance and a generalized distress in her life because of the apparent pervasiveness of birds. Mrs. Wilkes was unable to give any account of the onset of this fear, noting that she had been frightened of birds ever since she was a small child. In terms of daily life, when she left the house she would often have her husband depart first, stand by the car in the driveway and scan the yard for birds. If none were apparent, Mr. Wilkes would signal her to come out, at which time she would quickly scurry from the front door to the car, which her husband would open for her.

She was unable to visit friends' homes if she knew they owned a pet bird. She could not go into pet stores that sold birds, and was reluctant to shop at local supermarkets. This latter restriction had originated several years earlier when a live sparrow flew into the grocery store where she was shopping and fluttered about the ceiling. Upon inquiry, she stated that she could not buy fresh chicken, only frozen. This was because of her self-admitted irrational fear that the fresh, plucked, plastic-wrapped birds would somehow become reanimated and come after her. She knew this was unlikely with frozen chickens, however. The precipitant for her seeking treatment was her imminent departure with her husband on a long-looked-forward-to vacation in Jamaica. A few weeks earlier Mrs. Wilkes had heard a story from a friend who had stayed recently at the same resort hotel where the Wilkeses had reservations. Apparently the hotel had a large dining patio that had trees filled with parrots, cockatiels, and similar exotic birds that were so tame that they would fly down to the tables and peck tidbits from the diners' fingers. This story, unwittingly told by a friend who was ignorant of her bird phobia, filled Mrs. Wilkes with great distress and caused her to seek help before her departure.

Mrs. Wilkes had been happily married for over thirty years, and had several grown children and an accommodating husband who was puzzled by his wife's irrational behavior but did not make a major issue of it. He was supportive of her efforts to obtain help. Mrs. Wilkes had no other past psychiatric history or behavioral disorder and was rather embarrassed about seeking treatment for her phobia. It is worth reiterating that although certain aspects of Mrs. Wilkes's fear of birds bordered on the psychotic (e.g., her fear that dead birds in the poultry case at the supermarket would come alive), she was not psychotic and would admit sheepishly that although she really knew that the dead chickens wouldn't hurt her, she nevertheless could not control her fearful feelings. Mrs. Wilkes decidedly met the diagnostic criteria for simple phobia but for no other clinical condition or personality disorder.

Treatment planning. The usual client preparation process was completed without incident, and although Mrs. Wilkes remained curious about the origins of her bird phobia, she accepted the author's contention that it was unlikely that we could arrive at a clear etiological understanding (both her parents were deceased), and that in any event treatment could be effective without knowing the origins of her fears. She read and discussed *Living with Fear* and its accompanying description of and rationale for a program of therapeutic exposure. She was amenable to this approach, especially when it was made clear to her that it was the one most likely to yield rapid and long-term improvements.

Stimulus mapping of her phobia failed to reveal any significant elements that had a bearing on treatment. She was equally afraid of large and small birds, and their color, gender, or variety made little difference. Birds in a case were barely tolerable from a distance, if she was sure that they could not escape. She avoided eating chicken, game hens, or other poultry, and did not watch television programs or movies about birds or read stories about or look at pictures of them.

We constructed a hierarchy of potential anxiety-evoking stimuli, which ranged from looking at a color picture of a bird to being in a locked room containing several live birds on the loose. She agreed to begin our first session with my bringing a caged pigeon to our next meeting. Friends who worked in a laboratory that used pigeons for research agreed to let me borrow a pigeon and a clear plastic cage for a few hours.

Evaluation and Conduct of Exposure Therapy. I elected to evaluate my sessions with Mrs. Wilkes by using systematic behavioral approach tests conducted before and after each exposure therapy session. I would measure her approach behavior to the caged pigeon, along with her heart rate as she got progressively closer to the cage. By attaching a portable cardiotachometer to her finger I could record her heart rate as she approached the bird. Thus, before each session I could assess how close she would come to the bird, her subjective anxiety, and one physiological response (heart rate) at various levels of approach. This process would be repeated after each session. By systematically assessing her 'phobia' through the use of standardized behavioral approach tests, it would be possible to evaluate the effects of our intervention program through the use of a special type of research design called the "repeated pretest-posttest single-subject experiment" (see Thyer and Curtis, 1983).

Mrs. Wilkes arrived for her appointment on time. I seated her comfortably in my office and tried to put her at ease with some preliminary conversation. I explained that I did, as promised, have a caged live pigeon in an adjoining room. I gave her the rationale for the use of behavioral approach tests before and after each treatment session, explained the procedure, and obtained her consent. She waited in the hall while I placed the caged bird at the far end of my office, some eighteen feet from the door. I went to the hall, attached the cardiotachometer (a soft foam rubber clip) to her index finger, and asked her to give me a SUDS rating. It was a 95, and her heart rate was 110 beats per minute, mildly tachycardic. She agreed to accompany me back into the office and stood fifteen feet from the caged bird. Her SUDS went to 98 and her heart rate to 120. She agreed to come to within twelve feet, and we continued in this manner until she stopped six feet from the pigeon, saying that she had had enough. I praised her for her efforts, unclipped the cardiotach, and seated her about fifteen feet from the bird. I sat in front and to the side of her, between her chair and the bird, and quietly encouraged her to sit and look at the bird. Over the course of the next ninety minutes she remained with me in the room, interacting from a distance with the bird. As her SUDS scores declined, I asked her to inch her chair (which was on wheels) a bit closer to the caged bird. In this manner I eventually was able to get her to touch the outside of the plastic cage. At this "high point" of treatment I suggested that we stop, to which she agreed with evident relief. I reminded her that we needed to repeat the behavioral approach test once more, which we did. Both her SUDS scores and heart rate were lower during this second BAT, and her approach improved to where she could touch the cage. The data for the BATs conducted pre- and post- the first treatment session are depicted in figure 4-1. The data for the remaining series of four additional treatment sessions are depicted in figures 4-2, 4-3, 4-4, and 4-5.

As may be seen in figures 4-1 through 4-5, Mrs. Wilkes made consistent improvements at each treatment session. In these figures, the abbreviation OR stands for out of the room, IDT stands for indirect touch (i.e., touching the cage), and DT stands for directly touching the bird. She often could not start a new session at the point where she had left off at the previous session, but these mild regressions were quickly recovered. At the conclusion of the fifth session, she was comfortably holding the pigeon in her hand, was agreeable to allowing the bird to walk freely about the room and on the desk next to where she sat, would allow me to wave the flapping bird over and around her head, and even played "catch" with the bird, both tossing it to me and letting me toss it to her, accompanied, of course, by a great flutter of wings. She would permit the bird to be placed in her lap, on her head, and on her shoulder; both of us learned not to wear our best clothes during these sessions.

Mrs. Wilkes agreed to undertake certain extratherapeutic tasks, to be performed between sessions three through five. Examples included going for walks in her neighborhood; setting out bread crumbs and birdseed in her yard and stepping outside when birds were present; going grocery shopping in stores she had previously avoided, purchasing fresh chicken and preparing fresh chicken dinners for her husband (a treat he had not enjoyed in years!); visiting pet stores and asking to examine various birds, and feeding pigeons at the park. These tasks were accomplished successfully, albeit with some initial trepidation. Had there been significant problems, I would have accompanied her on some of these exercises.

When Mrs. Wilkes was free of avoidance behavior in the consulting room, was undertaking exposure therapy homework exercises comfortably, and reported that she no longer feared birds or dreaded her vacation (the precipitant to her seeking treatment), therapy was discontinued. A few telephone contacts were made in the week or so prior to her departure on vacation to confirm that all was well. Two weeks after treatment concluded, I received a postcard from Jamaica from Mrs. Wilkes: "Having a wonderful time! Wish you were here!" The postcard had a picture of a tropical bird.

SUMMARY

Matching Interventions to Client Problems

The technique of exposure therapy is a valuable clinical skill that most human service professionals should acquire. Given that the anxiety disorders are the most prevalent so-called mental disorders, and that the treatment of choice for virtually all anxiety disorders defined in the DSM-III-R usually involves some elements of exposure therapy, it seems appropriate that clinicians working with patients who meet the criteria for simple or social phobia, obsessive-compulsive disorder, agoraphobia, panic disorder and its associated phobic avoidance behavior, and posttraumatic stress disorder should be familiar with this approach. Carefully designed studies have examined the levels of client acceptance and the dropout rates associated with offering clients a program of exposure therapy; client acceptance is higher and dropouts are equivalent to those of conventional dynamic psychotherapies.

Components and Sequencing of Exposure-Based Interventions

Once it has been determined that a given client meets the DSM-III-R criteria for one or more disorders for which exposure therapy is an indi-

FIGURE 4-1 Behavioral Treatment of a Bird Phobia:
First Treatment Session (1 ½ hours)

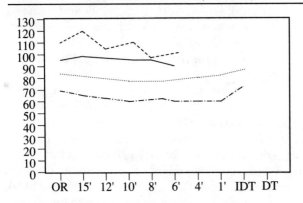

FIGURE 4-2 Behavioral Treatment of a Bird Phobia:
Second Treatment Session (1 ½ hours)

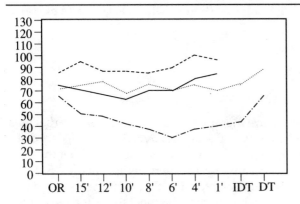

FIGURE 4-3 Behavioral Treatment of a Bird Phobia:
Third Treatment Session (1 ½ hours)

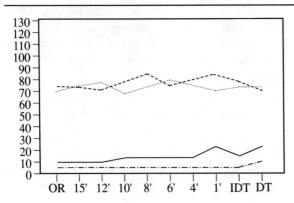

FIGURE 4-4 Behavioral Treatment of a Bird Phobia:
Fourth Treatment Session (2 hours)

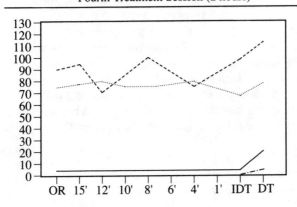

FIGURE 4-5 Behavioral Treatment of a Bird Phobia:
Fifth Treatment Session (2 hours)

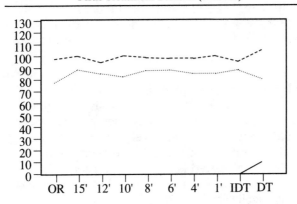

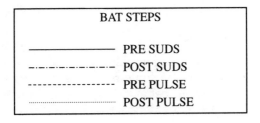

cated approach, the following processes go into the design and sequencing of this treatment procedure. First, careful stimulus mapping of the salient features of the client's anxiety-evoking stimulus is undertaken to determine the design and structuring of programmed confrontation exercises. Next, the client is aided in beginning this process of gradual exposure to anxiety-evoking stimuli so that he or she is able to remain in the proximity of the AES until he or she is calm, and can repeat this process over and over. Such exposure exercises may occur initially in the client's imagination, using simulated stimuli (e.g., rubber snakes as opposed to live ones), but real-life practice should eventually supplant such exercises.

In many cases clients can successfully undertake a program of self-conducted exposure therapy unaccompanied by an expensive therapist, guided instead by a self-help manual, a computer-assisted instructional program, or weekly visits with the behavior analyst (Ghosh and Marks, 1987). Self-conducted therapeutic tasks undertaken by the client outside of the consulting room, in the real-life environments where phobic behavior is most problematic, are essential to the process of behavior analysis and therapy, and vital to ensuring that treatment gains are maintained and generalized. Such requests of clients by the behavior analyst have ample precedent in the literature of psychodynamic psychotherapy, intriguingly enough, although the theoretical rationales for such endeavors differ (e.g., Herzberg, 1941; Omer, 1985).

Client progress should be reviewed regularly with the social worker, either over the telephone or in the consulting room. Interestingly, a recent controlled study has demonstrated empirically the value of therapeutic guidance for self-conducted exposure therapy supervised exclusively over the telephone (McNamee et al., 1989). If self-conducted treatment does not yield satisfactory results, therapist-assisted exposure exercises may produce the desired benefits. If local self-help or support groups for phobics are available, the client should be encouraged to explore these options as well (Thyer, 1987).

The use of single-system research designs to evaluate the efficacy of social work practice employing exposure therapies is especially helpful. Hudson and Thyer (1987), Thyer (1987) and Thyer and Curtis (1983) provide detailed descriptions and examples of such methods of practitioner-guided evaluative research.

CONCLUDING REMARKS

The origins of exposure therapy, although often purely empirical, may be tied clearly to advances in contemporary social learning theory, which forms the foundation of behavior analysis and therapy (Thyer, Baum, and Reid, 1988). It seems essential that social workers, psychologists, psychiatrists, and other human service professionals receive a thorough grounding in modern formulations of respondent, operant, and observational learning principles during their graduate training. Experiential practice in the conduct of behavior analysis and therapy during internship/residency programs, supervised by experienced behavior analysts, has reached the stage where the empirical literature suggests that such training should be mandatory (Thyer, in press). Any professional who provides so-called mental health services who remains unskilled in behavioral methods is at risk of engaging in unethical practice, and certainly is not capable of providing clinically anxious individuals with the therapies that they require.

CHAPTER 5

Case Management for Persons with Schizophrenia

Vikki Vandiver

Stuart A. Kirk

In this chapter, Vandiver and Kirk discuss how to do therapeutic case management for persons with schizophrenia. They define case management and review the empirical research and theoretical explanation for its effectiveness. They argue that this comprehensive intervention has the potential to become a residual category for all sorts of fragmented services that do not fit easily into other service delivery systems. Consequently, they carefully delineate well-explicited components of effective case management, including the roles of the case manager, the direct service intervention, and the active participation demands of the client. Case management is itself ongoing, without time limits, although the goals of integrating and maintaining the person in the community should have time frames. Thus, Vandiver and Kirk emphasize the need to match this intervention with appropriate clients, that is, persons with schizophrenia, and not use it for other clients for whom it might not be appropriate, such as people with an onset in childhood.

INTRODUCTION

Three decades ago, mental health professionals were unable to provide suitable care and services for the masses of discharged psychiatric patients who appeared at clinics, hospitals, and jails in the wake of the deinstitutionalization movement. Many patients were unprepared for release and the communities were similarly unprepared to receive them. The patients often had no family supports, no residence, an inadequate understanding of the use of medication, and few skills for community living (Torrey, 1983). Many found that life had gone from being a structured and controlled routine to being a turbulent struggle in communities unable to provide the constant contact and support that is often needed by those with severe psychiatric disorders (Mosher et al., 1980).

Unquestionably, deinstitutionalization occurred without planning for the community-based resources that would be required. Moreover, at the time there were only a few controlled studies to guide the development of community services (Wyatt, 1986). Although later research

(Beiser et al., 1985) reported the positive effects of community aftercare programs in reducing the negative symptoms of schizophrenia, initially there was a gap in scientific evidence on which to base aftercare services.

Psychiatric aftercare is essential for patients with schizophrenia who wish to live in the community. Aftercare services must be available and organized in ways that meet the multiple needs of the mentally ill. In addition to psychiatric aftercare, these needs include housing, food, safety, medical services, and employment. Patients also need social skills and supportive social relationships (Torrey, 1983). Case management was developed to attain these and other services for persons with serious mental disorders. In doing so, case managers assume the roles of broker-advocate, therapist-friend, and role model (Lamb, 1980).

Over the past two decades, legislation has encouraged the use of case management to assist people with mental illness in their transition from the hospital into the community (Okin, 1987; Talbot, 1979). In many community mental health centers (CMHCs), services are available to match patients' needs with community resources, increase their access to services, and improve their quality of life (Perlman, 1985). Unfortunately, many mental health agencies have not been prepared to meet the multiplicity of needs of this population. This chapter describes the characteristics of many of these patients, particularly those with schizophrenic disorders, reviews the nature and effectiveness of case management, and outlines interventions that practitioners may find helpful.

PROBLEM IDENTIFICATION

Many mental disorders lead to social, financial, and interpersonal problems that can strip people of strength, self-confidence, and appropriately assertive behaviors (Rapp and Winterstein, 1989). Schizophrenia is one such disorder; it diminishes a person's sense of competence and heightens his or her sense of vulnerability. With onset typically in adolescence or early adulthood (earlier for males than females), a diagnosis of schizophrenia usually means that the person has had hallucinations and delusions, and invariably has disturbances in several of the following areas: content and form of thought, perception, affect, sense of self, volition, relationship to the external world, and psychomotor behavior. Impairment usually is noted in the areas of work, social relations, and self-care (American Psychiatric Association, 1987). These problems must have at least a six-month duration to be considered as schizophrenia. Symptoms such as delusions, incoherence, and hallucinations (i.e., positive symptoms) can precede or follow symptoms of social withdrawal, lack of initiative, and marked impairment in personal hygiene and grooming (i.e., negative symptoms).

Other characteristics of schizophrenia can be seen in the impairment of routine daily functioning, such as work, social relations, and self-care. Schizophrenia is characterized by a lack of stable identity, poor problem-solving skills, disorganized and scattered cognitive processes, low motivation, passivity, a tendency to withdraw, occasional violent behavior because of a low tolerance for stress (Heinrich et al., 1988; Greenburg et al., 1988), medication noncompliance, or brain pathology (Shelton et al., 1988; Wolkin et al., 1988). Those with schizophrenia have a shorter life expectancy than the general population because of the increased rate of suicide as well as death from other causes. The dysfunctional traits may be symptoms of the psychopathology (e.g., disorganized cognition) or may be symptoms developed in response to long-term mental hospitalization (e.g., passivity). Regardless of the origin, these traits ultimately impair a person's social skills and capacities for self-help.

Schizophrenia is one of the most serious mental disorders in the country. Despite disagreements about exactly how it should be defined, what causes it, and how it should be treated, estimates of its prevalence and incidence have been relatively consistent. Prevalence is the number of persons with the disorder at any given time, regardless of its stage or duration in any one individual. Incidence is the number of new cases occurring in a given year. Because not every person who has the disorder is known or gets officially diagnosed, the prevalence and incidence rates typically are estimated. Most estimates place the number of persons with schizophrenia at about 1 percent of the population (in the 1970s, about 2 million), with the new cases each year at approximately 5 percent (about 100,000) of that total (President's Commission, 1978). Although the proportion is small, because the disorder appears at an early age and continues for long periods of time, it has a great impact on individuals, their families, communities, and national resources.

The course of the disorder varies among individuals, but has some overlapping features, from "subchronic," with positive and negative symptoms present for six months to two years, to "chronic," with acute exacerbation of positive symptoms for more than two years. Although DSM-III-R suggests that there is no "acute" type of schizophrenia, by defining schizophrenia as a disorder of more than six months' duration, it implies that there are acute features of the disorder (i.e., positive symptoms) that lend themselves to clinical intervention. When acute symptoms are present for less than six months, a diagnosis of schizophreniform may be given. This chapter focuses only on persons with schizophrenia who exhibit negative symptoms for more than two years and those who can be described as chronic with an acute exacerbation (e.g., reemergence of psychotic/positive symptoms as dominant). We will refer to these as chronic and acute features of schizophrenia.

Whether a person has lost previous skills because of long-term inpatient treatment or exhibits disorientation and confused thinking as a result of the disorder itself, the case manager needs to be familiar with the positive and negative features of acute and chronic schizophrenia.

Schizophrenia with acute features presents a clinical picture in which positive symptoms (e.g., hallucinations, delusions, agitation) dominate. Negative symptoms such as social withdrawal and apathy are present, but are secondary to the positive symptoms. The positive symptoms may be responsive to medication and low-grade therapeutic stimuli (Cancro et al., 1986; Hogarty, 1989). Too much social stimulation (e.g., group therapy) may be socially intrusive and lead to an acute relapse; too little stimulation, however, may exacerbate a tendency toward social withdrawal (Wing, 1985). Clients experiencing symptoms of acute schizophrenia require a decrease in psychosocial stimuli, such as communications, demands, and information (Ciompi, 1983).

Chronic schizophrenia, in contrast, presents a clinical picture in which the negative symptoms, such as social withdrawal, seem to dominate. These negative symptoms disrupt the person's ability to engage in social interactions outside the immediate family; this is especially true when functioning is impaired by apathy, lack of motivation, and decreased energy. Here, the case manager needs to focus on increasing the person's involvement with social, interpersonal, and environmental stimuli, as would occur by participation in psychosocial programs. This requires a cautiously graded increase of stimuli involving interpersonal communication and problem solving, as illustrated in table 5-1.

In essence, persons experiencing either an acute or a continuing psychotic episode are likely to have impaired social and self-help skills and lack social competency. Social isolation is a frequent consequence. Moreover, the longer the social isolation continues, the more the social skills tend to decrease (Anderson et al., 1986). This suggests that the timing of intervention is critical in the development of treatment goals aimed at resocialization, skills building, and stabilization.

CASE MANAGEMENT INTERVENTION

What Is Case Management?

According to Leonard Stein, one of the pioneers in community treatment models for the chronically mentally ill, "Long-term psychiatric patients are no different from the rest of us in needing a support network to maintain themselves in their environment. Unfortunately, however, their emotional disabilities are so serious and persistent that, without special help, they are unable to develop and maintain such a network. As a

TABLE 5–1 Classification and Characteristics of Schizophrenia (Acute and Chronic) and Related Case Management (CM) Practice Guidelines

DSM-III-R	Classification	Characteristics	CM Practice Guidelines
Schizophrenia (acute exacerbation)	A. Acute (duration of symptoms minimally 6 months)	1. Positive symptoms (hallucinations, delusions, agitation) dominate 2. Negative symptoms (social withdrawal, apathy) are secondary 3. Symptoms are responsive to medication 4. Requires low-grade therapeutic stimulation	A. Therapeutic intervention can be tailored around a DECREASE in psychosocial stimulation (e.g., communications, demands, information) B. Emphasis on relaxed, simplistic supportive interaction within a clearly defined environment.
Schizophrenia (chronic)	B. Chronic duration of symptoms generally 2 years or more)	1. Negative symptoms seem to dominate 2. Positive symptoms are present and require medication for symptom management and maintenance of daily functioning 3. Negative symptoms most amenable to CM intervention 4. Requires a high grade of therapeutic stimulation	A. Therapeutic intervention can be tailored around an INCREASE in client's involvement with social, interpersonal, and environmental stimulation B. Emphasis on gradual increase in involvement of client with support systems (e.g., day programming, etc.)

result, long-term psychiatric patients generally do poorly when living in the community: they live isolated lives, experience frequent crises, and have numerous readmissions to hospitals. This 'revolving door syndrome' is, in large part, a consequence of their inability to create and sustain a support system" (Stein, 1979).

In response to those needs, the National Institute for Mental Health (NIMH) developed Community Support System (CSS) projects in several states. These projects developed comprehensive service systems for adults with long-term psychiatric disabilities and included the following functions (Turner and Shifren, 1979):

1. Identification of CSS clients in hospitals and in the community and outreach of appropriate services

2. Assistance in applying for income, medical, and other benefits

3. Twenty-four-hour crisis assistance in the least restrictive setting possible

4. Psychosocial rehabilitation services

5. Supportive services for an indefinite period

6. Medical and mental health care

7. Back-up support for family, friends, and community members

8. Involvement of concerned community members

9. Protection of clients' rights, both in hospitals and in the community.

Finally, to cap this ambitious charge, it was suggested that "[t]here should be one person (or team) responsible for remaining in touch with each client, regardless of how many agencies get involved. This can provide the glue that binds otherwise fragmented services into arrangements that respond to the unique and changing needs of clients. This function is frequently referred to as Case Management."

Case management with those who have serious mental disorders attempts to cope with four realities of the human services (Stein, 1981). First, many clients have multiple problems as well as needs that change over time. Second, the resources and services available to meet those needs are fragmented because of categorical funding, professional specialization, geographical dispersion, and administrative decentralization. Third, no one profession, organization, or program has exclusive authority, responsibility, or accountability for the chronically mentally ill. Fourth, persons with chronic mental illness often are unable or unwilling to obtain the services they need.

Case management attempts to ensure that clients with multiple needs receive all the services they require in a timely fashion. This is accomplished through four core functions that appear in almost every description of case management: assessment, planning, linking, and monitoring (Moxley, 1989; Rubin, 1987). Case managers assess clients' needs initially and as they change over time. They develop an overall case plan that indicates the nature of the services needed by the client. They link the client through referrals and advocacy to the services and entitlements that are available. Finally, case managers continuously monitor and evaluate the match between the client's needs and the services received.

In addition, case managers often must assume responsibilities that include providing direct service, outreach, crisis intervention, and social support. They participate in face-to-face contacts with clients to facilitate client participation in the problem-solving process. They provide crisis intervention by, for example, helping clients obtain medical and/or psychiatric care or mediating a landlord-tenant dispute. They provide social support both in the context of the client–case manager relationship and by linking the client with peer groups through natural helping systems (e.g., churches or neighborhood community halls).

Far from being a new concept or practice, case management is basic to social work. Norman Lourie argues that it is the primary device for helping any individual with a disability. He claims that he has "never come across a human service agency dealing with individual or family, social, physical, or mental disability which does not subscribe to and claim to practice case management" (Lourie, 1978).

Studies of Case Management

Given the broad definitions of case management, an unlimited range of interventions for persons with schizophrenia could be considered components of case management. Indeed, given some of the more expansive definitions, everything could be considered an important part of case management with some clients in some circumstances. However, this section will review studies of interventions that meet three criteria:

1. The interventions were identified as examples of case management.

2. The studies made some attempt to evaluate the effects of case management using control or treatment comparison groups with random or matched samples assigned to both conditions.

3. The studies focused specifically on schizophrenic clients, or had schizophrenic clients as a majority of the study population.

The studies reviewed, therefore, suggest the effects of "case management" on severely disordered clients. These criteria excluded studies about closely related subjects, such as follow-up studies of the relationship of psychiatric outpatient services to rehospitalization and costs (Hafner and Heiden, 1989), innovative methods of financing case management services (Harris and Bergman, 1988), the effects of drug treatment (Hogarty and Ulrich, 1977), the combined effects of drug treatment and social casework (Goldberg et al., 1977), a five-year outcome study of case management that lacked a control group (Borland et al., 1989), reviews of studies of medication and various psychosocial interventions (Schooler and Hogarty, 1987), reports about promising psychoeducational approaches (Anderson et al., 1980), and so forth.

One study that met our criteria was conducted by Franklin et al. (1987) and evaluated a "generalist model of case management" with adults who had two or more admissions to mental hospitals during a two-year period and who were still living in the catchment area of a community mental health center in Texas. Over four hundred clients were randomly assigned to either an experimental or a control group. Approximately half of the clients had diagnoses of schizophrenia. The control group continued to receive those services from the community center that they would ordinarily receive; the subjects in the experimental group were divided into units of thirty and assigned a case manager.

The case managers had undergraduate or graduate degrees in various fields and had an average of four years of experience. During the project they spent 50 percent of their time "delivering nonclinical services directly to clients," 40 percent of their time "brokering services," and the rest in other activities. After twelve months, clients in the control group and the experimental group were interviewed and tallies were made of whether they had been rehospitalized, their quality of life from objective indicators, and their subjective satisfaction with aspects of their lives.

The results indicated that clients in the experimental group were more likely to have been readmitted to the hospital and to stay longer in the hospital than were clients in the control group. Also, clients in the experimental group used more community-based services than did those in the control group. On objective and subjective measures of qualify of life, the outcomes were about the same for both groups.

Interpreting the results of this study is difficult. Although the researchers used an appropriate control group design, the meaning of the findings is ambiguous. One ambiguity is related to the problem of defining desirable outcome variables; a second is the problem of measuring program implementation. The increased use of community services and hospitalization by the clients receiving case management services may or may not be a desirable outcome. The difference in use of services lends itself to two entirely different interpretations. On the one hand, one could argue that increased rates of hospitalization and the use of more community services (both involving more cost to the community) among those receiving case management services suggests that case management may be harmful to clients and expensive for communities. On the other hand, one of the purposes of case management is, in fact, to connect the client with more services in the community and to monitor the client's needs closely. Greater rates of hospitalization may be an expected result of closer attention to the client's functioning and needs. In short, good case management is not directed primarily at saving money, but rather at delivering services to an underserved and very needy population.

A second ambiguity in the Franklin et al. study is the omission of any detailed description of the nature of the case management services that were delivered. Other than telling us that some of the seven managers had undergraduate degrees and some had graduate degrees, we know nothing about their training, philosophy, viewpoint, or attitudes. More importantly, we know very little about what they did and with whom. What kind of services were offered, how were they delivered, how frequently, under what circumstances, involving what family or collaterals, with what intensity, and with which subgroups of clients? We are told that something called case management had few or paradoxical effects on clients, but we are not informed what that something really constitutes. Measuring program activity is as important to evaluation as measuring outcomes. One without the other provides limited guidance about what to do.

Bond et al. (1988) evaluated a case management program derived from the influential Program of Assertive Community Treatment originally developed in Madison, Wisconsin (Stein and Test, 1980). The program, called The Bridge, is sponsored by Thresholds in Chicago and has been described in detail in several publications (Witheridge and Dincin, 1985; Witheridge, 1985). Recently a controlled evaluation was done on the effectiveness of the program in preventing rehospitalization (Bond et al., 1988). The program, described as assertive outreach or assertive case management, is a psychosocial intervention designed to improve the community functioning of mental health clients with long or frequent hospitalizations. The program is characterized by the following features: intervention *in vivo*, that is, in the home; a focus on the neediest clients; an explicit mission to prevent unnecessary hospitalization and to meet everyday needs; a small (i.e., ten-to-one) client-to-staff ratio; a willingness to accept ultimate responsibility for the client; assertive advocacy on the client's behalf; anticipation and prevention of life crises; easy accessibility to staff; a total team approach; and a long-term commitment to clients.

The evaluation involved adult clients who had multiple prior hospital admissions (an average of over seventeen during their lifetime and four in the preceding year) who were diagnosed as having a major psychotic disorder or severe personality disorder (nearly 70 percent had schizophrenic or schizoaffective disorders). These eighty-eight clients were randomly assigned to either the experimental assertive outreach group or to an alternative treatment program (placebo control group) that offered a drop-in center that was readily accessible, but had low expectations of clients and considerably less outreach. All clients were interviewed at six and twelve months.

One of the striking differences between the groups after one year was that 76 percent of the assertive outreach group continued to be involved in services, whereas in the control group only 7 percent remained active and most never attended the drop-in center after their initial visit. The assertive case managers were very active in visiting their clients in their homes and making telephone and in-person contacts with collaterals. In terms of rehospitalization, the only outcome measure reported, those receiving assertive case management services had significantly fewer hospitalizations during the year than they had in the previous year, and significantly fewer hospitalizations than those in the control group. Those receiving assertive case management services also had fewer days of hospitalization than in the previous year and fewer than the controls.

The evaluation of the Bridge program suggests than an aggressive, outreach-focused service model can reduce hospitalizations and length of hospital stays, at least for severely disordered clients who are at high risk of rehospitalization. Unfortunately, no information has yet been published about the effects of assertive case management on other indicators of client functioning or quality of life.

Three community mental health centers in Indiana attempted to replicate Chicago's Bridge program. Adult clients with a history of psychiatric hospitalizations, 61 percent of whom were schizophrenic and 14 percent of whom were schizoaffective, were randomly assigned to either an assertive case management treatment or to a control group. The case management clients received outreach services similar to those at The Bridge, although services varied somewhat by center. The control group received regular services from the CMHCs. Over 160 clients participated in the evaluation, which took place at the three centers. An evaluation was made at the end of six months (Bond et al., 1988).

At two of the three centers, clients in the assertive case management group were less likely than the controls to be rehospitalized and they had spent fewer days in the hospital. The outcomes on other measures were less encouraging. There were no differences in quality of life, medication compliance, participation in CMHC programs, or police contacts.

A controlled evaluation of a case management program in Toronto provided follow-up data at six months and at twenty-four months after the program began (Goering et al., 1988). The program used a rehabilitation-oriented case management program modeled after programs developed by the Center for Rehabilitation Research and Training in Mental Health at Boston University. Eight rehabilitation case managers received intensive training in community service coordination skills that emphasized meeting clients' functional needs. The case managers were assigned to inpatient units, from which they drew their caseloads. They developed comprehensive rehabilitation plans for each client prior to hospital discharge. Caseloads averaged fifteen to twenty patients. Eighty-two clients were selected for the case management program and were matched with similar clients from an earlier study who did not participate in the case management program. After six months, the only significant difference was that the case management clients had higher levels of functioning than did the matched controls. After twenty-four months, however, there were a number of significant differences between groups. For example, the treatment group continued to have higher functioning, and, in addition, had more independent living situations and more social contacts. Contrary to the findings of Franklin et al. (1987), there were no significant differences between the treatment and the control group in rehospitalization rate or mean length of hospital stay. Treatment group clients, at the six-month mark, were more likely than controls to be using vocational, educational, housing, and financial services in the community; such use is one of the objectives of rehabilitation planning.

A different model of case management has been evaluated (Modrcin et al., no date). This model, described as a developmental-acquisition model of case management, focuses on the strengths of the client and environment, emphasizing client participation in case planning, aggressive outreach *in vivo*, teaching social skills, and active involvement with clients in the community (for detailed program descriptions, see Rapp, 1983; Rapp and Chamberlain, 1985; Rapp and Wintersteen, 1986).

The evaluation involved comparing the developmental-acquisition model with a more traditional model of case management, which had heavy caseloads, limited time to plan, was focused on pathology, and was office-based and reactive. The study design randomly assigned fifty-one adult clients to either of two case management models. The clients were somewhat different than in other studies; they were younger (mean age twenty-five) and 59 percent nonwhite. A majority (61 percent) had a diagnosis of schizophrenia. Pretest measures and four-month posttest measures were taken on a variety of outcome variables. The evaluation found that those in the special case management group had significantly more contact with case managers than did those in the control group.

After a relatively short follow-up period of four months, the special treatment group was rated as better adjusted to community living and more likely to be involved in vocational training, showed an increased tolerance for stress, and used leisure time more meaningfully. The experimental group did significantly less well on social skills as rated by the case managers, which was interpreted as perhaps a function of the greater knowledge and higher expectations held by the experimental case managers. No information about rehospitalization rates were reported.

The studies reviewed above concentrated on explicit "case management" interventions. Three other studies highlighted the effectiveness of closely related interventions with persons with schizophrenic disorders. In one of the early community treatment evaluations, Stein and Test

(1980) randomly assigned patients who were seeking hospitalization to either a "training in community living" program or to institutional care for as long as needed; both groups received posthospitalization community linkage. The community living training emphasized helping patients to secure material resources and to function in the community and manage their daily lives. The patients were evaluated fourteen months from the time of admission to either the hospital or the community living training program and then at four-month intervals over twenty-eight months. Patients were followed for more than two years by independent research personnel who gathered information in face-to-face semistructured interviews and by using standardized scales to assess symptomology, community adjustment, and self-esteem. At the fourteen-month evaluation period, patients exposed to the community living training program were significantly better than the other group in terms of the amount of time spent in independent living situations, time spent employed, amount of interpersonal contact, satisfaction with life, and symptomology.

When patients were discharged from the successful community living training program and integrated into traditional community programs, most of the beneficial differences disappeared. These results suggest not only that patients need help in acquiring the social competencies necessary to function outside the hospital, but also that services must be continuously available. Stein and Test (1980) make the crucial point that many of the traditional community programs are inadequate in meeting the continuing needs of severely disordered clients.

One of the pioneering studies demonstrating the benefits of social support and community living for the chronic mentally ill was conducted by Fairweather et al. (1977). The initial longitudinal study examined hospitalized patients en route to a community-based program. This program emphasized the importance of having patients assume responsibility for their actions, teaching patients social skills for daily living, and establishing an autonomous self-supporting community living facility. With the aid of key community mental health personnel, the facility became the basis for a group work project that provided meaningful employment (such as janitorial or gardening services) and a steady income. Results of this project indicated that with proper implementation, the program was more effective (when matched with controls) in terms of recidivism and employment than most other forms of aftercare. Its success resulted from the "ongoing support, especially during periods of crisis of one or two key individuals" responsible for the program. Although the study was limited in its full reporting of outcome measures, it lends support to the importance of social skills, social supports, and the use of significant persons (such as case managers) in an ongoing provision of high-quality services to a challenging and difficult patient population. Outcome measures from this study (abbreviated for the purposes of this chapter) showed that it was the supportive and democratic social situation of the training program that resulted in "more adequate adjustment" (e.g., less hospital recidivism and lower patient cost). A more recent review of the Fairweather program by Backer, Liberman, and Kuehnel (1986) found similar outcomes.

Hansen, Lawrence, and Christoff (1985) also provide evidence to support the role of case management in enhancing patient social competency through problem solving. Their study involved problem-solving training with seven recently discharged chronic psychiatric patients—mostly persons with schizophrenia—who attended a partial hospitalization program. The patients had difficulty with such interpersonal matters as using leisure time, work issues, budgeting, and medication compliance. The methods employed with patients included modeling, corrective feedback, role playing, and praise. Using a multiple baseline design, group skills training was shown to have an impact on problem solving in specific, coached situations and on skill generalization to novel situations. The maintenance effect of the training was evaluated at one- and four-month follow-ups. Social validation was accomplished by comparing the problem-solving competency of the patient sample with skills demonstrated by "normal" nonpsychiatric persons in the community. Using a nine-point Likert-type scale, patients scored significantly lower on problem-solving effectiveness than did the control (social validation) sample prior to training. However, following the training, no significant differences were found at both follow-up assessments between the patients and the controls in terms of ratings of problem-solving skills. Some of the limitations of this study are the small sample size, reliance on self-report rather than observation of demonstrated performance, and the failure to assess social problem-solving in vivo. Nevertheless, the study suggests that social problem-solving skills can be taught and that increasing patients' social competence may result in reduced readmission rates to inpatient settings.

Limits of studies. The studies reviewed raise several important questions. One concerns the intended objectives of case management with clients. The studies usually, but not always, measure relapse or rehospitalization. Despite their limits as outcome measures (Anthony, Cohen, and Vitalo, 1978), they are important indicators of the client's ability to maintain himself or herself in the community. Other measures of social functioning are used, and these too have their role in informing practitioners about the client's quality of life and social skills.

Relatively absent from the evaluations reviewed are any attempts to assess the extent to which the case managers were effective in achieving goals related to the service system itself. How effective were they in advocating for their clients, linking them with services, overcoming system barriers on the client's behalf, helping families care for their disordered relative, improving the accessibility of services, and creating new services where a need existed? There are many goals of case management that go beyond specific client characteristics and these also need to be evaluated.

In addition, most evaluations of case management have taken the "black box" approach. That is, they study the effects of "case management" without any attempt to operationally define it or to measure whether and to what extent it was differentially implemented in relation to clients in the treatment and control groups. When we learn that it is effective or ineffective in relation to some outcome indicator, we also need to know what "it" is. We need to know what components of the many activities that constitute case management were applied, whether some were more effective with certain clients than with others, whether some components affected some outcomes and not others, and so forth.

Finally, we rarely are informed in these reports of studies about which client characteristics, if any, are related to positive or negative outcomes. Do persons with schizophrenia do better than those with other psychoses or personality disorders? Do younger clients do worse than older ones? Are the prospects for women better than for men? These are important but complex questions that undoubtedly will be the focus of future research.

THE STRUCTURE OF CASE MANAGEMENT

Case management is essential for the care of those with severe psychiatric disabilities. But the concept of case management is so full of meanings that it is in danger of becoming a residual category, representing fragments of ideas that do not fit neatly into other service concepts or tasks that are left to be done after other things have been taken care of or have failed. Frequently, it seems that case management for those with mental disorders represents all the important tasks that are not viewed as part of office-based psychotherapy. One reason for the ambiguity of case management is that it is discussed simultaneously as a process, a role, and a structure.

Case management as a process attempts to arrange an integrated and comprehensive network of human services that is readily available and responsive to individual needs over time. Establishing such a network is necessary to assess client needs, identify and negotiate for available resources, and monitor and evaluate the client's progress. This involves extensive interpersonal contact with the client, the client's family or support group, and the staff of a variety of agencies. It also involves addressing the client's needs across all areas of functioning and within various physical and social environments. The process of case management reflects the variety of social work activities that are undertaken with persons with schizophrenia, ranging from advocating for their rights and entitlement in the community to providing direct service, social support, and skills enhancement. Thus, the case manager is involved in coordinating activities within one agency, as well as in spanning boundaries among separate organizations.

As a role, case management requires that a person assume responsibility for the processes described above. The role of case manager is as ambitious and complex as the process of case management, and is potentially so broad as to be without boundaries. Not surprisingly, it is also a role that is easily and frequently overloaded. To assess client needs, the case manager must be a social and clinical diagnostician. To develop a plan, the case manager must be knowledgable about community resources and skilled in developing comprehensive treatment plans. To link the client to the services, the case manager must be organizationally and politically sophisticated, understand the dynamics of referral, and be able to serve as an effective advocate. To monitor and evaluate, the case manager must know how to design, implement, and use information systems, have knowledge and skill in clinical and social measurement, and be able to perform supervisory tasks. In addition, the case manager must know how to provide social support, crisis services, clinical interventions, and other social services that may be needed. The case manager role thus requires that one be prepared to be caseworker, clinician, community organizer, supervisor, and manager. In light of this complexity, it is surprising that some of the case management literature describes these as paraprofessional rather than professional roles. Although there are certainly many tasks that can be undertaken by paraprofessionals, the need for skilled and knowledgable professional supervision is apparent.

In terms of structure, in order for case management to be effective, the role of case manager needs organizational legitimacy—that is, a structure that authorizes and supports the role and processes. The processes of case management are too expansive and the role of case manager too complex to exist outside of some authoritative structure. Many authors stress the need for a core agency to sponsor case management functions (Intagliata, 1982). Case management functions need to be anchored in an organization—whether it is a state, county, or local agency—with legal authority and fiscal leverage (e.g., service contracts, client vouchers, etc.). Good will, careful assessment and planning, and skilled advocacy on the part of a case manager may get a client services, but organizational legitimacy and sanction are needed to facilitate and sustain such efforts.

Case management requires an organizational setting that provides authority and continuity. Without authority, case management becomes freelance advocacy. Without continuity, it increases rather than decreases service discontinuity. Case management requires more than adding new responsibilities to existing clinical or administrative roles; case managers can be successful only if agency administrators have established interorganizational agreements and structures to facilitate their work and are willing to rearrange intraorganizational supervisory structures to support it.

DIRECT SERVICE INTERVENTION

The studies reviewed above describe several elements of interventions that suggest that a case management model is appropriate for working with persons with schizophrenia. Many of the studies that have reported positive outcomes involve:

- Frequent face-to-face contact with the client in the home environment
- Relatively low caseloads (twenty-five to thirty clients)
- Active assistance to clients through crucial telephone contacts (such as reporting utility problems)
- In-person contact with collaterals (such as family members or landlords)
- Client participation in community living skills training programs as a transitional service between hospital and community programs (to help client with, for example, budgeting and use of public transportation)
- Client participation in autonomous self-supporting community living programs (such as Fairweather Lodge) that emphasize democratic decision making.
- Support from one or two key personnel during crisis times
- Extensive training of case managers in meeting clients' functional needs

Intensive, task-focused case management services have reduced hospital stays and readmissions and increased clients' level of functioning and adjustment to the community. There also is evidence that case management can improve clients' use of vocational and educational services. To intervene effectively, the case manager needs to be able to think theoretically and practically about how to help the client with schizophrenia.

Case managers working with clients with schizophrenia should develop "treatment packages" of various interventions that will encourage resocialization, enhance skill building, and promote medical and social stabilization. The theory of self-efficacy, a component of social learning theory, is one among several theories (Roberts-DeGennaro, 1987; Liberman, 1988) that could explain effective case management. It is especially useful in enhancing clients' social competencies through self-help and social skills rebuilding. According to one leading theoretician (Bandura, 1986), the central premise of social learning theory is that behavior is determined by a continuous, reciprocal interaction among cognitive, behavioral, and environmental factors. The interaction of these is impaired for clients with schizophrenia. Bandura asserts that through various interventions, such as those that are key components of case management, individuals can improve their ability to perform certain cognitive and social activities.

In this context, self-efficacy is a person's belief in his or her capacity to organize cognitive, social, and behavioral skills into integrated courses of action. When an intervention enhances clients' beliefs about their ability to perform particular tasks, their self-efficacy is increased. The assumption is that a belief that certain actions can be accomplished will improve the likelihood of achieving the desired outcome. Promoting such courses of action is the goal of case management.

Clients' accomplishments are determined partly by how well they can orchestrate their existing skills. Bandura (1986) outlines three major techniques that help clients to effectively do this: direct performance, vicarious coping, and social persuasion. In direct performance, the case manager and client jointly perform and accomplish a task, such as a weekly visit to the grocery store to learn what foods to buy and how to manage money. In vicarious coping, the case manager and client role play and role model alternative ways to handle stressful situations, such as a visit to the food stamp office. Social persuasion uses cognitive appraisal through corrective feedback, verbal persuasiveness, coaching, and encouragement. Providing resource materials on employment opportunities or clarifying job assessment test materials are examples. Table 5-2 summarizes these various procedures.

Frequently, case managers work with people with schizophrenia who have difficulty in following through with life skills tasks, express confusion, or lack basic knowledge of community facilities. For some clients, grocery shopping or banking is a difficult task. Using social learning theory and self-efficacy guidelines, a case manager would approach these life skills tasks by becoming directly involved with the client in accomplishing them. For example, a case manager would participate in activities, such as banking, that allow the client to reach such goals of resocialization, skills building, and stabilization. This approach assumes that when clients believe in their own ability to master the situation, this belief itself promotes effective performance. This is not to imply that simply believing in the ability to accomplish a task will lead to improved functioning. It does suggest, however, that when the case manager and client collaborate as partners in the problem-solving process, the client has a better chance of improved functioning and performance.

TABLE 5-2 Case Management as Intervention: Methods for Efficacy Enhancement for Persons with Schizophrenia

Bandura's Category	Identified Client Problem	Client/CM Agreed-Upon Goal	Technique Used by Client	CM Intervention	Outcome Example
Behavioral	1. Difficulty following through with steps for daily living skills (e.g., shopping)	2. Increase personal control	3. Direct performance (or mastery of experience)	4. CM/client jointly perform agreed-upon task	5. CM/client do shopping/banking 2x weekly until client successfully accomplishes task independently
Social	1. Feels confused and ineffective in confronting or dealing with problematic circumstances (e.g., reporting stolen food stamps to welfare office worker)	2. Enhance social functioning via performance	3. Vicarious coping (or social comparison through vicarious experience)	4. Role modeling participational observation in which CM demonstrates alternative ways to handle stressful situations	5. CM/client role play pending visit to food stamp office
Cognitive	1. Has limited awareness of community and vocational resources; (e.g., misunderstands purpose of assessment information)	2. Increase social competency via knowledge	3. Social persuasion via allied influences (CM, rehab. worker)	4. CM offers corrective feedback, persuasiveness, encouragement, and coaching via use of problem-solving techniques	5. CM provides client with resource materials on vocational opportunities and gives feedback on vocational testing assessment results

These practice principles can be used with clients who display acute or chronic symptoms of schizophrenia. For example, with the acute client, the case manager simplifies incoming information when using social persuasion (e.g., giving feedback regarding vocational interests). This is consistent with the need to maintain a low-stimuli environment for acute clients. Once the acute symptoms have subsided or stabilized, and community, family, and social supports are in place, the case manager can reduce the amount of direct involvement in service acquisition. The time frame for intense services for acute clients can range from one to six months, with necessary booster sessions made available on an ongoing basis.

With the chronic client, the case manager maintains increased stimuli by means of role modeling conflict situations, offering corrective feedback, and working alongside the client to explore alternative ways of handling daily situations. Case managers assist clients in enhancing their self-efficacy through such exercises in social competencies. The time frame for successful demonstration of these interventions can range from six months to two years and interventions usually are performed in conjunction with additional ongoing outpatient support services, such as psychosocial rehabilitation programs.

The following guidelines may be useful for case managers working with persons with schizophrenia and their family or support groups.

1. Focus the intervention on "what can be" for the client as opposed to "what once was" (Anderson, 1986).
2. Create a noncritical, accepting relationship that is molded around realistic goals for clients (Wing, 1985).
3. Maintain a willingness to learn from relatives and clients (Wing, 1985).
4. Reinforce the induction of specific, positive expectations (Ciompi, 1983).
5. Promote the use of established community systems (e.g., Alcoholics Anonymous, YMCA, churches) as natural support systems.
6. Use as nontechnical, informal an approach as possible, one that is as close as possible to the way of life and needs of the client (Tranchia and Serra, 1983).

INTERVENTION LIMITATIONS

Schizophrenic disorders are mutlifaceted and influenced by cultural and social environments (Lewontin, 1984). Consequently, there is no complete theoretical framework that can be used to guide all the activities of a case manager in formulating and implementing interventions. Although many authors have suggested theoretical models (Liberman 1988;

Roberts-DeGennaro, 1987) that are useful in understanding the comprehensive scope of services necessary for the integrated treatment of persons with schizophrenia, there are many continuing uncertainties and limitations.

From a practice perspective, there is no generalizable model of case management intervention that applies to all diagnostic categories and behavioral levels. Social learning theory and the self-efficacy model have been used primarily with persons with phobias. They have not been fully developed for working in the community with those with schizophrenia.

Many of the case manager's roles require linking, negotiating, and obtaining access to services for the client. These functions appear to contradict the direct service role, in which activities are performed with, rather than for, the client. Nevertheless, there are many ways in which the case manager can encourage clients to become involved in advocacy on their own behalf. In this respect, both the direct service and indirect service roles of the case manager may have some congruent activities, even if the immediate objectives are quite different.

From an administrative perspective, case management effectiveness is maximized by small caseloads and intensive training, conditions that frequently are unmet. Large caseloads, in excess of forty high-risk clients, are relatively common for community-based case managers. Such high caseloads seriously compromise the effectiveness, delivery, and quality of care. Additionally, heavy clinical, clerical, and administrative demands often undermine the case manager's ability to provide an effective level of service.

Similarly, unless case managers receive training to recognize the variety of needs that people with schizophrenia have (e.g., high stimuli for chronic conditions versus low stimuli for acute symptoms), they will provide homogeneous treatment for a heterogeneous clientele without an appreciation of the variability of the disorder and its treatment implications. Therefore, program administrators must be willing to provide adequate education and training for staff and caseloads that maximize worker effectiveness.

Finally, not all clients are likely to benefit equally from case management. Some clients whose premorbid condition or onset of disorder occurred at an early age may not be easily changed no matter how active or strategic the case manager is with an intervention plan. Some clients will lack the cerebral integrity (Hogarty, 1989) to benefit from the cognitive restructuring that portions of the social learning theory and self-efficacy interventions suggest. There not only is considerable variability from client to client, but also variability within the same client over time, requiring continuous reassessment of the appropriateness of the interventions discussed in this chapter. Some clients improve with time and supportive case management intervention. Others may never become well; in these latter cases, case managers should not be angry with clients or blame themselves for "treatment failures." It is this variability among and within clients that makes a prescription for intervention (case management) more likely to work if applied with flexibility, consistency, caring, and a scientific knowledge base.

GENERALIZING CASE MANAGEMENT TO RELATED PROBLEMS

Falloon (1988) states that it is no surprise that competence in interpersonal skills is a significant determinant in the successful treatment and rehabilitation of all clients, not just those diagnosed with schizophrenia. It is this element of competence building through interpersonal and interactional skills training on which case management with persons with severe mental disorders is based. Using the techniques of planned teaching, support in real-life situations, role playing, assertiveness training, positive reinforcement, and family involvement, the case manager is able to apply an intervention that can substantially reinforce the learning process across many client problems. In this sense, case management as an intervention has applicability to most diagnostic disorders in which learning and coping processes are impaired. Specifically, case management intervention can be used with clients with a variety of psychiatric disorders as well as with moderate to mild levels of mental retardation. For example, case management can be used with clients who carry a diagnosis of bipolar affective disorders (manic-depression) and are in need of cognitive skills to improve their understanding and use of medication. Or, the case manager can assist the client in developing medication schedules that are compatible with the client's lifestyle, while at the same time helping the client develop the cognitive understanding of the importance of proper medication.

Case management is not, however, a panacea. There are mentally ill clients who simply need housing, or money, or friends, and these resources may be beyond the ability of the case manager to provide. Other clients may be too disturbed or mistrustful to be helped immediately by case management. For still others, the volatility of "expressed emotions" exhibited by family members may require an elevated level of clinical intervention, beyond the realm of case management (Leff and Vaughn, 1985).

For medical disorders, case management can be effective in assisting medically disabled or recovering clients by providing necessary information and coordinating transition services for aftercare. Hospital-based medical case management involves intervention planning and acting as liaison between the medical community and outpatient medical and social services. Much of a case manager's work involves discharge planning, placement, assisting patients in obtaining needed medical follow-up, and simplifying health care information provided by the physician to the patient.

Case management for persons with mental retardation can be particularly effective because of the long-term nature of the services needed by these clients and the importance to them of a consistent helping relationship. Here it is particularly important to emphasize behavioral and social skills that affect the client's ability to live and function in the community. The case manager can work with both client and family (or caregivers) in developing life skill programs that stress both their long- and short-term needs.

Case management services can be and are applied to many other human service populations, such as the physically disabled, the elderly, and the parents of the mentally retarded (Harrod, 1986). In all these areas, however, it is important to determine what consumers and their relatives want out of case management. Without consumer input, case management can simply become another mandated service driven more by bureaucratic necessity than clinical needs. Ultimately, case management is not a substitute for a comprehensive and integrated system of community treatment (e.g., rehabilitation, supportive housing, family and financial support). Case management is an intervention that provides continuity of care on a personal basis, while making use of a network of community resources and facilities.

SUMMARY

Effective case management involves many activities and roles. Active face-to-face involvement with clients and their collaterals is one particularly important task in working with persons with schizophrenia. It requires that case managers use core interpersonal interviewing skills, such as warmth, empathy, and genuineness. Case management activity can increase clients' community living skills, decrease the number of days spent in the hospital and the frequency of readmissions, and improve the level of functioning and community adjustment.

Persons with schizophrenia may have a variety of characteristics, ranging from positive symptoms (such as hallucinations and delusions) to negative symptoms (such as apathy and social withdrawal). Regardless of whether a client is considered to be in an acute or a chronic stage of schizophrenia, he or she will display impairment in any of the following areas: reduced self-help skills, decreased social skills, and lack of social competency. Case managers work with the client to develop a "treatment package," with the goal of addressing these impairments through (1) enhancing skill (re)building, (2) encouraging resocialization, and (3) promoting medical and psychological stabilization. These outcomes call for different treatment strategies, depending on the condition of the client and whether he or she needs high- or low-stimuli interventions. By developing treatment plans with clients, the case manager is also preparing them for active participation in a structured intervention.

Social learning and self-efficacy theory can be helpful in providing a framework for achieving treatment goals. The theory emphasizes that behavior is the result of continuous interaction of cognitive, behavioral, and environmental skills. Because these skills are impaired in persons with schizophrenia, clients should be helped to build their existing skills into integrated courses of action through the interaction between client and case manager. These interactions can be operationalized through three techniques. The first is a behavioral task that involves the client and case manager working side by side to accomplish an identified life skill task. The second is a behavioral task that involves vicarious coping, in which the case manager role models or role plays conflict situations with the client. The third is a cognitive task that involves social persuasion, in which client and case manager work toward cognitive competency via corrective feedback and problem-solving methods. Intervention is considered effective when it enhances clients' belief in themselves and their ability to successfully accomplish a task (i.e., self-efficacy). Belief in one's ability alone is not enough to create change, but it can be beneficial as one part of an effort to help clients improve their functioning. Other factors, such as medication and compliance (Hogarty, 1989), are known to influence outcome with persons with schizophrenia.

Finally, there is nothing extraordinary about the variability of the features of schizophrenia. People with schizophrenia are no different than other people who are constantly trying to adapt to an existence of competing internal and external demands, needs, and expectations. People with schizophrenia, however, have vulnerabilities that lead to breakdowns in social functioning (Cancro et al., 1986). Thus, one of the central aims of case management is to form a collaborative relationship with clients to help them adapt by building upon and extending their individual capacities and skills and by maximizing their use of existing community resources.

CHAPTER 6

Feminist Treatment for People with Depression

Nan Van Den Bergh

In this chapter, Van Den Bergh discusses a feminist approach to working with people who are depressed. She illustrates how the feminist approach incorporates a variety of theories while maintaining a perspective that emphasizes political change and personal empowerment. The clinical relationship developed with the client should emphasize egalitarianism. As Van Den Bergh illustrates, one structured component of this is the contract. Van Den Bergh also shows structure in her three-stage intervention. In all of the stages, the emphasis is on active participation as a technique to reduce the client's depression. In addition, Van Den Bergh highlights the importance of the societal antecedents that facilitate depression in women, and the usefulness of feminist treatment to both men and women social workers and for both men and women clients.

INTRODUCTION

Depression is the nation's leading mental health problem, affecting 8 million people annually (Wetzel, 1982). It covers a broad spectrum of moods and behaviors, ranging from normative disappointments to suicidally severe melancholia. "Depression" includes a definition of mood and certain specific symptoms, as well as a clinical syndrome.

PROBLEM IDENTIFICATION

Clinical Manifestations

Everyone at some time or another experiences some depressive symptoms related to the loss of objects, persons, or experiences. However, a constellation of those symptoms at one time, with significant severity and intractability, constitutes a clinical depression syndrome. The research diagnostic criteria for major clinical depression, as defined by Spitzer, Endicott, and Robins (1978), includes dysphoric mode that has persisted for at least two weeks, impairing one's social and/or occupational functioning, as well as at least five of the following symptoms:

1. Weight loss or gain
2. Sleeping too little or too much
3. Tiredness, fatigability, or loss of energy
4. Psychomotor agitation or retardation
5. Loss of interest or pleasure in usual activities
6. Decreased sex drive
7. Feelings of self-reproach or excessive guilt
8. Recurrent thoughts of death or suicide

Additionally, to constitute clinical depression, the above symptoms are present in the absence of schizophrenia or any other psychiatric disorder that could better explain the symptomology.

Predictors of Depression

A phenomenon that has warranted both study and conjecture is the significant difference between men and women in depression rates. It has been estimated that two to three times as many women as men report that they are depressed (DeLange, 1982) and that one out of every six women will become clinically depressed at some point in her lifetime (Wetzel, 1982). However, for bipolar affective disorders (which present with mood extremes from mania to depression) the sex ratios are about equal (Weissman and Klerman, 1987).

A clue to the greater prevalence of unipolar depression in women can be ascertained by examining several "at-risk" conditions and populations. Brown and Harris (1978) found that low socioeconomic status, the presence of more than three children under the age of fourteen, lack of a supportive partner, loss of one's mother before age eleven, and lack of a job increased depressive propensity. All of the above suggest that female heads of households, particularly those from poor, ethnic minority backgrounds, are at high risk for depression. In addition to the social structural variables related to an increased propensity for depression, certain social role variables have also been considered potent predictors. A 1980 survey in Michigan uncovered that depression in women was associated with perceiving one's partner as dominant, having a low sense of mastery and power, relying on others for achievement, and blaming oneself for others' difficulties (Haussman and Holseth, 1987). These factors suggest that adherence to the traditional female sex-role stereotypes of compliance, deference, and submission also predicts to the development of depressive symptomology.

Feminism as a mode of analysis concerns itself with the social structural factors, such as marriage, that affect women's lives, as well as the normative socialization practices, such as schooling, that affect women's development. A feminist perspective on the risk factors noted above is that women have devalued social status, in terms of the stereotyped sex roles to which they have conformed as well as in their impeded access to resources. The combination of pejorative attitudes towards women and blocked opportunities makes women vulnerable, leading to devaluation and depression.

Prior to discussing treatment approaches, it is appropriate to examine theoretical perspectives that have been generated to explain depression's etiology and treatment. In order to provide some comparative analysis, several theoretical perspectives on depression will be discussed, in addition to other explanatory propositions, prior to offering a feminist vision on depression's cause and cure.

TRADITIONAL EXPLANATORY MODELS OF DEPRESSION

Psychoanalytic Theory

The traditional Freudian view suggested that loss of an object or person was a reason for depression. Mourning as a normative reaction to loss includes feelings of dejection, a lack of interest in activities, and impairment of one's social and occupational functioning. Melancholia includes all of the above dynamics, and in addition the client experiences a pervasive loss of self-esteem. That dynamic is based on the client having previously incorporated into her own ego some identity with a person or an object. When she loses that person or object, there can be ambivalent feelings of love/hate. If the client has difficulty expressing anger at the lost person/object, she turns that psychic energy against herself in a self-reproaching manner, leading to reduced self-esteem and depression (Harris, 1987).

Ego Psychology Perspectives

According to one ego psychology perspective, depression is the outcome of conflict induced by a discrepancy between one's goals and the ability to achieve them. The basic goals that become stymied are desires to be (a) loved and appreciated, (b) strong and secure, and (c) good and loving. A breakdown in self-esteem occurs when the above goals cannot be met, which engenders depression (Harris, 1987).

Another ego psychology approach to depression defined by Bowlby (1980) suggests that mourning has three stages: (a) protest, (b) despair, and (c) detachment. In the protest stage there are persistent efforts to recover the lost person, with resulting disappointment, grief, and anger. The despair stage is characterized by a sense of disorganization accompanied by pain; it is at this stage that self-esteem is impaired and depression occurs. The detachment stage is related to an ability to begin accepting the loss and to move on with one's life.

Self-Psychology Approach

An interesting perspective on depression has been defined by Kohut (1977), who suggested that a lack of empathetic caretaking in one's childhood could lead to a fragmented, depleted self that is subject to depression. The lack of nurturing causes a developmental deficit whereby the individual experiences an inner world devoid of ambitions, ideals, or goals. An "empty depression," or sense of lack of meaning and purposefulness to one's life is the outcome.

Object Relations Perspective

This explanatory model considers the impact of one's relationship to external objects and their impact on personality development in explaining depressive potential. Between the ages of eighteen months and three years, children go through a developmental period in which they both begin to break their attachment to the primary caretaker (usually their mother) and also return to the caretaker for comfort/solace. Because girls identify with their mother, navigation of this rapproachement phase is more difficult for them than for boys, in part because of the independence imparted to boys. The sense of relatedness to their female caretaker provides females with an enhanced capacity for attachment/relatedness to others, but also makes them more vulnerable to depression when attachments are broken (Marcus, 1987).

However, for males, difficulty with the rapproachement developmental stage makes them vulnerable to depressive symptoms when they feel impaired in consolidating a self-concept and individuating. Hence, men are more prone to depression when their identity as an autonomous individual is threatened.

"Self-in-Relation" Explanation

Personality theorists using this perspective believe that dependence is the crucial variable related to depressive tendencies. A highly dependent individual is one whose self-esteem is directly correlated with the approval and support of others. Withdrawal of support lessens such a person's sense of worth; depression results. However, an individual with a healthy self-esteem will derive a sense of personal worth from internal sources or autonomous actions rather than external validation. Depression would result if the ability to self-actualize were impaired.

There are gender differences in how this theory explains depression. Men tend to become dependent on the achievement of goals or exceptional performance. When their accomplishment drives are stymied, self-esteem is negatively affected and depression can ensue. Women, who tend to be dependent on relationships for their self-esteem, experience depression when that relating propensity is curtailed through the loss of an attachment.

This theory explains a double bind experienced by women. In general, society views an orientation towards relationships as a sign of weakness (Jack, 1987); however, sex-role stereotypes suggest that women are to be valued based on their relationships to others. Hence, by pursuing what she believes is her proper role, a woman is set up to be devalued and depressed. Additionally, for women who choose to be independent and self-defined, stepping outside of societal expectations for female behavior sets them up to be devalued, which can lead to depression. Thus, women are in a double-bind, lose/lose situation. This perspective suggests that a self-esteem overly dependent on either the accomplishment of goals or attachment to others makes one vulnerable. Optimally, an individual should strive for balance between accomplishment and relatedness.

Cognitive Behavioral Perspectives

Cognitive behavioral approaches refer to a variety to techniques focused on modifying cognitions and using behavior therapy to promote change (Joseph, 1987). Beck (1972), the most notable cognitive therapist, has maintained that a significant part of the depressive syndrome is characterized by distortions in both thought process and content. A dysfunctional processing of information produces excessively negative evaluations of oneself, the world, and the future. Women who subscribe to sex-role stereotypes will have incorporated societal attitudes that can lay a foundation for pejorative cognitions about their capability to be self-actualized.

Beck also defined the importance of belief systems, or schemas, to one's mental health. Schemas are propositions about the world formulated through one's experiences; they constitute a vulnerability to events. If a woman maintains a schema of "I am valuable only when in a relationship," then loss of an attachment will produce cognitive distortions about her value and worth as a person, leading to depression.

Using the schema's paradigm, Beck defined two personality types and elaborated on the relationship between these models and depressive symptomology. An autonomous personality believes in preserving and increasing her independence, mobility, and personal rights. *Doing* is the theme of this personality schemata, and depression results when independent action is threatened. Hence, this personality type tends to fear connection and relies upon distancing to facilitate goal achievement. The socially dependent personality type wishes for acceptance, intimacy, support, and appreciation. This individual relies upon the social world for gratification, motivation, and direction. *Receiving* is the theme of this personality schemata; separation is feared and, if experienced, engenders depression.

The gender implications of this theory of depression are, again, related to the incorporation of sex-role stereotypes as schemas affecting one's automatic thoughts. If a male believes that it is his proper role to achieve, then failure to do so will precipitate cognitive distortions, such as "I am useless," and related feelings of despair. If a woman believes that her proper role is to be connected in a nurturant, caretaking role with others, then relationship problems will cause her to believe that "I am unlovable," leading to depressed affect.

CONTEMPORARY EXPLANATORY MODELS OF DEPRESSION

Gender Differences in Experiencing and Reporting Stress

This explanation for the greater prevalence of depression in women maintains that because women are encouraged to express their feelings more than are men, women are more willing to report depression. However, community surveys of mental status such as the Epidemiological Catchment Area Study of 15,000 individuals conducted in 1981 showed a two times greater incidence of depression in women than in men. For bipolar disorder, prevalence by gender was equal (Weissman and Klerman, 1987). Consequently, because the rates of depression are greater for women than for men in the general population and not just in clinical populations, that difference cannot be because women have a greater willingness to seek treatment for reported depression.

Genetic Explanation

This contention suggests that genetic factors are at the root of greater incidence of depression in women and maintains that a depression gene may be located in the X chromosome; because women are XX, this would explain the greater prevalence of depression in women. Research in this area has been inconclusive, to date. However, there does seem to be a genetic link in that women who are part of families where there has been a history of the disorder seem to have an increased probability of experiencing depression (Weissman and Klerman, 1987).

Endocrine Physiology Explanation

This explanation maintains that hormonal changes predict to a greater prevalence of depression in women. There has been some research substantiation that premenstrual tension and the use of oral contraceptives increase depression. However, there has been a lack of substantive proof that hormonal changes related to the postpartum period induce depression (Weissman, 1980). Additionally, hormonal alterations associated with menopause have not been proven to engender greater depression.

Psychosocial Explanations

Propositions in this area consider that women as a class have a long-standing history of disadvantaged status, which puts them at risk for depression. Both social status and learned helplessness hypotheses are espoused as part of this explanatory system. The social status hypothesis maintains that women's position in society has psychologically depressing consequences. Discrimination makes it difficult for women to achieve mastery by direct action and self-assertion. Inequality leads them to experience legal and economic helplessness, and forces them into a dependency status with associated low aspirations and poor self-esteem (Weissman and Klerman, 1987). Previously noted in this chapter were studies of populations at risk for depression that indicated that variables associated with poverty and limited social supports highly predict to depression. In *Lives in Stress: Women and Depression* (Belle, 1982) it was found that the women most likely to have poor mental health were ethnic minority females in lower socioeconomic groups who were single parents. These data suggest an interaction of racism, classism, and sexism that has a profound negative effect on minority women's mental health.

The learned helplessness hypothesis (Seligman, 1981) explains the negative outcome of sex-role stereotyping, which has been alluded to previously. Sex-role stereotypes suggest that women should be submissive, docile, receptive, and dependent. The message is one of helplessness; that women cannot take care of themselves and are dependent upon others for their well being. This sets up a dynamic in which a woman's locus of control is external to her self, preventing her from believing that she can acquire what she needs on her own in order to develop and self-actualize. In other words, oversubscription to sex-role stereotypes engenders a state of powerlessness in which a woman is likely to become involved in situations where she becomes victimized. Consequently, socially conditioned and stereotypical images produce in women a cognitive schema of helplessness that results in nonassertive behavioral propensities. For example, because young girls are socialized to be helpless, when they become women they tend to have a limited repertoire of responses when under stress (Weissman, 1980); e.g., they respond passively.

These are the most prevalent explanatory models for depression. Now let us examine how a feminist perspective can both explain depression's incidence in women and facilitate its treatment.

FEMINIST INTERVENTION

What Is Feminist Intervention?

Feminist intervention incorporates feminist values into a treatment process. Those values are concerned with the inequitable power relationships between men and women and are opposed to all "power-over" relationships, regardless of sex, race, class, age, etc., of the parties involved, that lead to oppression and domination. Feminism is a transformational perspective concerned with changing all economic, social, and political structures based on relationships between "haves" and "have-nots." As a result, it is a world view that can apply to any issue and is not limited to "women's issues" (Van Den Bergh and Cooper, 1986).

The impact of a feminist perspective on mental health began to be incorporated into the literature in the early 1970s as the feminist movement began to have an impact on society. Feminists who practiced in the mental health field began to view traditional psychotherapy as an agent of social control that maintained traditional sex roles by encouraging women to "adapt." Empirical validation that clinicians had a double standard of mental health for men and women was provided by the Broverman study (Broverman, 1970). Clinicians' judgments of traits of healthy women and healthy men paralleled sex-role stereotypes. Furthermore, concepts of mental health for an adult, sex unspecified, and for a man did not differ; however, concepts of mental health for a woman differed significantly from those for a healthy adult. These results demonstrate a double standard of mental health for women and men among mental health professionals (Kravetz, 1986).

Related to the theme of feminism as a transformational world view, Phyllis Chesler, in *Women and Madness* (1972), helped to define the view that women should seek to change rather than adapt to societal expectations of subservience and submissiveness. Additionally, engagement in feminist activism and development of feminist values were proposed as being therapeutic (Mander and Rush, 1974). Although feminism espouses the need for social change, it also maintains that the individual must be willing to take risks and action; hence, individual responsibility for improving one's life is inherent within the model.

Feminist treatment, consequently, is based on a cultural determinist view that women's mental health is directly related to their economic, political, and social status within society. Additionally, androgyny is espoused as a model for mental health, meaning that emotional well-being is related to the incorporation of both nurturant and achievement goals within one's life.

This is a general explanation of feminist treatment; now let us look at some of the principles undergirding its practice.

PRINCIPLES WITH FEMINIST TREATMENT

The Personal Is Political

This principle maintains that what a woman experiences in her personal life is directly related to societal dynamics that affect other women. In other words, an individual woman's experiences of pejorative comments based on her sex and of blocked opportunities are directly related to societal sexism. For ethnic minority women, racism and classism also are factors that affect well being.

The heart of a feminist perspective on mental health is articulated by this principle. The social worker's role is to assist her client in analyzing the relationship between her symptoms of distress and the constraints she has experienced in attempting to survive in a politically, economically, and socially oppressive society (Butler, 1985; Koschak, 1984; Gilbert, 1980; Rawlings and Carter, 1977).

Traditional Sex Roles Are Pathological

In feminist treatment clients are assisted in seeing how their distress may be related to oversubscription to sex-role stereotypes. This is a variation of a more traditional psychodynamic approach, which attempts to locate pathology within the client's ego functioning (Butler, 1985). Women are helped to see that they are asked, through normative socialization practices, to accommodate to a set of discriminatory role behaviors and sex-typed personality characteristics (Gilbert, 1980). By internalizing those traditional sex roles, women are inevitably set up to experience self-hatred and low self-esteem (Rawlings and Carter, 1977).

The significance of sharing this perspective with clients is crucial and can be easily incorporated into many of the more traditional treatment approaches discussed earlier. Psychodynamic, object relations, and cognitive behavioral explanations all address the significance of a loss of self-esteem as undergirding depression. Hence, social workers who utilize those approaches can add the additional analysis of how self-subscription to sex-role stereotypes leads to a sense of diminished self-worth, which lends itself subsequently to depressive symptomology.

Client Empowerment

Helping women to acquire a sense of power, or the ability to affect outcomes in their lives, is a crucial component of feminist practice. Empowerment means acquiring knowledge, skills, and resources that enhance an individual's ability to control her own life and to influence others (Smith and Siegel, 1985). Traditionally women have used indirect, covert techniques to get what they want, such as helplessness, dependency, coyness, and demureness; these strategies are used when more overt methods might cause retaliation and abuse.

As a first step in client empowerment, the social worker assists the client in defining her own needs. The therapeutic value of this process is that the individual can then derive a sense of purposefulness by clarifying personal goals. As noted previously in a discussion of ego psychology perspectives on depression, an individual needs to believe that she can achieve goals in order to have a sense of well-being.

Another empowerment goal is to provide clients with education and access to resources. This could include offering information on support groups or workshops that could be related to certain therapeutic objectives, such as assertiveness.

An additional component of this goal is encouraging the client to see that the direction and ability to change lie within herself. In other words, she cannot expect others to "fix" her; alterations in her life will result only from her own undertakings.

Egalitarian Therapeutic Relationship

This principle maintains that a social worker should not abuse her status as a professional to have a "power-over" relationship with her client. Obviously, there is an innate power differential between practitioner and client because the former has expertise and training as an "authority." However, the feminist admonition is to avoid abusing that status; "abuse" in this sense might be, for example, taking all credit for client change, or using terminology and nomenclature that are difficult for the client to understand.

The transference process can be used to model nonhierarchical relationships that the client can generalize elsewhere. Crucial to the development of an egalitarian process is reflecting back to the client significant changes she has made in becoming self-empowered (Butler, 1985; Koschak, 1984; Smith and Siegel, 1985).

This principle also suggests that some self-disclosure may be appropriate on the social worker's part. However, the focus of that sharing should be on the process that the social worker used to reach a goal similar to that which the client is pursuing.

This principle is related to the empowerment goal, in that the social worker must encourage the client to see that she can bring about change and take charge of her own life.

The social worker should model her concern for changed societal conditions that eliminate institutionalized inequalities by working on some social change projects, such as abortion rights, comparable worth, anti-apartheid activism, or environmental protection. Clients can be encouraged to engage in social activism themselves, as the experience of collective action can help to validate one's sense of self, personal worth, and power to change. However, judgment will have to be used as to whether this is appropriate, based on the client's current level of functioning and willingness to take risks.

FEMINIST TREATMENT WITH DEPRESSED CLIENTS

The process of feminist treatment is composed of three stages: (a) analysis, (b) empowerment, and (c) risk-taking support (Smith and Siegel, 1985). Each of these stages will be examined in the context of its application to work with depressed clients.

The Analysis Stage

The crucial first step and primary distinguishing characteristic of feminist treatment is helping the client to analyze how her problem is related to systematic difficulties experienced by women in a sexist, racist, and classist society. Moving in this direction is based upon having initially defined the "problem" to be worked on with the client, i.e., depression. After the practitioner and client have agreed that they will engage in a process to remediate the depressive symptomology, it is appropriate to elicit from the client her perceptions as to why she is depressed.

A skillful social worker can then make connections between the client's perceptions and how many women feel. For example, consider a client whose presenting problem is a sense of "hopelessness" resulting from a failed relationship. After providing empathetic support for her feelings, the social worker should help the client to see that she may have placed too much emphasis on relationships as indicators of her worth as an individual. The social worker then can help the client to see this as a normative dilemma that women face as a result of subscribing to sex-role stereotypes of women as primarily nurturers and caretakers.

The social worker and client then can explore the actual messages the client has received throughout her lifetime as to how she should act as a female child and adult woman. In weaving childhood experiences with current circumstances, the social worker can help the client to distinguish those behaviors that were essential to engage in as a powerless child from those that are appropriate for an adult. The client then can be encouraged to consider that her value and worth are more than her ability to look after other people's needs. A 1989 film, *Shirley Valentine*, addressed this theme, showing that it is appropriate for an adult woman to define her own expectation of life, despite others' assumptions that she should be a caretaker for their needs.

The Empowerment Stage

In the second stage of feminist treatment, the social worker and the client determine the underlying purposes served by the client's behavior and then redefine that behavior. This is experienced as an empowering process. For example, let us say that the client seeking treatment for depression because of a failed relationship is an adult child of an alcoholic. Because of the dysfunction within her family, the client normatively may have experienced a lack of nurturing that may have impeded her ability both to develop self-esteem and to eventually engage intimately with others as an adult. If the client also is an adult incest survivor, she can be helped to see that a variety of messages based on stereotypical sex roles may have encouraged her to be submissive and compliant and thus may have had an impact on her abusive experiences within the family. By looking at the varied forces that affected her as a powerless child, a client's guilt and self-reproach can be ventilated and reduced, allowing her to move from being a victim to being a survivor. With this particular client, that might mean encouraging her to see that she can break the cycle of destructive relationships by becoming more self-loving as well as more able to assert her needs for validation and support from herself and from significant men and women in her life.

Empowerment at this stage of therapeutic work means helping this client to realize that she does have choices and can pursue them by utilizing her ego strengths. Recognition of those strengths by engaging in values clarification work will enhance her ability to choose goals that are self-motivating. Additionally, reflection on the ways in which she coped with trauma as a child can be used to underscore that she is strong, that she can survive, and that she is capable of engaging in honest, intimate relationships with others.

Additionally, empowerment is experienced through the therapeutic relationship by the social worker mediating the client's tendency to be dependent, which is characterized by the client attributing change more to the social worker than to herself. It is crucial for the social worker to underscore to the client that the progress she has made is the result of the client's own motivation and follow-through.

The Risk-Taking Support Stage

The third treatment stage focuses on helping the client to assume responsibility for personal change. The social worker's role during this stage is to be both supportive and directive by helping the client to define behavioral alternatives. Additionally, the social worker should provide coaching—through role playing, modeling, and similar techniques—on how objectives can be achieved. The social worker also processes with the client all progress being made toward goals.

During this stage the client should be encouraged to develop forthright communication and to cease manipulative behaviors (Rawlings and Carter, 1977). For example, the depressed client historically may have used covert power in relationships by acting helpless and dependent, believing that those behaviors would elicit protective, caretaking responses from a significant other. However, women who behave that way may actually subject themselves to potential abuse by seeming to be victims. Encouraging alternative behaviors means supporting the client in expressing her opinions, feelings, and needs, as well as helping the client to establish boundaries of unacceptable behavior by others toward her.

During this stage, anger can be channeled into action and change. This becomes a crucial self-development process, as many women have difficulty expressing anger, again because of sex-role stereotypes concerning appropriate female behavior. However, as was noted above in the section on psychoanalytic explanations for depression, when individuals do not express their anger toward lost objects, the anger is turned inward and becomes a self-deprecatory force that reduces self-esteem, thereby precipitating depression. By channeling anger into action, a client gives up culturally determined self-deprecatory behavior and replaces it with personal power and self-esteem. By doing so, she can increasingly value herself and other women.

SUMMARY

Using a feminist approach to treating persons with depression includes aiding the client to see the similarities between her experience and that of other women. It also includes helping the client to analyze the impact of sex-role stereotypes on her experiences both as a child and as an adult in relation to the distress she is currently experiencing. Anger over pejorative and abusive behaviors she has experienced can be channeled creatively into goals that enhance her self-esteem and self-actualization.

Once the client has acquired a sense of empowerment by understanding her motivation for previous behavior, examining her ego strengths, and engaging in a goal-setting process based on intrinsic values, she can be encouraged to take risks with unfamiliar and challenging behaviors. Once she no longer sees herself as powerless, she can be supported in undertaking efforts to be more assertive and directive in living her life.

MONITORING PROGRESS

The monitoring of the client's progress toward her goals is most therapeutic when done systematically over the course of treatment and with standardized assessment tools. Depending on the client's particular circumstances, the social worker might consider assessing her assertiveness, as with the Assertion Inventory (Gambril and Richey, 1975) or the Simple Rathus Assertiveness Schedule (McCormick, 1984). Alternatively, the client's cognitive state of depression might be monitored, as with the Automatic Thoughts Questionnaire (Kendall and Hollon, 1980) or the Beck Depression Inventory (Beck, 1976). Finally, the social worker might consider assessing the client's emotional state, as with the Depressed Mood Scale (Radloff, 1977), or her frequency of self-reinforcement (Heiby, 1983).

In general, the social worker should select assessment devices along with the client, and select those that fit her specific situation. In addition, the social worker should share the observations with the client in open and frank discussions on a regular basis. This both facilitates an egalitarian relationship with the client and helps her to attain her goals.

GENERALIZING FEMINIST TREATMENT

Being a feminist social worker is not the exclusive domain of women; men who can apply a sex-role analysis within a therapeutic process also can use this approach. In addition, many men experience psychic distress as a result of their difficulty in conforming to male sex-role stereotypes and thus may be appropriate clients for a feminist treatment process.

This particular approach is particularly valuable for individuals whose mental health problem is highly related to their status as members of an oppressed group. Hence, clients experiencing anxiety or depression based on discrimination they have experienced as members of minority groups could be aided by employing the sociological analysis of "power-over" relationships included in this model. For example, an ethnic minority client who is feeling despair over continued disappointments in securing good jobs might be aided by analyzing the impact of institutionalized racism, classism, and sexism on his or her experiences.

One does need an ability to conceptualize in order to engage in the sex-role analysis inherent in feminist treatment. Hence, individuals who have impaired ability to abstract would not be optimal candidates for this approach. Also, individuals whose life experiences have been such that they have not personally encountered discriminatory behavior probably will not benefit from the political analysis inherent in this approach.

In summary, a feminist perspective on treating depression is a valuable approach to use for clients who are in "at risk" groups for clinical depression. This includes women, particularly those from lower socioeconomic groups who have had multiple responsibilities and limited social and economic supports. Its value as a therapeutic modality is in allowing clients to see that they are not idiosyncratically impaired and that they can become empowered by using their own internal resources to get what they need and to influence the world around them.

CONCLUSION

A feminist approach to treating depression emphasizes the utilization of a certain process undergirded by a particular ideological foundation. There is no particular structure that one must use; a feminist approach can be applied to several standard therapeutic modalities employed in treating depression, such as psychodynamic, ego psychology, object relations, or cognitive behavioral approaches.

The philosophical and ideological foundations of feminist treatment are the elimination of "power-over" dynamics in relationships, belief in the validity of redefining and renaming one's own reality and role in life (as opposed to adhering to stereotypes), and a belief that "the personal is political." This phrase means that what one experiences on an individual level, such as sexual victimization, job discrimination, or other pejorative treatment, is symptomatic of societal inequities. The realization that one's experience is not idiosyncratic or unique can be very empowering and often breaks dysfunctional learned helplessness patterns or negates cognitive distortions concerning one's inability to master one's environment.

There are three primary stages in the process of feminist treatment: (a) analysis, (b) empowerment, and (c) risk-taking support. As was noted above, the analysis stage includes an examination of how the psychosocial stressors related to one's depression may be based in inequitable and dysfunctional societal dynamics, such as discrimination based on sex, race, age, or class. In the empowerment stage, a client examines dysfunctional beliefs and actions in her own life, such as the belief that she never will be able to provide for her own needs, and is assisted in challenging them. This includes helping a client to see that she has choices and to use her ego strengths as well as other resources to pursue them. Taking risks by trying new behaviors, the last stage, requires that a client take responsibility for personal change and receive support in doing so. This may include a wide range of behaviors, from asserting her needs to honestly expressing feelings (especially anger) to leaving a relationship.

A feminist approach is dynamic, proactive, and can be applied by social workers of either gender who have analyzed their assumptions regarding sex roles and the differential treatment of women and men. It is directive and focuses on taking action, with the social worker being vigilant not to abuse the "power of authority" associated with being a credentialed mental health professional. The approach is wholistic, seeking client empowerment through the integration of one's psychic, physical, and spiritual strengths. As a transformational paradigm most basically concerned with the elimination of "power-over" relationships, a feminist approach can lend an egalitarian, empowering perspective to many therapeutic models and is not limited to "women's issues."

CHAPTER 7

Intervention with Suicidal Individuals

André Ivanoff
Nancy Jo Smyth

In this chapter, Ivanoff and Smyth delineate a comprehensive approach to working with suicidal individuals. As they illustrate the different dimensions of suicide (e.g., defining the specific problem), they show how to tailor the intervention to the various types of suicidal behaviors. This clearly reflects the importance of fitting the intervention procedure to the client problem. The comprehensive approach presented in this chapter reflects the active participation of both social worker and client in meeting objectives and reaching goals that enhance the client's reasons for living and decrease life-threatening behavior. Some components of this intervention include contracting, building problem-solving skills, cognitive restructuring, affective regulation, and building interpersonal skills.

INTRODUCTION

Depending upon which study is consulted, suicide is either the eighth or tenth leading cause of death in the United States. At a rate of 12.7 per 100,000 people, it results in about 30,000 deaths annually (NCHS, 1988a). Attempted suicide is estimated at a rate of 103 per 100,000 (Wexler, Weissman, and Kasl, 1978). Many people, at one time or another, consider suicide. What separates those for whom the thoughts are fleeting from those who decide that suicide is the only and best solution to their problems? For clinicians, the question most often is how to prevent suicide. How is hope regained? How do alternative solutions become possible and coping abilities improve? As we learn more about the multiple pathways to suicide, it becomes apparent that a permanent solution or formula for explaining suicide is unlikely (Maris, 1981).

BACKGROUND DISCUSSION

Suicide generally is preceded by observable forms of nonfatal suicidal behavior. Social workers are far more likely to encounter clients who are thinking or talking about harming themselves in ways labeled as "suicidal'' than they are clients who actually go on to kill themselves. Attempted suicide and other nonfatal suicidal behaviors traditionally have been viewed as problems primarily because they carry with them an increased risk of suicide. More recently, however, nonfatal suicidal behaviors, including suicidal ideation and attempted suicide, are receiving some attention as problems in their own right. Increasing evidence indicates that suicidal behavior does not follow a continuum from least to most serious, but that individuals who engage in different suicidal behaviors may also possess other differences that are important in effective intervention (Linehan et al., 1986).

Nonfatal suicidal behaviors include suicidal ideation (thinking about suicide), suicide verbalization (talking about suicide), and suicide threats (informing others of plans to engage in an act of self-harm). The term "suicide gesture" refers to an act of self-harm in which the intention to die is judged as low. The lethality, or medical seriousness, of a suicide gesture is generally, but not always, also low. "Attempted suicide" is regarded an an intentional but failed effort to die. British specialists use the term "Para-suicide" to describe all categories of nonfatal self-harm. Para-suicide is a deliberate, nonfatal act of self-harm; it describes a suicide-like activity without assuming that the intent is to die (Kreitman, 1977). The terms self-harm, para-suicide, and attempted suicide are used synonomously in the literature (Hirsch, Walsh, and Draper, 1982) and in this chapter.

The lack of an agreed-upon definition of suicide is the major obstacle to the accurate collection of suicide statistics and research findings and to the development of theory about the nature and causes of suicide. In clinical practice, there are two primary definitional questions: "What *is* suicide?" and "How do I judge the intention to commit suicide?"

The common definition of suicide is a simple one: "a human act of self-inflicted, self-intentional cessation" (Shneidman, 1976, p. 5). The focus is on the intent of the actor and on the goal of the action. Dimensions used in most classification systems include initiation, intent or motivation, and knowledge of the desired consequence (Douglas, 1967). Determining that a death is a suicide raises concerns about false positives (e.g., accidental overdoses mistakenly ruled as suicides) and false negatives (e.g., concealment of suicide evidence and mistaken ruling as accidental death).

Suicidal intent refers to how serious an individual is about achieving death (Beck, Herman, and Schuyler, 1974). It is an important concept in the assessment of suicide risk, as judgments of low intent frequently are labeled as less serious or "manipulative" acts. Despite the best research and clinical efforts, there is little evidence that distinctions among levels of intent can be accurately or reliably made after the fact. Whether or not an individual truly wanted to die is very difficult for a clinician to determine, as it is sometimes even for the individual himself or herself.

Attempted suicide or self-harm may be used by distressed or psychiatrically disordered individuals to escape, cope with, or solve problems, rather than to cause death. Differential assessment of suicide intent plays an important role in choosing appropriate management and intervention strategies. There is currently no widely accepted classification system in use for attempted suicide.

Theories of Suicide

Theories of suicide extend far back into recorded history. Early philosophical explanations debated the rights of an individual to end life versus the rights of the state.

Sociological theories.   Sociological research into the causes of suicide began with Durkheim's *Le Suicide* in 1897 and resulted in three categories of suicide: (1) egoistic suicide, the result of no or poor social integration; (2) altruistic suicide, the result of excessive integration and identification; and (3) anomic suicide, the result of losing integration through trauma or catastrophe (Durkheim 1897/1952). Current sociological theories still regard suicide as a function of social regulation and social integration; however, recently social meaning, norms, restraint, and the stability and durability of social relationships have been integrated into these theories (Henry and Short, 1954; Gibbs and Martin, 1964; Douglas, 1967; Braucht, 1979). Useful for predicting changes in suicide rates for total populations or subgroups, sociological theories are of somewhat limited utility for clinicians, as they are not useful in predicting individual behavior or in identifying individual strategies for change.

Psychodynamic theories.   According to psychodynamic theories, suicide is largely the product of internal, often unconscious, motives. Suicide is an unconscious hostile impulse toward an introjected and ambivalently viewed love object that is turned inward. In addition to aggression, Freud (1926) posited that factors such as maladaptive anxiety, guilt, dependency, and rage also result in suicide-prone coping mechanisms. Feelings of abandonment, helplessness, and hopelessness are also components of the psychodynamic formulation of suicide (Maltsberger, 1986).

Biological theories.   Biological theories suggest that genetic predispositions or biochemical imbalances precipitate drives toward suicide. Despite evidence linking genetic factors to major affective and psychotic disorders, no clear relationship to suicide has been found (Motto, 1986). There also is currently no biochemical indicator of suicidality that is useful in clinical work (Motto, 1986).

Cognitive theories. Cognitive theories regard suicide and suicidal behavior as caused by the belief that current problems are insoluble (Beck, 1963) and as an effort to communicate (Farberow and Shneidman, 1961) or solve these problems (Applebaum, 1963; Levenson and Neuringer, 1971). Hopelessness is the dominant characteristic associated with suicidal behavior (Kovacs, Beck, and Weissman, 1975). Suicidal behavior is variously regarded as an effort to get rid of problems through manipulation or death (Kovacs, Beck, and Weissman, 1975; Stengel, 1964) or as an effort to cope with extremely difficult life situations (Linehan, 1981; Linehan et al., 1986; Maris, 1971).

Learning theories. Learning theories describe suicidal behavior as a function of two factors: (1) past responses in similar situations, and (2) motivating, reinforcing, and environmental conditions. Suicidal behavior is acquired through social learning methods and becomes part of a repertoire of coping responses if it receives desirable consequences from the environment. Once learned, the probability of suicidal behavior is based largely on expectations of the act by the individual and others, the opportunity to engage in the act, and the presence or absence of preventive efforts by others (Diekstra, 1973).

Integrated models. Recently, clinical researchers have developed empirically based models of suicidal behavior that integrate elements of cognitive, psychodynamic, and behavioral theories (Clum, Patsiokas, and Luscomb, 1979; Linehan, 1981; Hawton and Catalan, 1987). Although these models are modified continuously as new evidence is available, their salience for clinical social work is based in the articulation of interdependence and dynamic interaction among an individual's intrapersonal, social, and environmental systems. This conceptualization acknowledges that not only does the environment influence individuals, but that individuals also influence their environments. By cognitively acting on incoming information and by objectively changing outside influencing events, individuals can play a role in creating their own environments (Bowers, 1973).

CLINICAL MANIFESTATIONS

A working knowledge of the risk factors associated with suicidal behavior is essential for identifying individuals at immediate and long-term risk. Risk factors are based on characteristics of populations in which rates of suicidal behavior are higher than the norm; it is important to note that these are population, not individual, risk factors. It is not at all clear how many or which risk factors place an individual at "high risk." Is more worse? Yes. Is not possessing many or even one of the characteristics a guarantee of low risk or insurance against suicidal behavior? Definitely not (Farberow and MacKinnon, 1974; Lettieri, 1974a, 1974b; Motto, 1986).

Based on environmental and individual changes, one may move in or out of risk populations. Although there are many characteristics that are shared by people who attempt and those who commit suicide, there also are differences between them. There are some risk factors for which information is available on either suicide or attempted suicide, but not on both.

Demographic Risk Factors

Demographic risk factors are sex, age, and racial or ethnic factors that increase the likelihood of suicide or suicidal behavior. Men commit suicide nearly four times more often than women and rates for both sexes are higher among those aged sixty-five and older. Suicide rates are almost twice as high among whites (13.9/100,000) as blacks (6.5/100,000). Among whites, rates generally increase with age; males aged eighty to eighty-four have the highest reported rates (61.6/100,000); however, among blacks and other racial minorities, rates remain relatively constant in later life, peaking at twenty-five to thirty-four years. Among youths aged fifteen to nineteen, suicide is second only to accidents as a cause of death (NCHS, 1988b). In contrast to patterns found in other age groups, the rate of suicide among males aged fifteen to twenty-four has increased markedly since 1960 (NCHS, 1988b).

Attempted suicide is not monitored or recorded in any systematic fashion in the United States. The ratio of female to male attempters is approximately 3:1. Rates peak between ages nineteen and thirty and then decline with age. Black women attempt suicide less than their white counterparts (Baker, 1984), perhaps because there is more support available within the black community for individuals who are alienated from the dominant society (Davis, 1979).

Social Environmental Risk Factors

Social environments linked to suicidal behavior have four characteristics: (1) lack of social support; (2) high negative stress; (3) links to others, or "models" of suicidal behavior; and (4) possible positive consequences for suicidal behavior (Linehan, 1981). Specific factors associated with suicide include unemployed or retired status (except among young employed professional women, for whom rates of suicide are increasing), immigrant status (Coombs and Miller, 1975), lack of shared social characteristics with neighbors (Braucht, 1979), and living alone (Bagley, Jacobsen and Rehin, 1976; Shneidman, Farberow, and Litman, 1970; Tuckman and Youngman, 1968). Women who attempt and later succeed at suicide are more isolated than other women and also may receive less helpful care from service providers (Wandrei, 1985). The quality of social support available to suicidal individuals is largely unknown; some data suggest that the relatives of attempters may be hostile (Rosenbaum and Richman, 1970), and that suicide victims may lack even a hostile support system.

Suicidal behavior is widely regarded as a response to stressful negative life events and loss in general (Birtchnell, 1970; Levi et al., 1966). Suicide attempters report higher numbers of distressing, uncontrollable events than do nonsuicidal depressed individuals (Paykel, 1979). Other studies have found that it is not the number or type of stressful life events involved that distinguish suicidal individuals, but the effect of events, i.e., the tendency for negative events to be regarded as more stressful by suicide attempters than by others (Linehan, 1988).

Most individuals experiencing stressful life events and low social support do not go on to self-harm or suicide. Those who do may have suicidal behavior in their problem-solving response repertoires and may have positive expectations about the consequences of such action (Kreitman, Smith, and Tan, 1970; Shaffer and Gould, 1987; Chiles et al., 1985).

Following para-suicide, major environmental changes may occur in a positive direction, such as improved family interaction (Rubenstein, Moses, and Lidz, 1958). This may increase positive expectations about suicidal behavior and may increase the risk of future attempts and of suicide.

Interpersonal Risk Factors

Interpersonal interaction patterns of suicidal and para-suicidal individuals are characterized by low levels of social involvement and lack of important social skills. Individuals who commit suicide also are less likely than the general population to ask for support or attention. Some data suggest that suicidal individuals may be less hostile and more passive and dependent than nonsuicidal individuals (Buglass and McCulloch, 1970; Kreitman, 1977).

Suicide attempters are likely to be dissatisfied with treatment and to report discomfort around people in general (Cantor, 1976). Their interpersonal relationships are often characterized by high levels of conflict. In conjunction with environmental factors, these characteristics suggest a lack of mutually satisfying relationships, which may increase emotional pain, the perception of unmitigated stress, and the sense that help is unavailable (Hawton and Catalan, 1987; Linehan et al., 1986).

Individual Risk Factors

Individual risk factors can be divided into three areas: cognitive, affective, and behavioral. As subsets of these, we discuss previous suicidal behavior and psychiatric disorder as correlates of increased risk.

Cognitive characteristics associated with increased risk include problems in cognitive style and content. Stylistically, suicide attempters are distinguished by rigidity (Patsiokas, Clum, and Luscomb, 1979), impulsiveness (Farberow and Farberow, 1970; Fox and Weissman, 1975), field dependence, and poor problem-solving ability (Levenson and Neuringer, 1971; Linehan et al., 1987). Cognitive content is dominated by hopelessness (Beck, 1963; Bedrosian and Beck, 1979), which is even more strongly associated with current suicidal intent than is depression (Beck, Kovacs, and Weissman, 1975; Kovacs, Beck, and Weissman, 1975; Wetzel, 1976). A strong relationship appears to exist between suicide and hopelessness; however, data are mixed regarding the relationship between attempted suicide and hopelessness in various clinical samples (Paykel and Dienelt, 1971; Wetzel, 1976; Rotheram-Borus and Trautman, 1988).

Behavioral risk factors are those activities or physical states associated with increased risk. A previous suicide attempt is the single strongest risk factor for future suicidal behavior. The presence of a suicide note at the time of a previous para-suicide has also been linked to subsequent suicide. Mixed evidence exists linking the lethality of a prior attempt to subsequent suicide or para-suicide; both higher lethality in prior attempts and no relationship between lethality and subsequent suicidal behavior have been found (Linehan, 1981).

Substance abuse and alcoholism are strongly associated with an increased risk of suicide in both adults and adolescents. Up to 20 percent of all suicides are alcoholics (Roy and Linnoila, 1986). Suicide attempters are highly likely to have used alcohol or drugs to alter their mood within twenty-four hours preceding hospitalization for the attempt (Chiles et al., 1986).

The presence of physical illness, whether terminal, chronic, or acute, is also linked to suicide and para-suicide. Efforts to obtain medical help often are made by those who are suicidal; most suicides and para-suicides have seen a physician within the six months prior to their act (Linehan, 1981; 1988).

Mental health or psychiatric disorders are global risk indicators. Only a very small proportion of suicides among either adults or adolescents appear to be free of psychiatric symptoms (Shaffer et al., 1988). Schizophrenic adults who feel hopeless (Beck, Kovacs, and Weissman, 1975; Wetzel, 1976) or are suffering from recurrent affective disorders (major depression and bipolar disorder) are diagnostic groups at highest risk. Sociopathy is linked with repeated attempts in adults. Evidence of a criminal record is also associated with increased risk among young men (Lettieri, 1974a; 1974b). Among adolescents who commit suicide, major depression is the most common diagnosis; schizophrenia is the least common, and evidence on manic-depressive disorders is mixed. Other disorders found among teenaged suicides include antisocial behavior and learning disorders (Shaffer and Gould, 1987).

ASSESSMENT AND MONITORING METHODS

Individual vulnerabilities, such as psychiatric disorders, poor problem-solving abilities, or inadequate coping mechanisms that increase vulnerability to suicide behavior, can be worsened by environmental stress. An ecological perspective assessing the interaction between individuals and their social and physical environments is important in understanding suicide risk. Although social workers practicing outside mental health settings may have few occasions to assess suicide risk, it is essential that they be able to make such assessments. In addition to mental health and counseling agencies, where one expects to find suicidal individuals, public assistance or child welfare settings, hospitals, and institutions such as nursing homes, juvenile detention centers, and jails are all settings where vulnerable individuals may be exposed to heightened environmental stress.

When a client in an agency setting presents several risk population characteristics, it is best to ask directly about previous suicidal behavior. As part of a general assessment interview, this question can be incorporated into discussing ways in which the client has previously tried to cope with his or her problems, a standard component in clinical social work assessment interviews (Hepworth and Larsen, 1986). Contrary to myth, it is not advisable to avoid discussing suicide, nor is there any evidence that simply asking someone about suicidal ideation or behavior plants the idea (e.g., ''Well, no, I hadn't thought of it before, but that's not a bad idea!''). In fact, clinical experience suggests that if clients are thinking about suicide, most feel relieved to be asked about it. Clients may be uncertain or fearful about the social worker's reaction to suicidal ideation and may hesitate to bring it up on their own; open talk about suicide and matter-of-fact questions can make discussion easier. Good questions to begin with are: ''Have you ever thought about doing or done anything to hurt yourself?'' or ''Have you reached the point where you've given up on yourself?'' The questions should be asked directly and the responses explored immediately if they are affirmative.

Although most clients do not seek help specifically for suicidal ideation, many do seek help for problems of depression or hopelessness tied to a downward spiral of mood, sense of self-worth, and success at solving or coping with life problems. Comments that require further exploration include indirect statements of how others might be better off if the client were gone, comments such as "I can't stand it" or "I'm at the end of my rope," or expressed wishes to be with dead relatives or pets. Such statements must be explored carefully in adolescents and adults for evidence of concrete thinking that may indicate a thought disorder. Direct statements of "wanting to end it all," "check out," or "go to sleep and never wake up" also require immediate follow-up inquiries directly about suicidal ideation and self-harm.

Finally, social workers may see clients who are referred to them for ongoing individual or family intervention following a suicide attempt. When suicidal behavior has occurred in the recent past, it is important to establish quickly whether ideation or intent remains. Whether the issue of suicide risk surfaces during the initial assessment or in some later contact, the social worker proceeds in a similar manner.

There are three foci of assessment in working with suicidal clients: (1) assessment of immediate and long-term risk of suicide and suicidal behavior; (2) assessment of the suicidal responses across individual, interpersonal, and environmental systems; and (3) assessment of the problems that precipitated the suicidal behavior across individual, interpersonal, and environmental systems.

Risk Characteristics

Although risk characteristics provide information about long-term risk, they do not predict the likelihood of future suicide or para-suicide. A number of suicide prediction scales have been developed to identify at-risk individuals. These scales alert the practitioner that a client falls into a risk population. However, individuals lacking one or many of the characteristics associated with suicide or para-suicide are not without risk, nor in any way immune to risk. Population risk characteristics are useful indicators of increased risk, generally at some unspecified time in the future. They do not provide information about the likelihood of suicide or para-suicide in the immediate future or next few days.

Unfortunately, in assessing immediate as well as long-term risk, there is no checklist of factors that can directly predict imminent risk. There are, however, direct and indirect indicators associated with suicidal behavior. Compiled originally by Linehan (1981) and updated to reflect new evidence, these indicators differentiate suicidal individuals from those who are not and describe circumstances that are associated with suicide or para-suicide within the next few days (Linehan, 1981).

Direct indicators of immediate risk include suicide ideation, suicide threats, suicide planning or preparation, and previous para-suicide at any time in the past. Indirect indicators of immediate risk include recent disruption or loss of an important interpersonal relationship, and falling into a population at-risk for suicide or para-suicide. Indifference to or dissatisfaction with treatment, recent medical care, current hopelessness, anger, or indirect references to or arrangements for death are also indirect indicators. Circumstances linked with suicide or attempted suicide in the next few days or hours are alcohol consumption, available or easily obtained suicide method, isolation, suicide note written or in progress, and precautions against discovery or intervention.

Functional Analysis

Assessment and intervention planning with a suicidal client are best conceptualized and conducted using what is known as a functional analysis. Based on the functional analysis interview model used in general clinical assessment (Pomeranz and Goldfried, 1970), it has been adapted for suicidal behavior by Linehan (1981). (See table 7.1.) For readers unfamiliar with this model of assessment, examples of questions used to obtain the information are suggested in the right-hand column of table 7.1.

Standardized instruments that are useful as adjunctive clinical tools include the Beck Hopelessness Scale (Beck and Weissman, 1974), the Reasons for Living (RFL) Inventory (Linehan, 1983), and the Suicide Intent Scale (Beck, Herman, and Schuyler, 1974). The RFL and other scales that measure associated problems of depression and life satisfaction can be found in Corcoran and Fischer (1987). Thorough clinical assessment requires a clinical interview, the use of standardized measures correlated with suicidal behavior, and ongoing monitoring of the specific thoughts, feelings, actions, and circumstances tied to this client's suicidal behavior (Blythe and Tripodi, 1989; Bloom and Fischer, 1982).

INTERVENTION

Crisis Intervention

To paraphrase a frequently cited expression, all forms of intervention are ineffective with a dead client (Mintz, 1968). Crisis intervention is the social worker's front-line strategy with a client at immediate risk of suicidal behavior. Intervention in crisis situations is described by Golan (1986) and summarized in Linehan (1981). Once the social worker determines that the client is at immediate risk, action must be taken to prevent further suicidal behavior. First of all, this means making certain the client is physically safe.

Is there someone in the client's home environment who is willing and able to stay with the client until the crisis passes? Is this individual willing and able to call emergency services for assistance if the client appears unable to maintain control? Does the client require hospitalization? A bias toward maintaining the client's sense of self-control and personal man-

TABLE 7–1 Functional Assessment of Suicidal Behavior

Information	Suggested Questions
A. Suicidal behaviors (ideation, threats planning/preparation, para-suicide)	A.
1. Identification and description	1. Have you had any thoughts of hurting or killing yourself? If so what were they? Have you recently (*fill in suicidal behaviors*)? If so, what did you do? Have you done anything to prepare for hurting or killing yourself? If so, what?
2. Dimensions of suicidal behavior (duration, pervasiveness, frequency, severity)	2. When did you first begin recently having these thoughts? How often do they occur? Each day? Each week? When you have these thoughts, how long do they last? Do the thoughts interfere with other things you're doing? On a scale from 1–10, with 1 being no urge at all to act and 10 being an overpowering urge to act on the thoughts, what is the worst these thoughts have been? How often does that happen? On the same scale, how strong are the thoughts usually? Yesterday? Today?
3. History of suicidal behavior (patient and family)	3. Same questions as above: What problems were going on in your life (or family members') that precipitated suicidal behavior?
4. Apparent situational determinants (preceding/ consequent events)	4. Are there particular items, situations, or interaction with others when you're more likely to _____? (*Go over each situation.*) What has happened after you've _____?

TABLE 7–1 *(Continued)*

Information	Suggested Questions
5. Apparent behavioral determinants (preceding/consequent events)	5. Describe what else you think before you _____. What are you usually doing before you _____? Describe what you think, feel, and do after _____.
B. Problems precipitating suicidal behavior; presenting problems	B.
1. Nature of problems: identification and description	1. What sorts of problems are happening in your life that make you consider _____?
2. Dimensions of problems (duration, pervasiveness, frequency, severity)	2. For each problem, when did this start being a problem, how often does it happen, how much does it in the way of accomplishing other things? (*Get more details.*)
3. Historical setting for problems	3. For each problem, has it ever happened before? If so, how did you handle it then? What else has happened in the past that you think may have contributed to this problem?
4. Current situational determinants (preceding/consequent events)	4. For each problem, who else is involved with the problem, when does the problem come up, what else is usually happening then, what's going on immediately before the problem, immediately after, what do other people do?
5. Current behavioral determinants (preceding/consequent patient behaviors)	5. For each problem, what are you usually doing/thinking/feeling before the problem comes up? During? After? In the long run, what happens as a result of the problem?
C. Patient/environment characteristics relevant to suicide risk	
1. Environmental characteristics that increase the risk of suicide and para-suicide (life events, social support, models, consequences of suicidal and nonsuicidal behaviors)	

TABLE 7-1   *(Concluded)*

Information	Suggested Questions
2. Patient characteristics that increase the risk of suicide and para-suicide (demographic variables; cognitive, physiological/affective, and overt motor behavioral patterns)	
3. Environmental and patient characteristics that reduce the risk of suicidal behaviors	
D. Patient/environment characteristics relevant to treatment	
1. Client assets (physical, aptitudes, abilities, interests, etc.)	
2. Patient deficiencies (physical, aptitude, abilities, interests, etc.)	
3. Environmental assets	
4. Environmental deficiencies	
E. Objectives	
1. Targets of modification (*list in priority order*)	
2. Outcome criteria and how progress will be measured (*list by target*)	
F. Interventions	
1. Immediate steps needed to reduce current suicide or para-suicide risk	
2. Intervention strategies (*list by target*)	

SOURCE: Adapted from Pomeranz and Goldfried (1970).

agement whenever possible should be demonstrated in assessing how best to deal with a crisis.

The decision to hospitalize a client is generally made in conjunction with a physician or emergency room staff. The question to ask yourself when considering this decision is "Can I prevent a suicide *now* by hospitalization?" Some psychiatric disorders linked to increased suicide risk, such as delusional disorders, depression, schizophrenia, schizoaffective disorders, and panic disorders, are best treated in the hospital during their acute phases. In other cases, however, the negative consequences of hospitalization—including social stigma, loss of feeling of control, and the potentially unfavorable treatment received from hospital staff—are worth consideration. Asking yourself "Does hospitalization prevent suicidal behavior from occurring in the future?" usually is not helpful. This question cannot be answered conclusively, and finds little positive endorsement in the empirical literature.

The use of contracts, both verbal and written, between social workers and suicidal clients is reported to be quite successful (Gibbons et al., 1978; Linehan, 1981). Here the contract refers only to suicidal behavior, not to other agreements for service. Prior to ending contact, whether in person or over the phone, the client is asked to agree not to commit suicide or harm himself or herself, and if he or she feels strong urges to do so, to contact the social worker or other stipulated service provider. If the client is unwilling or feels unable to enter into this contract with the social worker, a brief voluntary hospitalization may be discussed as a self-initiated method of helping regain control.

If a suicide attempt has already been made or is in progress when the social worker is notified, it may be necessary to call the police or emergency rescue squad for immediate action. If the social worker knows that local emergency services are not immediately responsive, an involved and supportive family member or friend may be called to go to the client and stay there until help arrives.

Planning for a Crisis

Ideally, the best way to manage a crisis is to predict and plan for it. If a client has attempted suicide or experienced intermittent intense suicidal ideation in the past, it is useful to acknowledge that the ideation will probably return periodically over the next few months. Viewing the ideation as a "habit" that you and the client will together develop ways to manage can be an adaptive problem-solving strategy.

Based on the coping resources and cognitive strengths identified during assessment (e.g., important reasons for living, any positive hopes for the future, supportive others), a plan for coping is developed. A useful product of this planning is a "crisis card," a business-sized card that has the phone numbers of emergency contacts on one side and a list of coping strategies to help maintain control on the other. Carried at all times by the client, the card can be used as a self-instructional device for periods when the client risks losing control and falling into suicidal behavior.

Legal Issues

Issues of legal liability and possible litigation in the event of a suicide warrant consideration. Many agency policies require social workers to enact coercive means of prevention, such as involuntary hospitalization, in all cases where the social worker is not confident that clients will not harm themselves. In circumstances where no policy exists, social workers must exercise greater self-awareness, risk assessment, and decision-making skills. However, malpractice suits are a very real possibility in the event of suicide or attempted suicide, based on the premise that the professional neglected to prevent the client's death or disability. Bad or negligent practice is measured in terms of professional practice standards and usually involves expert professional testimony to establish whether reasonable practice standards were followed (Perr, 1979). Good risk management procedures regarding suicide include immediate documentation of decisions, clear policies regarding the management of suicidal patients and strict adherence to those policies, and familiarity and compliance with relevant state laws (Perr, 1985). Given the possibile consequence, social workers in agency or private practice are prudent to practice within these guidelines.

Liability concerns provide one good reason for the use of professional consultation; in addition, the general need for ongoing consultation while working with suicidal clients cannot be overstated. The degree of judgment exercised and the types of decisions made require discussion with another professional, preferably one who is experienced with suicidal clients. The immediate and ongoing assessment of risk, the review of intervention strategies, and the exploration of other available prevention resources are three functions that this consultation can serve. Consultation can also help the social worker to maintain self-awareness and deal with personal responses engendered by the client's suicidal behavior. The possibility of losing a client to suicide or dealing with repeated para-suicide and the consequent feelings of frustration, anger, and impotence are reasonable and normal; however, they can prevent the social worker from being effective during this time.

Treatment of Choice

The treatment of suicidal behavior is ameliorative and preventive: to change the conditions maintaining or precipitating the current behavior and to decrease the likelihood that more severe behavior will occur. This treatment combines elements from several different treatment models and protocols (Clum, Patsiokas, and Luscomb, 1979; Gibbons, Butler, and Gibbons, 1978; Hawton and Catalan, 1987; Ivanoff, 1984; Liberman and Eckman, 1981; Linehan et al., 1986). Taken together, these components form a comprehensive treatment model. As a comprehensive model, it can be difficult to implement across all practice settings, and individual social workers may need to secure additional services elsewhere. Initial components include problem-solving set, contracting, referral and resource gathering, and medication evaluation. Four components make up a coping skills module, the middle phase of treatment: problem solving, cognitive restructuring, affect regulation, and interpersonal relations. Finally, maintenance and generalization of change are addressed through relapse prevention and follow-up strategies.

Research support. Based on the treatment outcome literature, there is no single best model of treatment to date. The recommended model is based on the treatment outcome literature and on the empirically derived characteristics of ideators, attempters, and suicides described earlier. It is important to note that the methodological quality of these studies is consistent. There also are few replicated components across the treatment studies.

Table 7.2 summarizes the attempted suicide, para-suicide, and self-harm treatment outcome studies by type of treatment, sample, design, and outcome related to suicidal behavior. Although it cannot be assumed that programs that are successful in reducing para-suicide are equally successful in decreasing completed suicides, the methodological problems in studying suicide and the statistical infrequency of suicide make this a next-best effort. Most studies compare the effectiveness of two treatments on suicidal behavior; because there are ethical problems in withholding treatment from suicidal individuals, the opportunity to use experimental designs is somewhat limited. Based on the treatment outcome research, several treatment components emerge as successful in reducing attempted suicide or self-harm: behavioral skills training, active follow-up, and medication.

Practice wisdom support. Many of the best-known suicide theorists and clinicians also have contributed to the empirical literature on suicide and suicidal behavior. Others, best known for their clinical contributions, include Shneidman, Farberow, Hendin, and Maltsberger. Although the recommended assessment and treatment model is presented from a cognitive-behavioral perspective, there are generally accepted clinical guidelines and principles that cut across major theoretical orientations.

Despair and giving up on oneself and the future have long been linked to suicide and suicide attempts. Freud's anxiety theory (1926) describes signal anxiety as an activating mechanism used by healthy, optimistic adults when self-regulation of emotional response is required. Bibring (1953) describes depression as a helpless and hopeless, rather than an activating, response to challenge. The ability to self-regulate emotional distress, learned as a task of separation, is critical in normal development. The absence of important sustaining resources—intrapersonal, interpersonal, and environmental—is cited often in the clinical literature on suicide (Maltsberger, 1986). Providing access to resources that the client can-

TABLE 7–2 Treatment Outcome Studies

Author	Sample	Design	Treatment	Follow-up Period	Results
Greer & Bagley (1971)	1 or more para-suicides; para-suicides who presented in emergency room (ER)	Q-Ex	1. prolonged contact (n=88) 2. brief contact, 1 or 2 sessions (n=76) 3. no treatment (n=47)	1–2 yrs.	(1=2) < 3
Kennedy (1972)	1 or more para-suicides; para-suicides under the care of general practitioners	Q-Ex	1. admitted to psychiatric tx center (n=142) 2. referred to a psychiatrist (n=32) 3. not referred (n=30)	1 yr.	1 < (2=3)
Chowdhury et al. (1973)	2 or more para-suicides; para-suicides admitted to poison center: studied on discharge	Ex	1. outpt. clinic, home visits, 24-hr. emergency service (n=71) 2. conventional care (n=84)	6 mos.	1 = 2
Bostock & Williams (1974)	3 or more suicide attempts, woman on a psychiatric inpatient unit	SSD-ABC	inpt. tx, including relaxation, systematic desensitization, operant shaping; outpt. follow-up (n=1)	27 mos.	no self-harm for last 18 mos. of follow-up
Ettlinger (1975)	1 or more suicide attempts; attempters admitted to hospital in need of intensive medical treatment	Q-Ex	1. intensive tx, contact w/relatives, planned follow-up (n=222) 2. less therapy time than in #1 (n=233)	5 yrs.	1 = 2

TABLE 7-2 (Continued)

Author	Sample	Design	Treatment	Follow-up Period	Results
Termansen & Bywater (1975)	1 or more suicide attempts; attempters presenting in ER	Ex	1. short-term intensive follow-up by MH worker (n=45) 2. same as #1, but by volunteer (n=32) 3. no follow-up	3 mos.	1 < 2 = 3
Bartman (1976)	2 or more suicide attempts; women on inpatient psychiatric unit for attempt	Ex	1. assertive training & milieu (n=7) 2. discussion control & milieu (n=7)	6 wks.	1 < 2
Welu (1977)	1 or more suicide attempts; attempters presenting in ER	Ex	1. outreach program (early engagement, biweekly contacts, visits (n=62) 2. standard program (n=57)	4 mos.	1 < 2
Gibbons et al. (1978)	1 or more self-poisonings; self-poisoning patients presenting in ER	Ex	1. time-limited task-centered casework in patient's home (n=200) 2. routine services, referral (n=200)	1 yr.	1 < 2
Hawton (1980)	1 or more self-poisonings; self-poisoning patients discharged from hospital after admission for overdose	Ex	1. domiciliary tx (n=48) 2. outpt. clinic tx (n=48)	1 yr.	1 = 2

TABLE 7–2 (*Concluded*)

Author	Sample	Design	Treatment	Follow-up Period	Results
Liberman & Eckman (1981)	2 or more suicide attempts; attempters on inpatient psychiatric unit (clinical research unit)	Ex	1. behavior therapy (n = 12) 2. insight therapy (n = 12); inpt., outpt., & follow-up	2 yrs.	1 = 2 at 2 yrs. 1 < 2, at 2, 12, 24 wks. (overall para-suicide rate lower than the rate prior to tx)
Draper & Hirsch (1982)	1 or more para-suicides; para-suicides admitted to hospital for para-suicide: studied on discharge	Ex	1. mianserin 60 mg. for 6 wks (n = 38) 2. nomifensine 150 mg. for 6 wks (n = 38) 3. placebo (n = 38)	3 mos.	1 = 2 = 3
Montgomery & Montgomery (1982)	3 or more suicidal acts; persons admitted to hospital for suicidal act: studied on discharge	Ex	Study A 1. mianserin (n = 27) 2. placebo (n = 21) Study B 1. flupenthinol (n = 14) 20 mg. mo. for 6 mos. 2. placebo (n = 16)	6 mos.	A: 1 = 2 B: 1 < 2
Ivanoff (1984)	1 or more suicide attempts; women on inpatient psychiatric unit (clinical research unit) admitted for attempt	Q-Ex	1. inpt. tx systematic desensitization (n = 4) 2. inpt. tx problem-solving training (n = 5)	6 wks.	1 = 2

KEY:
Ex = experimental design
Q-Ex = quasi-experimental design
SSD-ABC = single subject, ABC design
1 < 2 = 3 = group 1 had fewer suicide attempts than groups 2 & 3, which were equal in number of suicide attempts

not otherwise reach and teaching interpersonal and self-regulation skills address these deficits.

Narrowed and constricted cognition, accompanied by hopelessness that allows suicide as the only option to problems, is the most common cognitive characteristic of suicidal individuals. The immediate focus in treatment is on problem solving and broadening the client's range of felt options. Longer-term treatment focuses on the client's own ability to problem solve and avoid the cognitive errors that lead to suicidal behavior.

Practice wisdom also suggests the efficacy of general therapeutic and suicide contracts. Accessible help and clear expectations concerning response to suicidal behavior also are frequently noted.

Structure of the Intervention

An intervention plan is developed only after completing the functional analysis and assessment of problem areas. Attempting to base intervention on vague presenting problems can result in imprecise and ineffective intervention that serves to further convince the client that his or her problems are unsolvable.

Accordingly, a contract or agreement between social worker and client about the problems for work is important. In addition to describing the problems, a contract identifies the desired changes so that both client and social worker will know when the problem has been rectified or the goal accomplished. Individuals who are involved in the intervention plan should be specified and expectations that the client attend sessions and work actively on the problems should be agreed upon. If family members or others are involved, they should be clear about their roles in the intervention so that confusion does not result. The social worker's role in helping the client to work toward solutions to the problems and the social worker's response to any future suicidal behavior should also be made as clear as possible. The client has the right to know whether the social worker intends to encourage hospitalization, speak to family members if risk increases, or pursue involuntary hospitalization under set circumstances. Finally, the practicalities of role expectations, the extent and limits of confidentiality, and the expected number of treatment sessions should be discussed as a part of the contract.

Treatment Process: How to Implement the Treatment

Direct focus on the suicidal behavior and active problem solving are two hallmarks of prescribed intervention programs (Clum, Patsiokas, and Luscomb 1979; Hawton and Catalan, 1987; Linehan, 1981; Linehan et al., 1986). The social worker must first, however, adopt and convey to the client a problem-solving set or perspective toward suicidal behavior. Simply put, this means that suicidal behavior is considered a maladaptive solution and a response to some other problem. The social worker, taking the role of clinical scientist rather than omnipotent healer, works with the client to hypothesize and test alternative solutions to the problems that precipitate suicidal behavior. One function of the problem-solving set is to decrease the valence attached to suicidal thoughts and behavior by explaining them as responses to unsolvable problems. This in turn provides access to the problems precipitating the suicidal behavior and to the process of problem solving.

Once this occurs, the social worker can define and partialize presenting problems, establish priorities for intervention, and establish the contract with the client. Concerns related to immediate suicide risk and physical safety remain high priorities and strategies for managing crises should be in place before moving to other presenting problems.

Referral to other agencies. Referral to other agencies for primary or adjunctive service often is necessary. Suicidal clients frequently have multiple problems and may need the structure and support of, for example, a partial hospital program, supportive or supervised housing, substance abuse treatment, family therapy, or emergency food and shelter services. In many cases, social workers need to involve several agencies, requiring skillful case management. Consistency in therapeutic approach among all services is important to treatment outcome and roles of service providers must be clearly delimited. One typical case involved a repeatedly suicidal client who needed a crisis plan incorporating multiple service providers. The plan included the city police department, hospital emergency room staff, mental health crisis line, halfway house staff, and day treatment staff, in addition to the client and primary clinician. Each participant had a role in the plan and was involved in the plan's development. Implementing the plan required careful attention, coordination, and clear communication.

Medication evaluation. Suicidal clients almost always also experience psychiatric symptoms such as depression, anxiety, disordered thinking, or panic attacks; thus, a medication evaluation is recommended. Social workers who are not working in mental health settings are advised to develop a cooperative relationship with a psychiatrist. Likewise, if a client is already on medication, it is important to establish a relationship with the prescribing physician as soon as possible. Because the need for medication must be balanced with other considerations, including likelihood of lethal overdose and the client's impulsiveness, ongoing dialogue between the social worker and the physician is essential. Overdoses sometimes can be avoided by limiting the supply of drugs on hand through prescription or by having involved others store the medication and dispense it to the client.

Building coping and problem-solving skills. Following stabilization, the focus shifts to improving the client's ability to cope with and solve problems. Four skill components make up the coping skills module: problem solving, cognitive restructuring, affect regulation, and interpersonal relations. Although these components are presented separately, they operate in an integrated fashion; improved skill in one area will benefit other areas. Problem solving is both the perspective and the process in which other skills are used. Each skill is presented to and practiced with the client in the same manner. First, the social worker explains and demonstrates or models the skill. The client then rehearses the skill in the session. Finally, the client is given homework assignments to facilitate practicing the skill or components of it.

Problem solving. Problem solving is the primary component of the skills module. Active problem solving involves training the client to improve deficient problem-solving skills and encouraging and supporting the use of skills that have been inhibited. The social worker also provides direct information and offers feedback about the efficacy of proposed problem-solving solutions.

Effective problem solving involves four separate tasks. Clients may experience difficulty in one or more of them. Identifying specific deficits or inhibitions can help to target interventions. First, a problem must be recognized and accurately identified. In interpersonal conflicts, defining the problem as belonging solely to the other person is an example of flawed problem identification.

Second, alternative ways of solving the problem must be generated; the more alternatives an individual can generate, the better his or her ability to move from one to another when necessary. The suicidal individual sees only one alternative to his or her problem. Feeling trapped and seeing no way out demonstrates a lack of ability to entertain alternative problem-solving strategies. The client may say, "But there is *no other* way!" Third, the best solution to the problem must be selected and implemented. Faulty choice and implementation may result from poor decision making and judgment or from impulsiveness and failure to examine the consequences of an action. Finally, once the solution is implemented, its effectiveness must be evaluated for learning and future action. Sorting out the lessons in successful as well as unsuccessful problem solving is important to further development. For example, a client learned to control outbursts of rage at her toddler by using situational planning, a set of self-instructions during high-tension periods, and support from friends afterwards. With practice over time she was able to eliminate the outbursts and the feelings of self-recrimination that led to suicidal ideation.

The social worker's role in the change process includes several simultaneous activities. The first is to provide hope, in the absence of the client's own, that his or her problems eventually can be managed or solved. Although providing hope clearly is important in the beginning phase of work, it is also common for the automatic "what's the use? I may as well give up" thoughts to return intermittently as problem solving becomes more difficult for the client. Coping with problems continues throughout life: without a prior history of success and skill in coping, the future can seem overwhelming. The social worker should remain comfortable with the notion of lending hope to the client during the slow, gradual process of rebuilding the client's own internal resources.

Finally, the social worker's response to the client's efforts should be supportive and encouraging, but also corrective. If a client persists in maladaptive or ineffective problem solving, change has not occurred nor has the likelihood of future suicidal behavior decreased. Learning new ways of solving problems, however, is difficult. Each step toward adaptive problem-solving should be supported verbally, as clients may not recognize the accomplishment. Warmth in responding to not-quite-right efforts, help in adjustment, and the encouragement of continued effort are frequently repeated by the social worker.

Cognitive restructuring. Cognitive restructuring, the second skill component, is based on theories that dysfunctional thought and belief patterns play a key in maladaptive behavior (Beck, 1976; Ellis, 1962). Examples of dysfunctional thoughts are, "it's hopeless, there's nothing I can do"; "I can't do anything right"; or "the only way out is suicide." The client learns to identify and then to respond to dysfunctional thoughts by replacing them with more adaptive thoughts which, in turn, promote more adaptive coping.

Increasing awareness of internal dialogue and patterns of thinking can be done by simulating a problem situation (through role play or guided visualization) and asking the client what he or she is thinking at a particular moment. The social worker can model the process by speaking aloud his or her own thoughts while role playing a problem situation. Next, clients learn about the relationship between dysfunctional thoughts and strong feelings. For example, thinking "the only way out is suicide" is likely to result in feelings of hopelessness, whereas countering that thought with "there are options to suicide, I just can't see them right now" can reduce hopelessness and possible impulsiveness.

Clients then learn how to evaluate the adaptiveness of their thoughts and to replace any unrealistic or dysfunctional thoughts with those that facilitate coping. Asking such questions as, "what evidence do I have to support this belief?" or "what evidence do I have to disprove this thought?'' can assist in this evaluation process. Often the social worker can give the client specific tasks to do to gather evidence to invalidate an irrational belief. An example is asking a client to complete some relatively simple tasks to test the belief that ''I can't do anything right.'' By monitoring the client's thoughts across a variety of situations, the social worker and the client work to identify the dysfunctional cognitions that most commonly arise, evaluate the dysfunctional content, and then substitute more adaptive thoughts.

Affect regulation.   Affect regulation training involves developing skills to manage strong emotional responses to stressful situations through physiological regulation and general emotional coping (Linehan, 1984, 1987). Physiological regulation of affect involves identification of the physical sensations that are part of emotional responses, distinguishing one emotion from another, physical self-care, and relaxation strategies. First, clients learn how to identify physical sensations connected to the feelings they are experiencing by discussing the common physical sensations associated with specific feelings. This facilitates accurate labeling of feelings and allows clients to judge the intensity of what they feel.

Once the sensations of feelings are recognized, clients learn physical care and relaxation strategies. Physical care strategies include limiting caffeine intake and getting regular exercise, adequate sleep, and good nutrition; avoiding mood-altering drugs and alcohol; and treating any physical illnesses. Methods of relaxation range from simple to complex; from hot baths, deep breathing, massage, and listening to quiet music, to meditation or cue-controlled relaxation, in which relaxation is induced in response to a personally chosen word or signal, such as ''relax'') (McGlynn, 1985).

General emotional coping skills include two primary strategies, distraction and distancing. Distraction is turning one's focus to something other than the distressing situation—something that evokes an emotional response that is incompatible with the response evoked by the distressing situation. This is done by using visual imagery, purposely thinking about something else, or engaging in an activity. Distancing strategies that allow observation of feelings from a detached perspective also are useful. Examples of distancing tactics include focusing on physical sensations, focusing on details in the environment, observing patterns of self-thought, and writing in a journal.

Interpersonal relations skills.   Building interpersonal relations skills includes training in assertive and general social skills (Gambrill and Richey, 1988; Linehan, 1984). Assertiveness training includes distinguishing among assertive, aggressive, and passive behaviors, assessing situations requiring assertiveness, and learning specific assertive communication skills. These skills are using ''I'' statements, making clear requests, disagreeing effectively, staying focused, refusing requests/demands, and re-sisting pressure to withdraw refusals.

General social skills training includes strategies that are helpful in meeting people, indicating interest in and caring about others, and con-ducting conversations. Also included are relationship enhancement and conflict resolution skills. Excellent practice tasks and written exercises can be found in Gambrill and Richey (1988).

After learning adaptive coping skills in treatment, the client's task be-comes transferring these skills to real-world situations and maintaining them there once treatment is completed. Incorporating homework as-signments into the skill training module throughout treatment is an effec-tive method for accomplishing this.

Relapse prevention.   Relapse prevention (Marlatt, 1985) means pre-venting future suicidal behavior or limiting the degree of suicidal behav-ior should a lapse occur. Situations that have in the past resulted in sui-cidal behavior are identified by the social worker and client. Alternate coping responses to risk situations are then generated; often these re-sponses are developed through the coping skills module. Rehearsal and practice for relapse prevention rely on the same strategies used in learn-ing coping skills.

In addition to planning for high-risk situations, clients explore the short- and long-term consequences of suicidal behavior. For example, al-though a suicide attempt initially may mobilize significant others, effect-ing a short-term positive outcome, those same significant others may in the long run get hostile and withdraw from the client. Clients are thus taught to think past the immediate outcomes of a relapse and consider the longer-term consequences (Marlatt, 1985).

Active follow-up.   Active follow-up is the final intervention compo-nent. Follow-up has two objectives: to keep the client engaged in treat-ment as long as is required, and to solicit the involvement of any signifi-cant others. Client involvement is important, because many suicidal clients discontinue treatment prematurely. Follow-up letters, phone calls, and home visits increase the likelihood the client will follow through with treatment.

Similarly, involvement of significant others can facilitate clients' con-tinued involvement in treatment by providing concrete support, such as assistance with medication monitoring. Significant others are those peo-ple who are most likely to be in conflictual relationships with clients. In-cluding significant others in treatment has the potential to create mean-ingful change in clients' environments, thereby facilitating clients' change efforts.

Treatment Limitations

Success in treating suicidal behavior can be defined as the absence of suicidal thinking or action. It can also be defined more broadly as regaining the desire to live. Once an individual believes that death (or its suggestion) is the answer to life, the process of regaining hope and learning new ways of coping is slow and difficult.

There are many obstacles and limits to treatment of individuals who may be determined to end their lives. Foremost among these are environmental suicide potentiators: Is there ready access to the means to suicide? Are drugs and alcohol available? Are services or help unavailable? Both suicide and suicide attempts can occur impulsively, with little planning, when firearms, drugs, and isolation confront the vulnerable suicidal individual. This is particularly true among adolescents. Family environments also can potentiate suicide. Some families find it hard to acknowledge the severity of a member's problems and may not cooperate in obtaining help. Suicidal or depressed individuals who live in households where guns and drugs are openly accessible may impulsively use them. Surprisingly, high rates of suicide also occur in psychiatric hospitals and in jails, even though at-risk persons are under observation; such persons can persevere and find easily available methods, such as hanging.

Individuals who suffer from schizophrenia or other thought disorders and are unwilling to take medication often are not able to participate fully in treatment. The same is true for the substance abuser who is unwilling to obtain additional specific alcohol or drug treatment. Finally, there are individuals in multiproblem, chaotic life situations, such as economic duress, abusive relationships, substance abuse, and possible psychiatric disorder, who are unable to stop the turmoil and crises long enough to begin to learn new methods of coping. When feasible, short-term removal from the immediate setting may be the best way to begin change in this situation.

GENERALIZATION TO OTHER PROBLEM AREAS

The treatment components recommended in this chapter were all developed for and tested on the target problems associated with suicidal behavior. In this sense, suicidal behavior is the generalized problem.

Cognitive modification methods are integral parts of empirically validated treatments for depression, anxiety disorders, stress-related problems, and interpersonal deficits of both skill and inhibition. Problem-solving training has been found to be effective with depression, stress-related problems, and in a wide variety of programs seeking to prevent or decrease risk taking (e.g., smoking, drug use, and unsafe sex practices) related to health and emotional well-being. Interpersonal skill training has been found useful with individuals suffering from depression, social anxiety disorders, and marital dysfunction. It is also an important adjunct component in the treatment and prevention of drug use and other dysfunctional activities that are, to some extent, socially controlled (Bellack and Hersen, 1985).

A most challenging and fascinating extension of these treatment components, however, is their potential use for treating borderline personality disorder (Linehan, 1987; Turner, 1989). Although there is some overlap between the characteristics of borderline personality disorder clients and those of chronic suicide attempters, the extent of this relationship remains unclear. Borderline personality disorder is associated with long-standing patterns of myriad chronic self-destructive behavior, conflictual interpersonal relations, and inability to regulate affective distress. As with the model described for suicidal behavior, these programs include cognitive restructuring, interpersonal skills training, and affect regulation, but vary in their application methods and format.

CLOSING NOTE

Suicidal and despairing people are not sought out as clients. They can be frightening to the social worker's sense of personal equanimity and precipitate many sleepless nights. Few social workers prepare well or deliberately for the task of working with them until it is necessary. The introduction of this topic into the general social work practice literature suggests that some social workers want to examine issues of assessing and treating suicidal clients sooner rather than later.

CHAPTER 8

Competency-Based Treatment for Persons with Marital Discord

Catheleen Jordan
Norman H. Cobb

In this chapter, Jordan and Cobb show how to help couples in a dysfunctional relationship, focusing specifically on how to promote social competencies by developing functional social skills. One of the components of structure that they emphasize is defining the couple's problem by considering five areas of functioning: values, communication, negotiation and contracting, stress, and time management. Jordan and Cobb describe how to help couples with each of these problem areas to facilitate matching the client problem with specific clinical procedures. The components of the intervention are explained precisely, including a five-step protocol that uses active client participation, both in the session and in outside homework assignments.

INTRODUCTION

In this country approximately one in three marriages ends in divorce (Gambrill and Richey, 1988). This statistic does not take into account the number of marriages where spouses separate or desert the relationship and formal divorce proceedings do not occur. The statistics do not reflect marriages in which couples stay together although the relationship is characterized by marital dissatisfaction. Also, statistics are not available on the number of unmarried couples who experience the discord and frustration of living with another person. Barker (1984) reported that about 50 percent of wives have been hit by their husbands, at least 41 percent of married men and 20 percent of married women have been involved in extramarital affairs, and 80 percent of couples have considered divorce at some point in their relationship. Although the true extent of dissatisfaction and dissolution is difficult to estimate (both formally and informally), marriage and couple counseling is an important field for intervention by social workers and other helping professionals.

This chapter addresses dysfunction in intimate relationships and presents important interventions to build the skills and competence of partners. The problem is discussed in terms of background, clinical manifestations, and assessment issues, and how these aspects logically dictate the suggested intervention package. Although the terms indicative of marital relationships are used extensively in this chapter, the concepts and issues are relevant to all couples.

PROBLEM IDENTIFICATION

From a social learning–cognitive behavioral perspective, marriage relationships are seen as a product of the reciprocal interactions between marital partners in the context of their unique environment. Through the interaction of spouses' personal values, beliefs, and expectations, they create for themselves complex systems of individual and mutual behavior patterns. These strongly influence the satisfaction of the relationship and each partner's personal self-esteem or cognitive image.

Unfortunately, couples have varying degrees of skills with which to establish healthy systems of behavior. Although all couples could benefit from enhancing particular relationship skills, dysfunctional couples demonstrate significant deficits in these important skills. For example, many couples have rigid systems of verbalized or hidden rules, which might include: "Don't talk about our problems to others"; "Always say nice things about my body"; "Don't make a lot of noise when we're having sex." Many couples, particularly dysfunctional ones, lack the skills to discuss value differences and communicate the desire to negotiate solutions.

Background Discussion

Several theoretical models contribute to an understanding of couples from the social learning–cognitive behavioral perspective. Behavior modification emphasizes that partners' reinforced behavior increases and punished behavior decreases. Satisfaction or dissatisfaction is determined by the different levels of positive and punishing behaviors. Dissatisfaction can result from a high rate of punishing behaviors or a low rate of positive reinforcers (Jacobson and Dallas, 1981).

From social learning theory, Bandura (1977) emphasized that people's behavior is reciprocally determined in the give-and-take of relationships. For example, when two people communicate, the initial message has significant impact on the listener. The message not only defines the topic, but also alters the way the receiver thinks and reacts to the other person. When the listener returns the dialogue, the new message affects the thoughts, feelings, and reactions of the first person. The reciprocal give-and-take effectively changes each person in the process. Consequently, both partners carry a significant burden of responsibility for their mate's positive and negative behavior. If conversations about home chores frequently evolve into criticisms of the partner's attempts at housekeeping, the partner learns to avoid the task as well as the criticism.

Exchange theory demonstrates the reciprocal relationship between rewards and costs. Couples stay in relationships where the rewards are greater than the costs (Thibaut and Kelly, 1959). Research indicates that distressed relationships are characterized by greater numbers of punishing (vs. rewarding) events, and that negative exchanges are likely to occur in escalating chains of coercive behaviors (Patterson and Reid, 1970). Therefore, distressed couples are especially sensitive to the harmful effects of negative behaviors and interactions (Jacobson, 1984).

From a social competency perspective (Gambrill and Richey, 1988), basic skills are necessary for communication, sexual performance, employment, child rearing, and a host of other activities. Although different clinicians and laypersons may argue over the list of "necessary" skills, all agree that the lack of certain skills often contributes to couples' distress. Partners may lack basic communication skills, such as disclosing feelings, providing accurate empathy, communicating understanding, making requests, and negotiating conflicts (Gottman, 1979; Jacobson and Margolin, 1979). The skills approach in therapy allows couples and therapists to look beyond the idiosyncratic behaviors of individuals and focus on learning more effective and efficient tools for making changes in relationships. For example, a couple may report frequent arguments about a wide variety of issues. They may discount the interactions as "charming banter" or they may allow the dissatisfaction to question the authenticity of their commitment. In actuality, they may not have the skills to state their needs clearly or negotiate mutually satisfying solutions. These possible skill deficits, with their various clinical manifestations, are more readily assessed when viewed from the theoretical perspectives of social learning, exchange, and social competency.

Clinical Manifestations

Clinical manifestations are observed in at least one of five major areas of couples functioning: conflicting values, communication, negotiating and contracting, stress, and managing time.

Conflicting values. In the area of values, distressed couples experience difficulty in solving problems and correctly evaluating their relationship. Couples report differences between the early months of their relationship and their current situation. They frequently describe how similar they were in the beginning and how much the "other one" has changed. They are unaware of basic differences that previously were obscured by the excitement of dating and the "honeymoon period." Partners frequently become preoccupied with the conflicts or frustrations and discount the possibilities of the less obvious differences in values and perceptions. Consequently, a manifestation of value conflicts is recurring fighting over the same issues. Arguments may focus on the "correct" roles of males and females, differing attitudes about extended family members, disagreements about child discipline, disputes over intimacy, or personal uses of leisure time.

Communication.   Couples who interact poorly may be suffering from poor communication patterns in addition to differences in values, ideas, or needs. Poor communication is not a function of amount but, rather, an issue of quality. Some couples follow a totally honest, totally open communication style. As attractive as this may sound or even appear in treatment sessions, "totally open" may be a form of verbal brutality. Few relationships can survive long periods of unedited, poorly timed communication. Similarly, clients who communicate successfully at work are not automatically effective communicators at home. The expectations for communication at work and at home often are very different. The superior-subordinate interaction style at work does not work well in close interpersonal relationships (Bartolome and Evans, 1980; Bartolome, 1983, cited in Sekaran, 1986). Unfortunately, some partners assume a subservient role and fail to assert differing opinions, attitudes, or wishes. They may describe their spouses as bossy, opinionated, or overpowering. In other cases, couples who will not fight are possibly more dysfunctional than couples who continually fight. Additionally, couples may not listen to each other or tend to hear only the first part of their partner's messages.

Although a couple may "communicate" frequently about specific problems, the critical and oftentimes overlooked issue is the couple's lack of skills to resolve recurrent problems. Furthermore, the problems that they do solve characteristically result in one partner as the winner and one partner as the loser. One partner's resentment over past fights or solutions may indicate a failure to negotiate and safeguard the needs of both parties.

Negotiating and contracting.   Failure to negotiate agreements costs couples time, and unfortunately, many partners blame themselves for being inadequate, "always tired," "overwhelmed," or unable to handle all the pressures. For example, wives may report dissatisfaction because they perform more household and child-rearing tasks than their husbands and feel guilty about their fatigue and frustrations. The husbands, however, are not immune to these pressures, and a growing number report frustrations because of lack of time for family responsibilities. Couples may describe the loss of private and intimate time to be alone or with their partners.

Stress. Partners experiencing a great deal of stress may lash out at each other and focus attention on their partner's more irritating characteristics. Physical problems, such as elevated blood pressure, sleeping problems, and headaches, may indicate too much stress. After reviewing the literature on stress and life in dual-career and dual-earner marriages, we believe stress to be inevitable for modern families who report a moderate to high level of activities, such as work schedules, school programs, dance classes, meetings, schedule conflicts between family members, and so forth. Finally, individuals and couples experiencing predictable changes, such as marriage, birth, children beginning school, and so forth, experience significant stress (Andolfi, 1980). In essence, high levels of stress should be considered for every person in the 1990s.

Managing time. The failure to manage time effectively is only one of numerous sources of stress for couples. Individuals report not measuring up to their idealized image of a parent, house manager, lover, friend, employee, and the like. Partners report conflicting feelings about working outside the home, caring for extended family members or friends, or having insufficient time to be alone or pursue important ventures. They may report being overwhelmed by children who need time, partners who need support, houses that get dirty only hours after cleaning, or interpersonal problems and deadlines at work. Additionally, partners may correctly identify their marital relationship as the source of stress.

ASSESSMENT AND MONITORING METHODS

Initial contacts with couples may yield vast amounts of data. For example, many distressed couples show the tension in their faces, as well as in gestures and angry interactions. The very power of their emotions may cover up the basic skill deficits that produce a complex scenario of frustrations and disappointments. Other couples may be quite skilled at hiding their frustrations. For example, dual-career couples may present confident exteriors to colleagues and clients when they know, all too well, that their business personae are not working at home.

The complexity of clients' problems and personal styles dictates that assessments of couples in marital distress occur from a multidimensional systems perspective. Spouses are viewed as unique individuals interacting in complex relationships within the nuclear families, extended families, and community. Social workers must identify the unique expectations that spouses have for themselves and their partners. For example, are there conflicts resulting from value differences, or are there deficits in communication skills or in negotiating conflicts? Is the couple having problems because of inability to manage time schedules, or because of internal or external stress?

Assessment can be facilitated by the use of measurement instruments. There are two types, which are used for slightly different purposes: global measures and rapid assessment instruments.

Global Measures

Global measures are designed to look at overall conceptions of marital and family functioning. These usually are lengthy questionnaires or interview schedules that are completed at the beginning of therapy. A popular example is the Stuart clinical aids (Sheafor, Horejsi, and Horejsi, 1988), which include the Marital Pre-Counseling Inventory, the Family Pre-Counseling Inventory, the Sexual Adjustment Inventory, and the Pre-Marital Counseling Inventory. The Stuart questionnaires are suitable for beginning to look at the couple in the context of their individual, couple, family, and external systems (work, extended family, etc.) issues. Questions focus on such issues as the couple's adjustment and satisfaction, parent-child relationships, and personal life satisfaction. These questionnaires can be mailed in to be computer scored. Social workers can utilize the information to give an overview of couple and/or family functioning to aid in assessing, operationalizing, and prioritizing problems.

Other measures can be utilized to give a more specific view of the marital relationship itself. Fredman and Sherman (1987) reported instruments for measuring general marital satisfaction and adjustment, including the Locke-Wallace Marital Adjustment Test, The Spanier Dyadic Adjustment Scale, the Notarius and Vanzetti Marital Agendas Protocol, and the Udry Marital Alternatives Scale.

The Locke-Wallace Marital Adjustment Test is a fifteen-item questionnaire that has been used to standardize other marital adjustment instruments. The test measures global adjustment, areas of possible disagreement, conflict resolution, cohesion, and communication. Scores range from 2 to 158, with most nondistressed couples scoring above 100. Some of the questions may assume stereotypical roles for husbands and wives.

The Spanier Dyadic Adjustment Scale was designed to assess the relationship of either married couples or unmarried couples living together. The four subscales addressed in the test are dyadic satisfaction, dyadic cohesion, dyadic consensus, and affectional expression. The scale is designed to be used in whole or part; the subscales are designed to stand alone. The test is short and east to administer; each of the subscales has high reliability and validity coefficients, with the exception of the affect subscale, which, therefore, should be interpreted with caution.

The Notarius and Vanzetti Marital Agendas Protocol measures problems in the marital relationship in four sections. To complete the test, each spouse is asked to respond to a list of common issues couples face.

They read the list four times to respond to the following four issues: (1) relationship problems they may be experiencing, (2) spousal agreement about the seriousness of the problems, (3) expectations about the chances for problem resolution, and (4) assignment of spousal blame for continuation of problems.

The Udry Marital Alternatives Scale asks the couple to evaluate their thoughts about whether they could do better if they were married to someone else or not married at all. Two main factors emerge from the test, the spouse replacement factor and the economic maintenance factor. The spouse replacement factor refers to the likelihood of getting another partner as good as or better than the current one. The economic maintenance factor refers to the likelihood of maintaining or improving one's lifestyle if the spouse's income is lost. Studies suggest that couples with high scores on the test have a high probability of divorcing or separating. This test is helpful for couples who are trying to decide whether to stay together, and for those couples who have not evaluated what the alternative to marriage might be.

Fredman and Sherman (1987) also reported instruments for measuring communication and intimacy, including the Larzelere and Huston Dyadic Trust Scale, the Bringle Self-Report Jealousy Scale—Revised, and the Waring Intimacy Questionnaire.

The Larzelere and Huston Dyadic Trust Scale is an eight-item test that measures belief in the partner's benevolence and honesty. The text correlates highly with other measures of love and self-disclosure, but not with generalized trust or social desirability.

The Bringle Self-Report Jealousy Scale—Revised measures three factors: minor romantic, major romantic, and nonromantic. Fredman and Sherman give examples of each factor. The minor romantic factor presents situations such as: "At a party, your partner hugs someone other than yourself." An example of the nonromantic factor is: "Your brother or sister seems to be receiving more attention from your parents." The major romantic factor presents such situations as: "'Your partner has sexual relations with someone else." The text is a twenty-five-item questionnaire. Scores range from 0 to 100, with higher scores indicating more jealousy. Respondents rate how pleased versus upset they would be if confronted with specific situations.

The Waring Intimacy Questionnaire is designed to measure eight factors of marital intimacy: conflict resolution, affection, cohesion, sexuality, identity, compatibility, expressiveness, and autonomy. The test consists of forty items, and can be used to look at a spouse's perception of marital intimacy, and the discrepancy between the two spouse's answers.

Other instruments useful for assessing couples in the context of their family system include the Olson scales and the Beavers-Timberlawn scales (Fredman and Sherman, 1987). The most widely used of the Olson package of scales is the Family Adaptability and Cohesion Evaluation Scales III (FACES III). This scale measures four dimensions of family adaptability—chaotic, flexible, structured, and rigid—and four dimensions of cohesion—disengaged, separated, connected, and enmeshed. The 111-item self-report inventory is designed to be answered twice, first to assess the family as is, and second to assess the family as the member would like it to be. The discrepancy between scores on the "perceived" version versus the "ideal" version allow social workers to assess couples' marital satisfaction.

The Beavers-Timberlawn Family Evaluation Scale is a popular tool to observe family members as they interact. The social worker asks the family to "discuss as a group what you would like to change about your family." This interaction is videotaped and coded by trained observers on the following five dimensions: structure of the family, mythology, goal-directed negotiation, autonomy, and family affect.

Rapid Assessment Instruments

In contrast to these global measures, rapid assessment instruments (RAIs) are used for assessment but also have applicability in monitoring therapeutic progress. This monitoring can be more easily used in a practice evaluation design.

RAIs and other assessment measures can be used for the following specific problems:

1. To assess value conflicts. The Dunn, Dunn, and Price (1975) Productivity Environmental Preference Survey identifies potential sources of conflict. Areas measured include each spouse's preferences in functioning in the immediate environment, in emotionality, in sociological needs, and in physical needs. The Pendleton, Poloma, and Garland (1980) Dual-career Family Scales comprise six scales that measure working wives' view of the marriage. The six scales measure marriage type (traditional versus nontraditional), domestic responsibility, satisfaction, self-image, career salience, and career line. The Tetenbaum, Lighter, and Travis (1981) Attitudes Toward Working Women Scales identify sources of conflict when wives work or have careers.

2. To assess communication problems. The Bienvenu Marital Communication Inventory is a forty-eight-item questionnaire that measures relationship hostility, self-disclosure, regard, empathy, discussion, and conflict management. The Locke, Sabaght, and Thomes (Navran, 1967) Primary Communication Inventory is a twenty-five-item inventory that measures both verbal and nonverbal communication, as well as the individual's self-perception of his or her own com-

munication ability and the spouse's perception of the individual's ability. The Beier-Sternberg Discord Questionnaire is a ten-item instrument that measures the couple's discord or conflict, as well as their degree of unhappiness related to the discord. The popular Clinical Measurement Package (CMP) (Hudson, 1982) includes the Index of Marital Satisfaction, the Index of Sexual Satisfaction, Index of Family Relations, Index of Parental Attitudes, and Child's Attitude Toward Father and Child's Attitude Toward Mother. Each scale has a clinical cutting score. The CMP also has a new computerized version so that clients can quickly and easily fill out measures before each therapy session. The computer version also scores the instruments, interprets, and graphs the data (Hudson, 1989).

3. To assess negotiation skills. The Heppner Problem-Solving Inventory is a thirty-five-item questionnaire that measures the awareness of problem-solving abilities in the areas of getting along with friends, feeling depressed, choosing a career, and deciding whether or not to get a divorce. The twenty-item Infante and Wigley Verbal Aggressiveness Scale identifies each spouse's willingness to attack the self-concept of the other.

4. To assess stress and time management. The MacDonald Irrational Values Scale is a nine-item scale that measures spouses' irrational beliefs; it is based on the Ellis theory that maladaption and life problems are the results of irrational beliefs. The forty-item Weissman Dysfunctional Attitude Scale identifies attitudes and beliefs that may contribute to stress, and is based on the Beck theory model. The thirty-item Mackay and Cox Stress Arousal Checklist measures stress on two dimensions—stress and arousal. The first dimension measures feelings ranging from pleasant to unpleasant; the second dimension measures general sense of well-being. These instruments are reported in Corcoran and Fischer (1987) and Fredman and Sherman (1987).

COMPETENCY-BASED TREATMENT

Treatment of Choice

The treatment chosen for couples with marital problems is a skills-focused approach. The elements of the package are: values clarification, communication training, negotiation and contracting skills training, time management techniques, and stress management techniques. The intervention package takes into account that negative and positive behaviors in marital relationships occur independently (Jacobson, Waldron, and Moore, 1980; Wills, Weiss, and Patterson, 1974). Simply stated, decreasing the negative behaviors in the relationship does not directly increase the positive behaviors; consequently, certain positive behaviors may need to be learned. The skills perspective emphasizes the acquisition of positive behavior patterns. Research and practice wisdom support the effectiveness of learning positive behaviors.

Research support. The systematic approach to skills training has a long history of successful utilization (Curran and Monti, 1982; Gambrill and Richey, 1988; Carkhuff, 1971; Pierce and Drasgow, 1969). A systematic approach to teaching key elements of communication was successful for distressed couples in group settings (Wells, Figurel, and McNamee, 1975), with individual couples (Beck, 1976; Carter and Thomas, 1975), with dysfunctional families (Bright and Robin, 1981; Robin, 1982), with adolescents and their parents (Ostensen, 1981), and so forth. According to a study by Markman (1979), the positive effects of communication training continued for at least two and one-half years.

Communication training has been evaluated concurrently with other skills training. For example, Baucom (1982) studied the effectiveness of communication training and contracting with distressed couples. Similarly, communication training was used successfully as a stress reduction method with couples (Ewart et al., 1984).

Contracting and negotiation skills help couples resolve marital conflict and trials of daily living; however, individual and marital stress must receive direct attention. Research on the success of stress management techniques is quite encouraging (Cormier and Cormier, 1985). Various types of meditation helped clients reduce anxiety (Girodo, 1974) and drug usage (Shapiro and Zifferblatt, 1976). Relaxation training (King, 1980) reduced incidents of insomnia (Woolf et al., 1976), alcohol consumption (Marlatt and Marques, 1977), and stress (Woolfolk et al., 1982). For example, Denicola and Sandler (1980) used stress management successfully with parents who abuse their children. Charlesworth, Williams, and Baer (1984) combined progressive relaxation, autogenic training, stress hierarchy, imagery, systematic desensitization, cognitive restructuring, and assertiveness training successfully to reduce stress for white-collar workers.

Practice-wisdom support. Although few clinicians will be surprised by the fact that couples' conflicts frequently stem from differences in values, the effectiveness literature for values clarification is largely devoid of researched strategies to help clinicians. The marital therapy field has appropriately relied on such axioms as "couples fight about what 'should' occur in married life" (Stuart, 1980). Our practice wisdom emphasizes that the idealized picture of marriage contains numerous myths. Individuals, consequently, prepare themselves for marriage in order to fit these beliefs; however, only infrequently do an individual's values and myths match those of his or her spouse.

Partners frequently are not fully aware of how their cherished myths and/or values conflict with their images of themselves, the values of their spouses, and the values of society. For example, working women may fear that value conflicts between their work and home life will threaten their femininity or male support (Schwartz and Waetjen, 1976, cited in Sekaran, 1986). Similarly, males may feel threatened by normal home tasks that do not "fit" their definitions of what men "should" do. Partners need help clarifying discrepancies between their own images and the demands of modern home life. Many clinicians will not be surprised that Keith and Schafer (1980, cited in Sekaran, 1986) found that working couples with traditional male and female values experience higher threat to their mental health than do other couples.

A strong personal identity is hard to maintain when couples are directly or indirectly questioning and confronting each other's beliefs about the relationship (Brittan, 1973). Many practitioners emphasize that spouses with weak senses of identity have more conflict with their partners than do those with strong identities (Barry, 1968, cited in Stuart, 1980). Sekaran (1986) emphasized the importance of strong self-concept and self-identity to support working women, who must continually tolerate ambiguity that results from conflicts between their work world and home responsibilities. There may be conflict between partners when they fail to support each other as whole persons in each area.

Whereas values clarification enables couples to enhance their common understanding of each other's values, good communication serves as the vehicle to convey information about one's own values and show appreciation for one's partner's values. The majority of couples place very high emphasis on communication as a major criterion for marital satisfaction (Jacobson and Moore, 1981). Concurrently, clinicians know that communication problems signal distress in the couple's relationship (Gottman, 1979; Markman, 1979). Jacobson and Holtzworth-Munroe (1986) emphasized that regardless of whether poor communication is targeted as a causal factor of dysfunctional relationships or as a dominate component, the quality of communication is significantly related to the level of marital distress. Nonverbal elements of communication are important also. Mehrabian (1972) asserted that only 7 percent of the affective message is "heard" in the words. The remaining message is delivered through the vocal tone and facial expression. This evidence underscores the reality that communication is exceedingly complex, far more than most couples (and many professionals) realize. Watzlawick's description (Watzlawick, Beavin, and Jackson, 1967) of the multidimensional nature of communication is particularly useful and informative. Although the metacommunication and content of messages can enhance interaction, they often obscure the complex meanings within communication (Nierenberg and Calero, 1973).

In addition to the practice wisdom on the importance of communication, the therapeutic relationship requires that clients be willing to cooperate during clinical sessions and in the clients' day-in and day-out activities. Jacobson and Gurman (1986) emphasized this requirement with their expectation that couples be willing to enter into collaborative sets. The agreed collaboration requires an explicit commitment to compromise and change. Fortunately, an important goal of negotiation and contracting skills is the resolution of problems in such a way that both partners feel and believe that they gained from the resolution. For example, the research on household responsibilities clearly shows that wives are still performing two and one-half more hours of home tasks than their husbands (Pleck, 1982). In all families, but particularly in dual-career or dual-earner marriages, partners need to know how to negotiate and contract the division of labor in the home. Men frequently need to be encouraged to examine the consequences to their wives (and their marriages) of stressful and inequitable home and child-care responsibilities.

The very nature of spouses' stressed lives distracts them from using the obvious stress and time management skills. Many couples are unable to see the problem constructively, and they need an external agent, such as the therapist or other caregiver, to intervene and stop the cycle of increasing stress. Clinicians concur with McLaughlin, Cormier, and Cormier (1988), who studied dual-career women with children. They found a significant relationship between low levels of stress or distress and the high use of coping strategies and time management.

The Structure of the Intervention

The treatment package was first suggested by Jordan, Cobb, and McCully (1989) for dual-career couples and is adapted for use with other marital couples in distress.

Treatment process: how to do the treatment.   The five steps of the intervention package are goals and values clarification, communication training, negotiation and contracting skills training, time management techniques, and stress management techniques.

Goals and values clarifications.   The first step in intervening with distressed couples is to assist them in identifying the similarities and differences in their overall life and family goals. What did they expect the marriage to be like? How is it different? What do they like/dislike about their roles as spouse, parent, worker, in-law, friend, and so forth? What do they like/dislike about their spouses? The therapeutic aim at this stage is to help couples establish mutual and individual goals and values.

Practitioners can use rather simple procedures to enable clients to share their goals and values. For example, clients may be asked individually to list on paper such information as their preferences for the marriage, pro and con statements about their marital relationship, or positive and negative aspects of their roles as parents. Periodically during the listing of information, each client should be asked to share two or three ideas. This minor interruption stimulates clients' thinking and helps them clarify the task. Following the completion of the lists, clients share ideas from their lists and discuss similarities and differences.

Helpful variations on this procedure include asking spouses to list their expectations for their partners and compare that list with their expectations for themselves. Some partners, such as first-time parents, have been quite surprised at differences or conflicts in expectations. Many couples are surprised that the inclusion of an infant in the family initiates a change in roles toward more traditional family and marital roles. Only when this reality is addressed do partners gain the awareness to initiate strategies to avoid rigid and unhealthy traditional roles. For example, careful planning may ensure that fathers have more involvement with their children and that mothers avoid the onslaught of numerous overwhelming child-care tasks and expectations.

This activity can accomplish more than the mere listing and sharing of similarities and differences. Values that are assumed to characterize healthy relationships may be communicated to couples through the structure of the exercise. For example, wives and husbands may be instructed to separate their lists of work and home responsibilities. This strategy enables clients to separate the values of the work and home, and acknowledge the difference between the settings. By separating the two roles, partners can see themselves as competent within each setting and perhaps avoid or reduce the tendency of one set of expectations to infringe on the other.

Clients also may be asked to jointly list their goals for the family and their marriage. Couples may be encouraged to set goals in terms of future time periods, e.g., goals for the next four months, goals for two years or five years hence. The short-term and long-term consequences of each goal may then be explored.

The listing or comparison of goals and values frequently leads to important discussions and possible resolutions, because the therapeutic setting "gives permission" for discussion of sensitive issues or the presentation of topics that have never been addressed. Practitioners should emphasize that couples will benefit even more if this task is repeated at home. Some issues for discussion are: In what ways do the couple agree/disagree on the traditional or nontraditional nature of their relationship? In what ways are spouses' lifestyles, hobbies, and interests compatible? Which are compatible? Which are incompatible? What are the long-term plans for their family and what steps are they taking to make those plans materialize?

A matrix such as the one depicted in figure 8-1 may help couples to determine how each spouse rates the importance of work versus family life, and how each perceives himself or herself in terms of traditional or nontraditional characteristics. Each partner should select the category across the top of figure 8-1 that best describes himself or herself. Each should continue the individual classification by choosing the category on the left side of figure 8-1 that further characterizes him or her. Finally, each should mark the one square that corresponds (vertically and horizontally) to his or her choices. Partners can now disclose their positions and readily see their degree of match or mismatch. This visual representation frequently provides surprises and a tool for discussion at home.

Communication training. Communication skills training focuses on teaching couples both verbal and nonverbal elements of good communication. The framework developed by Gottman et al. (1976) for couples communication is used to teach couples how to listen and validate each other, how to level or communicate directly, and how to edit unproductive information. In order to listen and validate, couples may be taught to intervene in their own arguments, their faulty communication interactions, or their situations of possible misunderstanding. By teaching them how to call a halt to an interaction, both partners can agree that stopping a problematic interaction or asking for clarification and feedback is permitted. By using this strategy, partners demonstrate their caring and eagerness to understand.

The "stop-action" approach is easy to teach and use. The first step describes the stop action as a nonconfrontive request. For example, a spouse may ask a partner to set a time to talk about an issue or a conversation. The partner may say, "I am a little worried about our finances. I would like to set aside some time for us to talk about our money. When is a good time to talk so that we won't be interrupted by the kids or the television?" In the second stage of a stop action, a partner makes a direct request for feedback from the spouse. The request focuses attention on the possible impact of the message. To illustrate from the example above, the partner may ask, "Do you feel the need to talk about the money?" In the third stage, the partner is taught to respond to the request by stating what he or she thinks the partner meant by the request. The other spouse should be instructed to listen for possible misunderstandings between the original request and the interpretation (or feedback) provided by the partner. Partners should keep in mind that differences between initial

FIGURE 8–1 Sex-Role Orientations and Central Life Interests

Sex-Role Orientations*

	1 *HUS/WF both Trad'l*	2 *HUS- Nontrad'l WF- Trad'l*	3 *HUS- Trad'l WF- Nontrad'l*	4 *HUS/WF both Nontrad'l*
1. HUS/WF Work				
2. HUS Fam WF Work				
3. HUS Work & Fam WF Work				
4. HUS Work WF Fam				
5. HUS/WF Fam				
6. HUS Work & Fam WF Fam				
7. HUS Work WF Work & Fam.				
8. HUS Fam WF Work & Fam				
9. HUS/WF Work/Fam				

*Adapted from Sekaran (1986).

messages and perceived intent are common. Consequently, this commonality dictates the use of the stop-action steps.

The fourth step instructs partners to listen and respond to content and feelings in the original request. In the example above, the request asks for a time to solve problems and at the same time communicates a worry about the family finances. Partners commonly focus on either the request or the feeling and in doing so miscommunicate to their spouse. This failure frequently causes the worried partner to feel unsupported or not heard. The fourth step instructs partners to ask for clarification if both the feelings and the request are not heard. The fifth step asks the listener to summarize or paraphrase what he or she thought the partner intended by the message. The sixth step is important because the message is validated even though the listener may not agree or sympathize with his or her partner's concerns. The listener might say, "I certainly understand that you are worried about the family finances. Also, it is frustrating to try to find the time to sit and talk about it." Finally, the partner should check to see whether the impact of the message is in keeping with the intent. This evaluation allows partners to clarify any discrepancies that might still exist.

Leveling is recommended for the numerous couples who avoid conflicts and do not discuss problems. The first clear indication of couples avoiding topics may appear in the goals and values clarification period of this intervention package. The leveling technique consists of five steps. In the beginning, partners are taught to express their feelings despite their fears that something catastrophic will result. Partners may previously have avoided crucial topics for fear that their spouses will not love them any more or will leave them.

Unfortunately, these fears have a component of truth that practitioners should not deny or discount. The irrational aspect of fears, however, can be examined rationally in a worst-case/best-case discussion. For example, clients may be asked what they think will be the worst possible and best possible consequences of discussing an important topic with their spouses. The subsequent discussion should also consider less extreme consequences. In the process, the social worker teaches the client to examine decisions in a cost-and-reward framework. The ultimate decision point for overcoming fears about communicating rests on the determination that the rewards outweigh the costs.

The second step in leveling requires that partners examine their own feelings to help them better express their ideas as well as their feelings. Unfortunately, and quite surprisingly to most practitioners, many clients do not know appropriate words to express their feelings or they lack experience in expressing feelings with words. This is especially true for men who received little encouragement as children to verbalize their feelings. Clients can benefit from using a feelings chart or similar list of feeling words to help them associate words with their emotions. Various feelings lists categorize descriptive words and help clients to discriminate between words associated with frustration versus anger, happiness versus self-satisfaction, and so forth. For example, a wife may communicate her emotions more effectively to her partner when she expresses her frustration over the child-care responsibilities with feeling words such as "despair," "overwhelmed," or "pulled in different ways," rather than with angry words such as "bitter," "hate," or "detest."

The third aspect of leveling encourages partners to write feelings on paper and give each other time to read and think about them before responding. This approach short-circuits the tendency of many partners to respond prematurely with inappropriate or defensive words that do not communicate caring or a willingness to hear and support the other partner. This method helps reduce the fear of communicating on threatening topics.

The fourth step clearly addresses the need for partners to be more assertive in asking for what they want. Couples frequently lack workable agreements about the difference between assertive and aggressive behavior. They worry or fear that what they define as "assertive" will actually be destructive or demanding. An underlying theme, however, frequently is a belief that getting needs met is selfish or self-centered. Assertive partners sometimes are criticized for being too demanding, whereas their mates believe they must avoid assertiveness and resort to devious methods to meet basic needs.

Practitioners should help couples define and differentiate between aggressive and assertive. Additionally, the couple should discuss their right to have their needs met in loving relationships. A result of this discussion is at least a covert permission to ask each other and other persons to meet certain needs. The process of asking, however, does not come easily to many people. Couples should be encouraged to list their needs and share the needs openly with their spouses. Richard Stuart's Caring Days Model (1980, discussed later in this chapter) is effective for this task. Regardless of the approach, the mere process of asking and the concomitant permission to ask usually is well received by both partners.

The final step in leveling provides couples with a needed mechanism and permission to inform their spouses about their readiness to hear or communicate. In everyday life many demands, frustrations, or even positive mental states dispose someone to react in certain ways. Gottman et al. (1976) refers to this state of being or attitude as a "filter" that affects all incoming messages. For example, when working partners meet at home after work, they may need to "warn" their partners that they have had a horrible day or have a splitting headache. This final leveling skill may consist of an agreement between partners that each has the right, even the responsibility, to warn his or her spouse. While discussing this idea with clients, emphasize the therapeutic or care-giving aspect of this skill. A component of this agreement should include a listing of ideas for how the other partner might respond to the warning. For example, if the partner who has spent all day caring for the children announces that they have been "terrible," the other spouse will know that a good response is to take over and watch the kids for the remainder of the evening.

Whereas leveling encourages partners to communicate, editing is recommended for those couples who over-communicate about their problems. For example, they may have angry fights over every issue and, unfortunately, most of those arguments include all the problems at once. Characteristically, couples who over-communicate start fighting or discussing a concern, and fifteen minutes later the partners cannot remember what they originally discussed and usually failed to resolve.

In the simplest form, editing involves being polite to one's spouse. In treatment, couples may benefit from a brief discussion comparing how partners interact with friends or business acquaintances with how they interact with each other. Not surprisingly, most couples find that they are less polite to and thoughtful of their partners than they are of persons outside the family. They may nag, interrupt, put each other down, or bring up old unresolved issues. Couples should be reminded that although the home setting or marital relationship permits more honesty or directness, much of what happens in the name of openness is more properly characterized as honest brutality and, consequently, is quite destructive.

The principles of editing include the following:

1. Make requests in terms of what you can, rather than cannot, do (e.g., "I can go shopping with you, but only for one hour"—you edit out "I have a million things to do; how can you waste your time like that!").

2. Give sincere praise (e.g., "You were so thoughtful to give me this tie for my birthday"—edit out "even though it is a God-awful shade of purple and you know I hate that color").

3. Be considerate (e.g., instead of saying "Quit telling me how to drive," you edit this out and say nothing).

4. Listen and express interest in things that are important to your spouse (e.g., do not only talk about yourself; ask your spouse about his or her job, hobbies, day, etc.).

5. Don't interrupt your spouse; let him or her finish the conversation.

6. Say something nice that your spouse will like to hear, rather than putting him or her down.

7. Accept responsibility for mistakes you make, rather than making a self-put-down.

8. Stay in the present; don't dig up past grievances to manipulate and divert a conversation with your spouse.

9. Don't think only of yourself; be empathetic and try to recognize and act upon the wishes of your spouse.

When couples agree that the principles of editing will help communication, they should be encouraged to use simple methods to remind themselves and each other about the need for editing. For example, individuals may be instructed to plan discussions with their mates. The plan should focus on one topic that is central to a particular problem. Tangential or alternative problems should be delayed and even scheduled for discussion at a later time. Additionally, couples may be encouraged to openly allow one or the other person to interject in the discussion, "We are getting off the subject. This new problem is important; however, can we set aside time to talk about it, maybe this evening after supper?" This approach affirms the importance of the partner's concerns, but does not allow those concerns to interfere with the current issue. Similarly, couples need to be alerted to the simple technique of asking themselves silently if what they need or want to bring up in the discussion relates to the current issue or is merely tangential. Also, couples may need to inquire whether the initial topic is the problem that really needs their attention, or whether they need to agree to set it aside and change to the new topic. This technique allows for a clear and conscious break in the discussion and requires the concurrence of both partners. In short, editing may help couples communicate politely and rationally and avoid the seductive confusion of competing problems.

In another area of good communication skills, Gambrill and Richey (1988) made recommendations for improving verbal communication. Practitioners may give feedback about spouses' voice qualities, which communicate unintended messages. For instance, talking too loudly or too softly can communicate that partners are domineering or submissive, confident or sad. The tone in which they speak can indicate that they are depressed (flat, monotonous tone) or sophisticated (deep, resonant tone). People who vary the pitch of their voice are perceived as more dynamic and extroverted. Pace and clarity (that is, fast or slow) can communicate boredom or anger. Similarly, a gregarious person may be viewed as socially competent unless he or she monopolizes the conversation. Also, successful communicators balance general statements versus more detailed statements, because too many general statements may label someone as superficial, and too many details may bore others.

In the clinical social work setting, couples may benefit from the opportunity to give feedback to each other about tone and clarity of voice. For example, they may practice speaking with their voices clearly audible, neither too loud nor too soft. The voice should be warm, pitch and tone should reflect interest, tempo should be moderate. Although the physical proximity will vary with the situation, spouses should indicate interest and warmth.

Practitioners should also help partners become aware of the length of time that each person speaks. In arguments or discussions, one partner may be controlling the flow of information and the definition of the problem. Unfortunately, the quieter member is losing the opportunity and possible avoiding the responsibility to contribute information, personal feelings, or differences of opinion. Practitioners may want to teach clients appropriate and agreed-upon hand gestures that signal the desire to talk. For example, couples frequently agree that balanced dialogue is effective and that one partner tends to talk more than the other. Therefore, they can agree that holding up the hand with the index finger pointing up is an acceptable signal to change speakers.

Certainly, an equalization in the length of time partners speak facilitates self-disclosure and intimacy, but the listener also may facilitate communication through constructive feedback and active listening. Practitioners should model active listening and help partners to role play this skill. During this role play, couples also can practice exchanging feedback. They frequently need help discriminating between constructive and destructive feedback. If partners have difficulty making this distinction, ask them to give feedback for a few minutes then reverse roles and encourage each partner to return appropriate and inappropriate feedback to its source. Practice sessions in the office or controlled setting helps clients anticipate and avoid errors associated with too little helpful feedback or too much critical feedback.

In addition to verbal communication, focus clients' training on the very powerful nonverbal communication. For example, clients are quite surprised to learn that when communication is broken down into its parts—e.g., content, facial expression, tone of voice, and so forth—the largest percentage of the effective or "heard" communication actually is nonverbal. Unfortunately, clients and practitioners devalue the importance of these skills and overlook the necessity to learn and practice nonverbal skills.

Elements of appropriate nonverbal communication include (Hepworth and Larsen, 1986): facial expressions, posture, voice, and physical proximity. Desirable facial expressions include eye contact, a warm expression, eyes at same level as spouse's, facial expressions that change appropriately in response to partner's conversation, and mouth that is relaxed or that smiles when appropriate. Posture includes arms and hands that express appropriate gestures and a relaxed body that leans toward partner. Clients are more willing to pay attention to and practice these nonverbal skills when they realize their potential impact. Their importance may be emphasized by viewing a three- or four-minute videotape of a television show or home video with the sound turned off. Nonverbal communication that may have gone unnoticed when the sound was on becomes surprisingly vivid. After a discussion about the nonverbal messages, couples are more readily willing to practice and be sensitive to nonverbal skills.

Couples should be encouraged to practice their verbal and nonverbal communication skills. A few homework exercises facilitate communication and also enhance the relationship. A technique for increasing positive interactions between couples was described by Stuart (1980). The

FIGURE 8–2   Caring Days List

John					Caring Behaviors	Marie			
7/2	7/3	7/4	7/5	7/7	Ask me how my day went.	7/1	7/2	7/3	7/6
7/3	7/6	7/7			Call me at work just to say hi.	7/7	7/8		
7/4	7/6				Sit next to me when we watch TV.	7/7	7/8	7/9	
7/2	7/4	7/6	7/7	7/9	Compliment me when I look nice.	7/3	7/4		
7/4	7/5	7/9			Talk to me at breakfast and read the paper later.	7/3	7/4	7/5	7/7

SOURCE: Adapted from R. Stuart (1980).

Caring Days List (see figure 8.2) can be used to teach clients to communicate to their spouses discrete behaviors that are pleasing to them. The couple is then taught to watch for and record when each spouse performs the targeted behaviors. While the exercise increases the number of positive interactions in the relationship, the method requires couples to practice communicating their needs and giving supportive feedback.

An important exercise in the area of anger control (Deschner, 1984) uses communication as an important component to alter clients' environment. Steps include: (1) the client recognizing the signs that he or she is getting mad enough to be out of control; (2) communicating to the spouse that the angered partner needs to leave the situation and take a time-out; (3) thinking about the fight and focusing on what he or she did to contribute to the argument; and (4) returning to communicate his or her "technical error" and discussing better solutions.

In summary, both verbal and nonverbal skills can be taught by practitioner modeling, client rehearsal, feedback from practitioner and spouse, videotaping client's strengths and weaknesses, and homework assignments. Enhancing communication skills facilitates many areas of growth for troubled as well as healthy couples. Furthermore, these skills enable couples to learn from additional experiences. For example, Gambrill and Richey (1988) used role reversal with couples to increase their sensitivity to the opposite-gender spouse. Wives can take on the protector role by helping the husband on with his coat and opening the door for him; the husband can wait for the door to be opened, or sit quietly in a restaurant while the spouse orders for them both. With enhanced communication skills, these partners are enabled to exchange feelings and perceptions in a constructive, growth-producing manner. These skills also help couples negotiate other areas of their lives.

Negotiation and contracting skills training. When couples learn how to communicate well, they need a few additional skills to negotiate and contract areas of differences or conflict. Problem-solving techniques (Sheafor et al., 1988) may be used to look at all possible solutions. The steps include:

1. Writing or stating a clear description of the problem
2. Identifying each partner's stake in the problem
3. Brainstorming to come up with all possible solutions without making any judgments about any of the suggested solutions
4. Throwing out all solutions that are absolutely unacceptable to each member
5. Evaluating and ranking the remaining solutions, trying out the solution
6. Making modifications if necessary

Some clients are reluctant to review problem solving because they presume that they already know and usually use this easy, logical strategy. They should be reminded that the ease of use and the logic of the steps are misleading; people usually skip steps or fail to use the approach altogether. For example, people normally solve problems by looking for the first solution that is sufficiently logical and familiar. Unfortunately, the "familiar and logical" may simply be a repeat of previously ineffective solutions or a mismatch between a perfectly good solution and the wrong problem. The problem-solving approach facilitates a clear definition of the problem and a review of alternative solutions. Clients may also be helped by a reminder that one ingredient in successful problem solving is the long list of alternative solutions.

Contracts (Stuart, 1980) have also been used by couples to negotiate areas of conflict (see figure 8.3). *Quid pro quo* contracts make spouses' behavior contingent on their partners' performance. For example, the husband will take out the trash if, and only if, the wife cooks the dinner. *Quid pro quo* is more helpful when emotionally distant partners need to focus on positive, contingent behavior.

The good faith, or parallel, contract makes individual performance of behaviors independent of the other spouse. For example, the wife gets to go shopping for four hours on Saturday if she completes the laundry by Friday night. The husband gets to play tennis after he cleans the kitchen.

FIGURE 8–3   Contract

Targert behaviors: (a) *preparing food for the baby*
                    (b) *feedings*

HUSBAND:	WIFE:
Husband agrees to prepare food for evening and bedtime meals for baby.	Wife agrees to prepare food for morning and lunchtime feedings.
Husband agrees to get up for nighttime feeding on even-numbered days.	Wife agrees to get up for nighttime feedings on odd-numbered days.

Rewards for compliance with terms of the contract:
   Husband gets to take one night off per week to go out with his friends. Wife will stay with the baby or arrange for a babysitter.

   Wife gets to have time off to go shopping on Saturdays. Husband will stay with the baby or arrange a babysitter.

Contingencies for noncompliance:
   Husband forfeits night out and must give wife $20 for her shopping trip.

   Wife forfeits shopping trip and must give husband one additional night out with friends.

SOURCE: *Adapted from R. Stuart (1980).

Although this approach may feel rather mechanistic to many people, couples quickly recognize contracting as an effective way to get their needs met and ensure some equalization of power in couple relationships. The process reemphasizes the constructive necessity of stating needs and having some of them met.

Couples should be encouraged not to perceive family roles and responsibilities in male- or female-specific terms. When husbands and wives construct a simple chart describing the time and energy required of each person in their work outside or inside the home, they frequently are surprised at what the chart shows. Husbands and wives may be willing to take on extra roles when they realize inequities. This is facilitated when various chores are tied to clear-cut payoffs and benefits. For example, each partner may receive free time on the weekend in exchange for an equal amount of child supervision. Similarly, some wives are rather surprised when their self-described "macho" husbands are willing to accept child-care roles following a discussion about their husbands' childhood experiences (or lack of experience) with their own fathers. In essence, the therapeutic setting helps couples contract ways to manage their harried lives and their traditional-nontraditional roles.

Time management techniques. Time management is a therapeutic injunction to help couples prioritize their commitments and make time for important people, places, and events. Practitioners should help couples structure their time by encouraging them to establish and prioritize individual, couple, and family goals (Davidson, 1978; Ferner, 1980) and help clients keep in mind such obstacles to effective time management as procrastination and worry, perfectionism, fear of failure, avoidance versus confrontation, and overwhelming tasks (Curtis and Detert, 1981).

Couples should be encouraged to organize family life with a planned approach. For example, they should consider that each partner has home and family responsibilities. Similarly, if there are children, they should pitch in and perform those home tasks that are appropriate to their ages. Couples can list all of the individual and joint projects and rate each task. Top-priority tasks receive an "A," second-level tasks a "B," and so forth (Lakein, 1973). Partners then negotiate and schedule "A" tasks first. For example, home chores and responsibilities may be divided on the basis of expertise. The cooking is performed by the best cook, whereas checkbook/financial responsibilities are given to the one who spends the most money. Cleaning tasks may be divided according to certain payoffs. For example, cleaning bathrooms may be sufficiently unpleasant (to both partners) that the person who volunteers for that role need perform no other household cleaning duties (or receives special fringe benefits, such as a modest clothes-shopping stipend).

On another level, some couples may need to decide which home and family responsibilities are shared by the couple and which are performed separately (Smith and Reid, 1986). One couple may choose to share meal preparation responsibilities, but to have each partner maintain his or her own checkbook and possibly keep his or her money separate. Handling chores or responsibilities independently is an appropriate solution, especially if spouses have different standards of performance. Finally, when both partners have busy schedules, hiring household help may be efficient in terms of cost, increased personal or family time, enhanced mental health, or simply the good feelings derived from being cared for.

Mackenzie and Waldo (1981) made the following recommendations for time management:

- Log your time to find out where it goes
- Admit your time wasters (e.g., not setting deadlines, procrastination, etc.)
- Set goals
- Organize your home and office
- Learn to delegate
- Learn to avoid interruptions

- Be assertive
- Set deadlines for completion of important projects or activities
- Practice stress reduction techniques
- Take time to have fun

Practitioners may provide couples with this list of steps and guide them through a planning session. The process of practicing will be as beneficial as the outcome.

Stress management techniques.   Just as time management is an essential ingredient in couples' therapy, stress management is crucial to families in today's complex society. Couples should make a list of the stress points in their relationships and analyze them in terms of importance, strength, impact, and duration. This analysis often helps clients realize that stressors that previously were considered temporary or transitory are actually part of a long chain of ongoing struggles. Couples may need to determine whether the stressors are due to lack of organization or overwhelming responsibilities; if so, couples should be encouraged to develop time management techniques or to hire outside help.

Most empirically based programs (Friedman and Dermit, 1988) for stress management contain four components: self-monitoring, daily relaxation exercises, cognitive restructuring, and environmental alteration, such as time management. Other techniques to help reduce stress include meditation, self-hypnosis, and biofeedback. Practitioners may benefit from reading selections from Friedman and Dermit's (1988) list of recommended stress management texts, such as Gendlin, 1978; Girdano and Everly, 1986; Meichenbaum, 1983; Schafer, 1987. There is also a list of texts for your clients, including Mantell, 1988; Nathan, Staats, and Rosch, 1987.

Be ready to challenge any irrational beliefs or unrealistic attitudes that clients may have that contribute to stress. Cognitive restructuring (Granvold, 1988) is a technique that helps practitioners to challenge and dispute cognitive distortions. For example, the following distortions are common in couples with distressed marriages:

- Absolutistic/dichotomous thinking, such as seeing situations in a rigid good/bad manner
- Overgeneralization—applying information from one situation to an unrelated situation
- Selective abstraction—looking only at the negative information and ignoring the positive
- Arbitrary inference—mind reading and predicting negative outcomes

- Magnification and minimization—perceiving situations in the extreme rather than in a more realistic fashion
- Personalization—inappropriate self-blaming
- Negative attribution—attributing negative motivations to other's or one's own behavior
- Faulty interpretation—missing the intent of another's message

Clients usually are quite willing to examine a copy of the above list and recall examples of the distortions in their own lives. When exchanged in a warm, good-natured atmosphere, the label of "distortions" can more readily be accepted and incorporated. The practitioner should model for the client constructive ways for each partner to highlight or point out when their partner uses one of the common distortions. Similarly, the practitioner may want to intentionally exhibit one of the distortions and openly correct it. For example, the practitioner might say, "All clients benefit from learning about these distortions," and then, with humor and with a sense of the double-bind, say, "Oops! Did you hear *that* distortion? I'm sure not 'all clients' are capable of learning from their own distortions or overgeneralizations."

Treatment limitations.   A significant treatment limitation is the degree of the clients' motivation to change. Stuart (1980) reported that couples who come in for marital therapy are often taking one last chance to save the marriage before divorce. Therefore, one or both spouses already may have made the decision to leave the marriage. Treatment should, therefore, focus on giving the couple the maximum amount of hope and positive signs of change as quickly as possible to keep them in therapy. Techniques such as Stuart's Caring Days Procedure are designed to help spouses to recognize and begin reinforcing their partner's positive behaviors.

Other limitations are generalization and maintenance of the treatment. Just because couples learn to interact on a more positive basis in the consulting room doesn't mean that they will continue a satisfactory relationship once they leave. Generalization of positive changes learned in treatment must be transferred to the couple's external world by setting up homework assignments. This can help the couple to practice newly learned skills in the natural environment. Additionally, they can report how the practice sessions went and get feedback on improving skills.

Maintenance of change—that is, continuing the positive changes learned in therapy over time—can be encouraged by follow-up after the conclusion of therapy. At the final visit, present the couple with different situations that might occur, and help the couple to think through how their newly learned skills might be applied.

Generalizing the Intervention to Related Problems

Each element of the intervention package has been used in diverse settings. Values clarification is useful with adults and adolescents; communication training is a common component of many different strategies, such as group marital counseling, counseling with the chronic mentally ill, and business education. The remaining three have similar, yet less extensive exposure.

Research and practice wisdom support the generalization of this comprehensive treatment package to problem areas where interpersonal interaction is important for the maintenance of dyads or groups, and for the goal of growth and development for participants. Specific populations include adolescents and their parents, teams of professionals in medical or mental health settings, and business or management groups whose function and goals require close interpersonal support and cooperation. Many of the latter groups resemble a "marriage" of personnel to each other and the task at hand.

Self-esteem. Self-esteem is an important factor in treatment and this intervention package. Self-esteem is a much-talked-about idea, even though people define it differently. A helpful definition of self-esteem focuses on the cognitive image people have of themselves. For example, some people see themselves as succeeding at various tasks; others expect the worst of themselves. This image is largely learned from each person's complex array of people, life experiences, personal thoughts, and the like. Parents are very influential when they tell children that they are smart, dull, feminine, masculine, fat, skinny, and so on. These messages frequently are delivered verbally, yet more influential images are projected nonverbally. For example, numerous adults can recall the facial expressions their parents used to signal disapproval. Similarly, children and adults acquire the mannerisms, attitudes, and behaviors of important models, such as parents, friends, teachers, and movie stars, who are impressive for a variety of reasons. These images, attitudes, and the like, constitute one's self-image or self-esteem. Self-esteem is so much a part of people's lives that they are largely unaware of it until that self-image or self-concept is questioned.

In intimate relationships the self-esteem or self-concept of each partner affects the nature of the relationship. Rarely, if ever, are two partners so similar or complementary that their self-concepts mesh without occasional distress or outright hostility. Whereas all partners challenge each other and sometimes question their partner's behavior, distressed couples focus on their differences and emphasize the negative aspects of their self-image, such as beliefs of unworthiness or helplessness. Unfortunately, in some destructive relationships partners may emphasize the imperfections or insecurities of their mates in order to gain advantage. Therefore, improving the self-image or self-esteem is vitally important to healthy relationships.

The skills training addressed in this intervention package recognizes that insight into a person's low self-esteem is not as effective as building self-image through improved social competence. People's self-esteem improves when they gain the ability to interact more effectively with others. They see themselves as more in control of their environment when they get their own needs met and meet the needs of others.

As people's images of themselves improve, they can actively reconcile role and value conflicts with their partners. The cognitive dissonance between behaving in a new, effective manner and the old negative self-images often results in the alteration of the negative attitudes. Additionally, overcoming value conflicts allows partners to set new goals and interact in healthier patterns. Similarly, partners may also find that other people in their environment come to expect different interactions with them and, therefore, treat them in a more positive and affirming manner.

When communication, the primary vehicle for the resolution of value conflicts, is improved, clients frequently experience enhanced self-image, because they are able to effectively use communication as a tool to get what they want or need. For example, partners may feel that they are being taken advantage of because they are not getting what they need. Techniques of leveling may enable partners to clearly express their needs and, consequently, their partners know how to respond. They frequently are surprised to learn that their partners never knew of the previously unmet needs.

Similarly, negotiation and contracting skills are effective strategies for resolving long-standing disagreements or problems. Mastering these tools improves the sense of self-efficacy that comes from gaining the ability to negotiate solutions to problems. A byproduct of the contracting skill is the increased sense that it is worth the time and effort of making a contract to enable clients to fulfill their needs. Additionally, partners increasingly may see each other in a more valuable light and treat each other better.

Finally, reducing stress and managing time greatly improve clients' ability to gain control over difficult and demanding lifestyles. Persons armed with the skills from this intervention package are much more capable of meeting their own needs, interacting effectively with their partners and family, and gaining a more satisfying self-image.

SUMMARY

The social learning–cognitive behavioral approach teaches couples to take charge of their relationships, produce changes that best fit their own needs, and increase the rewards and lower the costs of being with their partner. The competency-based treatment package focuses on the following five areas: goals and values clarification, communication training, negotiation and contracting skills training, time management techniques, and stress management techniques. In general, the first three interventions are recommended as a sequence because of their logical and developmental nature. The last two intervention areas may be added as couples make sufficient progress in the other areas.

Goals and values clarification interventions frequently are helpful with couples who describe frustrations and conflicts over divergent opinions and perspectives. When couples complain about nonspecific frustrations and dissatisfaction, there usually are underlying differences in expectations or perspectives, in such areas as housekeeping standards, child-rearing styles, friendships at work, male-female roles, and expressions of intimacy.

Communication training focuses on improving partners' ability to express ideas or opinions and listen effectively to their partners. Couples who communicate about everything at once benefit from editing procedures; those who avoid intimate or disagreeable issues need methods of disclosure or leveling. Also, couples whose interactions get out of control should be taught to use time-out or stop-action procedures. Couples who frequently give mixed messages need to learn how to recognize and modify incongruent verbal and nonverbal messages.

The communication skills training helps couples develop their negotiation and contracting skills, which are especially helpful to couples who have recurrent problems. Techniques presented are problem-solving techniques, and *quid pro quo* and good faith contracts.

The time management interventions give couples tools to preserve the valuable human resources of time and energy. Couples need these skills when they feel continually overwhelmed, tired, or resentful of family or work demands. The intervention requires couples to prioritize and possibly reorder their time allotments and responsibilities. They are encouraged to give up activities that require inordinate amounts of time and hire outside help to alleviate pressures on the couple and family.

Finally, the last section of interventions focuses on stress management techniques. Practitioners should assess the amount of stress clients endure in terms of importance, strength, impact, and duration. The assessment can further differentiate between temporary or transitory stressors and long-term stresses. The intervention package includes such methods as self-monitoring, daily relaxation exercises, cognitive restructuring, and environmental alteration (such as time management).

Couples receiving competency-based treatment can be expected to generalize their learning to other settings. The skills perspective enables them to apply these tools in such related areas as work settings, relationships with friends and relatives, and parent-child interactions. Changes in clients' self-esteem should follow from the new or renewed sense of self-efficacy.

CHAPTER 9

Social Competence Promotion for Troubled Youths

Craig Winston LeCroy

In this chapter, LeCroy examines problems that are common in troubled youngsters and defines various risk-taking behaviors clearly and concisely. Such problems frequently result from peer pressure, and the author shows how to help promote social competence in adolescents. The intervention is a well-defined approach that develops social skills, problem-solving abilities, and cognitive skills. Structure is demonstrated by matching the particular need for interpersonal competency with the particular environment (e.g., family or school). LeCroy shows how to use an intervention in a well-defined and straightforward step-by-step protocol. Client participation is encouraged by the use of homework assignments, which generalize the treatment gains, and contracting, which is, as LeCroy illustrates, an important component of the intervention.

INTRODUCTION

Nancy was referred by the school social worker to an outpatient clinic that specializes in depressed children. She has been feeling lonely and frequently is seen at school by herself and appears to have few friends. Her parents report that she cries often and does not seem happy with her life. Tom was suspended from school because he and his friends were caught drinking alcohol on the school grounds. Tom has plenty of friends, but they frequently are in trouble with school officials and the law. Tom's parents are concerned about his alcohol use; he has been caught coming home intoxicated on numerous occasions. John dropped out of school at fifteen and has had a difficult time finding employment. He does not present himself in a very positive manner to employers, although he has had numerous job experiences. He lives with his mother and stepfather but does not feel welcome there and would like to become independent.

All of these young people lack certain social or life skills. With the necessary skills, they could lead more satisfying interpersonal lives. Nancy could be helped to learn friendship skills to address her feelings of loneliness. She could also be taught coping skills to address her negative and depressing thoughts. Tom could be helped by learning about the conse-quences of drug use and learning the skills needed to resist peer pressure. John needs to learn how to anticipate employers' concerns, present his qualifications confidently and assertively, and follow up with prospective employers.

The teaching of these skills to young people constitutes an approach referred to as social competence training. This conceptualization asserts that problem behavior in young people can be understood in terms of their not having acquired skills needed to cope with various situational demands. Social competence training emphasizes social skills: skills that are maximally effective in resolving the demands of problem situations while minimizing the likelihood of future problems (Goldfried and D'Zurilla, 1969). This approach perceives human development as a pro-cess of confronting a series of tasks and situational demands rather than as movement through stages. Promoting social competence in young people is an effective strategy for helping them to confront stressful or problematic situations. Adolescents need to acquire numerous social skills, because during this stage of life they develop new patterns of inter-personal relationships, confront new social experiences, and learn new behavioral responses (Jessor, 1982). Without adequate social skills, these experiences can become avenues to pregnancy, delinquency, drug abuse, and social isolation.

The extent to which adolescents successfully confront the complex demands and tasks of adolescence will have an impact on the course of their lives. Problem behaviors that begin in early adolescence are more likely to continue in later life. For example, Yamaguchi and Kandel (1984) have found that drug use in early adolescence is a strong predictor of drug use in late adolescence and adulthood. Young adolescents are vulnerable to serious social problems in our society: drug abuse, dropping out of school, unemployment, delinquency, early pregnancy, and poor mental health.

Research on the social problems of youth indicates that problems be-gin to develop between the ages of thirteen and sixteen. Indeed, research on adolescent development suggests that there are important differences between early, middle, and late adolescence. The young adolescent years mark beginning attempts to establish friendship, high degrees of anxiety regarding peer relationships, increased conformity with one's peers, and beginning attempts to acquire social competence (LeCroy, 1983). It is also during early adolescence that young people begin to experience their vul-nerability to some of society's external forces. Adolescents begin to con-front many social problems, and without requisite social and coping skills they become vulnerable to many situations that threaten their future po-tential.

PROBLEM IDENTIFICATION: RISK-TAKING
BEHAVIORS OF ADOLESCENTS

The risk-taking behavior of young people is a serious national problem. Successfully confronting the pressures of sex, alcohol, and drugs is a normal part of the process of growing up in American society (Jessor, 1982). Jackson and Hornbeck (1989, p. 833) state emphatically, "in our society, peer pressure to engage in early sexual activity and the availability of alcohol, drugs, and cigarettes virtually guarantee that every American young adolescent will be confronted with decisions about whether to engage in behaviors that could have life-long, if not lethal, consequences."

Use of Drugs, Alcohol, and Cigarettes

The combined effects of drug, alcohol, and cigarette use is taking an unprecedented toll on young people. Two-thirds of 1985 high school seniors had used alcohol in the past thirty days, and 5 percent had used alcohol each day for the past thirty days. Although studies document the decline in the use of marijuana, they also find large numbers of students using drugs such as crack and cocaine. It is estimated that 2.5 million eighteen-to-twenty-four-year-olds and 400,000 twelve-to-seventeen-year-olds had used cocaine in the past thirty days in a 1985 survey (National Institute of Drug Abuse, 1986). The initial use of these drugs is taking place at earlier ages; for example, 55 percent of high school seniors report alcohol use prior to the tenth grade. Although drug use has leveled off in the past several years, reports indicate that approximately 50 percent of those who had used drugs by their senior year initiated use prior to the tenth grade (Johnston, O'Malley, and Backman, 1987).

Sexual Activity

There are 12 million sexually active adolescents in the United States (Alan Guttmacher Institute, 1981). An increasing number of adolescents are becoming sexually active, especially young people under the age of sixteen. Girls fourteen years of age or younger continue to increase their rate of sexual activity. These younger girls tend not to use contraception and thus are engaging in high-risk behaviors. Almost half of these girls (42 percent) delayed using contraceptive methods for more than a year (Hofferth, Kahn, and Baldwin, 1987). In addition to the risk of unwanted pregnancy, young people are at great risk for contracting sexually transmitted diseases. One-fourth of all adolescents will have contracted a sexually transmitted disease before graduating from high school (U.S. Department of Health, Education, and Welfare, 1979).

Delinquency

Delinquency is also a concern because delinquent behavior begins and peaks in adolescence. By the age of fifteen, delinquent activity has reached its peak (Dusek, 1987). In one study (Institute for Juvenile Research, 1972) one-half of the fourteen-to-eighteen-year-olds surveyed had shoplifted. Census data show that an estimated 625,000 young people were admitted to juvenile detention and correctional facilities (Bureau of Justice Statistics, 1986). With regard to criminal offenders, one of every twenty persons arrested for a violent crime is under fifteen years old, and one in seven property crimes is committed by a person under fifteen years of age (Wetzel, 1987). In fact, ''youths are the segment of the population most likely to be victimized by a criminal, most likely to commit a crime, most likely to be arrested, and, after their early 20's, most likely to be imprisoned for committing a crime (Wetzel, 1987, p. 31).

School Dropout Rates and Unemployment

In the mid-1980s, 3.8 million young people aged eighteen to twenty-four quit school before earning a high school diploma (Bureau of the Census, 1985). Minority youth make up a disproportionate share of the total number of high school dropouts. There is reason to believe that the school dropout rate will increase because the educational system is unresponsive to the needs of non-college-bound youth. Whether they graduate from school or not, many young people have early negative experiences in their attempt to find employment. The unemployment rate for adolescents aged sixteen to nineteen is 15.8 percent (William T. Grant Foundation, 1988). The unemployment rate for minority youth is nearly double that of their white peers.

THE IMPORTANCE OF SOCIAL COMPETENCE

Clearly there are a multitude of life tasks that many young people are not prepared to address. Promoting social competence among young people is an approach that has been used both for problem prevention and problem remediation. Social competence training has taught young people the skills necessary to offset the influences and pressures to use drugs (Rhodes and Jason, 1988). It has also been effective in helping young adolescents prevent unwanted pregnancies. Schinke, Blythe, and Gilchrist (1980) discovered that successful coping with sexual behavior and responsible use of contraceptives result from a set of acquired social skills. Freedman et al. (1978) validated a conceptualization of delinquent behavior that is based on situational-specific skill deficits. Disadvantaged youth can be taught a skill-building process that helps them to overcome common skill deficits in seeking and maintaining employment (Staab and Lodish, 1985). It appears that many methods of socialization are inadequate in solving social problems of youth (described above), given the increasing number of youths who are involved in such problems. The promotion of social competence, which has been shown to be effective in solving or avoiding social problems of youth, is of critical importance to the successful socialization of young people.

PROMOTING SOCIAL COMPETENCE

The promotion of social competence as a framework for intervention represents a distinct move away from defect or medical models and places a greater emphasis on the environmental influences on individuals. It also emphasizes the positive aspects of functioning. Bloom (1977, p. 250) notes that ''of all the concepts that have been introduced to link individual problems to characteristics of the social system, the most compelling have been the concepts of competence and competence building.''

Wine (1981) notes that the defining characteristic of the competence approach is a concern with the effectiveness of the individual's interactions with his or her environment. Therefore, social competence deals explicitly with an individual's impact on the environment, as well as with the impact of the environment on the individual. In this manner, social competence is a transactional model of human behavior.

This approach to social competence recognizes the importance of overt behaviors, cognitive capacities, problem-solving abilities and coping skills, and the ability to produce appropriate matches between behaviors and situational requirements. Behavioral functioning involves a continuous interaction among behavioral, cognitive, and environmental influences. Although behavior is influenced by the environment, a person is one of the producers of his or her own environment. Through their transactions with the environment, people help shape the social milieu and other circumstances of their daily transactions. Internal personal factors (beliefs) form a reciprocal relationship with behavior to create expectations that influence behavior. In turn, environmental influences interact with behavior to affect a person's expectations of personal effectiveness or self-efficacy (Bandura, 1977).

Such multidirectional influence is best described by an example. A youth learns skills for resisting peer pressure to smoke cigarettes through modeling and role playing with others in a smoking-prevention group. Whether these skills hold up under natural conditions depends upon interactions among the person, the environment, and the person's performance. Personal sources of influence provide the initial stimulus (''If I smoke a cigarette my friends won't think badly of me,'' or ''I don't want to smoke because I know it's bad for my health''). The youth then selects a course of action ("No, thanks, I'm not smoking any more because it's bad for my health"). His or her peers may support this refusal by telling others the youth is no longer smoking, thereby influencing the environment by reducing the pressure to smoke. The youth's expectations are also influenced, because he or she has gained in his or her ability to make and implement responsible decisions.

The social competence approach has increasingly stressed the concept of self-efficacy and its importance in producing behavioral change. Self-efficacy provides a framework for studying stress and coping. Competence in coping with the environment is more than knowing what to do. It requires cognitive, social, and behavioral skills in dealing with situations that are ambiguous, unpredictable, and stressful. Bandura's model of self-efficacy assumes people use four sources of information for judging their capabilities to confront environmental demands. Most important is the performance mode, which relies upon information gained from previous experience in handling similar situations. In this way, experience with situations in which individuals have coped successfully builds efficacy. Research has found that lower perceived self-efficacy in stressful situations leads to a decrease in exertion of effort. People begin to give up easily and learn to anticipate failure. In general, we get information about efficacy expectations through vicarious channels. When we observe the successes or failures of others, our perceived efficacy is influenced. The intervention task is to understand these multiple sources of influence and make appropriate matches between an individual's competencies and the demands of the environment. Figure 9-1 shows the relationship between various competencies and environmental tasks or stresses for adolescents. Interpersonal competence revolves around three areas: cognitive development, problem-solving abilities, and social skills. At adolescence, the environment presents situations that demand competencies to deal with such issues as peer relationships, school, and family relationships. Such competencies as generating alternatives and thinking consequentially might be needed to address a situational demand such as deciding whether or not to have sexual intercourse when no contraception is available.

Social incompetence would be the result of a mismatch between a young person's ability to perform, given certain task demands imposed on the person. Problems develop when this imbalance occurs between a person's abilities and the demands present in the person's person-environment system.

RESEARCH SUPPORT

The bulk of research studies on social skills training have been with children and adults; however, an increasing number of studies have ex-

FIGURE 9–1 Social Competence Model

Interpersonal Competence		Environment (at adolescence)
Cognitive Development -reasoning abilities -interpersonal awareness	MATCH COMPETENCIES	Peer Relationships -anxiety over friendships -pressure to conform -sexual socialization
Problem-Solving Abilities -generating alternatives -thinking consequentially -means/end thinking	WITH DEMANDS OF THE ENVIRONMENT	School -entry into new peer groups -authority structure -exposure to drugs, sex, etc.
Social Skills -prosocial behavior -resisting peer pressure -negotiating abilities	← → TRANSACTING	Family -independence from the family -family versus peer relations -family conflict

amined social skills training with adolescents. Some of the earliest applications resulted from investigations at Achievement Place, a residential center for adolescents. These studies focused on conversational skills (e. g., asking questions, volunteering information) and used single-subject designs to evaluation effectiveness (Maloney et al., 1976; Minkin et al., 1976). Although the results support the effectiveness of social skills training, the skills being taught were simple and discrete and the researchers failed to provide any follow-up data.

One of the better-controlled studies that applied social skills training to delinquents was reported by Sarason and Ganzer (1973), who found that, compared to the control group subjects, the delinquents in the social skills training group had an increased internal locus of control and reduced recidivism rates at a three-year follow-up. Research continued in the area of juvenile delinquency and social skills training with the work of Hazel et al. (1981) and Goldstein et al. (1978). The program by Hazel et al. teaches eight skills: giving positive feedback, giving negative feedback, accepting negative feedback, resisting peer pressure, problem solving, negotiation, following instructions, and beginning conversations. Using a single-system design, the researchers found that the target behaviors improved over baseline levels. Goldstein et al. (1980) outline their approach to skill-streaming the adolescent and the research studies conducted to evaluate their procedures.

These early attempts to examine the effectiveness of social skills training lead the way for increasing applications of this model to other problem situations of adolescents. To name only a few areas, applications of social skills training have been made to:

- Developmentally disabled adolescents (Matson et al. 1988)
- Conduct-disordered adolescents (Tisdelle and St. Lawrence, 1988)
- Blind adolescents (Marshall and Peck, 1986)
- American Indian adolescents (Schinke et al., 1985)
- Disadvantaged adolescents (Staab and Lodish, 1985)
- Adolescents seeking employment (Hiew and MacDonald, 1986)
- School adjustment problems (Brown and Greenspan, 1984)
- Preventing unwanted pregnancy (Gilchrist and Schinke, 1985)
- Preventing substance abuse (Pentz, 1985)

Clearly, studies support the varied application of this model to numerous social problems in adolescence. Research must now be directed toward refining the intervention components, examining social competence treatment's efficacy relative to that of other treatments, and evaluating the long-term effects of the treatment. For example, Harwood and Weissberg (1987) argue that the use of video has great potential in the promotion of social competence in adolescents; would the use of video lead to enhanced learning or be effective in wide-scale applications?

Attempts to apply this model to the problem of adolescent aggression have been based on an integration of cognitive and skill-training strategies. Svec and Bechard (1988) suggest that metacognitive explanations of behavior are needed in the development of a model for reducing aggressive behaviors. Only a few attempts have examined the relative effectiveness of different training packages. For example, LeCroy and Rose (1986) examined three approaches to social competence training: social skills training, problem-solving training, and an approach that combined social skills training with methods of enhancing social cognitive skills. In general, all three methods were found to produce better results than the control group. There was some support for the combined model as the most effective across numerous measures of outcome. Of particular interest was that the social skills training group, in comparison to the problem-solving training group, did better on the problem-solving measure. Apparently learning social skills in different problem situations enhances young people's ability to problem solve. In a similar finding, Spence and Spence (1980) found that social skills training enhanced cognitive abilities, such as locus of control and self-esteem. More research is needed to tease out the differences between various social competence training packages.

Finally, evaluations have not always confirmed the long-term effects of social skills training. In a review of studies examining social skills training with adolescents, it was found that only 50 percent of the studies included a follow-up, and most of the follow-up measures were inadequate (LeCroy, 1983). Of related concern is the extent to which generalization of skills occurs following treatment. Many of the studies on social skills training focus on narrow aspects of social skills (e.g., eye contact, posture) and it is uncertain whether these skills will generalize to other complex situations where such skills are needed.

Strategies for promoting social competence consist largely of the techniques of social skills training and problem-solving training. Social skills training provides an environment for young people to experiment with new behaviors. It is usually done in a group format that provides support and a reinforcing context for learning new responses. Additionally, the group allows for extensive use of modeling and feedback, which are critical components of successful skill training. The following sections give an overview of the steps involved in social skills training.

DEVELOPING PROGRAM GOALS AND SELECTING SKILLS

In order to develop a successful social skills training program, it is important to identify the goals of the program; for example, the goal might be to manage one's anger in provocative situations. Once the goals of the program are decided upon, it is important to select the specific skills that are to be taught.

Depending on the type of problem situations being addressed, a number of different skills might be appropriate. For example, Hazel et al. (1981), in their juvenile offender program, focus on the following skills: giving and receiving feedback, negotiating, resisting peer pressure, and problem solving. Gilchrist and Schinke (1983) have discovered the skills needed for pregnancy prevention: discussing birth control, asking for information, refusing unacceptable demands, and problem solving.

In identifying social skills, it is important to break them down into their component parts so that they can be more easily taught. For example, Goldstein et al. (1980) define beginning conversational skills as including four component parts: greeting the other person, making small talk, deciding whether the other person is listening, and bringing up the main topic.

Constructing social situations that demand certain social skills also is an important part of social skills training. It is preferable that the social situations and skills be determined empirically. For example, Freedman et al. (1978) constructed problem situations that delinquents were likely to encounter, elicited responses to these situations, and then had the responses rated for competence. This allows a clear indication of what types of situations are problematic for delinquents and what constitutes an appropriate response to those situations. However, most practitioners develop their own problem situations for use in social skills training. For example, Gilchrist et al. (1985) use the following situation in their pregnancy prevention program:

> You are at a party with someone you've been dating for about six months. The party is at someone's house; their parents are gone for the weekend. There is a lot of beer and dope and couples are going into the upstairs bedrooms to make out. Your date says, "Hey, Lisa and Tom have gone upstairs. It's real nice up there—let's go—come on."

After goals have been defined and skills have been selected, the focus is on the process of teaching social skills. (For additional information on assessment and selection of skills, see Cartledge and Milburn, 1980; Goldstein et al., 1983; Rose and Edelson, 1987).

THE PROCESS OF TEACHING SOCIAL SKILLS

There are seven basic steps that leaders should follow in teaching social skills. Table 9-1 presents these steps and outlines the process for teaching social skills. In each step there is a request for group member involvement, because it is critical that group leaders involve the participants actively in the skill training. This keeps the learning experience interesting and fun for the group members.

Present the Social Skill Being Taught

In this first step, the group leader presents the skill being taught. The leader beings by soliciting an explanation of the skill, for example, "can anyone tell me what it means to resist peer pressure?" After group members have responded, the leader emphasizes the rationale for using the skill. For example, in teaching young people the skill of resisting peer pressure the leader might say, "you would use this skill when you're in a situation where you don't want to do something that your friends want you to do and you should be able to say no in such a way that your friends can accept your refusal." The leader then asks for additional reasons for learning the skill.

Discuss the Social Skill

The leader presents the specific skill steps that constitute the social skill. For example, the skill steps for resisting peer pressure are: good nonverbal communication (includes eye contact, posture, voice volume), saying "no" early in the interaction, suggesting an alternative activity, and leaving the situation if there is continued pressure. Group members

TABLE 9–1   Steps in Teaching Social Skills

---

1. Present the social skill being taught
   A. Solicit an explanation of the skill
   B. Get group members to provide rationales for the skill
2. Discuss the social skill
   A. List the skill steps
   B. Get group members to give examples of using the skill
3. Present a problem situation and model the skill
   A. Evaluate the performance
   B. Get group members to discuss the model
4. Set the stage for role playing the skill
   A. Select the group members for role playing
   B. Get group members to observe the role play
5. Have group members rehearse the skill
   A. Provide coaching if necessary
   B. Get group members to provide feedback on verbal and nonverbal elements
6. Practice using complex skill situations
   A. Teach accessory skills, e.g., problem solving
   B. Get group members to discuss situations and provide feedback
7. Train for generalization and maintenance
   A. Encourage practice of skills outside the group
   B. Get group members to bring in their problem situations

---

are then asked for examples of when they used the skill or examples of when they could have used the skill but did not.

Present a Problem Situation and Model the Skill

The leader presents a problem situation that demands the use of the skill being taught. For example, the following is a problem situation for resisting peer pressure (LeCroy, 1983):

> After seeing a movie, your friends suggest that you go with them to the mall. It's 10:45 and you are supposed to be home by 11:00. It's important that you get home by 11:00 or you won't be able to go out next weekend.

The group leader chooses members to role play this situation and then models the skills. Group members are asked to evaluate the model's performance. Did the model follow all of the skill steps? Was his or her performance successful? The group leader may choose another group member to model if the leader believes he or she already has the requisite skills. Another alternative being used increasingly is to show the group videotaped models. This has the advantage of following researchers' recommendations that models be similar to trainees in age, sex, and social characteristics.

Set the Stage for Role Playing the Skill

At this point the group leader needs to construct the social circumstances for the role play. Group members are selected and given parts to role play. It is important that the leader review with the group members in the role play exactly what their role is to be. Group members not in the role play are asked to observe the process. It is sometimes helpful if they are given specific instructions for their observations. For example, one member may observe the use of nonverbal skills; another member may be instructed to observe when "no" is said in the interaction.

Have Group Members Rehearse the Skill

Rehearsal or guided practice of the skill is an important part of effective social skills training. Group leaders and group members provide instructions or coaching before and during the role play and provide praise and feedback for improvement. Following a role play enactment, the leader usually will give instructions for improvement, model the suggested improvements, or provide coaching to incorporate the feedback in the subsequent role play. Often the member doing the role play will practice the skills in the situation several times in order to refine his or her own skills and incorporate feedback offered by the group. The role plays continue until the trainee's behavior becomes more and more similar to that of the model. Because it is important that overlearning take place, the group leader should encourage many examples of effective skill demonstration and follow them with praise. Group members should be taught how to give effective feedback prior to the rehearsals. Throughout the teaching process, the group leader should model desired responses. For example, after a role play, the leader can offer the first response and model giving feedback that starts with a positive statement.

Practice Using Complex Skill Situations

The group continues with more difficult and complex skill situations. More complex situations can be developed by extending the interactions and roles in the problem situations. Most social skills groups also incorporate the teaching of problem-solving abilities. Problem solving is a general approach to helping young people analyze and resolve interpersonal problems. Young people are taught to gather information about a problem situation, generate a large number of potential solutions, evaluate the consequences of various solutions, and outline plans for the implementation of a particular solution. Group leaders can give young people problem situations and have members generate alternatives and consequences, select a feasible solution, and make plans for implementing it. The problem-solving training is important because it prepares young people to make whatever adjustments are needed in a given situation. It is a general skill with large-scale application. For a more complete discussion on the use of problem-solving approaches, see Rose and Edelson (1987).

Train for Generalization and Maintenance

The success of the social skills program depends on the extent to which the skills that young people learn transfer to their day-to-day lives. Practitioners must always be planning for ways in which to maximize the generalization of skills learned and their continued use after training. There are a number of activities that help facilitate the generalization and maintenance of skills.

One important activity is to encourage overlearning. The more overlearning that takes place, the greater the likelihood of later transfer. Therefore, it is important that group leaders insist on mastery of the skills. Another important activity is to vary the stimuli when skills are learned. To accomplish this, practitioners can use a variety of models, problem situations, role-play actors, and trainers. The different situations and styles and behaviors of the people used produce a broader base to apply the skills learned. Perhaps the most important activity is to require that young people use the skills in their own real-life settings. Group leaders should assign and monitor homework to encourage transfer of learning. This may include the use of written contracts to perform certain tasks outside the group. Group members should be asked to bring to the group examples of problem situations in which the social skills can be applied. Lastly, practitioners should attempt to develop external support for the skills learned. One approach to this is to set up a "buddy system" whereby group members work together outside the group to practice the skills learned. (For examples, see Edelson and Rose, 1987).

TREATMENT LIMITS

Although numerous applications and much research support have been presented in support of a model for the promotion of social competence among youth, the model is not without problems and issues regarding its development as a treatment modality. In particular, three issues need further clarification: the conceptualization of social competence and social skills, the content of the treatment programs, and the applicability of the training.

There are many issues involved in determining the best way to conceptualize social competence. McFall (1982) believes that "the most important component in the evolving conception of social competence is the concept of a task"; that is, competence should be evaluated in reference to a particular task. In order to assess how adequately a person has performed a task, "one must understand these important features of that task: its purpose, its constraints, its setting, the rules governing task performance, the criteria for distinguishing between successful and unsuccessful performance, and how the task relates to other aspects of the person's life system" (McFall, 1982, p. 16). For example, with regard to setting, where does peer pressure occur? Also, we do not know much about the implicit rules governing situations in which young people are pressured into sex or drug use. Our attempts to address social skills should take into consideration the implicit organization and rules that govern such interactions.

Conceptual questions also arise concerning the reasons why some young people may fail to acquire social skills. It may be that young people never developed the necessary skills and therefore such skills are not in their behavior. Or, young people may possess the skills but may have substituted alternative behaviors that are dysfunctional. These conceptual questions require much more work and investigation.

Another issue concerns which behavioral units should be analyzed in attempting to understand problematic situations. Social skills training content has focused on narrow units (e.g., eye contact) as well as broadly based units (decision-making skills). Does the breadth or narrowness of the units taught have an impact on the effectiveness and generalization of social skills programs; if so, what kind of impact? The same question can be asked about the impact of an emphasis on overt skills versus cognitively based skills. Is an integration of both overt and cognitive skills the most desirable treatment package?

Although social skills training has been applied successfully to numerous social programs, there is a need for more research on the effectiveness of social skills training. For example, can social skills training programs produce additional treatment outcomes when used in conjunction with other treatment methods? What is the relative effectiveness of social skills training and family therapy for different adolescent problems? Future work is needed to address these issues.

SUMMARY

In a social competence model, the intervention is primarily behavioral or cognitive, depending on the client problem and the social circumstance. Client problems are defined according to the cognitive and skill deficits; once defined, these deficits then become targets for intervention.

Deficits are conceptualized as desired outcomes; therefore, a depressed adolescent is seen as someone with few friends who lacks friendship skills or perhaps someone who thinks "no one likes me." In this way, the intervention is more closely linked to the client problem. If someone is conceptualized as depressed, it is unclear how to help him or her; however, if this person in conceptualized as lacking friendship skills, it is clear that the intervention must focus on helping the person acquire those skills. It is in this manner that the practitioner must match the intervention with the client problem.

The components of the social competence model consist of the techniques of social skills training and problem-solving training. The first step involves defining the skill or competency that is to be taught according to the goals of the program. For example, if the program goal is to reduce fighting, the skills and competencies needed to replace fighting behavior must be defined. In addition to defining the competencies, the social circumstances in which the problem behavior occurs must be studied. What are relevant problem situations in which the fighting behavior has occurred? Once these basic components are developed, the practitioner follows a fairly structured process in teaching young people the needed competencies: present and discuss the social skill or competency, present a problem situation and model the skill; have the young person rehearse the skill, and give feedback to refine and modify the performance of the skill. Later the practitioner introduces more complex skill situations and teaches such accessory skills as problem solving.

In conclusion, the promotion of social competence in adolescents is a promising treatment model for helping young people. It has direct relevance to the tasks and demands that young people face in our society. It focuses on positive aspects of functioning and emphasizes the development of needed skills for young people. Social skills training has good empirical support and its application is clear and direct. Furthermore, the techniques of social skills training are applicable to various populations and problem configurations.

Young people need social skills to adapt to and cope with an increasingly complex society. To prepare young people for the future, we must teach them the necessary skills to confront, with self-confidence, the difficult social circumstances that await them.

CHAPTER 10

An Eclectic Approach for Persons with Drug or Alcohol Problems

Joel Fischer

In this chapter, Fischer shows how to use an eclectic approach with persons who have problems resulting from drug or alcohol abuse. As an eclectic approach, the intervention draws from several different theories and emphasizes the effectiveness of social learning theory. Fischer shows how to reach a well-defined understanding of the specific problem, one that is amenable to monitoring client change, and how to establish realistic goals. These components of structure are of particular concern with a controversial issue such as abuse of drugs and alcohol. The treatment plan Fischer illustrates tends to have well-organized and well-explicated components, and is a comprehensive approach to problems of drugs and alcohol. There is clear and unquestionable emphasis on the need for active participation of the client and contracting to help facilitate change. Fischer uses a variety of well-explicated techniques.

INTRODUCTION

There is little question that substance abuse is one of the hot topics of the 1980s and 1990s. Both the lay and the professional literature are rife with references to the problems and dangers associated with substance use and abuse—and rightly so. The direct and indirect costs of substance abuse—in terms of dollars and lives—are enormous.

On the other hand, the real issues involved sometimes are lost in the virtual national hysteria that has arisen since the days of the Reagan administration. The hysteria regarding drug usage in the United States has been well documented by Abbie Hoffman (1987) in his book *Steal This Urine Test*. Hysteria also can be seen, perhaps, in the statement of a graduate social work student who announced in class that an alcoholism expert in a lecture had asserted that 80 percent of human service professionals either have problems with alcohol themselves or come from families where at least one member does. Finally, the national preoccupation with substance abuse can be seen in President Bush's declaration in September of 1989 that ''the gravest domestic threat facing our nation today is drugs'' (*Honolulu Advertiser*, September 6, 1989, p. A-4).

Obviously, then, there is a great need for social work practitioners to get some kind of handle on the enormous range of problems associated with substance abuse, and perhaps to carve out some area of special understanding (or expertise) as a way of addressing some of these problems.

This chapter provides the basis for doing just that. Because of the complexity of and enormous literature on substance abuse problems, and the space limitations inherent in a book such as this, this chapter will not be a general treatise on the nature of substance abuse. Thus, many important and fascinating issues will not be explored, such as:

- Theories and research about the etiology and maintenance or continuation of substance abuse
- The existence of the ''addictive personality''
- The concept of addiction, per se (Peele, 1989)
- Total abstinence versus limited use of some substance for those recovering from abuse
- The pros and cons of twelve-step programs (Herman, 1988)
- The disease model controversy (Fingarette, 1988)
- Substance abuse prevention (Nathan, 1983) and education (Milgram, 1987) programs
- Public policy issues (Fraser and Kohlert, 1988)

Many of the references cited in this chapter, however, do address these issues, especially such recent books as Donovan and Marlatt, 1985; Miller and Heather, 1986; Lewis et al., 1988; Bratter and Forrest, 1985; McCrady et al., 1985; Galatner, 1983; Nirenberg and Maisto, 1987.

Instead of addressing the issues listed above, the focus of this chapter (in keeping with the purposes of this book) is on clinical implications of substance abuse. Substance abuse will be viewed essentially as a variety of problems in living that are manifested in biological/physiological, social, and psychological realms of human functioning. The use of the term ''problems in living'' is not intended to deny the powerful and significant effects of substance abuse. Rather, it is an attempt to destigmatize and delabel the problem, and is linked to the approach to intervention that will be described later in this chapter, especially in regard to the need for development of individualized goals and interventions.

Subsequent sections of this chapter describe some dimensions of the problems of substance abuse, both epidemiologically and clinically; present some assessment and evaluation guidelines; and focus most intensively on describing a program for clinical intervention with the problems of, and problems associated with, substance abuse.

PROBLEM IDENTIFICATION

Several substances typically are considered to have the potential to be abused, including alcohol, licit and illicit drugs, food, caffeine, and the nicotine in smoking and smokeless products. There are a number of commonalities among all these substances: all can be used by some people without any problems, whereas other people experience serious problems with their use; all involve short-term pleasurable activities with potential for long-term negative consequences; all involve biosocialpsychological phenomena; and all, when abuse is most extreme, seem to involve some aspect of "compulsiveness" on the part of the abuser in his or her attachment or involvement with the substance (see Miller, 1987).

This chapter focuses mainly on just two of the substances—alcohol and drugs. This is largely because of space limitations, but it is also because the assessment and intervention strategies for alcohol and drug abuse are relatively similar, and because social work practitioners apparently see more instances of alcohol and drug abuse—as identified problems, at any rate—than the other forms of substance abuse. However, it should be pointed out that the intervention techniques to be discussed in this chapter can also be applied to abuse of the other substances, and that the problems associated with abuse of these substances are not viewed as less serious than those associated with alcohol and drug abuse simply because they are not covered here.

Definition of Substance Abuse

Perhaps the most widely used definition of disorders associated with use of substances such as those described above is the one contained in the Diagnostic and Statistical Manual (DSM-III-Revised) of the American Psychiatric Association (1987; see also Maxman, 1986). This definition distinguishes between two major conditions associated with dysfunctional use of substances: substance dependence and (the more commonly used term) substance abuse.

Substance dependence refers essentially to a cluster of cognitive, behavioral, and physiological symptoms that indicate that a person has impaired control in the use of one or more substances and continues use of the substance despite adverse consequences (APA, 1987). The primary symptoms of dependence, according to DSM-III-R, include, but are not limited to, physiological tolerance and withdrawal. Tolerance refers to either the diminishing effects over time of a fixed amount of a substance, or the need to increase amounts of a substance in order to maintain the same effect. Withdrawal refers to the symptoms that occur when use of the substance is reduced or stopped. The symptoms of tolerance and withdrawal vary according to the specific substance and the frequency, amount, and chronicity of its use.

Substance dependence can show up in a variety of ways. DSM-III-R lists nine symptoms, three of which must be present for at least a month or have occurred repeatedly over a longer period for substance dependence to be present.

Substance abuse is referred to in DSM-III-R as a residual category in that maladaptive patterns of substance use are present that do not meet the criteria for dependence. These criteria, one of which must be present for one month or occur repeatedly for a longer period, are: (1) continued use of the substance despite knowledge of having a persistent or recurrent social, occupational, physical, or psychological problem that is caused or exacerbated by use of the substance; and (2) recurrent use in situations when use is hazardous (e.g., driving while intoxicated).

There are at least two problems with the DSM-III-R view of substance abuse. One is that it focuses mainly on the abuse, per se, and not on the myriad problems that could be associated with it. Thus, it implies that substance abuse is a more or less homogeneous problem, and, correspondingly, that treatment can be a more or less homogeneous activity (focused only on the abuse). The second problem is that the nine diagnostic criteria for substance dependence (of which at least three must be present) and the two for abuse all are indicative of very severe problems of substance use. Even though DSM-III-R recommends evaluating dependence (at least) as mild, moderate, or severe (or in partial or full remission), by no stretch of the imagination can the presence of any of those criteria be construed as "mild" (e.g., part of just one of the diagnostic criteria is "frequent intoxication or withdrawal symptoms when expected to fulfill major role obligations. . . ."; APA, 1987, p. 168).

It is especially important to recognize that substance abuse and the problems associated with it vary tremendously in severity from person to person. It would be overly simplistic to say that a person does or does not abuse some substance. A far more useful perspective—for both assessment and intervention—would be to view the use of substances on a continuum from nonproblematic to extremely problematic. In other words, deciding who has or does not have a problem with substance use depends on a variety of factors related not only to use (or misuse) of the substance, but also to the ways in which that misuse affects total functioning. Just such a continuum regarding problems with substance use has been proposed by Lewis et al. (1988), who conceptualize disorders associated with substance abuse as ranging along the following continuum:

1. Nonuse
2. Moderate, nonproblematic use
3. Heavy, nonproblematic use

4. Heavy use; moderate problems

5. Heavy use; serious problems

6. Dependence; life and health problems

This continuum allows for greater individualization in goals and techniques of intervention and avoids overgeneralized or stereotypical thinking about the supposed homogeneity of substance abusers.

The complexities of all of the above, then, necessitate some working definition of substance abuse that can help guide practitioners' activities. Such a working definition might be as follows: when use of alcohol or drugs (or, for that matter, any substance) affects an individual's biological/medical, social, behavioral, or psychological functioning, that problem can be viewed as one of substance abuse. This definition allows for the wide variety of problems typically associated with substance abuse to be viewed on the continuum described above. Thus, at one end of the continuum, few if any problems are associated with substance use, while at the other end of the continuum, serious problems exist in one or more areas of the individual's life. These problems could include dependence and/or abuse (as defined by DSM-III-R), and could also include the pattern that often brings people to the attention of professional helpers (voluntarily or involuntarily), the overwhelming involvement or attachment to the substance—the compulsiveness and inability to control its use that was mentioned earlier as a common characteristic of serious abuse of all the substances.

In line with DSM-III-R, this chapter focuses on the following classes of substances, individually or in combination: alcohol; amphetamines (e.g., "speed" and certain appetite suppressants); cannabis (e. g., marijuana, hashish); cocaine; hallucinogens (e. g., LSD); inhalants (e. g., glue sniffing); opioids (e. g., heroin); phencyclidine (PCP); and sedatives, hypnotics, and anciolytics. Throughout this chapter, the term "substance abuse" will be used in the general sense of problems associated with the use of any of the above substances, rather than the more narrow use described in DSM-III-R. Perhaps an even more appropriate general term might be "substance misuse," although this typically is taken to mean a less severe set of problems than "substance abuse."

Prevalence of Substance Abuse

The United States is a society of alcohol and drug users: some 90 million adults use alcohol on a regular basis (Miller, 1987). By the time they reach their mid-twenties, up to 80 percent of Americans have tried an illicit drug, and at any given time some 37 percent of high school seniors have had five or more drinks in one sitting within the preceding two weeks (Johnston et al., 1986). In other words, alcohol and drugs seem to be as American as apple pie and ice cream.

It is difficult to know precisely how many of the users of these substances actually have problems of abuse or dependence or misuse. Some estimates are available, however, from a community survey of three metropolitan areas that was conducted in the early 1980s (Robins et al., 1984; see also Helzer 1987). This survey examined lifetime prevalence of fifteen DSM III psychiatric disorders, with lifetime prevalence being the proportion of people in a representative sample who had ever experienced the disorder up to the time of assessment. Of all the disorders, by far the most prevalent was substance abuse, with 15 to 18.1 percent of the population being diagnosed. Of these, alcohol abuse ranged from 11.5 to 15.7 percent of the population, and drug abuse from 5.5 to 5.8 percent. These percentages translate into hefty numbers of the American population; with 1987 census figures showing roughly 185 million adult Americans, these data suggest some 3 million or more adult Americans, at some time in their lives, may have been affected by alcohol and/or drug abuse. Given that the 1987 census figures show roughly 89 million households, this means that up to 37 percent of American households may be affected.

The prevalence of alcohol and drug abuse does not appear to be different for blacks and whites (with the exception of one city in the community survey showing a slightly higher prevalence of drug abuse among blacks). However, the data are not as clear for other ethnic groups, for which few epidemiological studies have been conducted (Heath, 1987). There are few differences related to education regarding prevalence of substance abuse (again with one exception in one city that showed higher rates of alcohol abuse among non-college graduates). There are clearer differences according to gender: most data show higher rates of substance abuse for men than women, with this difference being greatest for alcohol abuse (a ratio of up to 5 to 1).

Although these data are startling, their true meaning becomes clear when examining the implications of these problems for everyday life. The direct and indirect costs—both in health terms and financially—of alcohol and drug abuse are immense. One of the leading experts on the topic, J. Danforth Quayle (1983), estimated, perhaps conservatively, that the price paid for health care, days away from work, and lost productivity amounts to approximately $70 billion per year. The medical risks are even more frightening, with a huge variety of illnesses associated with alcohol and drug abuse (Wartenberg and Liepman, 1987; Segal and Sisson, 1985). More importantly, estimates are that drug and alcohol abuse are related to the deaths of up to 130,000 people per year, including many innocent victims of people who drive while under the influence of some substance (Hoffman, 1987; Wartenberg and Liepman, 1987).

Add to all this the incalculable toll of substance abuse on individual functioning, family life, and employment, and it can be clearly seen that substance abuse is indeed one of the major problems of the era. Indeed, when the categories of substance abuse are expanded to include nicotine and food, with some 50 million smokers and 40 million overweight Americans (Miller, 1987), the enormity of the problem becomes even more apparent, with countless billions of dollars added to the costs to the nation, and hundreds of thousands of yearly deaths added to the numbers of deaths associated with alcohol and drugs alone (Wartenberg and Liepman, 1987; *Honolulu Advertiser*, April 4, 1989, p. D2).

Clinical Manifestations of Substance Abuse

Despite the many myths about the "typical alcoholic" or "typical drug addict," it would be inappropriate to try to characterize the clinical manifestations of substance use as though they apply to all people with substance abuse problems. The dangers here are stereotyping and overgeneralizing; it is perhaps better to err by individualizing than by assuming that all people are alike. This is not to say that there are not some commonalities among the manifestations of substance abuse. Rather, it is to say that the range of possibilities of clinical manifestations of substance abuse is so great that the real need for assessment and intervention is to be able to precisely pinpoint areas for change that are specific for each individual. This is one more rationale for use of the continuum of abuse—ranging from nonuse to misuse to serious abuse—described earlier.

Problems related to substance abuse can show up in all realms of human functioning. As mentioned earlier, DSM-III-R describes nine possible diagnostic criteria (or patterns of behavior) related to dependence (e. g., a great deal of time spent in trying to get, use, or recover from the substance; persistent desire or one or more unsuccessful attempts to cut down or control substance use), and two criteria or patterns related to "abuse." Not all of these need to be present either for the formal diagnosis to be made or for serious problems as a result of substance use to be present.

Similarly, DSM-III-R lists several categories of "organic mental syndrome" caused by the direct effect of various substances on the nervous system that could be present in any given case of substance misuse. These include intoxication, withdrawal, delirium, withdrawal delirium, delusional disorder, mood disorder, and other syndromes. Thus, the clinical manifestations of abuse could include one or more of these disorders as well.

In addition, any individual who misuses or abuses some substance could be suffering from any one of a number of medical problems associated with the abuse (Wartenberg and Leipman, 1987). These problems run the gamut from malnutrition to cancer to respiratory and cardiovascular problems to a variety of infections, such as hepatitis or even AIDS.

Finally, Lewis et al. (1988) list numerous problems that typically, but not uniformly, are associated with substance abuse. These include employment problems; problems with friends or neighbors; problems with spouse, children, parents, or other relatives; problems with arrests and the criminal justice system; financial problems; problems of belligerence, depression, anxiety, and so on. These numerous problems all are ways in which the clinical manifestations of substance abuse can be seen.

Practitioners who work exclusively with individuals who abuse only one substance may see more commonalities among presented problems than those who work with abuse of a range of different substances. However, when substance abuse as a whole is examined, it is obvious that it can manifest itself in so many ways, and in so many realms of human functioning, that it requires the practitioner to be especially sensitive and to be able to carefully assess each individual for the unique ways in which the problems may be manifested. The next section presents some guidelines and tools that emphasize the importance of such individualized assessment.

ASSESSMENT AND MONITORING

This chapter emphasizes the idea that problems associated with substance use should be viewed as "problems in living," leading to the necessity of individualizing goals and interventions. It is, therefore, probably no overstatement to say that the assessment of the client is the most important phase of the clinical process. This is because the assessment identifies the specific problems of each client, sets specific goals for each case, selects specific interventions tailored to the problems and goals, and develops a plan to monitor and evaluate the success of the intervention. Even though initial goals and interventions are selected, however, the assessment does not stop there; substance abuse involves such a complicated set of problems that goals and interventions may have to be reformulated constantly on the basis of new or better evidence, changes in the problems, or new problems arising. Indeed, the very complexity of the assessment process requires mastery of a great deal of material, much of which can be obtained from comprehensive guides to the assessment process (e. g., Donovan and Marlatt, 1988; Lewis, 1988; Baker and Cannon, 1988; Miller, 1981; McCrady, 1985; Sobell et al., 1988; Nirenberg and Maisto, 1987; Bratter and Forrest, 1985).

Assessment in this chapter is used for the purposes described above rather than for diagnosis. Diagnosis serves important purposes, including agency or insurance requirements. However, for reasons described earlier regarding problems with the DSM-III-R categories, the diagnosis, per se, is downplayed here in order to focus on the broader perspective of clinical assessment of not only the substance abuse itself, but also of the context and problems associated with that abuse.

Basic Principles

A number of basic principles underlie the assessment methodologies discussed here.

1. Substance abuse is a biopsychosocial problem that is very complicated and requires a multivariate assessment process to properly understand it. Thus, a variety of assessment methods must be utilized.

2. The problems of, and associated with, substance use occur on a continuum, from nonproblematic to severely problematic. Thus, the purpose of assessment is not to make a simplistic determination of whether or not an individual abuses some substance, but to examine the problem in all its manifestations.

3. There are a variety of interventions available to deal with the diverse problems associated with substance abuse. It is crucial for the practitioner to be aware of these interventions so that the best interventions available can be selected for each component of the problem.

4. The focus of assessment for substance abuse is largely on the present, especially on factors that might be maintaining the abuse. This is because factors that might be associated with the original development of abuse may not be the ones maintaining it; in fact, they may not be present at all.

5. The practitioner must be aware of the importance of socioeconomic, ethnic, and cultural variables in conducting an assessment. The basic principle is: the greater the difference between the practitioner and client (in values, attitudes, socioeconomic status, etc.), the greater the sensitivity required of the practitioner to properly understand the client's situation (see Lum, 1986, for a framework for conducting assessment that is attuned to sociocultural issues).

6. Assessment for substance abuse is very complex. Misconceptions associated with abuse, poor professional education in this area, difficulty of gaining cooperation from some clients, variability of problems associated with abuse, need to understand prior treatments with relapsed clients, and the covert nature of some problems of abuse all have been cited as reasons why assessment for substance abuse is especially difficult (Sobell et al., 1988). Thus, the practitioner

must take even more care than with other problem areas to ensure that he or she has done as thorough and sensitive a job as possible.

7. Despite the need to know as much as possible about the problem so that one can make a rational decision about the best available intervention, reality suggests that this must be balanced with the amount of time available to the practitioner, i. e., the cost efficiency of the assessment process (Donovan, 1988). In order to avoid practitioners becoming overwhelmed with assessing each case, Donovan (1988) describes the use of clinical hypothesis testing (generating hypotheses based on data collected) and segmented assessment strategies (funneling from very broad to increasingly specific foci in the assessment).

8. The practitioner who works with substance abuse needs an extensive body of knowledge to aid in understanding the variety of factors associated with the abuse. This includes not only knowledge that all practitioners might have about dealing with social and psychological problems (employment difficulties, depression, cognitive distortions, anxiety, and so on), but also knowledge about the specific substance of concern, including biophysiological factors, behavioral factors, cognitive-expectational factors, and social factors (Donovan, 1988).

Areas for Collection of Information

There are a number of areas about which practitioners should collect information to help in goal formulation and treatment planning. These have been hinted at above, but will be described in a little more detail here. Although the most common focus of assessment for substance abuse is the pattern of the abuse itself, the other elements described here are viewed as no less important in developing a comprehensive understanding of the client and the client's problems.

Medical information. Because of the numerous possible medical complications that could be associated with substance abuse, it is crucial for every client to have a thorough medical evaluation. In addition, it is important for practitioners to solicit information from clients about any physical problems as early in their contacts as possible in the event that referral to a physician is necessary.

Presence of related social/psychological disorders. In addition to the several substance abuse–related disorders described in DSM-III-R mentioned earlier, there are a number of problems of which practitioners must be aware. These include the behaviors, thoughts, and feelings associated with disorders involving depression, anxiety, sleep, eating, sex, and impulse control. Problems in any of these areas pose serious complications in the lives of clients who abuse some substance and will need attention if a comprehensive treatment program is to be developed.

Life stresses.   In addition to the above, there are any number of events that could complicate substance abuse patterns and, indeed, could even be associated with maintaining the abuse. These life stresses must be carefully assessed. They include problems with family, income, housing, and peer relationships.

Prior treatment history.   The practitioner must be informed about the client's attempts to receive treatment for any of the problems described above, or for the substance abuse itself. The practitioner then should determine the reasons for the success or failure of those programs and try to build on the successes and not duplicate the failures.

Client motivation and expectations.   The client may have a number of preconceived notions of what treatment may be like. These expectations can have a serious impact on the success or failure of treatment, and it is crucial for the practitioner to elicit these expectations from the client and to create positive expectations of success as part of treatment. Similarly, it is important to know and understand the client's motivation for seeking treatment. Obviously, the client's commitment to the process could be influenced by any number of factors, ranging from genuine desire for change to the desire to avoid some legal problems or dissolution of a marriage. This information allows the practitioner to make judgments about the extent to which he or she will need to emphasize enhancing the client's motivation as a major or minor part of the intervention.

Availability of social supports.   In making decisions about the type of treatment that will be recommended, the practitioner will have to understand the client's social support system, if indeed he or she has one (McCrady, 1985). The presence or extent of social support could have a bearing on the location of treatment (e. g., in- or outpatient), types of tasks and homework assigned the client, type of maintenance program, and so on.

Functional analysis of the pattern of substance abuse.   Ultimately, of course, the practitioner will have to do a careful assessment of the pattern of substance use and factors that may be associated with it, including antecedents that may be eliciting substance abuse and consequences that could be maintaining it. Sobell et al. (1988) have provided a comprehensive list of areas to be examined in such an assessment, including:

- Specific quantities and frequency of use of the substance
- Usual and unusual substance-use circumstances and patterns
- Predominant mood states and situations antecedent and consequent to substance use
- History of withdrawal symptoms
- Identification of possible difficulties the client might encounter in refraining from substance use
- Extent and severity of previous substance use
- Multiple substance use
- Reports of frequent thoughts or urges to use substances
- Review of positive consequences of substance abuse
- Risks associated with nonabstinence treatment goal

Other areas.   In addition to the areas described above, Shaffer and Kauffman (1985) offer a number of hypotheses to be tested in assessing substance abuse. These hypotheses—actually ''partial formulations''— include biological hypotheses (e. g., can the substance use be understood as an attempt to reduce dysphoria?), sociological hypotheses (e. g., does the substance use occur in limited or varied environmental contexts?), and behavior hypotheses (e. g., can the problems be understood as contingent upon the reinforcing properties of the substance?).

Methods of Data Collection

In order to collect information on the wide range of activities, behaviors, patterns, thoughts, and feelings described above, a number of different methods of data collection must be employed. These methods include interviews with clients and others, self-report measures, direct observation (influencing analogue measures), biochemical measures, and records.

Interviews.   The interview is, of course, the major medium for the collection of the information described in the previous section. This is as much the case in the area of substance abuse as it is in any other clinical area. Thus, standard social work intervention strategies are used to elicit and analyze this information. However, there are some specifics that differentiate interviews in this area from those in other areas (see, e. g., Shaffer and Kauffman, 1985). A summary of interviewing conditions that provide the most useful information in the area of substance abuse has been provided by Sobell et al. (1988, pp. 29–30) and includes the following: (1) when the client is alcohol- and drug-free; (2) when rapport is developed both by the practitioner's style and by stressing confidentiality and the importance of the information; (3) when terminology used is clearly understood by both parties; (4) when the focus of the interview is information gathering rather than social labeling; (5) when the client's self-reports are checked out against other sources; and (6) when data are gathered, to the extent possible, in a clinical research setting.

The interview typically contains both structured and unstructured portions. A very useful guide for the initial interview was developed by Lewis et al. (1988), along with a psychosocial and substance-use history form and a behavioral assessment and functional analysis interview form. A widely used structured interview format for assessment of alcohol abuse is the Comprehensive Drinking Profile (Marlatt, 1976; Miller and Marlatt, 1984), and a structured interview format for drug abuse, called the G-DATS, has been described by Boudin et al. (1977). Another structured interview format for both drug and alcohol abuse is the Addiction Severity Index (McClellan et al., 1988).

Self-report measures. Especially important areas for the collection of data on substance abuse are self-report measures and self-monitoring. These measures range from simple oral reports the client might make during the interview to the use of standardized questionnaires. For purposes of this chapter, these two types of self-report measures will be divided into two categories: standardized scales and self-monitoring.

Standardized scales. One of the fastest growing areas of assessment for substance abuse is that of standardized scales. Many of these measures have reported fairly good reliability and validity data. Standardized measures cover not only problems of abuse, but also problems that could be related to abuse, such as depression, anxiety, and cognitive distortions (see Corcoran and Fischer, 1987, for a collection of some 125 short-form measures for clinical practice; and see Hersen and Bellack, 1988, for a dictionary of well over 400 assessment procedures). Some of the most useful standardized self-report scales developed for assessing substance abuse are the Substance Abuse Problem Checklist (Carroll, 1984), the Michigan Alcohol Screening Test (Selzer, 1971), the Drug Abuse Screening Test (Skinner, 1982), the Hilton Drinking Behavior Questionnaire (Hilton and Lokane, 1978), and the Callner-Ross Assertion Questionnaire (Ammerman and Van Hasselt, 1988).

Self-monitoring. The second major type of self-report measure is called self-monitoring. Self-monitoring refers essentially to the client routinely recording, via diaries or logs, problems and behaviors related to abuse. This includes recording not only actual use patterns, but also problems associated with use and the urges and consequences related to use. Essentially, the process of self-monitoring involves training the client to record a variety of factors related to abuse, including some or all of the following: time, date, and amount of the substance; antecedents and consequences, including thoughts, feelings, and behaviors of self and others; and activities associated with substance use. These data are collected before, during, and after treatment and can be used as a basis not only for assessment, but also for evaluation. Of course, the practitioner's response to the client's efforts at self-monitoring can play a major role in how useful and accurate these data are (Sobell et al., 1988).

Reliability and validity of self-report data. A major concern about self-report data in the area of substance abuse is their reliability and validity. The prevailing myth is that such data are almost always suspect. In fact, a substantial amount of research shows that self-reports in the area of substance abuse can be both reliable and valid (Sobell et al., 1988; Ridley and Kordinak, 1988; Maisto and Cooper, 1980), including good agreement between self-reports and reports by collaterals (Sobell et al., 1988). The main cautions about these conclusions are that they apply mainly when the client is interviewed under the following conditions: he or she is substance-free, he or she is in a clinical/research setting, and he or she is assured of confidentiality.

Direct observation. Although rather difficult to implement in clinical settings, direct observation has been used in some instances to provide information on use of some substances (Foy et al., 1987). One type of direct observation involves the use of analogue measures, in which tasks are developed that are considered analogous to the natural environment in which a person must "work" to obtain a substance (typically alcohol). Another type of direct observation is where the client is placed in a simulated bar or living room environment and provided with the substance (again, typically alcohol), and then observed as to the patterns and amounts ingested.

Biochemical measures. A wide range of biochemical measures typically are used in comprehensive substance abuse programs. Although many of these are not available to the individual clinician (especially without research/medical supervision), they nevertheless add an important dimension to understanding the patterns of clients' substance use. These measures have been reviewed by Sobell et al. (1988); Foy et al. (1987); and Wells et al. (1988a and 1988b), and include blood-alcohol level analysis, liver function tests, Antabuse monitoring, urinalysis, breath alcohol tests, alcohol dipstick (for ethanol concentrations), and the sweat patch. Some of these tests are used for assessing recent use (e. g., breath and urine tests), and others for extended use (e. g., liver function tests).

Records. A final source of data is official records (Sobell et al., 1988). These records could include police, hospital, and school reports. Of course, these data may be incomplete or even biased (e. g., minority group members may be picked up by police for apparent illegal behaviors far more frequently than majority group or upper-income people displaying the same behaviors). Nevertheless, official records can form part of the basis for a comprehensive assessment, especially when used in context as only one source of data about the problem as a whole.

Integrative Formulation

The last part of the assessment process is to develop an "integrative formulation" (Siporin, 1975). The integrative formulation consists of a summary of the information collected by the practitioner, plus the practitioner's analysis of that information. The integrative formulation pulls together disparate pieces of information collected during the assessment, allowing the practitioner to reflect on that information and decide what it all means. If the practitioner is required to make a formal diagnosis, say, based on DSM III—R, this is where he or she would do this, adding to that diagnosis, ideally, the concept of the continuum described earlier in this chapter. The integrative formulation would then be used as the basis for goal setting and for the development of treatment plans.

Goal setting.   Goal setting is a particularly sensitive area for substance abuse treatment because it raises a number of difficult issues, foremost among them the issue of abstinence versus controlled use (especially of alcohol). Although this literature is too extensive to be covered thoroughly here (see recent reviews by Lewis et al., 1988; Maisto and Carey, 1987; Foreyt, 1987; Brownell, 1984), there does appear to be sufficient evidence to suggest that controlled use may be an appropriate goal for a small percentage of clients under very select circumstances.

Be that as it may, the setting of goals in the area of substance abuse should:

1. Reflect the broad ranges of problems identified in the assessment (not just the substance abuse, per se).
2. Be clear and precise.
3. Allow evaluations.
4. Include long- and short-term goals.
5. Add to specificity by identifying *who* is to change, *what* will be changed, *to what extent,* and under what *conditions* (Gottman and Leiblum, 1974; Brown and Brown, 1977). This will allow the practitioner to be as specific as possible in identifying specific areas of change.

Treatment plan.   The final part of the assessment process is developing a treatment plan that will address each of the problem areas and goals that have been identified. (One model of a treatment plan for substance abuse—including some very useful forms—is presented by Lewis et al., 1988.) The idea here is to select those intervention techniques that have the best evidence of effectiveness and apply them in a systematic way to each of the problems identified in the assessment. Although this may not always be possible, it is this effort to link previous research on effectiveness with a given client's individualized problems that is a hallmark of the eclectic approach.

Obviously, a number of factors in addition to previous research play a part in developing a treatment plan for substance abuse. These include issues such as: Will the treatment be in- or outpatient? How motivated is the client? To what extent are environmental factors involved? How extensive are the abuse and the problems associated with it? How familiar is the practitioner with the techniques recommended by the research and does he or she have the commitment to learn them?

The final step in the assessment process is putting everything into a written contract with the client. Not only will the contract itself be a positive force in structuring the treatment, but it also will clarify goals, time limits, mutual tasks and responsibilities, monitoring and evaluation activities, and precisely how and by whom the treatment will be implemented.

ECLECTIC INTERVENTION

This section focuses on specific intervention techniques that could be incorporated in a comprehensive treatment program for substance abuse. There is, in fact, no single specific treatment (or theory) of choice; rather, a number of different interventions can be applied, depending on the individual client, problem, and situation.

Research and Practice Support

Unfortunately, in the area of substance abuse there is no single intervention program with unequivocal support, nor single source of literature that one can turn to that clearly illustrates empirical support for one or more intervention programs. Indeed, the interventions described in this section are derived from several sources, including recent research.

1. Review of recent research on substance abuse (Matuscha, 1985; Merbaum and Rosenbaum, 1984; Ogborne and Glaser, 1985; Hester and Miller, 1989; Miller and Hester, 1986; Maisto and Carey, 1987; Stitzer et al., 1983; Ingram and Salzberg, 1988; Cox, 1987; Miller, 1985; Colletti and Brownell, 1982; McCrady and Sher, 1985). The upshot of all this research is that there are several techniques that

have been effective with some substance abuse clients under some circumstances, but no techniques that are effective with all clients under all circumstances. Further, although it appears that (with alcohol abuse at least) some treatment is better than no treatment, the type of treatment is not always crucial. However, there are many commonalities regarding treatment techniques in some of the most successful programs. The recommendations in this chapter will focus mainly on techniques that have been used successfully in several programs.

2. Less rigorous research, case studies, and practice experience. The literature on substance abuse is replete with hundreds of references to innovative programs, new techniques, small group studies, and case studies, many of which can be found in the references cited throughout this chapter. Although this literature is too immense to be reviewed comprehensively here, some of those reports are incorporated in the recommendations later in this chapter (see, e. g., *Social Casework*, 1989).

3. Adaptations of effective techniques. There are a number of techniques with substantial evidence of effectiveness in areas other than substance abuse (see Fischer, 1986, for a review of some of these techniques). Because the perspective of this chapter is that problems associated with substance abuse can be as serious as the abuse itself, and a number of these related problems have been treated successfully independent of treatment for substance abuse (e. g., problems of anxiety, depression), a number of these treatment techniques are incorporated in the recommendations here.

Basic Principles of Intervention

There are a number of basic principles of intervention that underlie the treatment recommendations here.

1. Treat the whole person. It is crucial to remember, first of all, that abusing a substance usually is not an independent problem—many other problems typically are associated with it; and second, that substance abuse rarely occurs in a vacuum. People exist in environments, and the successful treatment of substance abuse requires attention to assessment problems and the environmental context.

2. There is no single best treatment. The treatment always must be tailored to the individual client and problem. This matching of treatment to client is perhaps the key ingredient of an effective program.

3. Be prepared for failure. Work in the area of substance abuse is usually difficult and frequently unrewarding for the practitioner. On

the one hand, it is easy to begin blaming clients and/or feeling burned out, especially when clients are uncooperative or even disruptive. On the other hand, the intrinsic rewards of success are so great that they may make all the effort worthwhile. Typically, practitioners working in the area of substance abuse are unusually committed and have abandoned the "rescue fantasy" of being able to help everyone with everything. Indeed, sometimes they can reframe the difficulties as challenges, thus leading to a more positive, self-reinforcing outlook.

4. Attend to diversity in clients. In addition to the variations in client problems in this area, there is a tremendous diversity in other characteristics: race, gender, ethnicity, socioeconomic status, sexual orientation, and the like. Many of these variations can become barriers to successful interventions, especially if the practitioner views the client as "an alcoholic" or "a drug addict" and does not take into account his or her other human characteristics. This individualizing includes being aware of the client's world views; being sensitive to his or her culture, values, and norms; working to understand different patterns of communication; and using all this knowledge and awareness to create more individualized and sensitive intervention programs.

5. Use a variety of roles. One of the great strengths of social work is the wide variety of roles that can be employed in the client's behalf. If the practitioner views intervention as taking place solely in the clinical role, he or she could be undercutting the effectiveness of the program. Problems associated with substance abuse often involve the need for intervention with significant others and in the environment in such practitioner roles as consultant, advocate, and broker.

6. Attend to client motivation. Although poor client motivation frequently is used as an explanation (and sometimes as an excuse) for treatment failures, motivating the client to continue in treatment can be viewed as just one more challenge to the expertise of the practitioner. Indeed a number of successful strategies for enhancing client commitment in the area of substance abuse have been reviewed by Miller (1985), who describes several techniques that have been used successfully to enhance client motivation. These include giving advice, providing feedback, setting specific goals, role playing and modeling, maintaining continuity of contact, manipulating external contingencies, providing choice, and decreasing the attractiveness of the problem behavior. (A number of other procedures for enhancing client commitment are described in Meichenbaum and Turk, 1987; and Shelton and Levy, 1981.)

7. Focus on a positive relationship. Any intervention program should be grounded in the core interpersonal skills of effective practice. Empathy, warmth, respect, and genuineness—ingredients of a positive relationship—are the heart of all practice, but are especially important when working in the area of substance abuse. First, practitioners will find the clients are more willing to work and cooperate with practitioners who communicate high levels of these skills (Meichenbaum and Turk, 1987). This is particularly critical in the area of substance abuse. Second, there is clear evidence that the effectiveness of many intervention techniques will be increased when the practitioner implements them with high levels of interpersonal skills (Fischer, 1978). Thus, interpersonal skills—the relationship—and techniques bolster each other in enhancing overall practice effectiveness.

Intervention Techniques

The interventions described here, none of which rely on electrical or chemical interventions and thus can be used by social workers, have been synthesized from a variety of sources, as described earlier. Although, of course, these are not the only successful treatments, it is likely that combinations of these techniques, systematically applied to individualized components of clients' problems, constitute some of the more effective strategies available as of the early 1990s. Indeed, some of these treatments, when combined, have been called "ideal services" (Nathan, 1980). Obviously, because this is a multidimensional treatment program, not all of the techniques will be applied with all clients. Thus, the key, once again, is judicious matching of individual intervention components with client problems.

The individual components of this program are divided into twelve separate categories: detoxification and motivation enhancement, self-regulation and self-control, contingency contracting, stress-control training, aversive treatment, cognitive coping strategies, coping and social skills training, education about the substance, lifestyle intervention, marital and family counseling, community enforcement, and group support and self-help groups.

Detoxification and motivation enhancement. One of the axioms of treatment is that clients cannot be using or abusing substances if treatment is to be successful. Thus, a first step in treatment is to help the client withdraw from the substance he or she is using. This is usually a short-term process, but the period may also be an intense one, as the client may be experiencing some discomfort. There are several options for detoxification, depending on the extent of use, level of dependence on the substance, degree of social support, and resources available (McCrady, 1985; Lewis et al., 1988). The detoxification process could occur on an outpatient basis without involvement of a detoxification center; or in either a nonmedical (social) or a medical detoxification center, with both types of centers involving either partial or full hospitalization. Detoxification is the first step in a comprehensive treatment effort; however, a substantial part of the assessment, goal setting, and treatment planning could take place during this first step, and the detoxification effort can be coordinated with subsequent treatment to produce a more comprehensive and integrated approach for the client.

To the extent that the client becomes able to participate, this early stage begins the process of assessing and enhancing the client's motivation for treatment, using some of the techniques described in the previous section. In addition, if the client appears to be uncooperative, perhaps denying that he or she has a problem, specific intervention strategies to overcome this denial should be considered. Frequently, these strategies involve planned confrontations by family members, friends, or perhaps other group members in a detoxification program. These confrontations should be carefully planned and supervised, and could involve such techniques as family members making a list of specific incidents in which they were being hurt by the client's substance abuse and then rehearsing how to present these to the client. Other, more recent, variations of planned family confrontations include programmed confrontation and programmed request by the client's spouse, as described by Thomas and Yoshioka (1989).

Self-regulation and self-control. There is little question that after termination of the formal substance abuse program, the client will have to take control of his or her own program. The self-regulation, self-control component not only is intended to prepare the client to do just that, but also provides in-treatment benefits.

The very terms self-control and self-regulation imply that it is actually the client who generates and designs a unique self-improvement program, though this is not typically the case (Merbaum and Rosenbaum, 1984). In fact, the self-control package really is just one component of an overall comprehensive program in which the client learns certain techniques that he or she will continue to apply once the formal part of the program is completed.

A number of techniques for self-control components have been suggested by Nathan (1980), Merbaum and Rosenbaum (1984), and Kanfer (1986). Some of these techniques are:

1. Self-monitoring. Clients are taught to keep track of any substance-related thoughts, behaviors, or feelings, as well as amounts and cir-

cumstances of any substance use. The goal here is to increase awareness of patterns and urges so that the client can eventually engage in
some change activity. It also may be that the recording itself will have a
(positive) reactive effect.

2. Self-evaluation. Although related to self-monitoring, the focus here is
on setting goals and encouraging self-evaluation of adherence to these
goals.

3. Self-reinforcement. A crucial component of any intervention program,
self-reinforcement involves teaching clients to reinforce themselves—
covertly (through thoughts) and overtly (through desired activities)
for successful adherence to goals, successful completion of tasks, or
even partial successes.

4. Self-control manual. Clients are given training manuals that help them
develop comprehensive self-control programs.

Contingency contracting. The use of contracts increasingly is a part
of everyday practice in many social work organizations. Contracts have
numerous advantages, including ensuring explicitness, adding to structure, enhancing the client's commitment, clarifying goals, and clarifying
client and practitioner responsibilities. Contingency contracts, per se, go
a step further by actually spelling out relationships between desired behaviors and reinforcement for those behaviors (see Epstein and Wing,
1984). They provide for reinforcement of desired activities, such as self-
monitoring or adhering to a program of abstinence, and sometimes punishment for undesired activities or behaviors, such as nonadherence.

Contingency contracts for health and substance abuse problems were
recently reviewed by Epstein and Wing (1984). They describe numerous
characteristics of these contracts, including the variety of potential patterns of reinforcement, their use with several substance abuse problems,
inclusion of third parties in these contracts, and the use of behaviors that
are incompatible with substance use. Contingency contracts can be used
in a variety of ways to deal with problems of abuse, per se (e. g., adherence), as well as those only indirectly related to abuse (e. g., relationship
problems). As such, they are a flexible and important part of the practitioner's armamentarium.

Stress-control training. A key factor in helping clients overcome
problems of substance abuse is training them to deal with anxiety and
stress. It is not uncommon for practitioners to hear clients who have
abused alcohol or drugs for many years state that they never experienced
any anxiety in all that time; the alcohol and drugs prevented the anxiety
from occurring or killed it quickly when it did occur. Indeed, a major the-

ory of the etiology of substance abuse is that it serves a tension-reducing function.

The issue here, though, is to help clients deal with tension and stress once they have stopped using alcohol and drugs. Many Americans think nothing of using a glass or two of wine or a tranquilizer to help them navigate through a stormy emotional period. However, people with problems of substance abuse, once they complete treatment, usually have to control stress and anxiety without resorting to drugs and alcohol.

In these circumstances, clients can be taught to use a variety of relaxation and stress-control techniques. Many of these have been spelled out in Cormier and Cormier (1985). They include meditation and muscle relaxation, systematic desensitization, stress inoculation training, and emotive imagery. All of these techniques focus on providing the client with a variety of ways of dealing with stress and anxiety reactions, with stress inoculation training providing the broadest range of potential responses. In addition, all of these techniques can be taught by the practitioner during the treatment program, and can then be used as self-control techniques by the client once the formal treatment program is completed.

Aversive treatment.   Aversive treatments have a long and substantial history in treatment of substance abuse. Some degree of success in at least limiting consumption has been found for both chemical (using the drug Antabuse) and electrical aversion therapies. A technique called covert sensitization (Cautela, 1967) produces an effect similar to other "aversive therapies," but does so without the use of chemical or electrical aversion.

Covert sensitization pairs aversive images with images involving substance use. Clients are instructed to imagine a scene in which they are about to use alcohol or drugs, and to incorporate realistic, unpleasant information about the antecedents, location, etc., in the scene. In this way, clients are taught to imagine another scene—one of disgusting or repugnant responses, such as vomiting all over oneself—that, through repeated practice, becomes paired with the first scene. Clients also are instructed to imagine feeling total relief upon leaving the first scene and refraining from substance use.

Covert sensitization appears to be a moderately successful way of helping clients reduce urges to consume and levels of consumption. The research, however, is neither rigorous nor extensive enough to suggest that this should be more than one technique in a more comprehensive program.

Cognitive coping strategies.   The way people think about their problems is often strongly related to what they do about them. Thus, clients' self-statements, expectations, and beliefs may be critical factors in maintaining patterns of substance abuse. A number of cognitive techniques are available to help clients develop ways of coping with both life problems and urges to use some substance.

Cognitive restructuring.   Cognitive restructuring is a complex technique (some might say an entire approach to therapy) that focuses on identifying and altering clients' dysfunctional beliefs and negative self-statements or thoughts (Cormier and Cormier, 1985). Often a number of such dysfunctional beliefs and self-statements are uncovered in the assessment process (e. g., "I can never stop using"; "I need [substance X] to keep functioning"), and cognitive restructuring can be directed to altering those beliefs. This not only is beneficial in and of itself, but also can ease the way in other areas of the program by reducing resistance.

Guided imagery.   The focus of guided imagery techniques, such as covert modeling (Cormier and Cormier, 1985), is on helping the client rehearse adaptive rather than maladaptive (using the substance) responses to problems situations. Guided imagery can also be used to rehearse any task or activity that the practitioner suggests as a homework assignment.

Thought stopping.   The key components in a pattern of substance abuse often are the thought processes, which include obsessive thinking about the need and desire for a substance. This obsessive thinking typically takes place in the interval between the last use of the substance and the possible next use, and is one of the features of compulsiveness in substance abuse that was discussed earlier. Thought stopping is a fairly simple technique to implement and works to control unproductive, obsessive, or self-defeating thoughts by suppressing or eliminating them and teaching the client to switch to productive or reinforcing thoughts (Cormier and Cormier, 1985).

Coping and social skills training.   One of the keystones of effective treatment of substance abuse is a broad-based coping and social skills training program. Such programs foster a greater sense of self-efficacy (Bandura, 1977) or perceived control in clients by teaching them to cope more effectively with everyday problems in living (Marlatt, 1979). There are any number of social skills that might be the focus of such a program, and the determination of which skills are missing from the client's repertoire is based on information obtained from the assessment.

A number of skills have been the target in substance abuse programs: assertiveness, communication skills, job-hunting and interview skills, refusing the invitation to use a substance, and so on.

Most social skills programs incorporate similar techniques: modeling, coaching, rehearsal, reinforcement, and feedback. These techniques are applied in various ways and to varying degrees in developing an overall social skills training program that best meets the needs and aptitudes of individual clients. Social skills training is particularly amenable to implementation in groups, because groups provide greater potential for rehearsal opportunities. As such, social skills training has been a major focus of intervention in both residential and outpatient treatment centers (Monti et al., 1989; Ingram and Salzberg, 1988).

Education.   One component of a comprehensive substance abuse program typically is education about the substance itself and especially about the negative health and social effects of use of the substance. This education usually takes place through films, readings, lectures, and group discussions. Educational programs operate on two assumptions: (1) that the substance user may not know about the negative effects of substance use; and (2) that even if the client does know about such effects, it is a good idea to reinforce or update that knowledge.

Actually, evidence of the effectiveness of education as a sole or even just one component of a treatment program is rather skimpy. One way of bolstering its effectiveness is through the use of emotional role play, a technique with some evidence of effectiveness with smokers (Janis and Mann, 1977). In emotional role play, the client role plays some emotionally devastating scene (e. g., telling relatives that he or she has cancer of the liver brought on by too much drinking and will die in two months) as a way of breaking down defenses about use of a harmful substance. Such an experience can produce a change in the client's feelings of personal vulnerability, thereby opening the door for more serious consideration of the educational content.

Lifestyle intervention.   This is a catch-all phrase for using a number of interventions that focus on other problems in the client's life, whether or not they are related directly to the substance abuse (Marlatt, 1979). The idea here is that bringing these other elements of the client's life into balance (or within tolerable levels for the client) cannot help but have an overall impact on the client's level of well-being and self-efficacy. Lifestyle intervention can consist of a number of components, including:

- Supplementary counseling. This would include using any or all of the techniques discussed here plus others to deal with problems in the client's life. Such problems could include depression, anxiety, problems at work, money problems (perhaps calling for a referral for income supplementation programs), and so on. This also could include supportive counseling to help the client as he or she proceeds through the treatment program.

- Exercise and hobby programs. Once the client is cleared by a physician for participation, an exercise program can be a particularly useful antidote to substance use. Similarly, a hobby can occupy time that a client might otherwise spend thinking about or engaging in substance use.

- Substitution. The client can be taught to substitute desired alternative activities (e. g., jogging) for substance use.

Marital and family counseling. For those clients who are married or living with a family, consideration of that context is a major priority in a comprehensive program. As Lewis et al. (1988) state: "No substance abuser—in fact, no client—can be treated effectively unless his or her social interactions are taken into account" (p. 157). Attention to the client's social support system can be a major factor in attaining optimal effectiveness.

A focus on the marriage and family has numerous benefits: it can reduce pressures on the client so that he or she can be more successful in the program; it provides support to family members, who also may be suffering through the treatment program; it enhances follow-up and maintenance by teaching the spouse and family how best to deal with the client once he or she is discharged; and it enhances overall family functioning.

Because marital and family therapies and attention to environmental supports are trademarks of social work, there is little need to expand on this topic here except to note that there are several intervention programs available that focus on marital and family therapy in the area of substance abuse, per se (e. g., Lewis et al., 1988; Schlesinger, 1988; O'Farrell, 1987; Kaufmann, 1985; McCrady, 1986).

Community reinforcement. Because all clients operate in an environmental context, community reinforcement has shown particular promise as a way of enhancing the client's social support system. Although there is more than one variation of the program, community reinforcement is designed to restructure family, social, and vocational reinforcers in a manner that reinforces nonuse of the substance while discouraging further use (Miller, 1986). The components of community reinforcement programs range from buddy systems to family training to attendance at social clubs where the problematic substance is not available. But in all such programs, the focus is on reinforcing nonuse and helping clients avoid or deal successfully with situations that could result in use of the substance.

Self-help groups. One of the more controversial but most widely used interventions is the self-help group support operation, such as Alcoholics or Narcotics Anonymous. These organizations often are called twelve-step groups because they typically follow the twelve-step program outlined by the founders of Alcoholics Anonymous.

The controversy about these groups runs the gamut from scattered accusations of lack of evidence of effectiveness, to criticism from professionals who do not like to be out of control of treatment, to complaints from group members who do not approve of the philosophy and methods, and so on. But there are few professionals in the field of substance abuse who do not know numerous clients who say that ''A.A. (or N.A.) saved my life.''

Thus, it seems reasonable to consider such programs as important adjuncts to professional treatment programs. In the first place, they provide group support, not only during treatment but also on a permanent basis, long after the formal treatment program has been terminated. Second, they operate on a twenty-four-hour basis, with the client being able to phone a sponsor at any time of the day or night. And third, the absence of evidence does not automatically mean that such programs are not effective. The task of research (which is particularly complicated with such groups) may be to attempt to discover the characteristics of clients and twelve-step programs that are most optimally matched and to make referrals on that basis.

MAINTENANCE AND GENERALIZATION

Of what use is an intervention program that is successful during the formal treatment, but is unsuccessful once that treatment is terminated? That key question is addressed by maintenance programs in the area of substance abuse. Indeed, relapse—an uncontrolled return to drug or alcohol use—is perhaps the most important issue that the substance abuse practitioner must confront.

One report stated that almost 90 percent of clients treated for substance abuse relapsed within one year after termination of formal treatment (Polich et al., 1981). Although rates of relapse vary by substance, program, and other characteristics, it is almost a cliché to say that substance abuse remains one of the problems that is most refractory to successful treatment. Thus, it becomes the task of the practitioner to design into the client's treatment program a comprehensive antirelapse program that is geared toward maintaining treatment gains and generalizing them into the client's everyday life.

A Relapse Model

Much of the work on relapse has been pioneered by Marlatt (1979; Marlatt and Gordon, 1980; see also Lewis et al., 1988). Among his contributions are the identification of determinants of relapse and the development of a model of relapse that leads to specific intervention strategies.

Relapse episodes were classified by Marlatt and Gordon (1980) into two categories. The first is intrapersonal/environmental determinants, which is subdivided into categories of coping with negative emotional states (e. g., frustration or anger), coping with negative physical/physiological states, enhancement of positive emotional states, testing personal control, and giving in to temptations or urges.

The second major category is interpersonal determinants. This is subdivided into coping with interpersonal conflict, social pressure, and enhancing a positive emotional state (in an interpersonal situation).

In a study of these factors as determinants of relapse for alcohol, smoking, and heroin, Marlatt and Gordon (1980) found that 76 percent of all relapse episodes fall into just three categories: coping with negative emotional states (37 percent), social pressure (24 percent), and coping with interpersonal conflict (24 percent). The remaining 24 percent of all relapses fell in increments of from 3 to 7 percent into the other five categories.

These and other data led Marlatt to develop a model of the relapse process (Marlatt and Gordon, 1980). The model is based on the notions of self-efficacy and personal control, in that it assumes that a client who is refraining from using a substance experiences a sense of personal control that leads to a sense of self-efficacy. This perception continues until the person meets a high-risk situation, one that poses a threat to the client's sense of control and increases the risk of potential relapse. This high-risk situation is affected by covert antecedents, beginning with a possible lifestyle imbalance leading to the desire for indulgences or immediate gratification. This can lead either to urges or cravings mediated by expectancies for immediate effects of the substance, or to rationalization, denial, and apparently irrelevant decisions (choices that enhance the probability of a relapse).

Once the high-risk situation exists, if the client is prepared with a coping response, the result will be increased self-efficacy and lower probability of relapse. However, if no coping response is available, the result will be decreased self-efficacy plus positive outcome expectancies for the effects of the substance. This will lead to initial use of the substance followed by an Abstinence Violation Effect (AVE) that would include dissonance, conflict, guilt, and perceived loss of control. All of this results then in the increased probability of a relapse.

The whole model, then, from start to finish, follows the following steps:

1. Lifestyle imbalance
2. Desire for indulgence or immediate gratification
3. Urges or cravings
4. Rationalization, denial, and apparently irrelevant decisions

5. High-risk situation
6. No coping response
7. Decreased self-efficacy
8. Initial use of substance
9. Abstinence Violation Effect (AVE)
10. Increased probability of relapse

Use of this model in understanding determinants of relapse can be aided by the use of four new instruments that were developed to help predict clients' relapse potential. The first is the Relapse Precipitants Inventory (Litman, 1986), a twenty-five-item measure that appears to distinguish between relapses and nonrelapses. The second is the Coping Behaviors Inventory (Litman, 1986), a thirty-six-item inventory that evaluates a person's ability to develop coping strategies. The third is the Inventory of Similar Situations (Annis, 1986), a 100-item questionnaire designed to assess situations in which a client drank heavily over the past year. The last is the Situational Confidence Questionnaire (Annis, 1986), a 100-item instrument designed to assess self-efficacy in relation to a client's perceived ability to cope effectively with alcohol.

One of the major contributions of this generic relapse model is that it suggests a number of points for intervention that lead to several of the maintenance strategies discussed below.

Maintenance and Generalization Strategies

The literature increasingly reflects a good deal of concern about ensuring maintenance and generalization of interventions in all problem areas (Goldstein and Kanfer, 1979; Karoly and Steffen, 1980). This literature has produced a number of general principles regarding maintenance of therapeutic gains, including:

- Make sure that the behavior or activity is being performed at the desired level prior to termination.
- Try to approximate as much as possible the conditions of real life in your intervention program.
- Use more than one intervention agent (e. g., have the client rehearse with other practitioners, clients, etc.).
- Try to find events in everyday life that will help maintain the desired activity and build these into the program.
- Decrease the program gradually (do not end it all at once).
- Train the client to continue the activities in real life by having him or her practice them in advance of termination.

- Use real-life homework assignments throughout the intervention process.
- Gradually decrease the similarity between the artificial and real situations.
- Train others in the client's environment to maintain the desired behavior or activities (e. g., train in the use of contingency management). This is an especially important strategy for ensuring generalization.

In addition to these general principles, a number of maintenance strategies have been developed specifically in the area of substance abuse. A recent review of the outcome research for "aftercare" in the treatment of alcohol abuse shows that such programs contribute significantly to overall positive outcome (Ito and Donovan, 1986). Although several different aftercare or maintenance strategies were evaluated, the findings were consistent and substantial enough to suggest that such maintenance strategies be made a major part of every intervention program with substance abuse.

Several of these maintenance strategies have been described succinctly by Lewis et al. (1988, ch. 6; see also Daley, 1986). Many of them consist of continuing parts of the intervention program described in the previous section, so they need only be mentioned here. In addition, many also fit the specific stages of Marlatt's relapse model and will be briefly described.

Strategies related to relapse model.   These strategies can, of course be used at any time, but there is a particularly neat fit between the stages of the model and selection of an intervention. The idea here is to prepare the client in advance for dealing with any of the situations indicated in the model.

- Lifestyle imbalance requires development of a balanced daily lifestyle, including jogging, hobbies, meditation, and so on.
- Desire for indulgence requires substituting positive indulgences, such as recreational activities.
- Urges and cravings can be countered by preparing the client with coping imagery and stimulus control techniques.
- Rationalization, denial, and "apparently irrelevant decisions" can be countered by labeling these phenomena as warning signals and by teaching the client to use a decision matrix in which he or she lists immediate positive and negative consequences for using or not using the substance.
- High-risk situations can be dealt with by having the client use self-monitoring and self-evaluation skills that teach him or her to recog-

nize those situations and by teaching a variety of avoidance strategies.

- The absence of a coping response is dealt with by the use of skill training plus a technique called relapse rehearsal. Relapse rehearsal teaches clients to imagine a relapse situation in which they successfully use a coping technique to avoid using the substance.

- To counter decreased self-efficacy and positive outcome expectancies for using the substance, the client can be taught to use relaxation training, stress management, and efficacy-enhancing imagery. In addition, the client can be educated about immediate versus delayed use of the substance.

- To avoid initial unplanned use of the substance, clients can be taught the techniques of programmed relapse. This is a fairly tricky technique to use and is not recommended for most cases because it involves programming the first relapse (e. g., the first drink of alcohol) under the supervision of the practitioner. Other techniques include a contract to limit the extent of use plus a reminder card for what the client should do if he or she has a slip.

- For AVE, with its risk of relapse, clients can be taught through cognitive restructuring that a slip is actually a mistake to be learned from and does not have to lead to a complete relapse.

General maintenance strategies.   In addition to the strategies above that fit the Marlatt model, a number of other strategies and techniques could be considered, including the following:

- Use of booster sessions and follow-ups. These should be scheduled in incrementally increasing intervals following termination (e. g., at two weeks, one month, three months, six months, one year).

- Use of problem-solving training to help clients deal with life problems in a functional way without having to turn to substance use.

- Use of exercise programs to maintain the benefits of physical health.

- Continued membership in a self-help group with periodic follow-ups from the social worker (phone calls will do) to encourage the client's attendance.

CONCLUSION

As this chapter has illustrated, the problem of substance abuse and its modification is very complex. The essence of successful treatment is two-pronged: (1) critical use of the available literature to be informed about what works (with the awareness that new developments are appearing daily); and (2) careful individualizing of clients and problems so that specific treatment programs can be developed. It is hoped that the assessment and intervention guidelines presented here will be of use to students and practitioners who have made a commitment to working in this area. In the long run, it is this commitment that will lead to the greatest satisfaction and increasingly more effective treatment.

CHAPTER 11

Life Planning for People with Human Immune Virus (HIV) Disease

Harvey L. Gochros

In this chapter, Gochros shows how to work with persons with Human Immune Virus (HIV) disease. Gochros defines problems people face in the different stages of HIV disease and then focuses on life planning for each specific phase. As Gochros illustrates, the person adjusting to the progression of HIV disease faces different issues at different stages. The interventions range from stress management and will preparation to issues relating to death, dying, and dealing with loved ones. Clearly, this reflects the importance and usefulness of matching the client's problem with the particular intervention to help that problem. Using a task-oriented perspective, Gochros shows the importance of active participation by both social worker and client. Gochros also emphasizes the importance of keeping goals clear when working with people with HIV disease and of remembering that you are life planning.

INTRODUCTION

Never before has social work, or American society for that matter, confronted an illness quite like HIV disease. The combination of aspects of the disease make it a unique challenge to social work practice:

- It is an epidemic that profoundly affects almost every aspect of our lives and has a devastating impact on everyone involved with the infected person.

- It is a new disease, unknown until the mid-1980s, that probably has infected over a million Americans, over 100,000 of whom have been diagnosed with full-blown AIDS. It already has killed over 60,000 Americans (Centers for Disease Control, 1989), more than all the Americans lost in the Vietnam War, and hundreds of thousands of others in virtually every country in the world.

- There is an extremely long incubation period between infection by the Human Immune Virus (which causes the disease) and the actual appearance of the life-threatening consequences of the disease. Detectable physical damage or even symptoms of HIV disease may not occur for many years following actual infection by the virus. This extended latency period has contributed to underestimating its long-range impact on the thousands of people who already are infected but are not yet aware of their condition.

- HIV disease is not easily transmitted. Infection occurs only when fluids from an infected person that contain high concentrations of HIV enter the bloodstream of another person. Yet unfounded fears of casual transmission persist. HIV disease elicits irrational fears of contagion even among many people in the helping professions, including physicians, nurses, dentists, and other health care personnel who care for those infected.

- It attacks primarily already socially unpopular and stigmatized populations: homosexual men, drug abusers, the poor, and people of color.

- It is usually contracted through voluntary pleasurable acts (sexual activity and intravenous drug use) that may be illegal and/or considered immoral.

- It most often attacks young people, who are ill prepared, as are those around them, to deal with their mortality.

- There are no cures or vaccines available or in sight.

- It forces helping professionals to discuss and deal with not only such social taboos as sex and death, but also with controversial and anxiety-producing subcategories of these taboos: homosexuality and suicide.

- The major behaviors leading to infection, sexual activities and drug addiction, are among the most highly reinforced of human behaviors. Both can produce powerfully pleasurable experiences and both have deeply entrenched symbolic meanings. These factors contribute to the difficulty in modifying behaviors that contribute to HIV infection.

- It has uncovered the extent of previously hidden homosexual and bisexual behavior in our country and has forced society and the helping professions to reexamine their ethical and moral values about these behaviors.

In addition to these unique features, HIV disease has posed additional problems for social workers and others concerned with preventing the disease and serving those already infected: the very character and basic assumptions about the disease are changing rapidly. Just a few years ago, ''AIDS'' was considered an incurable, terminal disease with a life expectancy subsequent to diagnosis of just a few months. Relatively recent medical and pharmacological advances have significantly changed the prognosis for people with HIV infections.

Although it is still considered likely that anyone with an HIV infection will eventually advance to "full-blown AIDS," it is apparent that the life expectancy for those with AIDS is lengthening. It may come to pass in the 1990s that HIV disease will no longer be necessarily fatal, but instead will become a life-threatening but treatable condition, similar to diabetes or heart disease.

Not only are many people with HIV disease living longer, but they also are experiencing relatively good health in the lengthening periods between opportunistic diseases. This trend toward longer, healthier lives will have a major impact on the kinds of services that social workers will have to provide. Already the emphasis of social work treatment of clients with HIV disease is shifting from "death planning" to "life planning."

The character of the populations newly infected with the disease is also changing. HIV disease was originally considered a "gay plague," with most of those afflicted being young white gay males. Largely because of effective AIDS education within major gay communities, along with saturation of the host population, most members of that population who were going to become infected had been infected by 1990. Thus, the rate of new HIV infections among gay and bisexual men has decreased. Although the many thousands of gay men already infected will need attention for years to come, preventative and treatment services are gradually retooling to serve urban, black and Hispanic gays, bisexuals, and IV drug users, their sexual partners, and their children. Preventive programs such as drug education for adolescents, needle exchange programs for IV drug users, and outreach to homosexually active members of ethnic minorities will require further development and evaluation.

Finally, the very definitions of the disease are undergoing change. HIV disease was thought to be a disease that has three distinct stages, each with its own label:

1. Asymptomatic antibody positive—people who have been tested and found to have antibodies created by the immune system to ward off an invasion by Human Immune Virus, but who have not yet manifested any physical symptoms of the disease.
2. ARC (AIDS-Related Complex)—people who have some physical manifestations of the infection, such as swollen glands, oral thrush, night sweats, weight loss, etc., none of which are necessarily life threatening. (It should be noted, however, that people have died from ARC.)
3. "Full-blown AIDS" (Acquired Immune Deficiency Syndrome)— people who are HIV-antibody-positive and who have been diagnosed with a potentially life-threatening opportunistic disease, such as pneumocystis carinii pneumonia or Kaposi's Sarcoma, or other mani-

festations, such as AIDS-related dementia, that "take the opportunity" of a weakened immune system to attack the body. The Centers for Disease Control has designated certain diseases that attack people with a compromised immune system as diagnostic of AIDS.

More recently, however, many people who work with HIV disease are doing away with what they consider artificial and unhelpful labels for these three stages. Rather, from the detection of HIV infection onward, the condition should be referred to simply as "HIV disease." That term is used in this chapter.

The elimination of the ARC and AIDS labels, however, does not deny that many people with HIV infections go through some clearly identifiable phases as the disease progresses. Indeed, these phases determine which tasks require attention and the related interventions social workers might anticipate as they assist their clients in dealing with the various problems that the disease almost inevitably creates.

PROBLEM IDENTIFICATION

In the summer of 1989, the Centers for Disease Control (CDC) reported that the number of reported AIDS cases had exceeded 100,000. By that time, 56,468 Americans diagnosed with AIDS had died. More than half were gay or bisexual men who were infected largely through homosexual anal intercourse. The majority of the remainder contracted the infection through sharing IV needles or by having sexual intercourse with an infected individual.

There has been some debate about how accurately the CDC figures reflect the actual incidence of HIV infection. Many individuals who can afford "discreet" private physicians can avoid having the nature of their illnesses and deaths reported to any governmental office. Further, in many areas of the country antibody testing is done anonymously and thus there are no accurate data on the numbers of people who have tested positive. There also are no accurate data on the even larger number of people who are antibody-positive but have not been tested and thus do not know that they are infected.

The problem of obtaining accurate statistics from other countries around the world (and particularly in developing countries) is even greater. It is difficult to tell just how devastating HIV infection is now and will be in future decades throughout the world.

.The major targets of new infections in the United States are such underclass ethnic minorities as blacks and Hispanics, particularly those who are IV drug abusers, as well as those whom they have infected through birth, sex, or transfusions. Although the public still generally perceives HIV disease as a disease primarily of white homosexuals, people of color have been disproportionally hit by it (Raine, 1989). Black Americans comprise 12 percent of the United States population, yet 24 percent of persons with HIV disease are black. When Hispanics with HIV disease are added, the percentage of people with HIV disease from ethnic minorities rises to at least 40 percent. Furthermore, 70 percent of women with HIV disease are black or Hispanic, as are 71 percent of heterosexuals with the disease. Finally, 77 percent of infants with AIDS belong to ethnic minorities. These high percentages no doubt reflect the poverty and associated high incidence of IV drug use among these populations.

Being a member of an ethnic minority and being gay are not, of course, mutually exclusive. Of the 436 cases of AIDS among black men reported in San Francisco through February 1989, 294, or 67 percent, were in gay men. Another 59, or 14 percent, were both gay and IV drug users (Raine, 1989). Although social workers must certainly address the complex world of IV needle sharing among blacks and Hispanics, they must not lose sight of those heavily closeted, hard-to-reach ethnic minority gays and bisexuals whose cultures generally reject men perceived to be less than "macho."

Another population requiring greater attention is the increasing number of children and adolescents with HIV disease. As with their adult counterparts, these individuals and their families must deal with isolation, stigma, and rejection, along with the basic struggle for life and survival (Lockhart and Wodarski, 1989). In addition to offering individual and group support and counseling to these children and their families, social workers must consider legal and ethical issues associated with placing these children in institutions and foster care, develop culturally sensitive ways to address the specific concerns of minority ethnic families, and improve service delivery systems to the rising number of underclass families affected by the HIV epidemic. The HIV crisis forces us to try to understand the impact of poverty, ethnocentrism, racism, and homophobia on clients and on social work treatment and prevention efforts.

Perhaps the largest population drawing attention in the HIV epidemic is people whose viral infections have not yet manifested themselves in potentially fatal opportunistic diseases. There is no reliable count available of Americans who are infected with HIV but are unaware of their condition. Estimates range from 500,000 to more than 3 million (Beck, 1989). Worldwide estimates range into tens of millions. The possibility that even these figures may be too modest is heightened by recent studies that suggest that many people may harbor HIV infections for years before they test positive on standard HIV antibody tests. HIV-infected people, even those who seem to be in excellent health, can infect others.

As noted earlier, in the not-too-distant past, HIV infection was considered to be a death warrant, with an inevitable march to one or more fatal diseases. With recent significant medical advances in the treatment of the opportunistic diseases, there has been a major shift in the outlook for those with HIV infections. There is growing hope, if not conviction, that HIV disease will soon, perhaps within the next few years, become a manageable chronic but not necessarily fatal disease. In the spring of 1989, for example, the Food and Drug Administration approved the use of aerosol Pentamidine, which has been shown to be effective in impeding the progress of a form of pneumonia that most often has killed people with HIV infections.

The fact that people with HIV infections will be living significantly longer with their disease than had been true in the past brings hope to those infected, but poses serious problems in and stresses on the medical and social services that provide care for people with HIV disease. Hospital HIV wards are overcrowded and understaffed in many major cities, Pentamidine treatments cost about $1,800 a year, and AZT, the major available drug designed to fight the HIV virus—now frequently prescribed for people in the early stages of infection—can cost from $2,000 to $7,000 a year, depending on dosage. These costs take a heavy toll on the income of HIV-infected people, who may no longer be able to work and who may lack or have insufficient insurance coverage.

CLINICAL MANIFESTATIONS

Physical Manifestations

The physical manifestations of HIV disease vary from individual to individual, and over time as the disease progresses. A multitude of life-threatening as well as relatively minor but troublesome physical opportunistic conditions are associated with HIV disease. These include pneumonia, rare cancers, blindness, diarrhea, fatigue, and dermatological problems.

Psychological Manifestations

It is not surprising that high incidences of anxiety, depression, alcoholism, and other major psychiatric disorders are found in people infected with HIV. Learning that one has a potentially fatal disease that has painful and protracted physical, social, financial, and mental sequela, as well as attendant social biases and stigma ("AIDS is the punishment of God!" say some), can have severe psychological consequences. In addition, neurological infection of the brain and spinal cord may cause severe psychological problems. Indeed, dementia is a frequently encountered diagnostic indicator of an advanced stage of HIV disease and is often one of its most feared consequences. Suicidal rumination, threats, and gestures as well as actual suicides are not rare at several crisis points in the progression of the disease.

INTERVENTIONS AT EACH PHASE OF HIV DISEASE

People with HIV disease often encounter problems in almost every sphere of their lives: physical, social, emotional, sexual, economic, vocational, and spiritual. Indeed many people with HIV disease feel bombarded by such a range of problems that they seem to spend what remains of their lives going from one crisis to another. Although each person with HIV disease encounters a unique cluster of situations and reactions, some common problems are encountered by almost all.

The following sections discuss a sequence of seven phases through which HIV disease typically progresses, the specific tasks that usually confront people with HIV disease and those who are involved with them at each phase, and some of the social work interventions that have proved to be helpful.

1. With Persons at Risk, HIV Status Uncertain

As we enter the 1990s, it is unlikely that anyone who engages in high-risk sexual behaviors (e. g., receptive anal or vaginal intercourse without a condom with a potentially infected partner) is unaware of the possibility of HIV infection. Yet much confusion remains as to just what is safer sex. Unfortunately, it cannot be stated with certainty that particular sexual activities are absolutely safe. Sexually active people must be helped to understand the concepts of risk and probabilities. Once they understand these concepts, they can become informed about the wide range of sexual activities that exist between handshakes and coitus.

In many ways, the situation of HIV needle sharers is more complex and poses far more difficult problems both in prevention and in treatment. An addict generally will consider the long-range risk of HIV infection to be secondary in importance to getting a fix. There is nothing among IV drug users that is comparable to the gay community's own cooperative efforts to change risky behaviors. Further, IV drug use is often a product of poverty and racism, which remain unsolved problems.

Tasks.   Persons at risk for HIV infection who have not yet sought antibody testing often experience considerable anxiety regarding their drug and sexual behavior. They are confronted with two major decisions: whether to seek testing to determine their antibody status, and whether and how to modify or abstain from their high-risk behaviors.

Interventions.   The decision of whether to take an antibody test is simpler and more weighted toward the positive than it was a few years ago. Initially it was feared that the test might give too many false negative and positive results; that one might subject oneself to discriminatory practices—such as loss of job, insurance, or housing—should a positive HIV result become publicly known; and finally, it was argued, why subject oneself to the pain of knowing one is HIV-positive if there is nothing one can do about it anyway?

Currently, however, we know that existing tests are reliable, that anonymous testing is available, and that antidiscrimination laws are now in effect in many, but certainly not all localities, as well as in new federal legislation on the rights of the disabled. Also, there now are medications that, if taken at the first signs of HIV infection, will delay (but not stop) the progression of HIV disease.

Thus after discussion of the pros and cons of testing with a client at risk, and an assessment of the individual's support systems and anticipated behavior in the event of an HIV-positive result, the social worker might well support testing if anonymous or at least confidential testing is available and/or if supportive legislation is in force.

Another category of client who might be supported in seeking testing is the overanxious individual who is at low risk but perhaps has a high degree of guilt, who despite reassurance about his low-risk status can only be put at ease by being tested. The arguments for testing continue to grow stronger over time.

There are, however, many clients, "the worried well," who despite negative antibody tests continue to manifest high levels of anxiety. Krieger (1988) has suggested a five-step counseling approach to assist clients experiencing dysfunctional "AIDS anxiety." First, prepare the client by providing accurate, up-to-date information about the disease, its transmission routes, and its prevention. Second, assess realistically the client's risk of prior exposure to the virus. Has the individual really been at risk? Third, instruct the client in procedures to minimize or eliminate risks of future infection. Fourth, help the client find peer support to avoid patterns of both extremes of denial and despair in response to HIV risks. Fifth, address issues directly and indirectly related to the clients' "AIDS anxiety," such as guilt about sexual or drug behavior, attraction to dangerous sexual patterns and activities, concealment of risky behaviors from sexual partners, and latent or manifest homophobia.

Education and treatment programs to modify risky sexual behaviors also raise complex pragmatic and value issues. Preventive strategies that rely on simple "just say no" approaches are usually no more successful with sex than with drugs. Both sex and drug use are too powerfully reinforced and carry too much symbolic meaning to easily will away. Decades of efforts to curb adolescent sexual expression have proved the failure of simple moral suasion. Further, in the case of sex there are reasons to consider that attempts at abstinence may prove hazardous for some people and there are a number of relatively safe alternatives to abstinence (Gochros, 1988).

Discussions with sexually active individuals at risk for infection, therefore, should usually focus on modifying but not eliminating sexual activity. Explore the client's motivations for high-risk behaviors, and try to provide him or her with an understanding of relative sexual risks and the value of eroticizing safer sex.

Discussions of sexual matters are essential in providing help to clients with HIV disease. Thus the social worker must explore and overcome his or her own sexual biases and learn to directly and casually discuss explicit aspects of clients' sexual motivations, decisions, and behaviors (Gochros, 1986).

The social worker's approach to drug-related behavior that puts clients at risk for HIV infection is more complex. It is difficult to modify the drug addict's needle-sharing behavior when he or she is high on drugs. There is some evidence that supplying bleach kits (to clean used needles) and/or providing clean needles through carefully monitored needle exchange programs might reduce IV-transmitted HIV infection. Ultimately, however, reducing infection among IV drug users will require drug rehabilitation, control programs, therapies, and social reform that go well beyond the scope of this chapter.

2. With Persons Who Are HIV-Antibody-Positive, but Are Asymptomatic

As more and more people take antibody tests, voluntarily or involuntarily, many will discover that they are indeed infected with HIV, even though they display no symptoms of the disease. These people are confronted with a potentially agonizing paradox: their body contains the seeds of its own destruction, there is no known way to get rid of the invaders, and yet they feel fine. Further, there is no way to predict when, how, and even whether destructive manifestations of the illness will occur. Typically, people who are diagnosed as HIV-positive but are asymptomatic will alternate between feeling fine, especially if they deny the diagnosis, and feeling anxious, depressed, guilty, or irritable.

It should be noted, however, that several of my clients have reported a feeling of relief upon learning their antibody-positive status. Some had been expecting the illness to hit for some time and were relieved when it did. Others reported relief that they could now remove themselves from what they perceived as the arduous and usually unrewarding world of "sex and one-night stands." Still others felt relief because now, in their way of thinking, they had no excuse for not coming out to family and friends.

Tasks.   The person who has just learned of his or her positive antibody status must begin to integrate a new identity, an identity that may well set him or her apart from others in his or her own mind and perhaps in the minds of others.

For many gay people, acknowledging that they have HIV disease is a "second coming out" that is comparable to coming out as gay. Indeed, it has been suggested that the way people carry out and respond to their first coming out may be a good predictor to how they will handle dealing with informing others that they have HIV disease.

Many people in this situation will experience many of the reactions associated with crisis: denial, withdrawal, random impulsive behaviors, and fears of "going crazy." Some will seek out alternate explanations for their test results or begin doctor shopping. Some will consider suicide as a possible or only "way out."

The major tasks of this period for people with HIV infection are to seek early and competent medical treatment, learn what they can about their situation, rationally incorporate this new information, carefully appraise its significance, and develop a balanced perspective on the infection that includes both an awareness of the risks and the hope that medical advances will improve their prognosis. Perhaps the most difficult task is to learn to live with the uncertainty of when, how, and whether the disease will progress.

Guilt is a factor that may increasingly become an issue among HIV disease clients. Most of those who developed full-blown AIDS in the 1980s contracted the infection at a time when they and most others, including physicians and public health officials, did not know that their behavior could lead to a life-threatening disease. It can be anticipated, however, that people who became infected with HIV after the mid-1980s, when the media had made AIDS and its routes of transmission well known, may well experience a significantly higher degree of guilt, shame, and emotional trauma. These people will pose a challenge for social workers because of the feelings of guilt engendered by their belief that their behavior brought about their HIV infection.

Interventions.   The social worker often must deal with the crisis that an HIV-positive diagnosis generates. Standard crisis intervention strategies may well be called for (Golan, 1986). The social worker also must provide up-to-date information about the consequences of the test results and the range of courses that the illness might take. These activities must be based on a sound assessment by the social worker of the significance to the client of the diagnosis, and of the extent and accuracy of the client's information about the disease.

In this phase, as in subsequent phases, the social worker must be aware of the possibility of suicidal ruminations. These thoughts may simply be an effort by clients to take control of their lives in a period in which everything may seem out of control. People in crisis frequently expend considerable energy on bringing back some order and structure to their lives. In any case, suicidal thoughts should not be discounted; instead, the social worker should deal with them calmly and objectively. In any phase of HIV disease, suicide may be either a rational or irrational choice of an HIV-infected individual. However, as the prognosis for HIV disease improves, suicide may become a less rational choice.

Contact with a physician should be initiated by the social worker or the client as soon as possible after diagnosis, as there is growing evidence that early medical treatment, including the use of certain drugs, may well delay the progression of HIV disease. The social worker should be aware of the physicians in the community who are experienced at and capable of treating people with HIV infections. Do not assume that all physicians are equally qualified or even willing to treat HIV-related diseases. Homophobia is not unknown in the medical profession. HIV disease is a complicated syndrome that requires skill, sensitivity, and time on the part of physicians.

3. With Persons Who Have Begun to Experience Symptoms of HIV Infection

The first physical symptoms of HIV infection, such as weight loss, lymphadenopathy, diarrhea, and night sweats, cut through the denial of being infected and can be experienced as a major trauma: the disease becomes real. This stage of infection has earned its own acronym, ARC (AIDS-Related Complex), but is now considered only a phase of an ongoing disease process. In this phase of HIV disease, some individuals react with a frantic search for a cure, including medical, holistic, and nontraditional therapies.

Tasks.   People in this phase have less ability than in earlier phases to deny the significance of the disease in their overall life planning. They must make important decisions about medical treatment, reevaluate their long-term planning, and consider in great depth and detail the impact of the disease on their career, interpersonal relationships, and sexuality. Some will need to reevaluate now or later where to live, and perhaps consider a return to their family and home community. At this point many will want to decide whom to tell about their disease and when and how to tell them.

Interventions. This phase, like all of the significant phases of HIV disease, requires active listening and emotional support from the social worker, who must be knowledgeable about both the disease and the client's current situation. The social worker should explore the client's perception of his or her situation, correct any misinformation, and, if necessary, interpret the client's medical situation and treatment.

Of prime importance is to empower clients in as many areas of their lives as possible. Clients should be encouraged to take an active role in health and medical planning. Their right to know what is going on in their treatment and to share treatment decisions should be supported. Social workers may have to help clients sort out insurance and public welfare procedures and seek funding for the expensive medications required for preventive and therapeutic procedures. Preliminary discussions of future financial planning, including making a will, may be initiated but should not be forced.

Clients may experience fears of abandonment and should be assured of the social worker's ongoing support. Anxiety management and social skills training might be offered to deal with the interpersonal challenges that may lie ahead (Guay, 1989). Clients also may be responsive to explorations of philosophical and spiritual issues, either with the social worker or through referral to individuals or support groups within the community.

4. With Persons Who Have Developed Their First Opportunistic Disease

The actual diagnosis of AIDS is made only at the onset of an opportunistic disease that is recognized by the Centers for Disease Control as clearly indicative of AIDS. The client and others may have labeled the condition as AIDS much earlier if significant constitutional symptoms have been present (Guay, 1989). Clients may manifest a wide range of reactions to their illness, often rapidly going through and repeating the classic phases of grief, including shock, depression, anger, bargaining, and acceptance. It can be expected that many will anticipate a rapid death. The media have contributed to this ideation by portraying HIV disease as inevitably fatal.

Tasks. The social worker should anticipate that the onset of a life-threatening opportunistic disease is likely to result in a crisis situation not only for the client, but possibly also for family and lovers. Depression and panic are common reactions, along with recurring thoughts about illness and death and the possibility of suicidal rumination. People who are experiencing a first opportunistic illness, and the people who are important to them, must be given realistic hope, yet they must also prepare for the possibility of a protracted illness and death.

Interventions. In working with clients in this phase, the social worker must carry out the tasks that are associated with any major crisis confronting a client (Golan, 1979). The client must guard against such impulsive decisions as moving, divorcing, and quitting work. The social worker might want to help the client prepare a will, and perhaps a "living will" that specifies the type and extent of terminal care the client desires. Social workers may also act as brokers and advocates, if necessary, with the diverse agencies that will be involved in clients' care upon their return to the community.

To impress upon a client with HIV disease that an opportunistic disease is not necessarily fatal, the social worker may want to ask a volunteer who has survived his or her first opportunistic disease to visit the client in the hospital and demonstrate that many, and increasingly most, people with HIV disease survive their first disease and go on to live fulfilling and enjoyable lives.

To further help in dealing with the psychological trauma of facing a life-threatening illness, the social worker can also teach clients how to use the techniques of thought stopping, relaxation training, and visualization to manage potentially overwhelming feelings (Guay, 1989).

5. With Persons Who Have Survived Their First Opportunistic Disease

Because of significant progress in medical care and pharmacology, people with HIV disease are increasingly likely to survive their first opportunistic disease. Often, however, the progress of HIV disease is characterized by chronic fatigue and other painful and annoying, if not disabling, constitutional symptoms. The social worker may note that the client is slowly and subtly "winding down" or "wasting away."

Tasks. In this phase, clients must deal with two conflicting pressures. On the one hand, they will need to prepare psychologically, philosophically, practically, and perhaps spiritually for the possibility of death; on the other hand, they must reevaluate and readjust their life planning to take into account that they may live for many years. Whereas the goal for many people with HIV disease used to be to "live day by day," expanded life expectancies will necessitate long-range planning. This evaluation may provoke clients to review their hopes and ambitions and accept that they may never accomplish many of the life goals they had set for themselves. This can be a painful process.

There is a danger, however, that formerly active and accomplished individuals may withdraw prematurely from a productive, satisfying life. Shortly before he died, Hank E. Koehn (1988) a futurist, bank vice president, author, and founder and president of a consulting firm reported the following responses to learning that he had HIV disease:

> With no work to do, I was no longer reading and watching television. Instead, my days became empty. To fill the time, I began to sleep all day, as well as all night. Weeks before, while in the hospital, I had found that I could stare at "nothing" on the ceiling for many hours.
>
> In retrospect, the frightening fact was that I was content doing nothing. Everything, including reading, became too much of an effort. Nothing seemed worthwhile, since I only had a limited number of days. Because of my relatively strong personality, there was almost no one to challenge my approach to my remaining time among the living.
>
> I was well cared for in a comfortable home. I still felt deep inside that resignation seemed the civilized approach to my remaining life.
>
> During this time, the only trips outside my home were to my doctor's. . . . All of this made a continued resignation to dying very easy.
>
> Then one day, while talking with a friend, I asked again if he didn't think I had become too resigned, too easily. As we explored this thought, I became convinced that I had given up too quickly—even if giving up was the obvious course of action. From that point on I began to explore the alternatives. (pp. 21–22)

Finding these "alternatives" calls upon the creativity of client and social worker alike. Despite the improved prognosis for people with HIV disease, they must face numerous difficulties and losses. They may no longer be able to work, with a resulting loss of a sense of productivity and independence, not to mention loss of income. They may well lose their interest in sex, and even if they still have erotic urges, they may be reluctant to seek partners or engage in any sexual activity that could possibly lead to infecting a partner. Systemic illness and disfiguring dermatological problems may well impair their physical attractiveness and sense of well-being. Their energy may be easily depleted.

Further, it is not unusual for lovers and friends who have remained loyal to people with HIV disease throughout bouts of sickness to take the opportunity provided by this relative respite from illness to withdraw. Most difficult and important to people with HIV disease, however, is their loss of identity and sense of a future. They are now a "person with AIDS" and perceived by others, if not by themselves, as members of a stigmatized and isolated group.

It should be noted, however, that many clients in this phase of HIV disease do quite well and see this as a high-quality period of their life. They have survived a life-threatening disorder and experienced a new perspective on life. Some report enjoying their lives as they never had before. Often clients will demonstrate a functional denial of the apparent reality of their condition. They will treasure each day and celebrate every joy of life. Some report a rapproachment with family and friends and a spiritual reawakening. Often, however, this "high" sets the client up for discouragement and depression when new physical evidences of the HIV infection emerge.

Interventions. The social worker's role during this phase of the client's illness may be varied and complex, despite the fact that some clients may choose to avoid what they consider to be "morbid dwelling" on their disease while they are in this honeymoon-like phase. Some will choose to defend themselves against anxiety or depression through some degree of denial. For many, this is an effective and positive self-treatment that the social worker should not challenge.

Many, however, do not choose to deny the seriousness of their situation. For such clients, the social worker can initiate grief work to deal with the many losses clients are experiencing. At the same time, social workers must help clients maintain as active and fulfilling a life as possible within the constraints of the illness. To do this, social workers must accurately assess the clients' illness, attitudes, wishes, and resources.

Support groups for people with HIV disease are important resources. They reassure clients that they are not alone, provide models for behavior at various stages of the illness, and often provide a friendship network.

Clients need to continue to feel useful. Generally, they should be encouraged to continue to work as long as they enjoy their work, have a supportive work environment, and are physically able to do so. Even if clients must leave their work and seek other sources of support, there are other ways for them to maintain a sense of usefulness. Many are able to learn enough about their illness and its treatment to take an active role in their medical care decisions. Many also become active in coalitions that collectively press for the rights and needs of people with HIV disease. Others act as volunteers with AIDS caregiving services. Social workers can help their clients determine their needs for productivity and discover creative means for expressing them.

Social workers also must create an atmosphere in which clients can freely discuss their sexual needs and concerns. Although some clients will experience reduced or no sexual energy subsequent to a diagnosis of HIV disease, many still have sexual concerns. It has been proven that emotional stress can further compromise the immune system, and social workers should recognize that sexual release can help to reduce clients' emotional stress.

If a person with advanced HIV disease has a seronegative sexual partner, however, it is possible that conflict might develop over sexual needs. Discussions with clients and their partners can help them to consider options for meeting their assymetrical interests. Many clients with HIV disease will need information about safer sex if they are considering continued sexual activity. Social workers also may help clients think through the dilemmas posed by revealing their HIV infection to potential new sexual partners. The complex issues of how, when, and whether potential partners should be informed require careful consideration by both clients and social workers. Clients also may benefit from information on how to eroticize their safer sex activities.

Throughout these discussions of sexual behavior, social workers should keep in mind that sexual expression carries with it considerable symbolic meaning for people with HIV disease, as it does for everyone. Many people with HIV disease have learned to use their sexuality not only to achieve pleasure and intimacy, but also to enhance their self-esteem, solidify an interpersonal relationship, confirm their desirability, or overcome their loneliness.

HIV disease creates a number of obstacles to sexual fulfillment, however. The majority of infected individuals are concerned that they not pass on their disease to sexual partners. Some perceive themselves as hopelessly contaminated. Many who do not have regular sexual partners are torn between the desire for new partners and the need to tell them of their infection, recognizing that informing potential partners may well frighten them away. Social workers must first work through their own feelings about their clients' sexuality. Some may find the idea of a person with HIV disease remaining sexually active inappropriate and disturbing. For many people, however, including persons with HIV disease, sex is an important aspect of life and, indeed, may well be a celebration of life. Social workers should be supportive of clients' explorations of safe and responsible avenues of sexual expression.

This third phase is one in which problems with spouses or lovers come to a head. Couple counseling may be necessary to deal with the strains on the caregiving partner, especially in a relationship where one partner is HIV-positive and the other is not, as the caregiver strives to meet the partner's needs during a protracted illness. An important ingredient in this counseling is an assessment of the relationship, including a review of the characteristics of the relationship before and after one or both partners became infected. This might help to shift perceived responsibility for problems in the relationship from either the infected partner or the uninfected partner alone to both partners.

Both partners may need the social worker's support to understand each other's needs and communicate feelings directly and sensitively. The couple might choose to renegotiate their relationship, including allowing sexual expression outside the relationship. The healthier partner might also profit from the social worker's permission to express his or her feelings about being in a relationship with a person in an advanced stage of HIV disease.

Temporary or permanent separations may also have to be negotiated, with the social worker urging a slow and careful examination of the factors that lead to the need for separation. Sometimes the partner with HIV disease chooses the separation because he or she feels that whatever gulf has separated the couple in the past has been widened by the progress of the disease.

If the couple stays together, the social worker might teach them strategies, including ways to argue fairly and effectively, to deal with tensions and conflicts (Caldarola and Helquist, 1989).

In interactions with clients, social workers may choose to support clients' positive denial of the possible fatal nature of the disease. Clients and those who are close to them will need occasional breaks from focusing on the problems and the psychological stress generated by the disease. Clients can be taught various behavioral techniques to help them handle the chronic, recurring problems described above. These techniques include assertiveness training, relaxation training, cognitive restructuring, and social skills training (Guay, 1989).

The need for a case management role may well increase as housing, financial, and insurance problems emerge or intensify. Medical and drug bills may become overwhelming. Clients also may encounter problems in obtaining dental care. The social worker may need to direct special attention to clients' relationships with their physicians. Clients may need help in expressing themselves more assertively to physicians in order to get their questions answered and their needs understood and met. Social workers must support their clients' rights to adequate health care services.

6. With Persons Who Have Developed Subsequent Opportunistic Diseases

Subsequent bouts of life-threatening diseases, such as pneumonia, or a sudden intensifying of symptoms, such as a major increase in Kaposi's Sarcoma lesions, are especially difficult for people with HIV disease. When this occurs, clients can no longer deny that their illness is progressing and that they may well die from it. The "honeymoon" that followed the first onset of the disease is over.

Clients may be dealing with a plethora of opportunistic diseases, as well as pronounced weight loss, fatigue, muscular weakness, and disfiguring dermatological infections. They may also have symptoms of dementia, and fear losing the ability to care for their own basic needs.

It is at this point that many people with HIV disease lose hope for a "miracle" cure. They are physically and emotionally exhausted and this exhaustion may be shared by loved ones who have helped them prepare for death and then recovery time and again. This psychological see-saw of hope and despair is stressful and difficult.

Tasks.   People experiencing a second opportunistic disease or a re-occurrence of an earlier one may once again have to work through their grief. As in earlier stages, many people with HIV disease, and those in their environment, experience waves of anger that may be aimed in almost any direction. It is difficult to express one's anger toward a virus, and thus clients may direct their rage at family, friends, social service agencies, doctors, the president, or God.

As the bouts of opportunistic infections increase in frequency and/or intensity, people with HIV disease must deal increasingly with the likelihood of death. Many will try to make things right with their families.

There may be specific plans that clients want to make for their possibly imminent dying and death. Some may consider suicide. Others may want to disengage slowly from life, gradually withdrawing from family, friends, and their daily activities.

Interventions.   During this phase, the social worker most likely will continue to assist the client and his or her loved ones in carrying out grief work. To the extent that the social worker feels comfortable and competent, she or he may also help the client explore spiritual and philosophical aspects of the situation.

Discussions of suicide should not be avoided. Indeed, it is advisable to ask clients in this phase (and in earlier phases) of the illness whether they are considering suicide. The question will not cause the act. For some clients, preparation for suicide becomes the ultimate opportunity to exercise control over their own lives, even if they never carry out their plans.

The social worker may want to help the client differentiate between "rational" and "irrational" suicide. An irrational suicide is one done in haste, while under the influence of alcohol or drugs, or when individuals perceive suicide as their only option. A rational suicide, on the other hand, is one that has been carefully and soberly considered as the best of several options.

Suicide may be a difficult topic for many social workers to deal with because of their value systems, religion, or fear of shared responsibility for such a serious act. However, a nonjudgmental, supportive listener may be invaluable to clients who have found no one with whom they can calmly discuss their thinking and wishes.

The social worker will continue to carry out case management tasks. This may include exploring terminal care facilities. Work with the family may also come into greater focus. The client may wish to try to "make things right" with family, friends, and present or past spouses or lovers. This may involve working through a family's unresolved feeings about the client's homosexuality or drug use. There is no reason to believe, however, that a terminal disease will bring the family together and resolve conflicts, rejection, and emotional distance that has existed for decades. Death-bed resolutions of long-term conflicts occur more often in movies and television than in real life.

7. With Persons in the Terminal Phase of Illness

The medical consensus is that the majority of people with HIV disease will face death within a few years after the onset of their first opportunistic disease. Physical deterioration may be rapid or progress erratically. Often as the client's defenses weaken, he or she may experience severe dementia, blindness, and a host of other minor and major physical complications. Clients also may experience considerable pain, loss of control over body functions, confusion, and psychological withdrawal.

Improved medical treatment has saved more people with HIV disease, but in many cases it has also prolonged their dying. The fact that many people with HIV disease were young and in good health prior to their infection can prolong their dying process. People with HIV infections often have repeated close calls with death and surprise their doctors, families, and themselves with unexpected rebounds from the death bed.

Unfortunately, the bleak side of these unexpected returns to health is the often unexpressed fatigue experienced by family and friends: the psychological see-saw referred to earlier. Some secretly and guiltily wish that the client "would get it over with." This can be disturbing not only to the family, but to the medical staff and the patient as well. I have on several occasions sat with people in the terminal stages of HIV disease whose doctors had informed them that they were in their final days and given them "permission to let go," only to see them rebound and be back on their feet within a week.

Tasks.   The major task in this phase of the disease is to help the person with HIV disease to make the transition from life to a physically and psychologically comfortable death and to help the client and those who are close to him or her achieve peace of mind (Guay, 1989).

Interventions.   Just as interventions in the earlier phases of the disease focused on enhancing the quality of life of people living with the disease, towards the end of life, the interventions focus on enhancing the quality of dying.

Dying with dignity has become increasingly difficult in a technological age, and social workers may need to help their clients to achieve this (Larson, 1989). Social workers often are confronted with a medical staff that is committed to keeping patients alive as long as possible, yet is unwilling or unable to adequately ease their pain in their last days. Social workers may need to act as their clients' advocates in carrying out their wishes as to where and how they want to die.

Most people with HIV disease would prefer dying quickly and painlessly at home to dying gradually and alone in a hospital, hooked up to a variety of tubes and machines. If the patient chooses, the social worker may express his or her wishes about whether, when, and how to continue or stop life-saving procedures. At the same time, the social worker may attempt to overcome some physicians' reluctance to prescribe adequate pain medication. Fear of causing addiction and other rationales for withholding adequate pain medications from dying patients are unconscionable.

It is more important than ever at this phase for the social worker to be a good listener and to offer reassurance and caring. Physical touching and holding may be all that is wanted and needed toward the end. The social worker also may help the client assess whether he or she has finished his or her "work" and then give the patient permission to let go and peacefully die.

The social worker's final efforts may be with family, spouses, lovers, and friends, dealing with unresolved guilt, anger, and other unfinished grief work.

GENERALIZING THE INTERVENTIONS TO RELATED PROBLEMS

There can be considerable transfer of learning between our understanding of work with HIV disease and work with other human problem areas. Perhaps the greatest similarity is found between work with people with HIV disease and work with those who are aging. Both groups tend to experience grief about a multitude of losses: health, productivity, sexual interest and desirabiity, attractiveness, friends, family, social acceptability, and a sense of a future, to name a few.

In both situations, the social worker must be able to facilitate any necessary grief work. In aging, of course, the grief work, as well as acceptance of mortality, stretches over a period of many years, whereas the person with HIV disease must deal with his or her grief and probable death in a few months or (at the present time) at most a few years. Although aging is not necessarily easy, there are more institutionalized supports and services for those who are aging than there are for those who have HIV disease.

SUMMARY

As can be seen from this chapter, the complex and varied tasks associated with HIV disease require a diverse collection of social work roles and skills. Case management is required to meet the basic human needs of people with HIV disease, including advocacy and brokerage to help the client obtain adequate nutrition, housing, medical care, hospice or long-term nursing care, and financial planning and assistance.

Support groups with skilled group leaders provide invaluable assistance to people at various stages of HIV disease as well as to their families, spouses, and lovers. Such groups help them avoid feeling alone and provide them with models for resolving many of the common problems they are likely to encounter.

Social workers can support and help the coalitions of people with HIV disease that increasingly are acting as their own advocates to protect and assert their rights, demand a better level of service, and attack bureaucratic obstacles to their receiving experimental medications as well as other services. The coalitions also question what some consider to be excessive profits drug companies and others are making at their expense.

Such coalitions serve a latent function of providing another means of empowerment for people with HIV disease, who often feel that they have lost some degree of control over their own lives. The coalitions can serve as major allies, as well as occasional critics, of social workers working with people who have HIV disease. As a note of caution, social workers must guard against the temptation to discount these coalitions' criticisms of social workers and their agencies as simply the product of dementia or misdirected anger associated with the disease process.

Finally, social workers themselves must use their social development skills to assure that basic human needs of people with HIV disease are met, not only by their own organizations but also by all relevant organizations and groups of professional helpers and through humane and supportive public policy and legislation.

CHAPTER 12

Experiential Focusing with Mexican-American Males with Bicultural Identity Problems

Fernando J. Galan

In this chapter, Galan shows how to use experiential focusing techniques in working with Hispanic males with identity problems. Galan discusses the development of identity problems in relation to acculturation and biculturation in Hispanic families. In some families, a male child may be placed in the roles of surrogate adult and spouse because he is the only family member who can communicate with the English-speaking outside world. Using Gendlin's (1978) step-by-step method, Galan shows how to define the components of experiential focusing. The very process of developing such protocols helps demonstrate how structure can be applied to work with clients regardless of the theory behind the methods used.

INTRODUCTION

Little has been written about the impact of acculturation on personality development in bilingual/bicultural children, especially in a family in which the mother speaks only Spanish and is culturally traditional and the father speaks only Spanish or is physically absent. Part of the paucity of practice knowledge can be explained by the fact that contemporary research has focused predominantly on generational rather than cultural differences in families. Where cultural differences in the Hispanic family have been examined, bicultural effectiveness interventions have helped practitioners address family conflicts (Szapocznik et al., 1984). And although there may be cause to suggest that bilingual children of monolingual parents perceive their world in broad terms, it remains unclear how developmental issues affect their emerging bicultural identity.

Issues of ethnic identity among indigenous bilingual/bicultural Mexican-American adolescents become more salient in succeeding generations, as thousands of Mexican children become naturalized. For Mexican-born children who later become citizens of the United States, ethnic identity may not be a serious problem because they were Mexican citizens first and American citizens second. For indigenous native-borns, however, developmental issues of separation and individuation in adolescence may get muddled with intergenerational culture conflict.

This may lead to blurred boundaries in a family and confusion in the definition and implementation of family roles. When children are placed in family roles in which they have no choice, they may develop strong emotions towards parents.

The purpose of this chapter is, first, to discuss the difficulties associated with the stress of acculturation in Mexican-American family functioning. Second, the chapter will define and explore two variations in family roles that may occur during the development of identity formation among Hispanic male children: (a) the adultification of a child, and (b) the spousification of a child. Third, the chapter examines the clinical manifestations or themes of psycho-emotional stress that indigenous, native-born Mexican-American children may face during childhood and adolescence as a result of parental bicultural tension. An appreciation of the influence that acculturation stress has on family dynamics will help social workers understand how children may bear the brunt of a parent's inability or unwillingness to adapt to the larger Anglo society.

When a parent's coping responses in situations outside the family are inappropriate or maladaptive, a child may be called upon to manage family stress. Understanding how a parent's inability to function outside the family can lead to a child's identity problems will help social workers to better appreciate the impact that acculturation stress has on family functioning. Later discussion will focus on directions for a treatment process and specific techniques for treating the emotional consequences created by role confusion.

CONCEPTS OF BICULTURAL FAMILY FUNCTIONING

As bicultural individuals from ethnic minority backgrounds learn the values and behaviors of the majority culture, and as these become part of their world view and coping repertoire in social situations, such individuals are said to become acculturated. Hispanic children are raised with a particular set of family values and behaviors and are exposed to and incorporate a different societal set of values and behaviors as they are socialized in school or work settings.

Mexican-American, Chicano, or Mestizo are terms used to refer to an individual born in the United States of Spanish-Indian-African cultural heritage. For the purposes of this discussion, they refer to individuals whose socialization and childhood and adolescent development have occurred in families residing in the United States. The bicultural socialization has occurred both in the family and in school. A Mexican-American family refers to a family in which the children have been socialized with this dual perspective.

"New Americans" is a term that refers to foreign-born individuals whose early childhood and adolescent development typically have occurred in another country. Children of "new Americans" who are exposed to bicultural socialization in human development can also be referred to as Mexican-Americans.

Bicultural conflict occurs when an individual's family values and behaviors are different from those of the society at large; there is a high degree of incongruence, or contrast, between family values and societal values. Although bicultural conflict need not necessarily be a problem, it can lead to bicultural tension. Typically, "new Americans" who have immigrated to the United States experience bicultural conflict immediately, whereas native-born Mexican-Americans usually experience conflict when they enter child-care or school situations outside the home.

Bicultural tension occurs when an individual's available coping skills are based on only one value system: either that of the family or that of society. The individual therefore is not able to use his or her coping skills in both family and societal situations. For example, if an individual learns coping responses from the family, such responses are used to adapt to family situations. Those same family-prescribed coping responses, however, may be socially problematic and not useful in adapting to situations outside of the family.

When adaptation is difficult, particularly adaptation to the majority culture, issues of adjustment may surface. The pressure to adapt to one's environment is, in part, integral to mastery of situations outside the family. Individuals who are not able to develop coping responses to adapt to societal situations experience stress that can sometimes be displaced on other family members.

STUDIES OF ACCULUTURATION STRESS

Research with Cuban immigrants "clearly indicates that the acculturation process in many instances results in the disruption of the traditional closely knit family" (Szapocznik et al., 1979). These changes can lead to behavioral disorders in family members (Scopetta and Alegre, 1975). Szapocznik and Truss (1978) have observed that "since youngsters acculturate more rapidly than their parents, the substantial intergenerational differences in acculturation that develop in the family may either precipitate or exacerbate existing familial, and particularly, intergenerational disruption" (Szapocznik, 1979). In relation to the functioning of individual family members, Szapocznik and Kurtines (1980) suggest that "the nature of the relationship between the individual's acculturation process (monocultural or bicultural) and the degree of plurality of the cultural context has important implications for the psychosocial adjustment of individuals and families of the migrant culture" (Szapocznik, 1979, p. 322).

Research on the functioning of individual members in Hispanic families, however, has been scant. Research on mothers of adolescents suggested that acculturation-related disorders in nuclear families are accompanied by intergenerational acculturation gaps in which middle-aged mothers and their adolescent sons tend to be at the acculturational extremes (Szapocznik and Truss, 1978).

> In pathological families, mothers tend underacculturate (individual–social context interaction), exhibit rigid and neurotic patterns of behaviors (either a clinical determinant or outcome of the individual–social context interaction), and tend to abuse sedatives and tranquilizers (behavior with biosocial and physiological consequences); sons tend to overacculturate (individual–social context interaction), exhibit acting-out syndromes (either a clinical determinant or outcome of the individual–social context interaction), reject their culture of origin, and abuse illegal drugs such as marijuana, Quaaludes and cocaine (behavior with biosocial and physiological consequences). The data from these studies reveal that in addition to the normative linear component of the acculturation process, there is another component which is pathological and non-normative and that is frequently reflected in severe overacculturation in youngsters and severe underacculturation in parents (pathological individual–social context interactions which are associated with pathological behaviors). (Szapocznik, 1979)

Where one parent is culturally traditional (high adherence to family values and low adherence to societal values) and a child is more acculturated (integrated family and societal values) or assimilated (high adherence to societal values to the exclusion of family values and behaviors), the child may be cast in the role of helping a parent relate to society. Interactions with the representatives of social systems can strongly affect the individual's or family's self-esteem (Cohen, 1970). Acculturated or assimilated children who speak Spanish and English usually have the coping skills necessary to adapt to societal situations, whereas their monolingual parents may not. "Dual-frame-of-reference" children are placed in family roles that correspond to the needs they help their "single-frame-of-reference" parents meet. "In all, it is very clearly manifested, that the Mexican-American family tends to come into conflict with the dominant society because the value system contrasts sharply with that of the minority, and because no substantial effort has been made to adapt services to the basic difference in consequent diverging needs" (Saenz, 1978). As the children develop coping responses and skills in the majority culture, and as they discover a new power to manage societal situations, they may find themselves in conflict with one or both parents, whose coping repertoire is limited to family situations. Perceived threats to family unity may precipitate crises. There has been little research into the dynamics of strain in families in which individual members are at different levels of acculturation. As mentioned above, children who have the coping skills to adapt to both family and societal situations may find themselves plunged into adult roles in order to help alleviate family stress. The literature is remarkably void of descriptions of the outcomes of these dynamics relative to their influence on the identity formation process in Hispanic children. Consequently, we know little about the choices or consequences that bilingual/bicultural children face when pressured to act in adult roles in behalf of parents. Practice evidence suggests that the tension these children experience often gets displaced as anger in situations outside the home, such as the classroom or church study group.

ADULTIFICATION AND SPOUSIFICATION

Adultification occurs when a child assumes adult roles before adulthood. *Spousification* occurs when a child becomes adultified and subsequently bonds emotionally as a spouse with a parent. An adultified male child, for example, is one who assumes and carries out adult roles in the family. A spousified male child is one who, as a result of carrying out adult roles in the family, becomes emotionally overinvolved with his mother and in effect replaces his father as his mother's spouse. Adultification becomes spousification when emotional bonds are developed between a parent and a child whose imposed family role is that of the absent adult. When a parent's overinvolvement results in a child perceiving that his or her worth is contingent on taking care of the adult's emotional needs, and when a parent's fear of inadequacy and failure keep the child emotionally bonded as a spouse, a child cannot easily establish personal boundaries and an identity apart from the parent. Identity diffusion results. For example, when a mother develops resentment toward the father and when the child may also have preexisting resentment toward the father, the common emotions that both mother and child experience may contribute to their bonding. In dysfunctional families, role integrity is lost and spousification may provide a creative yet maladaptive antidote to family disintegration.

Bilingual/bicultural children whose independence is stifled by a parent's inability to be independent or responsible become exploited by their circumstances. Their ability to make choices is hampered by role confusion. On the one hand, what they want becomes entangled with what they need to do to maintain family functioning. The pressure on children who feel forced into adult roles in order to compensate for a parent's inability or unwillingness to cope results in tension. The parent's relative powerlessness to manage life in the new language or value system creates stress in a spousified child. Chronic stress results when a spousified child's own fear of inadequacy and failure is not addressed because of the parent's own inability and fears. The failure of a monolingual parent to alleviate the tension the child is experiencing renders the child powerless.

An emotionally overburdened child in a spousified role can develop symptoms similar to those of post-traumatic stress disorders. Adultification in itself, without spousification, is less likely to create role confusion than it is to create pressure.

In traditional family cultures or in low socioeconomic family situations, where interdependence and cooperation are operational values, children learn to adapt their roles to fit the needs of the family's limitations. Because children may have coping responses and skills that help them adapt in the majority culture, they may be called upon to be advocates, cultural translators, or problem solvers in a family. This has been observed repeatedly as later generations help traditional parents adapt to the majority culture and thus increase their family's overall adjustment. Bilingual/bicultural children often are called upon to translate and mediate in situations involving their monolingual Spanish-speaking parents and monolingual English-speaking representatives of society. That children respond to these situations and exhibit their bicultural skills to help their parents is not in and of itself a problem. Bilingual/bicultural children who navigate between two languages and two cultures often develop incredible mediation abilities and sophisticated code-switching responses, as well as a high level of social sensitivity and an appreciation of the difficulties encountered by those who speak only Spanish. That they are referred to as "being like two people" is a tribute to an adaptive biculturality.

Thus, bicultural socialization is not inherently pathological. Nor does temporary adultification in itself necessarily create permanent role confusion. The negative circumstances in the environment that surround the acculturation process (in which a family finds itself changing from being solely monolingual/monocultural in the language and culture of origin to becoming bilingual/bicultural in succeeding generations) usually produces the stress attributed to role conflicts in the family. The acculturation stress of a family in transition in an environment of poverty, powerlessness, humiliation, lack of opportunity, and social injustice is sometimes too much for parents to manage. Spousification of children might not occur if negative circumstances in a family's environment were eliminated and appropriate supports were available for families undergoing the intergenerational transitions of acculturation. Many of the difficulties experienced by Mexican-American adolescents result from the inability of schools, media, neighborhood, and community to provide positive bicultural images and the skills with which to master their bicultural environment.

Adultification: The Child as Adult

Adultification affects different children in different ways. Some minority children are not able to make a transition from child to adult early in their lives. Being placed in adult roles can put immense pressure on youngsters and lay the foundation for a series of developmental difficulties, especially with the separation and individuation tasks of adolescence. Rinsley (1971) has observed that a child who develops significant psychopathology, who is "perceived and accordingly dealt with as something or somebody other than what he in fact is may suffer various degrees of distortion of his developing identity."

Bateson discusses the concept of the "double bind." He describes this as a learning context in which the growing child is subjected repeatedly to incongruent, mutually exclusive messages for which no resolution is possible and concerning which no further discussion can be developed. This situation exists when a child grows up with family values that are substantially different from societal values at school and gets one set of messages from parents and another set from teachers. Examples include when a parent tells a child cooperation is an important value and a teacher says competition is an important value; when the family extols interdependence and teachers reinforce independence; when the family imprints that *respect* for people is based on status and age and teachers program that all people should be treated with equal respect. An adultified child may feel cultural pressure to represent family values in social situations and, consequently, experience tension when trying to be loyal to parents and simultaneously act in an adaptive manner. Children who are placed in situations where they are expected to act as adults may experience developmental pressure that could force a denial or postponement of aspects of innocent and carefree childhood in order to protect parents.

Adultification presumes what Rinsley (1971) refers to as adultomorphization, in which the parent:

> . . . projects into the child their own reservoir of magic-omnipotence and infantile gradiosity. Such a child becomes, in the parent's mind, a powerful, omniscient being, through identification with whom the parents seek to achieve a proxy sense of mastery and accomplishment. But through the very process of adultomorphization, the parent poses for the child impossibly high standards and expectations of intellectual and emotional achievement, leading to ineluctable failure, which only further infantilizes him. (Rinsley, 1971, p. 11)

Spousification: The Child as Spouse

Where a child, in the role of an adult, becomes emotionally bonded to a parent, the child becomes a symbolic husband or wife. Rinsley (1971) identified two circumstances "in which the parent's depersonification of the child into a symbolic spouse is most likely to occur and have a particularly pathological effect upon the child's psycho-social development."

The first circumstance involves "narcissistic, unemancipated parents who obsessively and repetitively press the child into service as a means of wresting independence from their own parents" (Rinsley, 1971). The second circumstance involves the biological parent who "is bereft of a 'real' spouse as a consequence of abandonment, separation, divorce, or death" (Rinsley, 1971). In the latter circumstance, the parent attaches to the child as a substitute for the departed or emotionally absent husband or wife.

Inferences drawn from experience with Mexican-American adolescent cases suggest that a male child becomes spousified as a result of an emotionally or physically absent father. The clinical subjects were male school dropouts or students who had been identified as "at risk," harshly physically disciplined sons, or oldest sons, all of whom had clearly defined bilingual/bicultural coping skills and who perceived their fathers as "weak," "helpless," "sexually distant," or "emotionally unavailable" in regard to their mothers. The mothers were perceived by their sons as "needy," "unable to handle crisis alone," "unaware," and "tolerant of their husband's distance." When the son became emotionally involved in protecting his mother (*"le tengo que ayudar"*—"I have to help her"), a clearly traditional rigid male role expectation, the boy replaced his father. This contributed in part to identity conflict and blurred boundaries between child and adult roles. Additionally, tension in the spousified son created an array of themes of conflict. Experiential social work treatment of the son would later demonstrate the clinical manifestations of psychoemotional stress associated with spousification.

CLINICAL MANIFESTATIONS

Practitioners need to understand and be sensitive to manifestations of tension experienced by adolescent males who have been spousified. Knowledge of the themes of conflict and tension are essential in formulating a solid assessment. Families under acculturation stress engage in communication styles that influence the dynamics of role definition and role assignment. For native-born Mexican-American males who have been or are in spousified roles, various themes of psychoemotional stress may be faced during adolescence. In some cases, tension derived from spousification can be observed in childhood.

Self-Judgment and Guilt

The boy who "replaces" his father realizes a sense of power in being able to act in ways that his father is either unable or unwilling to act. When his mother looks to him to perform roles prescribed for his father, and as she rewards his behavior with loving gestures, a sense of guilt may surface in the boy for "usurping" his father. The guilt may give rise to a need to punish himself because, by stepping in and acting in his father's place, his actions automatically announce that he is in charge, not his father. By taking the role of spouse, the boy relegates his father to an ambiguously defined figurehead. Because the boy's actions, not his intentions, remove the father from a decision-making role, a sense of culpability may be assumed.

Resentment

Spousified sons exhibit enormous rage at their mothers for manipulating them into impossible positions. They become angry because they perceive their mothers as weak and unable to manage for themselves. They may rationalize that if their mothers were socially competent, they (the sons) might not have to assume decision-making roles.

Additionally, spousified sons may feel anger because they perceive their mothers as requiring attention and incapable of being left alone. Spousified sons may get upset at their mothers' need for intimacy and may become angry that they feel pressured to protect them.

Older spousified adolescents may develop distorted views of and repressed rage toward women, whom they perceive as needy. They may become attracted to "masculine, assertive" women who are perceived as "self-sufficient." And although their source of self-validation may be rooted in the need to protect and please women, they may concurrently retreat from intimacy in future relationships because they fear they will be pressured into always having to protect women.

Spousified adolescent males may be angry at their fathers, whom they perceive as being not "strong enough" to take care of their family responsibilities. Spousified males may see their fathers as weak, helpless, powerless, and indifferent, as "talking tough, but not being tough." Because of years of bonding, adolescent males who believe that their fathers are irresponsible have great difficulty in confronting their fathers, much less their own feelings about their fathers. Resentment toward fathers is rampant among spousified males. Its root appears to be a fundamental perception that "Dad abandoned his role and, in doing so, forced me into it." Integrity, extent of perceived real love of family, and self-respect are areas in which spousified males may have unresolved feelings toward their fathers.

Problems with Separation and Individuation

Spousified adolescent males who work toward their own goals and experience degrees of success may feel that they have abandoned their family. They may believe that they are selfish and that pursuing their own aspirations hurts the family. Questions about whether or not they can or should leave the family, especially the mother, can create anguish. Fear of success may be rooted in fear of separation and individuation, especially if a spousified son believes or knows that without his help his mother's willingness or ability to manage will be severely impaired. Codependent behaviors and exaggerated levels of responsibility have been observed among spousified sons because their own needs do not get met or are repressed.

Blurred Identity and Distorted Role Modeling

Because an adultified or spousified son may not be allowed to express his anger, it may become internalized and self-hatred may develop. This self-hatred may serve to hide enormous rage and may manifest as a narcissistic personality disorder. With fathers not providing clear directions for what males do and do not do, spousified sons get their structure for behaviors and mannerisms from mothers.

Although they want their fathers to be strong and provide direction, adolescent spousified sons get mixed or no messages about what masculinity is from their absent or seemingly weak parents. Thus spousified sons may become obsessed with images of strong men who are in charge. They also may wonder whether they are adequate as males. Spousified sons may not have a normal frame of reference for male behavior because their fathers have modeled a weak or an absent figure.

Support groups focused on men's issues often provide a context for men to discuss their lack of relationships with their fathers. When men are sad about a father–son relationship that never materialized, they may long for male intimacy and yet struggle through distorted perceptions of what it means to be close to another man, how intimacy can be structured, and whether they can achieve it. Although virtually no research has examined the association between adolescent male spousification and adult capacity for male-to-male intimacy, practice wisdom suggest that spousified adolescents long for male role models.

Shame and Humiliation

Prolonged spousification of adolescent sons inevitably raises the theme of conflict. Separation and individuation may become difficult to accomplish and, as the spousified son reaches the late teen years, shame and humiliation for having trampled on Dad may begin to set in. Where there is evidence of a deteriorated or nonexistent relationship with the father, a spousified son may think that he is to blame for his father's indifference or distance. He also may believe that he can never bond with his father because he has humiliated his father and validated his incompetence. Spousified sons may feel ashamed of and embarrassed by their fathers. Developmental issues relative to autonomy and self-fulfillment may be eclipsed by spousified sons' beliefs that they do not deserve success because of what they have done to their fathers.

ASSESSMENT AND MONITORING

Separation and individuation issues in adolescent human development complicate identity formation. When a child or adolescent in a spousified role is also physically abused, he receives mixed and unclear messages about what he is supposed to do in a family. The Mexican-American child who is adultified and spousified has outstanding roles in the family that may not be brought into a treatment situation until later in life. The following case study provides an example.

Ramiro Lopez became acculturated in school, where he learned English while speaking Spanish at home. His mother was culturally traditional, monolingual in Spanish, and had little understanding of societal institutions. His father also was culturally traditional, spoke little English, and developed a life primarily with other Spanish-speaking workers.

Ramiro's mother was dependent, fearful, and at times hysterical. The only way Ramiro could take care of himself was to take care of her. When Ramiro was eleven years old, his father chose not to involve himself with creditors. Ramiro's mother asked Ramiro to help out. Ramiro's ability to speak English made it possible for him to relay to creditors his mother's plans to catch up on account payments. As Ramiro assumed an adult role, his mother began to applaud his efforts. Ramiro felt both helpful and loved for his actions.

As Ramiro continued to assume adult roles for his mother, she began to confide more in him. She discussed with him money management, plans for home repairs, and the schooling of her two younger daughters. The emotional bonds intensified to the point that Ramiro and his mother discussed every aspect of family life. Even when Ramiro's father could participate in family decisions, both Ramiro and his mother chose to hold discussions when he was away from the house.

Later, when creditors demanded that some financial commitments be made, Ramiro made them on directions from his mother. She believed she would be able to count on her husband's paycheck. When Ramiro's father was laid off temporarily and was home one day, creditors called the house to talk to Mr. Lopez. Even with his limited English, he learned of the commitments "he" had made. When Mr. Lopez confronted his wife, she told him that Ramiro had spoken to the creditors. When Ramiro got home from school, an angry Mr. Lopez physically abused him for interfering in his business and "lying" to him. Unable to stand up for himself, Ramiro watched as his mother assumed a "what can I do?" attitude.

The subsequent distancing between Mr. and Mrs. Lopez intensified Ramiro's pressure to act in behalf of his family by helping his mother, even though he was aware of his father's disapproval. Ramiro and his mother both colluded to keep secrets from Mr. Lopez, he to protect his mother from getting yelled at by his father, she to protect him from getting hit by his father.

Comprehensive assessment of acculturation stress in the Lopez family would later reveal spousification of the adolescent male as a factor in precipitating jealous tension in the father. The father's loss of control of family administration, as well as his perceived powerlessness and loss of self-respect, would later surface as enraged envy of his son's abilities. As Mr. Lopez withdrew from intimacy with his wife, Ramiro was blamed. Mrs. Lopez's need for emotional intimacy, coupled with Ramiro's need to protect her in order to protect himself, led to his becoming spousified. With Mr. Lopez clearly relegated "out" of family decision making, Ramiro became the object of his father's displaced anger. Envy and rage would later be viewed as emotional precipitators for the father's abusive behaviors.

When a child is pressured to do more than he or she is able or willing to do, he or she may develop fears of inadequacy. In part, these fears result from the child being placed in situations in which he or she *is* inadequate, such as trying to fill the role of an adult spouse or a parent. When a spousified son is constantly expected to fill adult roles, his inability to do so may seem to "prove" that he is incapable of being a husband or father. This may lead to a deep sense of inadequacy as a male. To be subsequently punished by his father for his attempts to protect the family and ensure its survival may contribute to the son's distorted sense of self and to feeling shame.

EXPERIENTIAL TREATMENT

The processes of successful treatment of spousification in Mexican-American adolescent males have received little attention in the literature. Consequently, there is little scientific documentation of efforts.

Rinsley (1971) suggests separating the adolescent from the family through admission into full-time residential treatment. The author of this chapter believes such treatment to be excessive, ineffective, and inaccessible to large numbers of Mexican-American families, who do not have insurance coverage and are not likely to appreciate or endorse the rationale of residential treatment.

Szapocznik and others at the Spanish-Speaking Family Guidance Clinic in Florida have experimented successfully with outpatient intervention through the use of one-person family therapy (Szapocznik et al., 1980) and bicultural effectiveness training (Szapocznik et al., 1984). These are treatment interventions based on helping clients to adapt to biculturality. Interventions based on this philosophy are supported by research that suggests that adjustment to bicultural contexts necessitates an ability to act appropriately in either cultural context. Their work with Cuban families whose individual members are at different levels of acculturation and acculturation stress have realized fascinating results, such as the treatment of related or behavioral disorders through the enhancement of biculturalism in family members, an improved flexibility of family roles, and more openness in family functioning. As of this writing, a literature search disclosed no entries regarding family therapy with Mexican-American families related to the treatment of spousification in adolescents.

In the treatment of the spousified child, it is important to eliminate the rigid role that resulted from the emotional conditioning between parent and child that intensified the triangulation of the child. Appropriate techniques can unravel the web of triangulation and facilitate communication in the marital dyad. Such resolution also temporarily frees the adolescent for important self-liberation and empowerment work. Structural family therapy techniques show promise in helping family members to address the various relations among members as they affect how decisions in the family are made. The spousified child has a series of tasks to work through as part of treatment intervention:

1. Awareness and education about spousification
2. Exploration of cognitions (thought forms) and affect (feelings) related to relationship with spousifying parent
3. Exploration of self-image that has developed as a result of being spousified
4. Review of situations where parent may have been traumatized, thereby forcing child into adult role
5. Exploration of complementary behaviors that child learned in order to protect traumatized parent or cope with parent's inability to adapt
6. Awareness of child's participation with spousifying parent in decision making to the exclusion of other parent
7. Exploration of child's feelings about replacing other parent
8. Exploration of child's core survival thinking about his behavior vis à vis spousifying parent's love (examination of codependence)
9. Uncovering of child's deep-seated emotions through (a) awareness of the process of spousification; (b) how the imposed adult role was a form of emotional manipulation; (c) awareness that the child's intense need for nurturance may have led to intense denial of that need; and (d) how child was "expected" to have emotions of adult and spouse
10. Exploration of child's powerlessness to freely pursue his interests and associated addictive patterns of pain control

11. Uncovering of child's emotions about himself (self-derogation, self-denial, and self-destruction) and manifested behaviors (anger at self, guilt, and shame)

12. Uncovering of child's emotions towards parents (anger, resentment, bitterness)

13. Uncovering of child's emotions toward life (anger, fear of judgment)

During treatment, the spousified son's work on separation and individuation from parents may become intensified as he staunchly defends his "illusionary self," which was created by the confusion of roles. Separation and personal integration work using transactional analysis techniques, Gestalt techniques, and self-image modification usually are necessary before any restructuring of new beliefs and clearing of repressed emotions can be effective. Personal leadership building, assertiveness training, and personal problem-solving skill development can later assist the empowerment process toward independence. Social workers should remember that the "escape to freedom" philosophy may be one of great emotional pain for an adolescent male child, but with the establishment of liberation and empowerment to individuate, termination of short-term treatment comes within reach. Additional post-treatment follow-up may address regret, grief for the loss of "self," and guilt for perceived interference with the other parent's role as spouse. These and other associated feelings may suggest that the work of personal integration, separation, and individuation has, in effect, occurred, and that the client may need assistance in releasing the past and forgiving himself.

At the point in the treatment process when repressed emotions surface and are identified, the social worker needs to use techniques to manage and clear the feelings that have surfaced. One set of techniques is experiential focusing. Experiential focusing techniques are structured methods designed to direct the client's attention to his or her physical or internal sensation (bodily) experiences (Gendlin, 1978). These bodily experiences have a profound influence on one's life, one's insights, and one's goals. Focusing is based on the assertion that differences in effectiveness of treatment can be measured not so much by what clients talk about as by how they talk; that is, change seems to occur when the client's discussion reflects change in his or her internal experiences, those internal sensations that are meaningful to the client. Gendlin has labeled these experiences the "felt sense." By focusing on these bodily experiences, clients obtain a special kind of internal experience pertinent to insight and change.

Focusing has been shown to relate to client change (see, e.g., Gendlin, 1973; Gendlin, 1978; Kantor and Zimring, 1970) and clinician's empathy (Corcoran, 1982). Unlike many experiential techniques, focusing is structured in a step-by-step format. Information on focusing is available in book form (Gendlin, 1978) and on audiotape (Olsen, 1978). The focusing techniques that follow have been developed specifically for Hispanic males with identity problems. Used with one or both parents, these techniques are designed to allow the client to disidentify by projecting the emotions and images generated as a result of emotional tension. Through the use of projection, the client becomes involved in an internal dialogue that is nonthreatening and serves (1) to clear the feelings he is having and (2) to dissipate the symbols associated with those feelings.

The first technique is the Affective Release Process. This is used to release any feelings about self, others, or life. The Image Dissipation Process is the second technique. It is used to release the past through an imaging procedure that dissipates the symbols associated with the feelings. As part of the procedure, the client is also directed to make verbal statements of forgiveness.

Emotional Accessing Technique

As preliminary work before using either process, the social worker can ask the client to use his own body to locate where he is experiencing feelings. This is accomplished by using the Emotional Accessing Technique. Successful use of this technique enables the social worker to gain access to an image somewhere in the client's body of the tension being experienced, which can help social worker and client identify the actual feeling producing the tension. This is accomplished by first asking the client, ''Where in your body do you feel the tension with your parent?'' When the client identifies a specific place in his body where he feels the tension (for example, the stomach), the social worker then asks the client to *imagine or make up a picture of what the tension looks like.* The client then can describe or draw the image in the specific place in his body where he is experiencing the tension (for example, a thick, dark, heavy black knot in the stomach). In order for the social worker to gain access to the actual feeling the client is experiencing as a result of the tension, the final step of this technique requires the client to enact the image that has just been identified in a specific place in the body. The social worker plays the part of the client in this simple role play. This is accomplished by asking the client, ''What is the tension that I am feeling?'' The client, playing the part of the dark knot, would respond by identifying the actual feeling being experienced. The ''dark knot'' might say, ''The tension is because I am scared.'' The social worker might be able to identify, for example, that the client is experiencing real fear of a parent; that fear was accessed by guiding the client through a projective process. In this way, the social worker can help the client learn to identify his own feelings.

Additional treatment strategies could further identify where in time and space the fear was created; what the client did to protect himself;

what interpretations or beliefs he made about self, others, or life; what factors kept the fear in place; what kinds of behaviors were developed as a result of the fear and continue; and what skills and behaviors can be developed to address the abatement of the fear. Although further intervention may be necessary and is not delineated here, the three steps of the Emotional Accessing Technique accomplish the identification of the feelings that can eventually be resolved through the use of the experiential techniques described in the next section of this chapter.

Experiential Techniques

Affective Release Process. The purpose of this process is to address methodically the feelings that the client has just accessed by having the client put into words what he feels and express himself assertively in a manner that helps resolve the issue. Clients often are reticent in expressing their feelings in a session, particularly if they have experienced previous difficulty in personal assertiveness or if their trust of others has eroded over time. Therefore, it is important that the social worker guide this process in a professional, nonjudgmental manner that conveys a sense of safety.

The expression of feelings that the client has for a parent can occur in the absence of the parent. In using the Affective Release Process, the social worker asks the client to imagine that the parent with whom he is distressed is sitting across from him. The social worker can ask the client to describe the parent as if he or she were indeed in the room: how the parent is dressed, how his or her hair is combed, how he or she is sitting, etc. Carefully describing the person with whom one is distressed creates a more vivid image and helps feelings come to the surface more easily. The actual steps of the Affective Release Process follow.

Step 1: Have the client state, as if the person with whom there is distress were actually present, all of the things he does not appreciate about him or her. The social worker asks the client to express all of the feelings he is experiencing to the image he has described of the person. Specifically, the social worker guides the process by explaining that the client needs to begin expression with the following phrase: "[Actual name of person with whom client is distressed], what I don't appreciate about you is. . . ." (Example: "Mom, what I don't appreciate about you is that you didn't stand up for me when. . . .") As the client feels freer to express all the things about which he feels tension, the social worker provides support by quietly echoing what the client has just said and by asking the client, "What else do you not appreciate about Mom?" Additionally, the social worker can not only help the client express his feelings about the person with whom he is distressed, but also unravel feelings the client may have about what the person did. The practitioner can support the expression of more feelings by asking, ''What else do you not appreciate about what Mom did?'' or ''What else do you not appreciate about what happened to you?''

This step continues until the client has completely expressed all the feelings he has about the person. This single step should not be time limited; social workers should not interfere with the free flow of feelings once the client begins to express them. Notes from practice reveal that clients may use an entire counseling session for this one step. Additionally, as social workers allow clients the freedom to direct their own work, clients may end sessions with a greater sense of trust in the social workers.

Step 2. Have the client state, as if the person with whom there is distress were actually present, all of the things he does appreciate about him or her. In this step, the client is asked to focus on the things that he does appreciate about the other person. This step provides the client with an opportunity to acknowledge positive feelings he has for the person and a perspective for those feelings. It recognizes that although clients can have negative feelings about a significant other relative to specific negative experiences, they may also have overall positive feelings about their relationship with that person. As clients have the opportunity to express their general feelings about the relationship, this step brings a sense of balance to an otherwise difficult review of an experience.

It is important to note, however, that some clients may bring to their treatment a historical perspective that is not positive because of a turbulent and distrustful relationship with a significant other. This has been observed in clients who have been abused, neglected, or who have suffered chronic tension as a result of multiple traumatic experiences. These clients may choose not to express what they appreciate about people with whom they are distressed because positive feelings do not exist.

Step 3: Ask the client whether there is anything else he would like to say to the person with whom there is distress. This step provides an ending to this structured manner of self-expression and an opportunity for the client to acknowledge his general feelings toward the person. The social worker can guide the client by asking, ''Is there anything else you would like to say to Mom?'' or ''Is there any final thing you would like to say now to close?''

Clients may seem quiet at the conclusion of this technique. This may suggest that the client is tired after having expressed deep feelings; it may suggest that the client is reflective about his realization of how he really felt; or it may be a natural response to the completion of the process. As the client is provided with the structure in which to express all of his feelings relative to the discomfort that caused the tension, the resolving of affect becomes an empowering tool.

Image Dissipation Process.   People create symbolic images of their experiences with themselves, others, and life. Symbolic images convey meaning and feeling. Clients who experience difficult and traumatic events in their lives may suppress feelings associated with the tension of those events. Because defense mechanisms allow people to postpone or deny feelings about difficult events, they may not have complete awareness of the underlying emotions that influence their motives and behaviors. Based on this understanding, the Emotional Accessing Technique described earlier provides the social worker with a structured way in which to achieve consciousness of underlying feelings through the identification of a symbolic image.

Having completed a process that has cleared the affect identified through the symbolic image, it is now desirable to structure for the client a way in which to dissipate the symbolic image. The rationale for dissipating or dissolving the symbolic image of the client's tension is the connection between images and emotions. Although emotions represent one system of communication and images represent another, their connection occurs when the messages of emotions become converted as a body of information to symbolic images. Symbolic images become encoded with the information of emotions.

A whole-person approach to clearing tension would necessarily suggest not only the clearing of affect, but the clearing of images as well. Because individuals' feelings about themselves, others, and life are encoded in their symbolic images, the dissipation of the mental picture created to identify the tension accomplishes an important therapeutic task. This is the release of the body of information from the emotions of the tension through the dissipation of the sensory agent that carries them.

The Image Dissipation Process accomplishes a second important task, namely, the forgiveness of self. This is important when the client makes a connection between the image of what happened and his own culpability. As symbolic images act as sensory agents of emotions and become internalized in the client, they can serve as springboards for the development of negative or illusionary thinking about the self. In clients who bring to their treatment sessions strong internalized negative feelings or beliefs about themselves, the release of feelings and the dissipation of symbolic images from role tension may not be enough. Observations from practice have shown that clients who use negative experiences to judge themselves suffer relentless stress. The symbolic images become not only the sensory agents of the emotions of the difficult experience, but also register the emotions the client had about himself in that experience. Where internalized judgment of self occurs as a result of a difficult experience, it becomes additionally important to dissipate the symbolic image because it also acts as the sensory agent of nonforgiveness.

The preliminary client preparation work the practitioner does before using the Image Dissipation Process (IDP) involves bringing the client's attention back to the symbolic image that was accessed earlier. The practitioner can explain to the client how mentally dissolving or destroying the symbol of the tension can help remove the sensory push that would bring the emotions to the surface all over again. Additionally, the practitioner can explain that the faculty of the imagination is used to complete this process. Successful outcomes of the therapeutic use of the imagination in practice have been observed to result in client perceptions of peacefulness and empowerment.

Step 1: Ask the client to focus his thinking on the symbolic image. The social worker asks the client to identify the image and what it looks like. (Example: The client describes the tension as being like a dark, heavy black knot in the stomach area.)

Step 2: Ask the client to use his imagination to expand the symbolic image, making it larger and larger until it dissipates (changes or explodes) and then tell what he sees afterwards, if anything. The social worker is helping the client to mentally dissolve the symbolic image. Additionally, the social worker is interested in the next symbolic image that surfaces, because it determines whether this step will need to be repeated.

Step 2-A: Ask the client to repeat aloud a set of positive affirmations and a statement of forgiveness of self. This step is led by the social worker, who models for the client self-talk that acknowledges the release of any judgment the client has of himself. (Example: The social worker may say, "Repeat with me . . . with all of my power, with all of my protection, with all of my love, I forgive you, John, for the image of the dark, heavy knot.") With the completion of both parts of this step, the client has dissolved the symbolic image and cleared himself of any self-judgment that was or could have been derived from the tension of the negative experience.

If the client imagines a new symbol after dissolving the original one, repeat steps 2 and 2-A. This process continues until the client no longer imagines any symbols or until the client imagines a symbol with which he is comfortable and that he wishes to keep.

Step 3: Ask the client to re-image the area in the body where the original symbolic image was experienced. The purpose of this step is to determine whether the symbolic image has completely dissipated. (Example: The social worker says, "John, go back and re-image your stomach and tell me what you see.") Successful outcome of this step results when the client reports that the symbolic image is gone, that the sensory agent identified with the tension has been eliminated. When the client reports that the symbolic image is cleared, the process ends.

As a part of this step, a client may report that another symbolic image exists. The social worker should determine whether the client is comfortable with the new symbolic image. If the client wishes to dissolve this and any new symbolic images, the social worker should guide the client through the process again until the client is comfortable. If the client wishes to keep a new symbolic image because of a positive association made with it, the social worker ends the process by acknowledging the value of the positive outcome of the creative process.

If a client has difficulty with the concept of dissipation, the practitioner can ask the client to imagine a procedure through which the symbolic image can be dissolved or eliminated. It has been observed in practice that clients have imagined the symbols being erased, painted over, torn, and covered, all with the same result of eliminating the sensory agent, which is the goal of this technique.

GENERALIZING THE INTERVENTION TO RELATED PROBLEMS

The evaluation of the impact of experiential treatment techniques has been encouraging limited to Mexican-Americans. In terms of the special population of Mexican-American males with identity problems, clinical trials are currently being conducted to study the effects of these specific experiential techniques. Practice experience and evaluations of treatment suggest that the techniques are successful with ethnic minority clients and overburdened adolescents experiencing role tension from acculturation stress. Additionally, the use of these techniques has been successfully evaluated with treatment of war veterans experiencing symptoms of post-traumatic stress disorders; treatment of high-risk antepartum obstetrical patients experiencing symptoms of pregnancy-induced hypertension, diabetes, and hyperemesis gravidarum; and treatment of adults who were molested as children and who are experiencing intimacy dysfunction in marriage. In some cases, clinical analysis of high-risk antepartum obstetrical patients who are adolescents and of ethnic minority background has revealed preexisting role tension from acculturation stress.

No empirical data have been set forth in the literature that support the validity or reliability of these specific techniques, although research on other Gestalt techniques has been encouraging (see Simkin and Yontef, 1984). Clinical case studies suggest that these techniques have application in helping to address not only the role tension associated with acculturation stress, but also tension associated with post-traumatic stress. Gerber posits that "the most powerful of all healing modalities is the patient's own mind. Positive, spiritually uplifting verbal affirmations may be used to change negative message tapes that may be playing through the subconscious mind. Transformational healing images are also of benefit, especially when visual imagery is combined with the use of affirmations"

(Gerber, 1988). Recent works by professionals in the helping professions suggest that, although empirical data are incomplete and many of the methods that address affective and self-image modification work have validation only in observations from practice, the direction in which these techniques are developing shows much promise.

CONCLUSION

Much work has been completed in the past few years in building knowledge of the treatment of behavioral disorders related to acculturation stress in families. Although biculturality and generational conflict can contribute to acting-out and disengagement, both also can lead to a higher-level integration of the personality. As practice-based research reveals the intricacies of identity formation in bicultural males, more in-depth analysis may support biculturality as a phenomenon that is dynamic and self-affirming.

CHAPTER 13

Psychodyamic Treatment for Persons with Borderline Personality

Kevin Corcoran
Cele Keeper

In this chapter, Corcoran and Keeper review one of the most clinically complex and challenging client problems, the borderline personality. The intervention reflects the dominant theoretical approach to this personality disorder, an ego-dynamic approach. Although this type of intervention is frequently considered to lack structure, the authors emphasize the importance of accurate assessment and appropriate short- and long-term goals. The long-term needs of persons with this problem require that the intervention be adjusted to the client's particular borderline symptom. Some of the components have fairly structured definitions; for example, the social worker should clearly define how to be consistent with the client, or what self-defeating behaviors will be confronted.

INTRODUCTION

One of the most complicated and confusing clinical problems social workers face is the client with a borderline personality disorder. Although the borderline personality has been the topic of study for nearly three decades, it only recently received conventional recognition from the American Psychiatric Association by inclusion in the third edition of the *Diagnosis and Statistical Manual* (DSM III-Revised). As recently as 1975, Wiedeman opened a chapter on borderline personality by stating, "although not officially recognized, the diagnostic term 'borderline' has attained *de facto* recognition through common usage" (p. 423). The topic itself is often spiritedly debated. Is it a disorder that reflects the development of a more formal psychotic condition, such as schizophrenia? Is it sufficiently different from other personality disorders to warrant diagnostic consideration? Does it actually exist at all?

The confusion is a consequence in part of the very nature of personality disorders; few have clear boundaries to enable easy differentiation from other disorders. The borderline personality disorder is very similar to the schizotypical, antisocial personality, an identity disorder, and features of cyclothymia, which is a condition characterized by mood instability. In addition, persons with personality disorder often have more than one type. For example, narcissistic and histrionic personality disorders often present sufficient borderline symptoms to warrant both diagnoses. The borderline client, moreover, is confusing and controversial because of the primary theory underlying development and treatment of borderline personality disorder; namely, ego-oriented, psychodynamic theory and treatment, which are complex and are questioned by many other theorists. We will focus on these perspectives in this chapter.

PROBLEM IDENTIFICATION

A person with a borderline personality is characterized by pervasive patterns of instability in several aspects of life. He or she may show instability in identity, interpersonal relationships, and mood. The pattern of instability tends to be consistent across the client's interaction with different people, in different social environments, and over time. That is, the symptoms are numerous and occur in a variety of contexts. The unstable identity tends to be the most common symptom, and may be seen in the client's self-image, acceptance of values, sexual orientation, and long-term commitments, including interpersonal relationships and career goals. The client may also complain of boredom or feelings of emptiness. You might observe that the client has intense involvement and emotional investment in a person he or she just met; a new lover, for example. Yet the client may quickly disdain this person because of a seemingly inconsequential event.

You might find this client complimenting you for helping so much, and yet at the very next session he or she may be enraged at you, claiming the money and energy spent on coming to you for help are wasted. The person with a borderline personality might seem anxious and irritable with you, and then both affective states may seem to pass in a few hours or a day or so. In periods of high stress, transient psychotic symptoms may appear. At times it might seem that the more you try to oblige this client, the more difficult he or she becomes. You might find yourself at a loss for what to do to help this client.

The reason for this potential response to the borderline is the very nature of the problem as it is manifested in the treatment process. The struggle with what to do in the intervention is due, in part, to the complexity of the borderline character, as well as the interpersonal dynamics of the intervention method, which utilize transference and countertransference. The treatment may seem to lack well-established, structured techniques. The components of treatment often are quite conceptual and are not always easily replicated. Further, little empirical evidence is available about specifically when to do what in the treatment process. We know what some of the components of helping effectively are (for example, a constant holding environment where the social worker consistently responds with unyielding limits and acceptance of the client), but we may not know how to actually do this or when in treatment it is optimal.

Determining how to work effectively with a person with a borderline personality can be facilitated by being flexible about the specific borderline characteristics of attention during a session and establishing concrete treatment goals, both short term and long term. For example, a meaningful short-term goal might simply be to keep the client in treatment, because persons with borderline characteristics tend to prematurely terminate treatment more than do most other clients, especially if the problem does not warrant hospitalization (Gunderson et al., 1989). A meaningful and relatively concrete long-term goal might be to enhance the client's identity, as manifested by improved self-esteem and less feelings of emptiness.

You can enhance your ability to work effectively with this problem by achieving a thorough understanding of the development of the borderline personality and the dynamics of clinical work, which often relies on the transference relationship. In this chapter we provide an introduction to both the theoretical development of the borderline personality and effective methods for helping this type of client. We encourage you to learn more because of the complexity of the topic and the limitations of a single chapter.

Theoretical Considerations

The most widely accepted perspective on the borderline client is based on the psychodynamic development of the individual. The theory is an ego-oriented one, which emphasizes the development of the ego and ego functions, such as judgment and reality testing; this contrasts with more traditional Freudian theories, where the emphasis is on the id. The theory, then, is neo-Freudian, and integrates such work as Margaret Mahler's psychological development theory, Erik Erikson's psychosocial development theory, and Jean Piaget's cognitive development theory.

The essential features of the psychodynamic theory concern the developmental failure in which one's ego functions are not fully acquired. Ego functions allow for adaptive capacity, or the ability to respond adequately to the environment. For example, perception and judgment influence reality testing and are ego functions. If a person misperceives the environment or uses bad judgment in response to the environment, then the ability to adapt may be impaired. The borderline syndrome is characterized by gross fluctuations in perception, cognition, and affect in terms of self-perception and the perception of others (Kernberg, 1976).

Generally, the borderline personality has an intact ego, but it is impaired and lacks sufficient ego strength. Ego strength refers to one's adaptive capacity, the autonomy of the ego from the id, and thus the ability to tolerate frustration and anxiety in order to resist regression. Because of the absence of sufficient ego strength, the borderline personality may regress and use functions of the id and primary processes. Consequently, at times the borderline personality may be out of touch with reality and show psychotic features. At other times the person may adapt well to the environment, reflecting good ego functioning. An illustration of impaired ego functioning is a client's poor judgment and lack of established cause-and-effect relationships. For example, a young man may know the risks of intravenous drug abuse but continue to use intravenous drugs nonetheless. Alternatively, he may recognize the need for treatment, a sign of the ego's adaptive capacity, but seek treatment while under the influence of drugs.

The lack of ego strength results from insufficient mastery in one's early development. The basic position of the theory is that the borderline personality has not successfully mastered developmental issues that begin at birth and continue through adolescence (Masterson, 1976) and thus has an impaired ability to adapt to the environment. Early development is most important to the theory, and lack of ego strength results when the infant is not allowed to develop a basic sense of trust in himself or herself or others, particularly parents (Kernberg, 1975; 1976). Because the infant lacks a basic sense of trust, he or she in turn is not able to develop a sense of autonomy; "pseudo-autonomy" develops instead. This occurs at a time in cognitive development when the infant is acquiring a sense of the permanency of objects, called object constancy. The borderline has not had sufficient nurturance and opportunities to interact with a psychologically safe environment to develop the full realization of object constancy in interpersonal relationships. The sense of mistrust and pseudo-autonomy are the foundations of the borderline personality. This is further seen in the separation individuation process, in which the infant gradually emerges from a symbiotic mother-child unit to become an autonomous person (Mahler, Pine, and Bergman, 1975). If the infant is not allowed to experience adequate trust, development of the ability to tolerate frustration and anxiety is thwarted. During this phase, the child develops representational thought and symbolization (Piaget, 1953), which are used to maintain the image of one's mother while she is absent. If the infant lacks trust and object constancy, he or she will become overwhelmed and frustrated by the mother's absence. In order to preserve the positive images of his or her mother, the child will dissociate from these images and see himself or herself as a "bad" child abandoned by the mother (Kernberg, 1975; 1976). The child consequently experiences rage and separation anxiety and develops a negative self-image, all of which are characteristics of the adult borderline personality disorder. This dynamic process is the basis of the defense mechanism of "splitting" (see below), and is used throughout the borderline personality's life (Masterson, 1976). Additionally, the infant's feelings of abandonment result in the reactive fantasy, "If I grow up, I'll be alone," which helps explain the immaturity characterizing the borderline personality.

Winnicott (1969) suggests the continuation of the borderline development may be thwarted by having a parent who responds consistently, setting firm limits and sticking to them, and yet maintaining a loving, nurturing, and soothing relationship. This "constant holding environment" strengthens the child's positive image, allowing him or her to see the parent as both gratifying and frustrating. It helps the child learn impulse control, which decreases the fear of his or her own aggressive tendency (Kernberg, 1975).

These developmental issues are seen again during adolescence, when the separation individuation themes are recapitulated (Masterson, 1972). Here the child struggles with dependency on and independence from the family. If the child lacks an adequate sense of trust, acts of autonomy (or pseudo-autonomy, as real autonomy requires basic trust) are again experienced as abandonment, leading to what Masterson (1975) calls "abandonment depression."

Defense Mechanisms

To understand the borderline personality, it is important to be familiar with common defense mechanisms. Defense mechanisms are used to control anxiety and frustration. The four most common ones seen in a borderline person are splitting, acting-out, projective identification, and denial (Kernberg, 1975, 1976; Masterson, 1972).

Splitting, as alluded to above, is the polarization of two images and the disowning of the positive one and acceptance of the negative one. Kernberg (1975, 1976) sees the core cause to be the borderline person's inability to integrate the loving and hating aspects of one's self-images and the images of others.

Acting-out is the predominant symptom of borderline adolescents, according to Masterson (1972). It is a dysfunctional coping mechanism that is employed when anxiety cannot be tolerated and is warded off by acting out the ego-dystonic impulse. Acting-out may be manifested in negativity, school truancy, running away, aggression, stealing, and other forms of antisocial behavior.

Projective identification is the dissociation of uncomfortable features of the personality and the projection of these features onto another person, which results in an identification with the other person because of the perceived similarity. The borderline person also tries to get the other person to conform to the projected qualities. For example, a teenage boy who hates his father will believe his father actually hates him. The youngster may continuously misbehave in order to get his father's disapproval, resulting in behavior that confirms the projected impulse. This is something you will need to be particularly sensitive to in treatment, as your client may try to facilitate negative transference by getting you angry, frustrated, and ineffective.

Denial, the fourth common defense mechanism, is when the client denies to himself or herself, and frequently to others, the existence of an emotion, thought, or action that is unacceptable to the ego; the impulse to feel, think, or behave is called ego-dystonic or ego-alien.

Assessment and Monitoring

The above theoretical discussion, although brief, illustrates that the borderline personality is truly complex and elusive. It is easy to overlook the personality pattern because of the variety of clinical symptoms, as well as the person's tendency to function well at times. Accurate assessment is critical because, as we will discuss in the section on treatment, it is important to establish goals and be consistent throughout the intervention process. It is helpful to diagnose and monitor the client problem with standardized assessment tools and rapid assessment instruments for specific symptoms.

The first issue, of course, is to identify or diagnose the borderline personality. The DSM-III-R requires that the client meet at least five of the following eight criteria:

1. Unstable and intense interpersonal relationships
2. Impulsivity in two or more areas in life, such as drug or alcohol use or sexual behavior, that is self-damaging
3. Unstable affect that lasts anywhere from a few hours to a few days
4. Inappropriate anger or the inability to control anger
5. Suicidal threats or self-mutilating behavior
6. Disturbed identity in two or more areas, such as self-image, values, or career choice
7. Chronic feelings of emptiness or boredom
8. Efforts to avoid abandonment

These criteria have numerous possible manifestations. Because of this, you might find certain semi-structured interview schedules helpful in reaching a diagnosis. One that is most widely used and has had some empirical support for its reliability and validity is the Diagnostic Interview for Borderline (DIB) (Gunderson, Kolb and Austin, 1981). The DIB is a 160-

item interview that takes approximately an hour to complete. The interview has a high degree of sensitivity and specificity for differentiating clients with borderline personality from nonborderline clients (Kolb and Gunderson, 1980), as well as for differentiating borderline persons from depressed or schizophrenic patients (Gunderson and Kolb, 1978). It also has been shown to have good concurrent validity by correlating with such criteria as depression, hostility, and impulsivity (Soloff, 1981). There have been some mixed results with the concordance with other methods of diagnosing the disorder (Nelson, 1985), but the DIB generally identifies borderlines as well as—if not better than—other methods (Tarnopolsky and Berelowitz, 1987). Other useful methods for evaluating clients for borderline personality are checklists, including the DSM-III criteria (Sheehy, Goldsmith, and Charles, 1980), the Ego Functions Inventory (Perry and Klerman, 1980), and two self-report measures (Conte et al., 1980; Hurt et al., 1984).

In addition to a semi-structured interview, you might find it helpful to monitor specific symptoms of your client. Because the borderline client often requires long-term treatment (from two to three years), you will find that different symptoms are the focus of your sessions at different times in the treatment. For example, abandonment depression may be the focus early in treatment, when you and your client are establishing a meaningful therapeutic alliance, and again during termination; thus you might want to monitor your client by measuring his or her depression, with the Depressed Mood Scale (Radloff, 1977), early and towards the end of treatment.

You might also decide to monitor symptoms more specific to the borderline personality, such as impulsivity, distorted perception, or defense mechanisms. There are four instruments you might find valuable:

- The Cognitive Slippage Scale (Miers and Raulin, 1985), a 35-item measure of cognitive distortion
- The Intense Ambivalence Scale (Raulin, 1984), a 45-item measure of the existence of simultaneous and rapidly interchangeable positive and negative feelings
- The Magic Ideation Scale (Eckblad and Chapman, 1983), a 30-item measure of beliefs, including invalid causation
- The Splitting Scale (Gerson, 1984), a 14-item measure of the defense mechanism that involves the radical shift in evaluation of self and others

When using these or other monitor devices, it is important to keep your work in perspective. First of all, clients with borderline personality are notorious for quitting treatment before much success has occurred (Gunderson et al., 1989); consequently, you may need to monitor your initial goals frequently earlier in treatment until the borderline client is indeed committed to continuing. Secondly, once you have the client's commitment, it is important to remember that change does not occur quickly; thus, you might administer your measures every few weeks or so.

PSYCHODYNAMIC TREATMENT OF THE BORDERLINE PERSONALITY

Research Supports

The research on the borderline personality has tended to focus more on the reliability and validity of the construct than on the effectiveness of different treatment methods. This focus has been from the perspective of the value of the psychoanalytic model, as recently reviewed by Shapiro (1989), and more conventional research methods, as reviewed by Tarnopolsky and Berelowitz (1987). There have, however, been several in-depth case reports, although these procedures are beyond the focus of this section. The basic outcome of the research into the construct has been the creation of assessment tools, as discussed above.

The most noted controlled study compared supportive psychotherapy, psychoanalysis, and expressive psychotherapy (Kernberg et al., 1972). The study was conducted on an inpatient unit, and borderline clients were reported to respond well. Other, less complicated studies have focused on pharmacotherapy. As Tarnopolsky and Berelowitz (1987) summarize, the effects of medication on the psychotic-like symptoms and affective symptoms were noted when the client was experiencing those dimensions of the condition. They suggest that future research needs to include the impact of psychotherapy.

The majority of the research has focused on the validity of the construct and thus the ability to measure the borderline personality. The above discussion of the Diagnostic Interview for Borderlines is an illustration of these efforts. It has been shown to be reliable in actual interviews (Kroll et al., 1981), and case notes (McGlashan, 1983) and for agreement between interviews and notes (Armelius, Kullgreu, and Renberg, 1985). Research also has supported the value of the DSM-III criteria for identifying the borderline construct (e.g., McGlashan, 1983), and a DSM-III–derived structured interview (Stangle et al., 1985). As reviewed by Tarnopolsky and Berelowitz (1987), the lengthy interview process, usually six sessions, used by Kernberg and his associates (Kernberg et al., 1981) has not had adequate support for its reliability. In part this is because of the level of pathology the process attempted to measure and the length of the assessment, which may reduce reliability.

The research on the assessment and measurement of the borderline construct tends to identify rather clear characteristics. As Tarnopolsky and Berelowitz (1987) summarize, the core characteristics include ''unstable interpersonal relationships, with idealization and denigration of others, intense unpredictable feelings, and impulsive, often self-destructive behavior'' (p. 726). Some of the other most defining characteristics are stress-related psychotic symptoms and regression.

As is evident from the above theoretical discussion, many of these characteristics reflect what have been defined as ego functions. Whether or not the specific dynamic-oriented intervention we are about to discuss is the most effective means of helping clients with this problem awaits future research.

Structure of the Treatment

There are four general approaches to treating the borderline client: psychoanalysis, analytically oriented psychotherapy, dynamically oriented psychotherapy, and supportive psychotherapy. Goldstein (1985, 1988) defines these on a continuum from insight-oriented and exploratory to supportive and care giving. Let us briefly consider each of the four approaches.

Psychoanalysis involves four or five weekly sessions, and is frequently conducted by having the client recline on a couch and free associate. All three of these components (frequent sessions, reclining, and free association) facilitate an intensive transference relationship. In essence, the client transfers or displays feelings and thoughts, as well as defenses against them, to the clinician. The emotions and cognitions may be real or fantasied. The crucial component of change is considered to be the resolution of the transference relationship by means of insight; consequently, the clinician relies on interpretation of the transference. This form of treatment is the least advisable for a borderline client because the regression is far too great for the client's weak ego functions.

Analytically oriented psychotherapy involves less frequent sessions than psychoanalysis, usually two a week. The clinician uses interpretation as much as possible, but does not rely on free association or a couch to develop the transference relationship. Transference is encouraged so that the client can gain insight and change. The borderline personality's tendency to regress and to distort the relationship with the clinician is seen as facilitating the transference relationship.

Dynamically oriented treatment focuses on the client's daily activities, with particular attention given to how these events correlate with the client's past. Assuming a fairly active stance, clinician and client together try to understand the current interactions from the basis of the client's sensitivities, vulnerabilities, and distortions. The clinician uses techniques similar to those of the support approach (see below), but may include partial interpretation. The role of transference is minimized in dynamically oriented treatment.

Supportive treatment is especially appropriate for persons with disturbed ego functions; its purpose is to help build a weak ego. Supportive psychotherapy uses education, suggestion, clarification, reassurance, and instructions; it rarely includes interpretation, because the client's ego is not sufficiently strong to tolerate the anxiety and frustration that facilitate insight. The clinician attempts to maintain his or her neutrality, and the sessions tend to focus on the daily activities that resulted from the client's impaired ego functions.

Supportive psychotherapy may be particularly useful in agency settings because all too often there is not sufficient time for the long-term treatment needed to help change the enduring traits of the borderline personality. Further, in agency settings you, the social worker, may be the first professional a person with a borderline personality encounters. This may be because of the crises the client experiences and the fact that borderline clients are often ordered to treatment by the legal system because of antisocial behaviors. However, as Freed (1980, p. 3) points out, "limitations of time and staff, treatment methods and the client's lack of motivation contribute to the despair of the social agencies in treating these people."

Therefore, even though the therapeutic need of the borderline client is for substantial change in the personality structure and interpersonal behaviors, in agency settings it is very likely that the initial treatment will need to be supportive. It will also be beneficial to direct your attention to concrete social services. Here you should not rule out or discount the value of goal-directed short-term treatment. Your focus should be on small, manageable immediate issues, such as arranging placement in a day treatment program or referring the client to services where long-term treatment is available. As Freed notes, providing concrete services can be "a means of reaching the client" (1980, p. 554). However, it may follow that the client does not receive the treatment services needed. Even if you make a referral in good faith, the borderline person may very well feel neglected, abandoned, or "passed on" in spite of your well-meaning intentions.

Choosing your approach.   When long-term treatment is available, you must take an approach that facilitates the development of the client's ego functions (i.e., ego building). It will be necessary for you to use your own ego to act as an auxiliary one for the borderline client (Eckrich, 1985). For example, you will need to use good judgment and constancy to facilitate such client ego functions as judgment and the sense of object constancy. In this sense, it is important for your client to identify with you and transfer the feelings and thoughts, along with the accompanying defenses, to your clinical relationship. Needless to say, this requires (a) that the agency permit long-term treatment; and (b) that you have the capacity to work with very difficult persons.

Forming a therapeutic alliance.   Freed (1980) elaborates on the capacities a social worker must have to work with a borderline client. Her suggestions include that you reach out to form a therapeutic alliance and offer support and understanding that were missing from the client's early relationships. You must not be passive, and you must establish yourself as someone who will focus on reality issues and problem solving. It is necessary to establish an atmosphere of mutual respect and an expectation of achieving successful results. It is also helpful to set up ground rules and a contract with the client that state that impulsive acting-out will cease and that the pressures to do so will be discussed in treatment. You must be caring and nurturing, and must make this evident early in the course of treatment. If the client has a family, Freed believes strongly that you should engage them in the treatment process.

Freed further asserts that to effectively help a borderline client you must be flexible and creative. You must have a feel for when to get close to the client and when to honor the client's fear of intimacy. Setting limits and having clear and well-defined expectations are very important. A reality orientation is necessary in order to give the client the positive modeling needed to work through the splitting of good and bad object representations. Finally, then, the borderline client can integrate these into a whole and gain the ability to appreciate that people can have some good and some not-so-good qualities.

Even after the borderline client has made a commitment to continue treatment, you should bear in mind that these clients have high dropout rates (Gunderson et al., 1989). Once the client has established a meaningful level of trust in you, long-term work may begin. Numerous issues will be presented once you have established the necessary trust. Rage, depression, fears of abandonment, a history of unstable personal relationships, lack of identity, feelings of emptiness, complaints of nonreality, gripes about past social workers by whom the client felt deserted, and constant job friction all will be grist for the therapeutic mill. They should be discussed, with your client ventilating and then receiving reality-based feedback.

Setting goals.   There are many long-term goals for the borderline client. Freed delineates ten:

1. Integrate good and bad splits
2. Accept the primary ambivalence rather than fight it

3. Bring primitive idealizations and projective identification within reality contexts and develop normal repression

4. Develop mature dependence through the therapeutic relationship

5. Establish efforts at mastery, impulse control, and frustration tolerance

6. Engage the ego in realistic planning and healthy coping behavior through the problem-solving process

7. Feel better about oneself, accept these good feelings, and achieve an improved self-image by reducing self-defeating behaviors and recognizing accomplishments

8. Accept one's separateness and wholeness

9. Establish the capacity to relate to others and allow others to relate to oneself with trust and warmth; permit closeness without fusion, separateness without abandonment, and individuality within the social and family context

10. Meet concrete needs and use the therapeutic experience to build relationships and trust

Effective Interventions.   With such a complex client problem and elusive goals, you might ask, "What can I actually do to help the borderline client?" In the past two decades, the approach to treatment of the borderline personality has, in fact, developed from a highly supportive approach (e.g., Zetzel, 1971), where the client was thought to be unable to internalize a sufficiently stable ego identification, to use of interventions that are much more encompassing. The current mode of thinking, supported by Kernberg (1975), Masterson (1976), Buie and Adler (1982), and others, is aimed at the resolution of the pathological distortions through the use of intensive psychotherapy. Essentially, as Freed asserts, you will want to use "confrontation, insight, interpretation, supportiveness, availability, crisis intervention and transference," (Freed, 1980, p. 555).

Adler (1985) outlines a three-phase intervention. The first phase is concerned with establishing and maintaining a dyadic relationship in which the therapist can be used by the client as a holding self-object. The second phase facilitates the resolution of the transference so that the borderline client sees the clinician more realistically. Assuming the success of these two phases, in the third phase the client generalizes the knowing, esteem-building, and loving experience from the clinician to a significant other.

More specificity to the components of effective treatment is delineated by Waldinger (1987). The eight basic components discussed below tend to be accepted by most authors working with borderline clients, even though there is disagreement about the use of the four approaches outlined earlier.

1. Establish stability in the framework of the treatment.   This means setting regular appointment times and expressing your expectations that the client will keep the appointments and pay the fees. Feelings about missed or changed appointments must be addressed openly and honestly and without exception. If you make exceptions, the borderline client may very well distort this and perceive you as manipulatable, weak, and not a constant holding environment. That is, you will be seen as an untrustworthy and unconstant object relationship; and such relationships were, theoretically, part of the origin of the client's problems.

2. Keep increasing your activity as a clinician.   With the borderline personality you must always be active. This serves to emphasize your presence, anchor the client in reality, and minimize the distortion of the transference relationship. A couple of ways to establish yourself as active are to verbally support self-enhancing relationships and confront self-defeating behaviors.

3. Tolerate the client's hostility.   You must be able to withstand verbal assaults from the borderline client without withdrawing or retaliating. This enables the client to begin to examine and master his or her pattern of relating to others. Remember, as was mentioned in the discussion of projective identification, often the borderline client will actively try to get you to confirm the projected qualities. If you get angry and tell the client off, you are simply confirming a distorted perception, for example, that "you never really did care." The ability to tolerate your client's behavior requires that you be secure in your own sense of self and not internalize or overreact to the client's behavior.

4. Make self-destructive behaviors ungratifying to the borderline client.   Borderline clients are very skilled at remaining unaware of self-destructive behaviors that they use to gratify wishes and allay anxiety. For example, a client might mistreat a date such that the person never calls again; after all, the client "knows" that the other person really was not interested in him or her anyway, and the fact that the other has not called just confirms it. It is your job to point out repeatedly to the client the adverse consequence of such self-defeating behaviors. Other self-destructive behaviors that are commonly seen with borderline clients include sexual acting-out, drug and alcohol abuse, and inappropriate bursts of anger, either in terms of the intensity of the anger or the circumstances stimulating the anger. In confronting the self-defeating behaviors you should focus on the outcome of the behavior rather than on the client's stated intent. This will help the borderline client learn cause-and-effect relationship and object consistency, which were not mastered in his or her early development.

5. Establish a connection between the client's action and affect in the here-and-now. Because the borderline client's actions frequently serve as a defense against the awareness of uncomfortable feelings, you must aid the client in acknowledging and understanding that his or her communication through action has a defensive function. For example, the ungracious dating behavior mentioned above defends the client against feeling fears of abandonment.

6. Block acting-out behaviors. The borderline client uses acting-out as a resistance to awareness of transference and, therefore, to growth. It will be necessary for you to set limits on behaviors that threaten the safety of your client, yourself, or the treatment. For example, you should refuse to see the client if he or she arrives for treatment under the influence of drugs or alcohol.

7. Focus early clarifications and intervention on the here-and-now. That is, similar to the dynamically oriented psychotherapy discussed above, you should avoid being manipulated to examine the past for the past's sake. Early family interpretation, for example, will be counterproductive. It is important for you to focus on immediate and dangerous acting-out behaviors. You might want to use current behaviors to illustrate the influence of past development, but keep the focus of your attention on the immediacy of how the client is behaving.

8. Pay careful attention to your countertransference feelings. This component is often one of the most difficult, especially to novice practitioners. By constantly monitoring your countertransference reactions you will minimize your own acting-out of feelings. In this sense, you must strive to be neutral. Neutrality is difficult with borderline clients, however, because they are masters at manipulation. You should use your countertransference feelings to further help your client change by confronting him or her and illustrating how he or she provokes others.

This last component has been a source of controversy, especially in terms of when in the sequence of the treatment process it should be used (Goldstein, 1988; Waldinger, 1987). Clinicians who work with borderline clients disagree over whether transference interpretation is actually helpful early on in the treatment or whether creating a holding environment is the style that is essential. A few words on these two positions may be useful.

Kernberg (1975) maintains that the primitive defenses of the borderline client (e.g., splitting and denial) will ensure that he or she will distort your comments. He further asserts that by clarifying such misperceptions early in the session, primitive defenses can be replaced by higher-level ones, a stronger ego will result, and the client can then make use of the comments. Masterson (1976) agrees, and sees the main task as controlling the acting-out by repeatedly clarifying the self-destructive nature of such behaviors. By doing so, you are making the behavior ego-dystonic, which means that it is alien to the wishes of the ego. Masterson further asserts that when this is accomplished, the client is able to accept your comments without gross distortions.

The ability of the borderline client to make use of your interpretation may be dependent on other variables. For example, the client's level of anxiety, how he or she relates to you, and whether there is some current stress between the client and you (such as might be the case with an upcoming vacation), all can affect the intensity of the client's transference and his or her tendency to distort interpretations. This is why, in part, Freed (1980) stresses the need for you to be flexible and creative and to use your own good judgment in working with a borderline client.

The holding environment position is dramatically stated by Buie and Adler (1982) and Adler (1985). They claim that the core of the borderline pathology lies in a failure to develop holding and soothing introjects as an infant. They, therefore, do not propose to "undo what is already there and malformed (as Kernberg and Masterson propose) but to create what never existed" (Waldinger, 1987). This position requires the client to use the clinician as a holding self-object that performs the soothing and holding functions the client cannot perform on his or her own. You might provide a soothing and holding function by such supports as hospitalization, telephone contacts between sessions, and additional appointments. While on vacation, you might send a postcard. Freed (1980) cites a case example in which the social worker made herself available for telephone interviews and occasionally called the client "just to keep in touch." This may also help to facilitate the transference relationship such that the client's affects and thoughts can be discussed in treatment. It is not the content that effectively helps the client, Buie and Adler (1985) claim, but that the clinician is stable, caring, consistent, nonpunitive, survives the client's rage, and continues to serve as a holding object that was absent in the client's early development.

GENERALIZING THE INTERVENTION TO RELATED PROBLEMS

Much of what we have discussed above is applicable to work with other personality disorders. Clients who are maladaptive, who suffer from feelings of dissatisfaction, despair, and emptiness, who make the rounds of therapists hoping to find relief from their pain, fall into the antisocial, borderline, histrionic, and narcissistic personality disorder classification. At times it is not easy to differentiate entirely among the four, and indeed clients present overlapping characteristics and features that make the diagnosis that much more difficult.

There are a few relational capacities that you should look for when generalizing the dynamically oriented treatment to any of these personality disorders. Silver (1985) favors looking at relational capacities as a means of determining therapeutic strategies. Has the client sustained an important relationship for at least a year, or could he or she do so? If not, chances are this client is too fragile for intensive psychotherapy. Can the client develop an empathetic therapeutic bridge with the therapist? If the early developmental damage experienced is too extensive, this capacity may not be there and crisis intervention and short-term treatment approaches may be the preferred interventions. Does the client have the capacity to soothe, comfort, and solace others and, in turn, be comforted and solaced by others? If this capacity is present, long-term treatment has a better chance of success. In all cases, negotiating a therapeutic contract is essential to minimize undesirable effects. Borderline clients tend to expect magic from their social workers and "they impose on them the fantasy of original nurturer" (Silver, 1985, p. 366). It is imperative, then, that the client know what can realistically be expected from your social work intervention.

Because repression is not a very stable form of defense for these clients, Silver goes on to assert that a great deal of unconscious material is also available from the beginning of assessment. It is wise to be cautious about making interpretations too early, however, as this can be devastating for these clients and may contribute to mild psychotic symptoms. This, in fact, is why psychoanalysis is rarely warranted with borderline or other personality disorders.

There has been a great deal of discussion regarding the differentiation of borderlines from narcissistic personalities. A few words to differentiate borderline and narcissistic disorders for the purpose of treatment may be in order. The borderline is brittle, self-devaluing, erratic, and full of rage. The narcissistic personality fears humiliation, is cold, relates poorly, and covers it all with grandiosity. The borderline is hostile and may direct it toward himself or herself, but more likely directs it toward others (Freed, 1980). The borderline client is clingy, demanding, angry, and dependent. The narcissistic client may bore the social worker with self-preoccupation, and be aware of the social worker only when idealizing, mirroring, or attempting to seduce him or her. You will need to keep these differences in mind when working with both the borderline and the narcissist. Empathy is essential when treating the narcissistic person. However, if you are seduced into becoming an idealized figure for the narcissistic client, he or she may distort or change perceptions and turn against you.

SUMMARY

This chapter reviewed the theoretical considerations of the borderline personality disorder, although briefly, and outlined some of the more salient features of working with clients with this clinically challenging disorder. The research in this area tends to be more idiographic than monothetic, with a reliance on case studies and clinical observations. Sample-based research is beginning to emerge, especially in the area of assessment and diagnosis.

Our examination of the treatment strategies for the borderline client reveals several general characteristics: creation of a constant holding environment, use of supportive techniques, the availability of the social worker's ego as an auxiliary ego for the client, the use of confrontation, and the importance of consistency and commitment. Transference and countertransference were outlined as major factors in treating the borderline client.

We supplied guidelines for distinguishing between clients with borderline personality disorder and those with narcissistic disorders and discussed the use of empathy in treatment. For narcissistic personalities, empathy is the essential ingredient (Kohut and Wolff, 1978); however, too much empathy may be seen as a sign of weakness by clients with borderline personality disorder. When working with clients with borderline personality disorder (as well as those with other personality disorders, especially narcissism), it is very important that you maintain a strong toehold on reality and constantly monitor the pitfalls of countertransference. Failure to do so will only be used to support the client's distorted perceptions. Establishing explicit short-term and long-term goals is helpful in this regard. By successfully maintaining your own sense of reality, confronting the client's distorted reality, and providing a constant holding environment where the client can learn trust in self and others are some of the first steps to effectively helping a borderline client change.

CHAPTER 14

Mediation Techniques for Persons Involved in Disputes

William R. Nugent

In this chapter, Nugent discusses interpersonal, nonviolent conflicts and shows how to use mediation to resolve such disputes. The fact that these disputes exclude violent conflicts illustrates the important principle of defining what specific problem to use with an appropriate intervention. Mediation itself has several well-defined components that help to arrive at mutually agreeable outcomes in a dispute. The components of mediation include establishing rapport, ventilating feelings, caucusing, defining the problem, generating solutions, and implementation. Drawing from a variety of theoretical perspectives, Nugent also shows how to use techniques such as reframing. The importance of client participation in problem solving and contracting is also illustrated.

INTRODUCTION

Numerous practice settings can present the social worker with interpersonal conflict and the practice-related problem of helping to resolve it. Examples include:

- You are a school social worker who is asked to intervene with two students who were about to come to blows over some issue.

- You are a social worker in a residential program for adolescents, such as a runaway shelter. The mother of a client, during a visit to see her daughter in the shelter, suddenly becomes very angry, grabs her daughter, and threatens to "knock her block off."

- You are doing community organization work and are faced with a dispute between a group of residents in a neighborhood and a minority family that has just moved to the area.

- You are working as a community mediator for a county court system. You are asked to help resolve a dispute between two neighbors over a barking dog.

- You are working as a therapist and are asked to help a divorcing couple work out a divorce settlement.

In each of these situations, the social worker is faced with a dispute and the task of helping resolve interpersonal conflict.

Conflict is an inevitable aspect of life and interpersonal relationships. Strayhorn (1977, p. 1) writes, "Conflict is the rule, not the exception, in human relationships." In and of itself, conflict is neither "good" nor "bad," adaptive nor maladaptive. What is of critical importance is the manner in which individuals involved in a dispute attempt to manage the conflict. Properly handled, conflicted situations present a wonderful opportunity for the enrichment of interpersonal relationships and the growth of individuals and society. Improperly managed, conflict can lead to numerous destructive outcomes, such as the deterioration or destruction of relationships, families, and, in some cases, human beings, as in the case of physical violence and war.

Some all-too-commonly used procedures for resolving conflict are adversarial and have "win/lose" outcomes. With such approaches, one party in a dispute "wins" (for example, is "right" or is the last person standing after a fist fight) and the other "loses" (for example, is "wrong" or sustains the most physical damage in a fist fight). Unfortunately, regardless of who wins or loses in an adversarial approach to conflict resolution, the relationship loses. Thus, if the disputants are involved in some type of ongoing relationship, whatever it might be, it is of great importance to avoid win/lose approaches to conflict resolution.

A far more desirable approach to resolving conflict is a cooperative one in which outcomes are "win/win." Such an approach leaves all persons with the sense that their needs have been met. More importantly, the relationship involved wins in that it continues and becomes stronger, deeper, and richer than before the conflict was worked through.

This chapter presents one win/win approach to conflict resolution. You will learn a strategy, an overall plan, for settling disputes. This strategy is essentially a problem-solving approach to conflict resolution. You will also learn several specific intervention procedures that help implement this win/win strategy. These interventions are drawn from a number of areas, including methods of community conflict resolution, the hypnotic work of Milton H. Erickson, cognitive-behavior therapy, a number of systems of marriage and family therapy, and the writings of social workers. The role that you will have in helping resolve disputes will be that of a *mediator*, and the process itself will be called *dispute resolution* or *mediation*.

PROBLEM IDENTIFICATION

Disputes, Conflicts, and Their Manifestations

Conflict arises any time people involved in relationships, such as friends, family members, co-workers, or neighbors, have differing needs, wants, desires, expectations, goals, or means of achieving certain ends (Strayhorn, 1977). The aspects of conflict that the social worker will want to observe are not only the content (i.e., the issues over which persons differ) of the conflict, but also the means being used to attempt to resolve the conflict. Indeed, the conflict itself is not the problem. Rather, it is the means being used to attempt to resolve the conflict that is the problem to be worked on. This is an example of a principle of problem formation and resolution developed by Watzlawick, Weakland, and Fisch (1974): the attempted solution to a difficulty (such as conflicting goals, desires, expectations, etc.) can lead to a "problem." When this happens, it is the attempted solution that becomes the target of change, not the difficulty that spawned the attempted solution. Thus, the social worker in the role of mediator will work to interrupt the ongoing problematic attempts at conflict resolution that disputants have been using and involve them in a cooperative, win/win dispute resolution process.

There are a number of common indicators of ineffective and adversarial methods of conflict resolution. They are the indicators of attempted solutions to conflict that have created a problem for those involved, and include:

- Anger that increases in intensity over the course of the attempted resolution
- Movement towards more aggressive, hostile, forceful, destructive, and nonpeaceful resolution tactics
- Mistrust that increases in intensity
- Increased polarization of persons in the dispute, who become more firmly entrenched in rigid positions, demands for particular "solutions," and perceptions of one another
- Movement away from negotiation tactics
- Blaming stances and message styles
- Increased use of "obstructive message styles," such as overgeneralizing and speaking about general ways of being (Strayhorn, 1977)
- Misunderstanding of other people's views, positions, needs, etc.
- A "tunnel vision" negative view of other persons (Beck, 1988)
- A negative bias in attribution of motives to other persons involved in the dispute (Beck, 1988)

The greater the number and intensity of these indicators in any dispute, the more volatile and problematic the methods being used by disputants in an attempt to resolve the conflict are.

Assessment and Monitoring

As the social worker helps people resolve disputes, he or she may want to evaluate objectively any interventions used as part of the process. There are a number of objective assessment tools available. The particular measurement instrumentation used will depend upon the relational context in which the conflict occurs, such as marriage, family, professional, business, peer-relationship, and so forth. For example, the State portion of the State-Trait Anger Scale (Spielberger et al., 1983) might be used to monitor the level of anger felt by disputants. The social worker might work with the disputants to develop a self-anchored scale to measure specific aspects of the conflict (Bloom and Fischer, 1982). Self-anchored scales are easy to construct, client- and problem-specific (Bloom and Fischer, 1982), and some research has suggested that they can have psychometric characteristics comparable to those of standardized Likert-type scales (Nugent, 1991). "Thought listing" procedures may be used to assess and monitor cognitive aspects of conflict in a more qualitative manner (Cacioppo and Petty, 1981). The following are excellent sources of measurement instrumentation: Hudson (1982); Corcoran and Fischer (1987); Chun, Cobb, and French (1975); Comery et al. (1975); Goldman and Sanders (1974); and Goldman and Busch (1978, 1982).

The social worker can use data gathered from his or her measurement procedures and single-case design methodology to monitor graphically how the dispute resolution process is progressing, as discussed in chapter 3 of this book. At the simplest level, the social worker may make repeated measures of aspects of the dispute (such as levels of disputants' anger) during the dispute resolution process, plot the resulting measurements on a graph, and thereby monitor progress (or lack thereof) using an intervention-only design. More complex evaluation procedures also may be used.

THE DISPUTE RESOLUTION STRATEGY

The dispute resolution strategy may be described as a five-phase problem-solving process:

1. Establishing rapport and dissipating or altering "nonfacilitative" or "negative" feelings

2. Defining the conflict issues in behavioral or negotiable terms from the viewpoints of all involved parties

3. Generating as many alternative "solution options" as possible

4. Choosing from the alternative "solution options" and creating a composite plan for resolving the dispute

5. Implementing the composite plan and evaluating its effectiveness

This process, though modeled in five sequential and distinct phases, should not be taken to be linear. You may need to return to a previous phase one or more times during the course of helping to resolve a dispute. Indeed, the first step, establishing rapport, is a continuous process that must be maintained throughout the entire conflict resolution endeavor.

Specific Intervention Tactics

Several specific intervention procedures that help the social worker to implement the overall strategy will be described in this section. The specific intervention techniques to be discussed, and the phases of the conflict resolution process in which they are useful, are listed in table 14-1.

Establishing Rapport and Dissipating Feelings.   The mediator must first establish rapport with each person involved in the dispute. Rapport may be defined as a warm, empathic relationship within which the disputants have a sense of trust in the mediator (Welton, Pruitt, and McGillicuddy, 1988). According to Welton et al. (1988), rapport serves a critical function:

> Rapport contributes to successful mediation in several ways. It facilitates mediator influence over the disputants and makes the disputants more committed to the mediation process. . . . Rapport may even contribute to one disputant's taking the needs of the other disputant more seriously, since the mediator, who is trusted, is seen to take these needs seriously. . . . (p. 182)

The mediator also must facilitate the dissipation, as much as possible, of strong ''nonfacilitative'' feelings. A ''nonfacilitative'' emotion is one that hinders the creation of a cooperative, mutually satisfying resolution to a dispute. Examples of such feelings are anger, resentment, hate, fear, and confusion. Anger especially must be safely and effectively dissipated. When disputants are in the grip of such feelings they are unlikely to work to understand other disputants or to negotiate win/win solutions. Indeed, disputants in the grip of strong feelings may be hindered in any attempts to cooperatively resolve a dispute by the phenomenon of ''mood congruent recall.'' This term refers to the apparent inability of people to bring to mind memories that are inconsistent with a specific mood, such as hostility or depression (Barlow, 1988). For example, a husband who is feeling hostile towards his wife will have great difficulty remembering incidents in which his wife did something that left him feeling warm and affectionate towards her. This will remain true until his hostile mood has changed to one that is more amiable towards her.

TABLE 14–1   Intervention Procedures for Dispute Resolution Phases

Phase I: Establishing Rapport and Dissipating/Ventilating Feelings

Interventions (use A., B., and C. in an opening statement during a joint meeting)
  A. Establishing rules for interactions
  B. Establishing psychological contracts
  C. Defining participants' role behaviors
  D. Active listening
  E. Caucusing
  F. Reframing

Phase II: Defining the Conflict

Interventions
  A. Use of behaviorally specific language
  B. Reframing
  C. Listening for implied definitions of the dispute

Phase III: Generating Alternative Solutions

Interventions
  A. Caucusing
  B. Brainstorming
  C. Reframing

Phase IV: Choosing Alternatives and Creating a Plan

Interventions
  A. Rating alternatives
  B. Caucusing
  C. Quid pro quo contract negotiations

Phase V: Implementing the Plan and Evaluating Its Effectiveness

Interventions
  A. Quid pro quo contract
  B. Agreeing upon follow-up meetings

Four specific intervention procedures that are useful for establishing rapport and dissipating strong feelings are: (1) imposing structure and defining roles (Levi and Benjamin, 1977); (2) active, or empathic, listening (Gordon, 1970; Hepworth and Larsen, 1986; Alexander, 1979); (3) caucusing (Welton, Pruitt, and McGillicuddy, 1988); and (4) reframing (Watzlawick et al., 1974; Fisch et al., 1982; Watzlawick, 1978; Bandler and Grinder, 1982).

The goal of mediation is the production of a solution that resolves the dispute. Consequently, it involves both task and process components (Levi and Benjamin, 1977). An intervention that helps achieve both process and outcome goals is the imposition of structure upon the interactions between disputants (Levi and Benjamin, 1977). This can be achieved through several techniques that are described below.

Establishing ground rules for the mediation process. The mediator can impose structure by describing rules governing participants' behavior during the mediation process. The rules used, such as no interruptions while another is speaking, can be designed so as to help facilitate the development of rapport and hinder the escalation of nonfacilitative emotions and behavior.

Establishing a psychological contract with all participants involved in the conflict resolution process. This contract calls for each participant to adopt, as much as possible, a problem-solving orientation during the conflict resolution process. It also calls for each participant to express his or her feelings and views openly and honestly, but in a manner that follows the structure of the mediation process and behavioral ground rules for participants laid out by the mediator.

Defining the role behaviors of all participants. This is done, in part, through the psychological contract already discussed. Role behaviors are further prescribed by the mediator, who describes her or his own functions in the process. It often is useful to define one of the roles as that of translator. This role requires the mediator to work to alleviate misunderstandings between the disputants that seem to result from misperceptions and misinterpretations of what others are saying. It also is useful to frame the role of the mediator as one of helping each participant get, as much as possible, what he or she wants during the resolution process. In other words, the process is framed as a cooperative win/win procedure from the beginning of the mediation.

The opening statement. Each of these procedures can be implemented in an "opening statement" made by the mediator at the beginning of a mediation session. The mediator takes a few minutes in a joint meeting of the disputants to clearly verbalize ground rules, get all parties to agree to the psychological contract, and define the role behaviors of participants. The first few minutes of a mediation session can be very important to the ultimate success of the mediation work.

Active listening. Hepworth and Larsen (1986) and Gordon (1970) give in-depth discussion on what active or empathic listening is and how it is done, so I will not spend a lot of time on the "how tos" of this procedure. The reader probably has already encountered this interpersonal communication method and has a sense of its value. There is both practice wisdom and research evidence that suggest that this technique is helpful in facilitating change.

It is almost impossible for a social worker (or anyone else) to be too proficient at active listening. It is important in conflict resolution work to listen not only for feelings but also for how disputants interpret events, behaviors, and situations. Numerous writers have pointed out that it is not the events, behaviors, or situations that cause people distress, but rather the symbolic meanings they attribute to these things (Beck, 1976, 1988; Burns, 1980; Watzlawick et al., 1974; Watzlawick, 1976, 1978).

Disputants often will confuse a possible solution to a conflict situation with the needs or wants that are at the heart of the dispute. For example, a young woman in a residential program for adolescents who was in a dispute with a young man over a missing radio said, "I want him arrested! I know he stole it and I am sick of having things stolen! There have been a bunch of my things stolen and no one cares. No one, not even the counselors, has done anything about my things." The mediator, using active listening, noted to the young woman, "It sounds like you're really sick of things disappearing and no one paying attention to your complaints. It also sounds like the most important thing to you is that you find a way to get people in the shelter to respect your belongings. More importantly, you need to feel that your things are safe in the shelter . . . to feel that you have some space of your own and a sense of security for your stuff." This statement by the mediator apparently functioned to separate the potential solution of arresting the young man (which, it turns out, meant in the young woman's mind that others in the shelter would be frightened and therefore leave her things alone) from the more fundamental issue of the young woman wanting to feel that her belongings were secure. Up until this point, the young woman has been rigidly stuck on having the young man arrested as the only possible solution. Subsequent to the active listening statement, the young woman became open to a number of alternative possibilities.

Caucusing.   Caucusing refers to the intervention tactic of meeting separately with each person (or group) involved in a dispute (Welton et al., 1988). This is to be distinguished from joint, or conjoint, meetings, in which all persons involved in the conflict are present. There are a number of potential outcomes from caucusing that facilitate cooperative dispute resolution and win/win outcomes:

- Reductions in levels of anger, tension, and defensiveness
- Acquisition of information about interests, assumptions, and interpretations underlying the conflict
- Increased levels of rapport between mediator and disputant as a result of the mediator's ability to focus on the individual (or individual group).
- Increased effectiveness of brainstorming for alternative solutions and increased willingness to consider alternative resolutions to the conflict
- Increased ability of the mediator to focus responsibility for coming up with creative alternative solutions on the individual or individual group

- Increased ability of the mediator to influence the behavior of individual disputants

Most of these advantages accrue because of the absence of the other persons involved in the dispute. Blades (1984), Evarts et al. (1983), Kolb (1983), and Witty (1980) discuss the theoretical reasons for use of caucusing. Welton et al. (1988) present experimental evidence demonstrating the facilitative effects of caucusing. Taylor, Barry, and Block (1958), Dunnette, Campbell, and Joasted (1963), and Bouchard (1972) give research evidence of the superiority of individual brainstorming over that done by a group of individuals.

There are a few disadvantages to caucusing. Welton et al. (1988) note that disputant statements in caucus sessions are likely to be less accurate than those in joint sessions. Also, occasionally a disputant may be able to coopt the mediator. Marriage and family therapists have warned about the dangers of being told something by a spouse or family member in an individual meeting session that the person wants kept confidential, a situation that can accuse substantial difficulties if managed improperly. Also, poorly timed caucus sessions may interrupt joint problem-solving discussions between disputants. Finally, problems may arise if the disputants who are not involved in the caucus sessions talk with friends, relatives, or other supporters and are influenced by input from these sources.

Reframing. Reframing is a useful and versatile intervention technique (Watzlawick et al., 1984; Watzlawick, 1978; Bandler and Grinder, 1982). This procedure also is called relabeling (Weeks and L'Abate, 1982) or redefining (Hepworth and Larsen, 1986). Watzlawick et al. (1974, p. 95) write that to reframe means, ''. . . to change the conceptual and/or emotional setting or viewpoint in relation to which a situation is experienced and to place it in another frame which fits the 'facts' of the same concrete situation equally well or even better, and thereby changes its entire meaning.'' To reframe some event, behavior, or situation means to change how it is interpreted, which changes the meaning that the event, behavior, or situation has for the client. The person's world view, perception, understanding—in a sense their "truth"—has been altered (Watzlawick, 1978). By changing the interpretation, the person's emotional response also changes. Thus, reframing can be used as an intervention to alter intense emotions and problematic behavioral expressions of emotion (Nugent, 1989). Reframing also can be used to break up the rigid, limited view of a situation that persons involved in a dispute may hold. It also can be used as a means of changing disputants' perceptions so that they may become more open to considering alternative solutions to a dispute. Indeed, sometimes simply reframing how something is interpreted can eliminate a problem, with no other intervention needed.

One of the clearest, and perhaps most creative, examples of reframing comes from the clinical work of Milton Erickson. Erickson was approached by the mother of a fourteen-year-old girl who had become obsessed with the idea that her feet were too large. The mother told Erickson that the girl had become more and more withdrawn over the past three months and that all the mother's efforts to reassure her daughter had failed. The girl had become very seclusive. Erickson, being a medical doctor, arranged to give the mother a physical exam at her home with the daughter in attendance. In Haley (1973) Erickson recounts:

> When I arrived at the home, the mother was in bed. I did a careful examination. . . . The girl was present. I sent her for a towel, and I asked that she stand beside me in case I needed something. . . . This gave me an opportunity to look her over. She was rather stoutly built and her feet were not large.
> Studying the girl, I wondered what I could do to get her over this problem. Finally, I hit upon a plan. As I finished my examination of the mother, I maneuvered the girl into a position directly behind me. I was sitting on the bed talking to the mother, and I got up slowly and carefully and then stepped back awkwardly. I put my heel down squarely on the girl's toes. The girl, of course, squawked with pain. I turned to her and in a tone of absolute fury said, "If you would grow those things *large* enough for a *man* to see, I would not be in this sort of situation!" The girl looked at me, puzzled, while I wrote out a prescription and called the drug store. That day the girl asked her mother if she could go to a show, which she hadn't done in months. She went to school and church, and that was the end of three months' seclusiveness. (p. 198)

Erickson managed to change this girl's view of her feet, and put an end to an increasingly rigid pattern of behavior, with this one intervention. Other specific examples of reframing can be found in Haley (1973), Bandler and Grinder (1982), Weeks and L'Abate (1982), Watzlawick et al. (1974), Watzlawick (1978), and Hepworth and Larsen (1986).

There are two general ways in which a person's interpretation of events, behaviors, or situations may be reframed: the "systematic" procedure, and the "finesse" procedure. The cognitive-restructuring methods described by writers such as Burns (1980), Beck (1976, 1988), Williams (1984), Deschner (1988), and Persons (1989) are excellent examples of the "systematic" approach to reframing. The systematic approach has considerable clinical and experimental evidence of its effectiveness. Williams (1984) gives a good overview of evidence of its effectiveness in the treatment of clinical depression. Deschner (1988) gives clinical and experimental evidence of its impact in helping to decrease the frequency of physical abuse in battering couples. Barlow (1988) discusses evidence of its effectiveness in treatment of social phobias. Beckham and Watkins (1989) review research on the systematic approach. Nugent (1990) gives some experimental and clinical evidence concerning its effectiveness in altering frequency of episodes of explosive anger.

The following steps are involved in the systematic approach to reframing:

1. Frame part of the dispute between the involved parties as resulting from possibly erroneous perceptions. Explain how feelings and behavior appear to result, at least to some extent, from how a person thinks. For example, in families disputes can arise from individuals incorrectly "mind reading" the intentions and feelings of another family member.

2. Inform the person about any of a number of distorted thinking patterns, described by Burns (1980), Williams (1984), and Beck (1988), that seem relevant to the conflict. A list of these distorted patterns is provided in table 14-2.

3. Have the disputant relive in imagination a relevant part, or parts, of a conflict situation. During this revivification, have the person be alert for and identify "automatic thoughts" that seem to just pop up in the person's mind and are assigned the value of "truth" without any reality testing. Beck (1988) gives a description of this technique, which he calls the "instant replay."

4. Help the disputant to identify distortions in his or her automatic thoughts and challenge their validity by reality testing (Williams, 1984). This can be done by having the person write down accurate, distortion-free alternatives to the automatic thoughts. Reality testing also can be done by helping a disputant come up with some means of determining which of his or her views of an event, behavior, or situation are valid (Burns, 1980; Williams, 1984; Beck, 1988).

The systematic approach to reframing has been used most often in clinical contexts. However, you can adapt this reframing approach to any context in which you have good rapport with and will have multiple contacts with the disputants.

The "finesse" approach is exemplified by the reframing done by Erickson that is described above. In this approach, the mediator creates in his or her own mind an alternative interpretation of events, behaviors, or situations and attempts to communicate this alternate meaning to the disputant in such a way that he or she accepts it in lieu of the interpretation he or she has been holding. I label this the "finesse" approach because it is less obvious and less direct and takes more creativity and flexibility on the part of the mediator.

This approach to reframing has two fundamental steps:

1. The mediator creates an alternative interpretation, or framing, of an event, behavior, or situation that is different from that held by the disputant. This interpretation must fit the event, behavior, or situation

TABLE 14–2 Several Cognitive Distortions and Their Definitions

MIND READING: Assuming that one knows the thoughts, feelings, motives, intentions, etc., of another without him or her explicitly communicating them.
Example: Jane sees Bob frowning and thinks he is angry at her.

FORTUNE-TELLING ERROR: Imagining some event or happening in the future and then acting (i.e., basing one's subsequent behavior) as if this event or happening had already occurred.
Example: Joe imagines asking Sue out on a date and that she will turn down his request. So he does not ask her out.

OVERGENERALIZATION: Thinking that a particular behavior, event, or situation represents a never-ending exclusive pattern. This pattern may be involved with a phenomenon called mood congruent recall described by Barlow (1988).*
Example: A traffic light turns red as Jim is driving across town. While sitting at the light, Jim thinks to himself, "These lights always turn red for me."

PERSONALIZATION: Imagining that (1) the behavior of others is directed at oneself; and (2) that one is responsible for events, the behavior of others, or situations that one actually has little or no influence over.
Example 1: Jackie sees two people laughing at a table next to hers and thinks they are laughing at her.
Example 2: Joe's son is arrested for smoking marijuana, and Joe thinks that it is all his fault that his son got into drugs.

MAGNIFICATION: Blowing the significance of an event, behavior, or situation out of proportion.
Example: Betty gets a B on an exam and feels that she is a failure as a person.

MINIMIZATION: Belittling or minimizing the importance of some event, behavior, or situation.
Example: Eric goes through a master's degree program with all As and thinks, "It really means nothing."

CLAIRVOYANCE ERROR: Assuming that others can read you well enough to know what you need or want without your actually letting them know (sometimes this assumption is turned into an expectation or demand of another person).
Example: Kim gets home from work needing some comforting from Ed. She expects him to "know" she needs comforting without her telling him (and becomes resentful when he does not comfort her).

BIASED ATTRIBUTIONS: Attributing only negative (or positive) motives or interpretations to the behavior of another person. This distortion may also be related to the phenomenon of mood congruent recall.*
Example: Over time Jane comes to interpret all of Bill's behavior as coming from his "lack of concern for me."

TABLE 14–2   *(Continued)*

SELECTIVE FOCUS: Noticing only a particular type of event, behavior, or situation consistent with a particular belief, and ignoring (or failing to notice) those that are inconsistent with the belief.

Example: Bob has come to "believe" that his son "has no respect" for him. He notices behaviors that his son engages in that fit this belief, but fails to note times when his son behaves in ways that are inconsistent with this interpretation.

*Mood congruent recall refers to the phenomenon that human beings, when in a particular mood (such as feeling angry or depressed), will have an easy time remembering events that fit this mood and will have a very difficult time remembering events that do not fit this mood. See Barlow (1988) for a discussion.

---

involved and the framing used by the disputant, but also must entail different meanings and imply alternative solutions to those attempted by the disputant.

2. The mediator then must communicate this alternative interpretation to the disputant in such a way as to maximize the probability that he or she will drop the old interpretation and accept this new one.

There are a number of ways to create an alternative interpretation. You may directly change the meaning ascribed to the stimulus. For example, verbal labels such as "insensitive" that are used in a negative or pejorative manner can be reframed by merely redefining the meaning of the label. Thus, the label "insensitive" might be redefined to mean "defending oneself from being hurt." The label "submissive" might be redefined from a negative meaning to "seeking authority and direction." Weeks (1977) and Weeks and L'Abate (1982) give numerous other examples.

Time may be used as an element in reframing. For example, a disputant said, in an earlier example, "I want him arrested! I know he stole it and I am sick of having things stolen! There have been a bunch of my things stolen and no one cares. No one, not even the counselors, has done anything about my things." This person's perception of the situation and her proposed solution (having the other person arrested) might be reframed by the response, "Yes, you are angry at having your things turn up missing and *up to this point you have not thought of another way of getting what you want* besides having him arrested." The italicized portion of this statement (if accepted by the disputant) essentially puts the conflict into a frame of reference in which other solutions are possible but not imagined or thought of at this time. The implication is that, as time goes on, other solutions may be found that are satisfactory.

Another way in which reframing can be done is context reframing (Bandler and Grinder, 1982). This form of reframing is based upon the assumption that all behavior can be viewed as appropriate, given a relevant context. Thus, the practitioner finds a context in which a behavior, currently being rigidly framed in an all-or-nothing manner as problematic, would likely be viewed as positive. When done successfully, the rigid cognitive frame created by the disputant is disrupted, opening up the possibility of alternate solutions. Emotional responses can also be affected, both in intensity and in type of response. An example of this latter effect is that of a single mother whose son had been arrested for selling marijuana. This caused substantial conflict at home. The boy apparently had established a fairly substantial dealership. The mother framed the situation, in part, as the boy being "unbelievably bad," a problem that resulted from her "being a failure as a mother." This view was very rigid. The situation was reframed by having the woman imagine what the young man would need to do in order to establish a successful automobile dealership. She described tasks such as marketing, advertising, and public relations. This allowed me to reframe the situation to show that she had done quite a good job as a parent. Her son obviously had the ability to do all these things—he had to have done them to establish his drug dealership. Although it was quite unfortunate that he had chosen to sell an illegal product, she might well imagine how successful he might be if he were to choose to market a more socially acceptable product. The woman accepted this reframing and manifested quite different feelings and views of herself and her son.

There are some exercises at the end of this chapter that will help you to gain some skills at finesse reframing.

How a reframed interpretation is communicated to a disputant is critical to the success of this technique. You can increase the likelihood of acceptance by pacing the client prior to verbalizing the reframed interpretation (Bandler and Grinder, 1975; Lankton and Lankton, 1983). Pacing refers to meeting the client at his or her frame of reference prior to leading him or her into a new one. This can be done in the following manner:

1. Summarizing, via an active-listening type of paraphrase, the disputant's perceptions.

2. Using the disputant's language in this paraphrase. For example, if the disputant is an adolescent, you will not want to use words that are unlikely to be in his or her vocabulary.

3. Bridging from this pacing over into the reframed interpretation.

For example, let us return to the statements by the disputant, "I want him arrested! I know he stole it and I am sick of having things stolen! There have been a bunch of my things stolen and no one cares. No one, not even the counselors, has done anything about my things." In this situation, no one knew where the radio was or whether or not it had been stolen. The young woman's insistence that the young man be arrested inflamed him and inhibited the consideration and adoption of alternative solutions. The young woman's view, framed in her statements above, might be paced and then reframed in the following manner:

1. "Yes, you are very sick of your things disappearing."

2. "You are also sick of seeing other people around here react to your complaints in ways that seem uncaring."

3. "You also sound very angry that no one has yet responded to your complaints in a way that you see as caring."

4. "It sounds like one of the most important things to you is to know that your things are respected and that you have some private space."

Items 1 and 2 are pacing statements that utilize the woman's words "sick" and "cares." Item 3 is a pacing statement that bridges into a reframing using the time dimension. Item 4 is a reframing that may alter the young woman's proposed solution from aggressive retribution (throwing the accused young man into jail) to meeting needs of privacy, respect, and security. If the young woman accepts this reframing, a plethora of alternatives becomes available.

Historical evidence provides some practice wisdom concerning the effectiveness of finesse reframing from the context of international politics. One example is that of King Christian X of Denmark, who reframed a request from a special Nazi emissary for a solution to Denmark's "Jewish problem" by replying, "We do not have a Jewish problem; we don't feel inferior." Later, after the Germans issued an order that all Jews had to wear the Star of David, the king again reframed the situation by announcing that, because there were no differences between one Dane and another, the German order applied to all Danes and that he would be the first to wear the Star of David. The Danish population responded overwhelmingly to the king by wearing the Star of David and the Germans ended up canceling the order (Watzalwick et al., 1974, pp. 105–06). Fogg (1985) gives other approaches to, and examples of, reframing conflict.

Defining the conflict.   Reframing is an intervention that not only can be used to help defuse strong feelings, it also is useful during the problem definition phase. Most often disputants have unknowingly defined a dispute in such a manner that it cannot be resolved without one of the persons involved losing in some way, if it can be resolved at all. For example, when people argue over exactly how some past event occurred, there is little chance that the dispute can be satisfactorily settled. Reframing the dispute into something that can be settled is a very useful intervention tactic in such cases.

Consider again the young woman who says, ''I want him arrested! I know he stole it, and I am sick of having things stolen! There have been a bunch of my things stolen and no one cares. No one, not even the counselors, has done anything about my things.'' It would be very easy in this case to become involved in a no-win game of trying to determine whether or not the young man really did steal the woman's radio. With the dispute defined as, at least in part, ''did he or did he not steal the radio,'' the mediator can rest assured that the young man will fight vigorously to prove he did not, while the young woman will fight to prove he did. This is a win/lose definition of the conflict. Reframing the dispute into one in which the young woman finds a satisfactory means of feeling that her belongings are safe in the shelter changes the problem from one with essentially one solution (a verdict about the young man's guilt or innocence) into one with many alternative paths to resolution. Always listen carefully to how disputants are implicitly defining the conflict. Many times you will hear alternative definitions of a conflict implied by what disputants say, even though the exact content of their words may clearly define a dispute in win/lose terms. Once you hear such an implied alternative definition, you can reframe the dispute in these new terms, often with great success.

Another useful intervention during this phase of the conflict resolution strategy is the use of open-ended questions to elicit behaviorally specific definitions of behaviors that are being interpreted in ''problem'' terms. For example, a father complains that his son ''needs to show more respect for authority.'' The mediator might ask, ''How would you like for him to show you respect?'' as a means of eliciting behaviorally specific descriptions of ''respectful'' behavior. Strayhorn (1977) refers to this procedure as ''asking for more specific criticism.'' It is also useful to ask for specific examples of desired (or undesired) behaviors.

Generating alternative solutions.   In this phase, a useful intervention is brainstorming (Levi and Benjamin, 1977). This can be done in a caucus session, or by having disputants in a joint session write down alternatives (Levi and Benjamin, 1977). In brainstorming, the mediator has the disputants create as many alternative solutions (including wild, creative ones) as they can without evaluating the feasibility of the alternatives. Premature evaluation of alternatives tends to inhibit the creative process.

Choosing alternatives and devising a plan.   Useful procedures during these phrases are rating alternatives and use of a quid pro quo contract. Rating alternatives involves having disputants rate their level of satisfaction with a given alternative (Levi and Benjamin, 1977). This can be done by having each person rate his or her satisfaction on a scale from

-10 (totally dissatisfied) to $+10$ (totally satisfied). The disparity between scores can serve as an index of the degree of disagreement between disputants, and the sum-of-all-ratings for a given alternative can serve as a useful index of "total satisfaction" with an alternative. This procedure can be used by the mediator to operationalize the ideas of "maximal mutual satisfaction with a solution" and "win/win solution." The mediator works with disputants to develop a planned resolution that has the highest sum-of-all-ratings, and smallest discrepancy between ratings, among a set of possible solution plans. The plan with the highest sum-of-all-ratings and smallest difference between ratings will be the one that entails the greatest mutual satisfaction among disputants.

A quid pro quo contract is essentially an agreement between disputants that says, "I will do this, if you will do that," with the "this" and "that" spelled out in clear, behaviorally specific terms. There are a number of studies demonstrating the effectiveness of negotiating and contracting as a behavioral change procedure (e.g., Jacobson, 1978). The contract, which is best written and signed by all disputants, should specify who will do what with whom in what manner and when or in what situations or contexts. For example, a mediator might write the quid pro quo contract shown in table 14-3 for two neighbors involved in a dispute. Each disputant, along with the mediator, gets a copy of this written agreement.

There are several important things in this written agreement. First, it clearly specifies who will do what, when, and in what manner. Second, the agreement alternates listing what different disputants will do. It has been found that having a number of actions to be carried out by one disputant listed in their entirety prior to listing the actions to be performed by a second disputant can sometimes lead to an agreement being rejected. A disputant seeing a long list of things that he or she agrees to do, without the list being "broken up" by things the other disputant agrees to do, can get the feeling that he or she has "lost." Finally, the agreement does not contain professional or technical language or jargon. It is best to write an agreement in language that disputants will understand.

Implementing and evaluating the plan.   After an agreement has been reached, it is implemented by the disputants. It is important to evaluate the effectiveness of the agreed-upon settlement. This can be done by agreeing to a future meeting in which the agreement is once again discussed. Many times unforeseen difficulties in satisfactorily carrying out an agreement can threaten to rekindle a conflict. By having an agreed-upon future meeting to discuss such possible difficulties, the mediator can head off a renewal of the conflict.

TABLE 14–3   Sample Quid Pro Quo Contract

DISPUTE RESOLUTION AGREEMENT

Joe Jones agrees to keep his dog out of John Smith's flower bed.

John Smith agrees to call Joe Jones on the phone and discuss any incidents involving Joe Jones' dog on John Smith's property before calling the animal control center.

Joe Jones agrees to have his dog, "Growler," complete a dog obedience class within six months from today, July 19, 1989.

John Smith agrees to construct a fence around his flower bed within six months from today, July 19, 1991.

Signed: _____
           Plaintiff

Signed: _____
           Defendant

Signed: _____
           Mediator

Date: _____

GENERALIZING THE DISPUTE RESOLUTION STRATEGY

The role of mediator is useful in many practice situations, several examples of which were given in the beginning of this chapter. The mediator role is "generic" in the sense that it can be used across a very broad range of settings and contexts. You need not be a marriage and family therapist in order to find yourself in the midst of an interpersonal dispute. Regardless of the practice setting, you will find the techniques discussed in this chapter appropriate and effective.

Especially exciting from a community practice perspective is the growing trend in many states to establish citizen dispute resolution centers. These practice settings entail invaluable community service and work. Persons involved in disputes with others in the community, whether they be neighbors, people in business, friends, or family members, come to these centers in order to peacefully and productively resolve their conflicts. Many such centers provide alternatives to the court system. Social workers who serve in such centers will find the techniques in this chapter especially useful.

CONCLUSION

The problem-solving strategy described in this chapter provides an overall plan for the dispute resolution process. The listing of interventions in table 14-1 provides a possible sequencing of intervention procedures as you work through this process. These interventions have been matched with the strategy step in which you may find them most useful. However, as noted earlier, the dispute resolution process is not linear. You may find yourself moving to and from any one of the problem-solving steps more than once during the mediation process. More important than trying to fit the dispute resolution process into a neat and invariant sequence of steps is becoming skilled at using all of the intervention procedures as well as a creative flexibility in sequencing (and even combining) these interventions.

The systematic approach to reframing is less useful in contexts in which you have limited contact with disputants. For example, in some county court mediation settings the mediator will meet with disputants for at most an hour or an hour and a half. In this setting, the systematic approach to reframing is not as useful as the finesse approach. In contexts in which you will have more prolonged contact with disputants, say, several meetings over several days or even weeks, you will find both reframing approaches useful.

Finally, keep in mind that the interventions presented in this chapter are like tools. Tools can be used in a variety of ways and need to be used to fit the job at hand. Some of the procedures discussed in this chapter may be more useful in some contexts than in others. Given the practice wisdom and research evidence about the tools described earlier, it would seem that the creative and thoughtful use of these tools can lead to productive, win/win resolutions to interpersonal conflict across a broad range of practice settings.

REFRAMING EXERCISES

1. For each of the following "negative labels" come up with one or more interpretations that are "positive." For example, for the label "nosy," as in "he is really nosy," you might reframe it to mean, "a person who is very curious and inquisitive." In each of the phrases below, the negative label is italicized.

   A. He is *nerdy*.   She is *stubborn*.   He is *ornery*.
   B. She is *reclusive*.   He is *passive*.   She is *submissive*.
   C. He is *too self-critical*.   She is *too seductive*.
   D. She is *insensitive*.   He is *impulsive*.   She is *oppositional*.
   E. He is a *cry-baby*.   She is *too withdrawn*.   He is a *dumb jock*.
   F. She is *stuck-up*.   He is *wandering*.   She is *too controlling*.

  G. He is *oversensitive*.   She is a *nymphomaniac*.   He is *manipulative*.
2. For each of the situations below, find one or more contexts in which the italicized behavior would be considered appropriate, even desirable. Then, write out a statement you might use to do a context reframing of the behavior. You may reframe the meaning of the behavior as well as do a context reframing.
  A. A mother complains to you that her daughter, ". . . *sleeps with every guy she meets*. She meets some new boy, and the next thing you know she is in bed with him."
  B. A father complains that his son, ". . . *never does any work around the house*. All he does is watch TV. He's a lazy bum."
  C. A supervisor complains about a subordinate, "She never *does things the same way twice*. She always wants to *do things some new-fangled way* rather than standardize them as the agency's regulations require."
  D. A son complains about his father, "He is always on my back. He is *always telling me what to do*. I can't stand him."

CHAPTER 15

Planned Short-Term Treatment for Persons with Social and Interpersonal Problems

Richard A. Wells

In this chapter, Wells describes an approach to using planned short-term treatment for persons with social and interpersonal problems that includes many aspects of a structured intervention. For example, Wells describes how to contract with the client with an emphasis on well-defined goals. He also describes how to develop a well-defined and strategic (i.e., planned) intervention that includes active participation by social worker and client, including homework. The specific interventions Wells discusses are assertion, stress management, and interpersonal skills, all of which comprise well-defined and replicable components.

INTRODUCTION

The short-term or brief methods of psychotherapy have been practiced since at least the beginning of this century, yet it is only in the past two or three decades that they have been widely recognized as useful and legitimate ways of helping people. This chapter will describe and illustrate an approach to short-term intervention, combining the methods of brief therapy with key aspects of social skill training, that is particularly suitable for many of the social and interpersonal problems met in the clinical practice of social work.

Social skills are the verbal and behavioral elements that influence and govern our immediate interpersonal interactions (Becker, Heimberg, and Bellak, 1987). Beginning a conversation with a new acquaintance, asking someone for a date, refusing an unreasonable request from an importuning relative, and reducing tension while carrying out a demanding task are specific examples of social skills. There are a multitude of others, all as mundane and yet as vital to effective living. They can be seen as falling into a number of related clusters, with the skills of stress management, assertion, and communication regarded as the most important. Individuals differ in the degree to which they have mastered and can utilize the social skills most relevant to their particular life stage or situation. From a social skills viewpoint, many of the distressing emotional reactions people endure or the social or interpersonal problems they experience stem from the absence (or inadequate employment) of necessary social skills. As a consequence, a well-researched model (Hollin and Trower, 1986) has been developed for training people in the skill areas where they are deficient or awkward.

Although this chapter will examine a particular approach to short-term treatment, the reader should be aware that there is actually a family of brief psychotherapies (Wells and Giannetti, 1989) that share a common emphasis on time limits, focus, and action. Before looking at the use of social skill training in brief interventions, it is a good idea to review the basic principles of short-term practice. As I pointed out in another work (Wells and Phelps, 1989), the critical elements of brief psychotherapy, whatever its methodology or objectives, include the following:

1. Therapist and client concentrate on a key area of personal or interpersonal concern, providing a clear and impelling focus for the therapeutic efforts.
2. The therapist takes a direct and active role in promoting client function and, at the same time, displays a positive belief in the client's capacity to change.
3. Tasks are given to the client to perform outside the therapeutic session, making a clear demand for activity rather than passivity.
4. The therapist works within a time-limited context, usually explicitly conveyed, further emphasizing the immediacy and urgency of the change process.
5. The client in brief psychotherapy is expected to act rather than to suffer and to become an involved participant in the therapeutic process. (Wells and Phelps, 1989, p. 4.)

If the planned and explicit use of time is seen as a key dimension of short-term treatment, as Hoyt (1989) has suggested, then three models of brief intervention can be utilized in practice: brief treatment within designated time limits; recontracting following an initial time-limited intervention; and intermittent brief treatment.

Brief Treatment within Designated Time Limits

In this, the most basic model of brief treatment, the social worker agrees to see the client for a stipulated number of sessions (from one to sixteen sessions is the usual range), after which treatment is terminated. In an earlier work (Wells, 1982), I have recommended that the client should be seen for a follow-up interview a month or two after the termination of active treatment. The following is an example of this brief treatment model.

> John, an unmarried man in his middle twenties, was shy and ineffectual in his relationships with people. Despite a socially and economically advantaged background and a science degree from a prestigious university, he seldom dated and had few friends. Ten sessions of brief treatment focused initially on expanding his conversational and communicational repertoire, and then worked on developing more adequate assertive skills. A follow-up interview, three months after termination, found John continuing to use his newly acquired skills in a positive way in his life.

Time-limited intervention is the most familiar model of brief therapy and perhaps its commonest form. Its prevalence in practice is suggested in the work of Gibbons and her associates (1979), who conducted a large-scale study in which task-centered casework (Reid and Epstein, 1972) was offered to 200 individuals following emergency hospitalization for suicide attempts. They found that, for 54 percent of this group, time-limited intervention—averaging nine sessions—was feasible and effective.

Recontracting Following an Initial Time-Limited Intervention

With some clients, it is necessary to continue treatment beyond the original series of sessions. In some instances, social worker and client may decide to begin long-term treatment at this point, but in many cases an additional period of time-limited intervention is all that is required. For example, client and social worker may agree that goal achievement at the expected termination point (or at a follow-up session) is insufficient, and further work in the target problem area is needed. The following case, described in more detail in an earlier work (Wells, 1982), illustrates this possibility.

> Mr. F., a single man of twenty-five, was both anxious and depressed about his difficulties in relating to women. He seldom dated, was highly self-conscious when talking to women, and characterized himself as a "sexual failure." A twelve-session intervention concentrated on building his heterosocial dating skills (Gallassi and Gallassi, 1978) and, via task assignments, encouraging and monitoring his increasing contacts with women. By the end of these sessions he was dating regularly, but a follow-up interview a few months later found that this initial progress had dwindled. A further eight-session intervention focused on reducing the cognitively induced anxiety that was impeding his utilization of his newly acquired skills.

Recontracting may also be necessary in those instances where the client wishes to focus upon a problem that was of low priority when the initial work began, but still continues to be troublesome. A study of task-centered intervention referred to earlier (Gibbons et al., 1979) found that 17 percent of clients were seen beyond the contracted time-limits. This study does not clarify whether the extension involved continued work on the original problems or work on new areas. However, it is interesting to note that this finding is very close to that reported by Parad and Parad (1968a, 1968b) in another large-scale study of short-term treatment, who found that 14 percent of their population required a time extension.

Intermittent Brief Treatment

Finally, although many clients benefit from a single episode of brief treatment, there are others who, for various reasons, may need periodic interventions. These contacts may occur in response to the ordinary vicissitudes of living, which some individuals find difficult to manage, or may result from particularly stressful circumstances or life-choices that the client is experiencing. For example:

> Mr. D. originally was seen for four sessions in order to help him make a decision about whether he would remain in an unhappy marriage. The intervention consisted of assisting him in evaluating the pros and cons of the marital relationship and rehearsing and coaching him in ways of constructively expressing to his wife his dissatisfactions. Almost a year later he was seen for a further six sessions, following his separation and divorce, because he was experiencing considerable stress in dealing with these events, and with his reentry into the "single" world.

Budman and Gurman (1988), as well as Minuchin (1974), suggest that this form of brief therapeutic practice resembles that of the traditional family physician, a professional who was available on an as-needed basis, depending upon the nature of the life stage the client was in or the demands of a specific problem situation. As with the family physician, relationship between social worker and client in short-term psychotherapy can be a continuous one, even though actual therapeutic contact may occur at widely spaced intervals.

PROBLEM IDENTIFICATION

In order to work comfortably and effectively as a short-term therapist, the social worker needs theoretical or conceptual frameworks that are hospitable to the current practically oriented mode of direct helping utilized in these approaches. It is important to remember that no theoretical framework in the therapeutic arena, with the exception of social learning theory (Bandura, 1969, 1977), is supported by any substantial body of empirical research. Most theories are simply explanatory schemas that particularly clever therapists have devised as a way of explaining the development of human problems and justifying a particular method of therapeutic intervention. The theorists of psychotherapy, beginning with Sigmund Freud and continuing through Carl Rogers, Eric Berne, Joseph Wolpe, William Glasser, Virginia Satir, Jay Haley, and many others have each offered somewhat different viewpoints on the nature of social and interpersonal difficulties and, of course, varying prescriptions for how therapists can help to correct clients' problems.

The Social Skill Perspective

The social skill perspective stems from a social learning theory base and therefore is much better supported empirically than most theoretical frameworks. As is true of any theory, however, it serves a major function of explicating client problems and predicting how they should be treated by the practitioner. Because of its emphasis on the current, here-and-now functioning of the client and its specification of a structured, education-ally oriented approach to treatment, the social skill training approach is one that is readily adaptable to the practice of short-term treatment.

Many of the problems encountered in social work practice stem from the difficulties individuals experience in effectively managing their lives and their relationships, which can be seen as the manifestations of social skill deficits. From a positive perspective, social skills are the learned behaviors we use "when we meet people for the first time, make small talk, encourage acquaintanceships and make friends, adapt to groups, and negotiate countless other social interactions" (Herbert, 1986, p. 11). The social skill training approach places the social worker in the role of an educator (Guerney, Stollak, and Guerney, 1971) who identifies the missing or poorly developed skills and teaches them to the client. This involves an emphasis on increasing social competencies, rather than the conventional therapeutic focus on diagnosing pathology and decreasing the negative behaviors or characteristics of the client. As Hollin and Trower (1986) note:

> In keeping with the philosophy of learning new behaviors, the [social skills] movement was also away from a traditional pathology, or "medical" model in which behaviors are to be eliminated, and towards a "constructional" approach in which new, socially acceptable and competent behaviors are trained. (p. 2)

Consonant with the focus of most short-term therapy, the social skill perspective is essentially ahistorical. The clinical issue is what skills are missing or deficient, and therefore need to be taught; client and social worker spend little or no time attempting to understand why these skills have not developed. As Becker, Heimberg, and Bellak (1987) suggest in their exposition of social skills training in the treatment of depression, inadequacies in skill performance can arise from a number of different sources:

a. Insufficient exposure to interpersonally skilled models at key developmental periods.

b. Insufficient opportunity to practice important interpersonal routines at key developmental periods.

c. Learning of inappropriate or maladaptive interpersonal behaviors at key developmental periods.

d. Failure to "discard" old behaviors and adopt new ones during periods of transition, that is, entry into adolescence or adulthood.

e. Decaying of specific behavioral skills due to disuse, as in the case of a newly divorced individual who must now enter the singles' world.

f. Failure to recognize the appropriate or inappropriate times for the execution of specific behavioral routines.

g. Failure to execute adaptive behavior because of a belief that it will not produce the desired results or one's belief that he or she cannot perform the required behavior adequately. (Becker et al., 1987, pp. 4–5)

The practitioner of short-term therapy may gather enough background, in the initial interview with the client, to make an educated guess as to which of the first five sources of skill deficit might apply to a given client. This can then be utilized, briefly, in structuring a rationale for the client concerning the relevance of social skill training, but, as was noted above, the specific origins of skill deficiencies are not relevant to their remediation. However, the last two sources suggested by Becker and his colleagues identify the possibility that the individual possesses the requisite social skills but that cognitive factors—faulty discrimination or inhibiting beliefs—are hampering their utilization. In such cases the social worker will need to buttress social skill training with work on reducing the impeding cognitions or, from a constructional perspective, increasing positive, guiding cognitions. Indeed, most current versions of skill training recognize the need for such additions (Bellak and Hersen, 1978; Kelly, 1982; Lange and Jakubowski, 1976).

There is a wide variety of identifiable social skills but, as I noted in the introduction to this chapter, the most important are those concerned with stress management, assertion, and communication. Where these vital skills are lacking, insufficiently developed, or inadequately applied, the likelihood of problematic social or interpersonal situations is greatly increased, along with an accompanying increase in such uncomfortable and debilitating emotions as anxiety and depression. For some troubled individuals these problematic situations represent crises; for others they are persistent or chronic difficulties. The following example from practice will illustrate a crisis exacerbated by social skill deficiencies.

When Sally, a thirty-year-old single woman, was first interviewed she was so distraught that it was difficult to obtain a coherent picture of her situation. Between bouts of crying, what emerged was that she lived at home with her widowed mother and two other family members. Over the past year Sally had become increasingly perturbed by her mother's negative and demanding attitude toward her and her mother's blatant favoritism of a younger, married sister.

Sally described her mother as critical of her in many ways—for being overweight, for wanting to have a life of her own, for not being married—and as seldom positively recognizing the effort Sally put into attempting to please her. One of the other members of the immediate household was the maternal grandfather, who was elderly and quite ill, and Sally's mother expected her to assist in his care, yet never credited her for her help. At the same time, Sally's younger sister frequently would leave her two preschool children with the mother, who would uncomplainingly look after them.

Remember that, as with any conceptual framework, a certain amount of translation of clients' expression of the problems they are experiencing is necessary in order to see whether these difficulties are manifestations of social skills deficits. Most clients do not share the same vocabulary as social workers, or the same viewpoint about the etiology of their difficulties. Clients by and large tend to describe their past or immediate life situations and to tell stories about the difficulties they are enduring, and to ascribe these problems to either the bad motivations and intentions of others, or to the vagaries of misfortune or fate.

In the case described above, Sally did not say, "I have a great deal of difficulty being assertive with my mother and some real problems in managing stress without becoming very anxious," although—from a social skills perspective—this was certainly the social worker's view of her difficulties. Instead, she wept profusely, described incidents that portrayed her mother as vindictive and her sister as scheming, and conveyed the overall impression that she (Sally) was the unfortunate and helpless victim of these nasty and insensitive individuals. As Harry Stack Sullivan (1954) once observed, much verbal description is neither lie nor truth, but what he characterized as "best appearance," that is to say, an exposition casting the narrator in the most favorable light.

Because social skills are what we do or say in actual encounters with others, their presence or absence is best judged by literally observing clients in interaction with the key people in their lives. A number of scales are available that can be used in clinical practice to identify and assess social skill deficits (Corcoran and Fischer, 1987), but to be most meaningful these must be connected to illustrative incidents and episodes drawn from the client's own presentation. In conjoint family or marital interviews we can directly observe and assess interpersonal interaction. In many cases, however, the social worker is dependent on an individual client's verbal descriptions of his or her ongoing life and must infer from these how the client actually is functioning in relation to social skills.

In a number of instances the client may supply a sufficiently detailed picture of his or her current interactions that the deficient social skills will be obvious. In other cases the therapist may have to ask the client to carry out a brief behavioral enactment (Flowers and Booraem, 1980; Wells, 1982) of a troublesome situation in order to gauge the extent of social skill deficit. Be aware, however, that clients often disguise their deficiencies with global phrases or censored descriptions that may omit or favorably portray their own behaviors.

For example, a client may be describing a troublesome interaction with another individual and say, "I told him not to do it but he wouldn't listen." This is a global descriptive phrase characteristic of conversation and does not literally mean that the client spoke to his antagonist in a forthright, assertive manner. Particularly where there appear to be a number of instances of such difficulty in interpersonal relations, the social worker should ask the client to demonstrate, in a behavioral enactment or rehearsal, how he or she literally acts in such situations. The enactment will be much more likely to reveal whether the client's apparent assertiveness is present or whether the phrase "I told him not to do it" stands for one of the many combinations of ambiguous wording, inaudible tone, downcast eyes, and unconvincing expression that would make the client ineffectual in conveying his or her intended message.

INTERVENTION

Short-term methods typically are action-oriented (Wells and Phelps, 1989) and, especially where the focus is on social skill development, call for the social worker to take an assertive, direct teaching stance. This is in sharp contrast to the mainstream long-term approaches, predominantly influenced by psychodynamic or Rogerian theory, that emphasize the achievement of "insight" and "growth" and call for a relatively passive, reflective role from the clinician (London, 1986). It is not necessary, in my opinion, that clinicians have unique and esoteric knowledge, but it is vital that they be able to apply their knowledge in a skillful manner that is directed toward the expressed goals and better interests of the client. All of the social skills discussed in this chapter are as applicable to social workers, as practicing professionals, as they are to problem-beset clients. Vattano (1978), for example, has described the teaching of stress-management skills to social work students for their personal use in professional situations. Cunningham (1978) describes similar training for undergraduate social work majors in their beginning professional use of assertiveness skills. I was not so fortunate as to receive this kind of skill training in my earliest professional education, but since then I have tried to develop the skills, drawing on many helping sources. My experience has been that the more effectively I have been able to utilize appropriate social skills in my own professional (and personal) life, the more effectively I have been able to teach them to clients.

As I have emphasized, the most essential social skill areas are stress management, assertion, and communication. Each of these areas addressed important aspects of living, and without a reasonable mastery of such skills in daily life, the individual will be prey to depression or anxiety, the unfortunate victim of insensitive others, or the heedless perpetrator of rash and hasty actions. Some further description will highlight the nature and relevance of each area.

Stress management (Meichenbaum, 1975; Vattano, 1978) is concerned with organizing and conducting one's daily life in a way that reduces the common tensions and pressures that can arise from a variety of everyday sources. Stress can also arise as an individual attempts to negotiate major life transitions of many kinds, as the following example shows.

> Ms. J., a divorced woman in her early thirties, had worked for a number of years in a clerical position in a large service organization. She recently had sought and attained a promotion from this routine and structured job to a much more demanding position in direct sales. Although pleased with the greater financial rewards of the new position, she was finding its relatively unstructured nature difficult to manage. Like many prospective clients, she initially ascribed the anxiety she was experiencing to her own character flaws; with explanation from the therapist she was able to see her difficulties as stress-related and to work productively on developing these skills.

Within this skill cluster the individual may use specific relaxation procedures as well as cognitive devices that promote a positive sense of purpose and well-being. The goal of stress management is not to achieve or maintain complete calm but to keep realistic tensions at endurable levels and to keep stress from detracting from the utilization of one's normal abilities.

Assertiveness has to do with the ability to stand up for one's legitimate rights without unduly detracting from the rights of others (Alberti and Emmons, 1974; Lange and Jakubowski, 1975). The ability to make requests of other people in clear, direct words is a key assertive skill, as is the ability to deny unreasonable or unwanted requests from others in a forthright, nonhostile manner. With Sally, the client described earlier in this section, assertive skill training concentrated on simple, straightforward requests to her mother for some time together. Later coaching on assertiveness focused on how to tell her mother directly that her critical manner was hurtful to Sally.

As with other skill areas, it may be important in assertiveness training to teach clients not only the necessary verbal and nonverbal skills, but also how to modify any cognitive factors—unrealistic or distorted expectations or assumptions—that may impede the utilization of the skills (Goldfreid and Goldstein, 1980).

Communication includes skills that range across a wide variety of contexts (Kelly, 1982; Perry and Furukawa, 1986), and may be specific to the nature of the relationship in which the individual is functioning. Some communication skills, for example, are concerned with initiating conversations, others with expressing feelings. Broadly speaking, all of the skills in this area are extremely helpful in such important life tasks as developing friendships or entering new social groups. John, the young man described at the beginning of this chapter, was taught how to begin conversations with friends, both on the telephone and in face-to-face interaction. As he became more adept at these skills he was coached in how to end conversations gracefully, a problem that, in his previous state of minimal social contact, he had seldom encountered.

Other communication skills are concerned with the more intimate relationships of life—spouse to spouse, or between parent and child—and emphasize not only clear and direct verbalization but also the expression and empathic understanding of deeper feelings and emotional states (Birchler, 1978; Guerney, 1977).

The Structure of Interventions

Within the context of short-term treatment, skill training may be utilized in two major ways: teaching aspects of skill training or undertaking full-scale skill training.

In the first kind of utilization, various aspects of skill training are drawn upon to supplement the common methods of brief therapeutic helping. That is, the social worker teaches the client a particular aspect of a social skill as opportunity and need arise within the course of more conventional time-limited treatment. The following is an example of this.

> In the case of Sally, described earlier, initial treatment was essentially crisis intervention (Hansell, 1975), one of the family of short-term therapies. Within a supportive relationship, she was assigned tasks designed to increase her perception of being in control in her life, thus reducing her emotional turbulence. Over the four sessions the therapist worked with her, opportunity soon arose to teach her some simple stress-management skills, and, as described above, to coach her in making direct, assertive requests to her mother. As her desire was to continue to live within the family home, but with lessened conflict, this was sufficient to stabilize her situation. A follow-up contact four months later found the gains she had made were continuing.

In using skill training in this manner, I do not even identify it as such to clients, but simply present the skill elements as helpful strategies for dealing with particular problems in life. For example, with a client who is struggling with how to talk more effectively with a significant other, it is useful to role play in the therapy session. The modeling or coaching examples I utilize are certainly drawn from the clinical research on communication skills or assertiveness, but they are embedded within the therapeutic conversation of the session. There is no intent to deceive the client by incorporating skill training in this way. The clinical issue is that in short-term work the social worker should do no more than is necessary to help the client satisfactorily within the duration of the selected time limits. Particularly if the client already has some base of social skill—though ineptly used, perhaps—behavioral rehearsals of selected skill components within the immediate session, and the assignment of related tasks outside the therapy hour, are sufficient to stimulate the desired change.

In the second kind of utilization, the social worker finds that he or she must undertake full-scale skill training with a particular client. In such cases the client's lack of ability to be assertive or to cope with stress is so pervasive that training must begin with relatively undemanding situations, before proceeding to the most troublesome ones. Social skill training in this more wholesale approach has three major phases:

1. The range of problematic situations where the client's skill deficits occur are specifically identified, and usually are arranged in order of the complexity of skill involved or their emotional demand. In assertiveness training, for example, a client might identify asking a clerk in a store to take back a defective purchase as not too difficult, but find responding to unfair criticism from a supervisor to be quite problematic.

2. The client is taught the component skills of the selected areas through a modeling and rehearsal process, beginning with the least complex skills in the least demanding situation and proceeding, step-by-step, through the more demanding situations. Again using assertiveness as an example, the earliest training might involve coaching the client to make his or her request in very simple, clear language and in an audible voice.

3. Real-life tasks are assigned at each step of the training process, in order to give clients the opportunity to test their developing capabilities. Because the client and the social worker are working on skill development in relation to situations drawn directly from the client's life, it is usually quite easy to identify relevant tasks at each stage of the training. As with any employment of tasks, however, the clinician must be careful that the task is not only pertinent to the client's life, but also one that the client is capable of carrying out. The fine art of task giving is discussed in detail in such works as Levy and Shelton (1989), Shelton and Levy (1981), and Wells (1982).

A case I described in an earlier work (Wells, 1982) offers a final illustration of the application of social skill training in clinical practice. Mr. J., a physically handicapped, mildly retarded man in his late thirties, reluctantly applied to a family service agency because of temper outbursts that were jeopardizing his job at a large industrial organization. He had been told by his immediate supervisor that he must "get counseling" or risk losing his job.

Mr. J. had been employed as a freight elevator operator for about two years and took an almost fierce pride in the reliable and responsible performance of his duties. He had a moderately impairing handicap which placed some limitations on his physical capacities and at times made his speech slurred and difficult to understand. His education had been mainly within "special class" settings in the public school system and had given him only the most rudimentary academic skills. Despite several earlier attempts at vocational training at various social agencies, he had not been able to gain any marketable technical skills. His present job represented the best position he had been able to attain in his work career.

In the sometimes insensitive atmosphere of the working-class world, he frequently encountered teasing and deprecating remarks from his fellow workers. This rough bantering created some stress, but in addition, Mr. J. described himself as being extremely upset over what he regarded as the lazy and slipshod work habits of certain co-workers. Brief behavioral enactments during the initial interview suggested that he possessed reasonably adequate assertive ability in situations where stress had not risen to too high a level. However, tension had been building over many months, and the angry incidents that had precipitated his referral both occurred on days when his dissatisfaction with himself, his job, and his co-workers had become particularly acute.

In both of these episodes Mr. J. had become verbally abusive, had shouted threats at other employees, and in one instance had thrown a piece of heavy equipment across the room. Mr. J. was realistically afraid that he might lose his job if he was not able to convince the firm that he could control his temper in the future. He expressed discouragement about his handicaps, and the restrictions they placed upon him, but viewed these as limitations within which he had learned to live.

An agreement was negotiated with Mr. J. to concentrate on developing workable methods of temper control, and the therapist suggested that this goal was attainable within six sessions. It was explained to Mr. J. that his angry outbursts could be seen as accumulated reactions to the stress he was encountering on a daily basis. This rationale was discussed with him and illustrated through the various situational and attitudinal factors he had described. He was told that the method of intervention would involve teaching him several ways of reducing stress in order to prevent its building up to unmanageable proportions. He was also informed that this approach would require that he practice the stress-management techniques at home so as to gain proficiency, test and refine them in the actual work setting, and, finally, keep a daily record of tension-producing situations in order to follow his progress.

The actual intervention utilized an adaptation of the stress-innoculation model developed by Meichenbaum (1975) and, following these guidelines, emphasized (1) the development of behavioral skills in relaxation; and (2) attention to any cognitive cues that were engendering tension. Relaxation techniques involving muscular release and deep breathing (Benson, 1974) were taught during the first three sessions, and Mr. J. practiced these daily at home. He was asked to keep a very simple diary noting the occurrence and nature of any troublesome incidents at work.

The overall strategy, as in much brief therapy, was to provide Mr. J., as quickly as possible, with some tangible means of reducing stress. It was felt that once his general tension level was diminished he would be better able to see how some of his own attitudes were contributing to his stress. Perhaps fortuitously, a minor incident came up on his job during the second week of treatment. Because this situation was not too demanding, Mr. J. was able to handle the pressures reasonably well and this bolstered his confidence in himself and, implicitly, in the treatment program. Fortified by his developing skills, and this beginning success, he coped with some further difficult incidents over the following week with equal aplomb.

Work on stress-reduction techniques continued over the final three weeks of the contact. This concentrated on further refinement of Mr. J.'s ability to relax himself and focused on using such key words as "relax" and "calm" as relaxation signals that could be utilized unobtrusively in public situations. In these final sessions the focus also incorporated general discussion of the realistic pressures of factory work. Additionally, Mr. J.'s demands upon himself to perform, as well as his feeling of being trapped in a dead-end job, were identified as factors that were contributing to his overall level of stress. Within the general context of short-term treatment, the therapist's effort was to make Mr. J. more aware of the impact of his own attitudes upon his difficulties rather than to resolve the difficulties.

A follow-up session with Mr. J. three months later found him coping well with the day-to-day pressures of his job. He described a few episodes that had been upsetting to him, but he had been able to handle each without any undue outburst of anger. Although he was not using the stress-management techniques consistently, it was apparent that he was able to call upon them as needed to reduce or control immediate tensions. An unplanned follow-up took place about two years later when the therapist encountered Mr. J. by chance on the street. Mr. J. volunteered that he was successfully maintaining his job and still occasionally used ''those relaxing things you showed me.''

GENERALIZING THE INTERVENTION TO RELATED PROBLEMS

This discussion of the use of social skill training within planned short-term treatment has concentrated on the three major skill areas of stress management, assertion, and communication. There are a number of other areas in which specific skills have been identified and, in general, the same training model described earlier in this chapter can be utilized in their development. A sampling of the skills discussed in Hollin and Trower's *Handbook of Social Skills Training* (1986, vols. 1 and 2) includes the following:

- Parenting skills
- Heterosocial (dating) skills
- Problem-solving skills
- Friendship/conversational skills
- Sexual skills
- Sociocultural skills
- Job-finding skills
- Interview skills
- Job-management skills
- Negotiation skills

In addition, skill training has been included as a critical component in the treatment of some of the most serious mental health problems. For example, Scott and associates (1984) describe the use of skill training procedures in the treatment of a child-abusing parent. The client, a single parent, was trained sequentially in assertion, child-management, and problem-solving skills in a multiple-baseline design that monitored change in key areas of the parent/child relationship.

In another example, Goldstein and associates (1978) have incorporated stress-management training into short-term aftercare treatment with schizophrenics and their families as one means of reducing the impact of interpersonal conflicts that can lead to relapse and rehospitalization.

Finally, in a work I have cited earlier in this chapter, Becker and associates (1987) have developed a highly focused skill training approach to the treatment of major depressive disorder. Supporting research studies (Bellak, Hersen, and Himmelhoch, 1983; Hersen et al., 1984) report data indicating that the skills training approach is as effective in the treatment of the disorder as commonly used antidepressant medications.

These are a few examples of how the social skill training model has been applied in other treatment areas or in the development of further aspects of human skills in living. Although one must always be cautious about "bandwagon" effects in the therapeutic arena, there is reason to be optimistic about the utility of the social skill approach, not only in short-term treatment, but also in a number of related areas of concern to the mental health professions.

SUMMARY

As noted earlier, difficulties in social skill areas may be identified either through the assessment typically conducted during the initial clinical interview or through the employment of a number of clinical assessment scales (Corcoran and Fischer, 1987). Few clients ask explicity for training in a specific social skill, although their descriptions of their problems in living offer many clues concerning skill deficits. Matching the skill area to be utilized with the client's problem(s) requires knowledge, on the clinician's part, of the essential component skills of each of the major skill areas so as to ascertain their absence (or ineffectual utilization) in the client's life. This process may be aided by brief role plays as well as by the aforementioned scales.

There are three major components in training for any of the specific skill areas:

1. Identify the range of real-life situations where the client has difficulty with the target skill. Arrange these in a hierarchy from least demanding to most demanding, so that training can begin with situations where success is most likely.

2. Utilize modeling and role rehearsal to teach the client the specific elements of a designated skill, practicing these within the session until a reasonable degree of proficiency is attained.

3. Through task assignments, have the client try out each level of skill attainment in appropriate real-life situations. Feedback from assignments can be utilized to further refine the client's skill level as well as to deal with any cognitive factors (irrational beliefs, expectations, negative self-dialogue, etc.) that may be affecting performance.

There will be times when a given client needs training in more than one skill area. In some of these instances the sequence of skill training may be important. Generally speaking, where the client is experiencing discernible amounts of tension or anxiety in his or her life, stress management should be the first area for intervention. Once the individual is coping more adequately with stress, training in other needed areas—

assertiveness or more effective parenting skills, for example—can proceed. On the other hand, in a case where stress management was not a primary issue, Scott and associates (1984) sequentially trained a child-abusing parent in assertion and child-management and problem-solving skills.

References

Adler, G. 1985. *Borderline Psychopathology and Its Treatment.* New York: Jason Aronson.

Alberti, R. E., and Emmons, M. L. 1974. *Your Perfect Right.* San Luis Obispo, CA: Impact Press.

Allan Guttmacher Institute. 1981. *Teenage Pregnancy: The Problem That Hasn't Gone Away.* New York: Guttmacher Institute.

American Psychiatric Association. 1987. *Diagnostic and Statistical Manual of Mental Disorders,* 3rd ed., revised. Washington, DC: American Psychiatric Press.

Ammerman, R. T., and Van Hasselt, V. B. 1988. The Callner-Ross Assertion Questionnaire. In M. Hersen and A. S. Bellack (eds.), *Dictionary of Behavioral Assessment Techniques.* New York: Pergamon.

Anderson, C. M., Hogarty, G. E., and Reiss, D. J. 1980. Family treatment of adult schizophrenic patients: A psychoeducational approach. *Schizophrenia Bulletin* 6: 490–505.

Anderson, C., Reiss, D., and Hogarty, G. 1986. *Schizophrenia and the Family: A Practitioner's Guide to Psychoeducation and Management.* New York: Guilford Press.

Anderson, S. C. 1989. Goal-setting in Social Work Practice. In B. R. Compton and B. Galaway (eds.), *Social Work Processes.* Belmont, CA: Wadsworth.

Andolfi, M. 1980. Prescribing the families' own dysfunctional rules as a therapeutic strategy. *The Journal of Marital and Family Therapy* 6: 29–36.

Andrews, J. G., and Harvey, R. 1981. Does psychotherapy benefit neurotic patients? A reanalysis of the Smith, Glass and Miller data. *Archives of General Psychiatry* 38: 951–62.

Angus, L. E., and Marziali, E. 1988. A comparison of three measures for the diagnosis of borderline personality disorder. *American Journal of Psychiatry* 145: 1453–54.

Annis, H. M. 1986. A Relapse Prevention Model for Treatment of Alcoholics. In W. R. Miller and N. Heather (eds.), *Treating Addictive Behaviors: Processes of Change.* New York: Plenum.

Anthony, W. A., Cohen, M. R., and Vitalo, R. 1978. The measurement of rehabilitation outcome. *Schizophrenia Bulletin* 4: 365–83.

Applebaum, S. A. 1963. The problem-solving aspects of suicide. *Journal of Projective Techniques* 27(1): 259–68.

Armelius, B., Kullgrean, G., and Renberg, E. 1985. Borderline diagnosis from hospital records. *Journal of Nervous and Mental Disease* 173: 32–34.

Atkinson, J., et al. 1988. Prevalence of immunodeficiency virus. *Archives of General Psychiatry* 45 (September): 859–64.

Austin, M. J., Kopp, J., and Smith, P. L. 1986. *Delivering Human Services*. New York: Longman.

Azrin: N. H., Naster, J., and Jones, R. 1973. Reciprocity counseling: A rapid learning-based procedure for marital counseling. *Behavior Research and Therapy* 11: 365–82.

Backer, T., Liberman, R., and Kuehnel, T. 1986. Dissemination and adoption of innovative psychosocial interventions. *Journal of Consulting and Clinical Psychology* 54: 111–18.

Bagley, C., Jacobsen, S., and Rehin, A. 1976. Completed suicide: A taxinomic analysis of clinical and social data. *Psychological Medicine* 6(3): 429–38.

Baker, F. M. 1984. Black suicide attempters in 1980: A preventive focus. *General Hospital Psychiatry* 6: 131–37.

Baker, T. B., and Cannon, D. S. (eds.). 1988. *Assessment and Treatment of Addictive Disorders*. New York: Praeger.

Bandler, R., and Grinder, J. 1975. *Patterns of the Hypnotic Techniques of Milton H. Erickson, M.D.*, vol. 1. Cupertino, CA: Meta Publications.

_____. 1982. *Reframing*. Moab, UT: Real People Press.

Bandura, A. 1969. *Principles of Behavior Modification*. New York: Holt, Rinehart, and Winston.

_____. 1976. *Social Learning Theory*. Englewood Cliffs, NJ: Prentice-Hall.

_____. 1977. Self-efficacy: Toward a theory of behavior change. *Psychological Review* 84: 191–215.

_____. 1986. Fearful expectations and avoidant actions as co-effects of perceived self-inefficacy. *American Psychologist*, December, 1389–91.

Barker, R. 1984. *Treating Couples in Crises*. New York: Free Press.

Barlow, D. 1988. *Anxiety and Its Disorders*. New York: Guilford Press.

Barlow, D. H., Hayes, S. C., and Nelson, R. O. 1984. *The Scientist Practitioner*. New York: Pergamon.

Barnes, D. 1987. Brain damage by AIDS under active study. *Science*. 235 (March 27): 1574–77.

Barry, W. A. 1968. *Conflict in Marriage: A Study of the Interactions of Newlywed Couples*, 273. Ann Arbor, MI: University Microfilms.

Bartman, E. R. 1976. Assertive Training with Hospitalized Suicide Attempters. Doctoral diss., The Catholic University of America.

Bartolome, F. 1983. The work alibi: When it's harder to go home. *Harvard Business Review* 61(2): 67–74.

Bartolome, F., and Evans, L. P. A. 1980. Must success cost so much? *Harvard Business Review* 58(2): 137–48.

Baucom, D. H. 1982. The relative utility of behavioral contracting and problem-solving/communications training in behavioral marital therapy: A controlled outcome study. *Behavior Therapy* 13: 162–74.

Beck, A. 1972. *Depression: Causes and Treatment*. Philadelphia: University of Pennsylvania Press.

Beck, A., and Weissman, A. 1974. The measurement of pessimism: The hopelessness scale. *Journal of Consulting and Clinical Psychology* 42(4): 861–65.

Beck, A. T., Herman, I., and Schuyler, D. 1974. Development of Suicidal Intent Scales. In A. T. Beck, H. L. P. Resnick, and D. Lettieri (eds.), *The Prediction of Suicide*. Bowie, MD: Charles Press.

Beck, T. T. 1963. Thinking and depression. Idiosyncratic content and cognitive distortions. *Archives of General Psychiatry* 9: 324–33.

_____. 1976. *Cognitive Therapy and the Emotional Disorders.* New York: International Universities Press.

_____. 1988. *Love Is Never Enough.* New York: Harper and Row.

Beck, D. F. 1976. Research Findings on the Outcomes of Marital Counseling. In D. H. L. Olsen (ed.) *Treating Relationships.* Lake Mills, IA: Graphic.

Beck, M. (1989). AIDS, *Newsweek* 114(1):571c.

Becker, R. E., Heimberg, R. G., and Bellack, A. S. 1987. *Social Skills Training Treatment for Depression.* New York: Pergamon.

Bedrosian, R. C., and Beck, A. T. 1979. Cognitive aspects of suicidal behaviors. *Suicide and Life Threatening Behavior* 9: 87–96.

Beidel, D. C., Turner, S. M., Stanley, M. A., and Dancu, C. V. 1989. The social phobia and anxiety inventory: Concurrent and external validity. *Behavior Therapy* 20: 417–27.

Beiser, M., Shore, J., Peters, R., and Tatum, E. 1985. Does community care for the mentally ill make a difference? A tale of two cities. *American Journal of Psychiatry* 142: 1047–52.

Bellack, A. D. and Hersen, M. (eds.). 1978. *Research and Practice in Social Skills Training.* New York: Plenum.

_____. 1985. *Dictionary of Behavior Therapy Techniques.* New York: Pergamon.

Bellack, A. S., Hersen, M., and Himmelhoch, J. M. 1983. A comparison of social skills training, pharmacotherapy and psychotherapy for depression. *Behavior Research and Therapy* 21: 101–7.

Belle, D. 1982. *Lives in Stress: Women and Depression.* Beverly Hills: Sage.

Benson, H. 1974. Your innate asset for combating stress. *Harvard Business Review* 52: 49–60.

Berman, J. S., Miller, C. R., and Massman, P. J. 1985. Cognitive therapy versus systematic desensitization: Is one treatment superior? *Psychological Bulletin* 97: 451–61.

Birchler, G. R. 1978. Communication Skills in Married Couples. In A. S. Bellak and M. Hersen (eds.), *Research and Practice in Social Skills Training.* New York: Plenum.

Birtchnell, J. 1970. The relationship between attempted suicide, depression and parent death. *British Jounral of Psychiatry* 116: 307–13.

Blades, J. 1984. Mediation: An old art revisited. *Mediation Quarterly* 3: 59–95.

Bloom, B. C. 1977. *Community Mental Health.* Monterey, CA: Brooks/Cole.

Bloom, M. 1975. *The Paradox of Helping: Introduction to the Philosophy of Scientific Practice.* New York: Wiley.

Bloom, M., and Fischer, J. 1982. *Evaluating Practice: Guidelines for the Accountable Professional.* Englewood Cliffs, NJ: Prentice-Hall.

Blythe, B. J., and Tripodi T. 1989. *Measurement in Direct Practice.* Newbury Park, CA: Sage.

Bond, G. R., Miller, L. D., Krumwied, R. D., and Ward, R. S. 1988. Assertive case management in three CMHCs: A controlled study. *Hospital and Community Psychiatry* 39: 411–18.

Bond, G. R., Witheridge, T. F., Dincin, J., Wasmer, D., Webb, J., and DeGraaf-Kaser, R. 1988. A controlled evaluation of the Thresholds Bridge assertive outreach program. Paper presented at the annual meeting of the American Psychological Association, New York City, August.

Borland, A., McRae, J., and Lycan, C. 1989. Outcomes of five years of continuous intensive case management. *Hospital and Community Psychiatry* 40: 369–76.

Bostock, T., and Williams, C. 1974. Attempted suicide as an operant behavior. *Archives of General Psychiatry* 31: 482–86.

Bouchard, T. 1972. Training, motivation, and personality as determinants of the effectiveness of brainstorming groups and individuals. *Journal of Applied Psychology* 56: 324–31.

Boudin, H. M., et al. 1977. Contingency contracting with drug abusers in the natural environmental. *International Journal of the Addictions* 12: 1–16.

Bowers, R. S. 1973. Situationism in psychology: An analysis and a critique. *Psychological Review* 80: 307–336.

Bowlby, J. 1980. *Loss: Sadness and Depression.* New York: Basic Books.

Braff, D. 1989. Sensory input deficits and negative symptoms in schizophrenic patients. *American Journal of Psychiatry* 146(8): 1006–11.

Bratter, T. E., and Forrest, G. G. (eds.). 1985. *Alcoholism and Substance Abuse: Strategies for Clinical Intervention.* New York: Free Press.

Braucht, G. N. 1979. Interactional analysis of suicidal behavior. *Journal of Consulting and Clinical Psychology* 47(532): 653–669.

Briar, S. 1973. Effective Social Work Intervention in Direct Practice: Implications for Education. In S. Briar et al., *Facing the Challenge.* New York: Council on Social Work Education.

Bright, P. B., and Robin, A. L. 1981. Ameliorating parent-adolescent conflict with problem-solving communication training. *Journal of Behavior Therapy and Experimental Psychology* 12: 275–80.

Brittan, A. 1973. *Meanings and Situations.* London: Routledge and Kegan Paul.

Broverman, I., et al. 1970. Sex role stereotypes and clinical judgments of mental health. *Journal of Consulting and Clinical Psychology* 34: 1–7.

Browell, K. D. 1984. The Addictive Disorders. In C. M. Franks, et al. (eds.), *Annual Review of Behavior Therapy,* vol. 10. New York: Guilford Press.

Brown, G., and Harris, T. 1978. *The Social Origins of Depression: A Study of Psychiatric Disorders in Women.* London: Tavistock Publications.

Brown, G. M., and Greenspan, S. 1984. Effect of social foresight training on the school adjustment of high-risk youth. *Child Study Journal* 14: 61–77.

Brown, J. A., and Brown, C. S. 1977. *Systematic Counseling: A Guide for the Practitioner.* Champaign, IL: Research Press.

Budman, S. H., and Gurman, A. S. 1988. *Theory and Practice of Brief Therapy.* New York: Guilford Press.

Buglass, D., and McCulloch, J. W. 1970. Further suicidal behavior: The development and validation of predictive scales. *British Journal of Psychiatry* 116: 483–91.

Buie, D., and Adler, G. 1982. The definitive treatment of the borderline patient. *International Journal of Psychoanalytic Psychotherapy* 9: 51–87.

Bureau of the Census, Department of Commerce. 1986. *School Enrollment—Social and Economic Characteristics of Students: 1985.* Washington, DC: Government Publications Office.

Burns, D. 1980. *Feeling Good: The New Mood Therapy.* New York: Signet Books.

Butler, M. 1985. Guidelines for Feminist Therapy. In L. Rosewater and L. Walker (eds.), *Handbook of Feminist Therapy*. New York: Springer.

Caccioppo, J., and Petty, R. 1981. Social Psychological Procedures for Cognitive Response Assessment: The Thought Listing Technique. In T. V. Merluzzi, C. R. Glass, and M. Genest (eds.), *Cognitive Assessment*. New York: Guilford Press.

Caldarola, T., and Helquist, M. 1989. Counseling mixed antibody status couples. *Focus: A Guide to AIDS Research and Counseling* 4(9): 1–2.

Cancro, R., Kane, J., Dubuvsky, S., and Liberman, R. 1986. *Managing the Schizophrenic Patient in an Era of Psychosocial Rehabilitation*. Intelligence Reports in Psychiatric Disorders. Cedar Grove, NJ: HealthScan, Inc.

Cantor, P. C. 1976. Personality characteristics found among youthful female suicide attempters. *Journal of Abnormal Psychology* 85: 324–29.

Caragonne, P., and Austin, D. M. Final report: A comparative study of the functions of the case manager in multi-purpose, comprehensive and in categorical programs. School of Social Work, University of Texas, Austin, TX, no date.

Carkhuff, R. R. 1971. Training as a preferred mode of treatment. *Journal of Counseling Psychology* 18: 123–31.

Carkhuff, R., and Berenson, D. 1976. *Teaching as Treatment*. Amherst, MA: Human Research Development Press.

Caroll, J. F. X. 1984. Substance abuse problem checklist: A new clinical aid for drug and/or alcohol dependency. *Journal of Substance Abuse Treatment* 1: 31–36.

Carter, R. D., and Thomas, E. J. 1975. Modification of Problematic Marital Communication. In A. S. Gurman and D. G. Rice (eds.), *Couples in Conflict*. New York: Jason Aronson.

Cartledge, G., and Milburn, J. F. 1980. *Teaching Social Skills to Children*. New York: Pergamon.

Cautela, J. R. 1967. Covert sensitization. *Psychological Record* 20: 459–68.

Centers for Disease Control. 1989. *HIV Surveillance Report*. August.

Charlesworth, E. A., Williams, B. J., and Baer, P. E. 1984. Stress management at the worksite for hypertension: Compliance, cost-benefit, health care, and hypertension related variables. *Psychosomatic Medicine* 46(5): 387–97.

Chesler, P. 1972. *Women and Madness*. New York: Doubleday.

Chiles, J. A., Stroshal, K. D., McMurtray, L., and Linehan, M. M. 1985. Modeling effects on suicidal behavior. *Journal of Nervous and Mental Diseases* 8: 477–81.

Chiles, J. A., Stroshal, K., Cowden, L., Graham, R., and Linehan, M. 1986. The 24 hours before hospitalization: Factors related to suicide attempting. *Suicide and Life Threatening Behavior* 16(3): 335–42.

Chowdury, N., Hicks, R. C., and Kreitman, N. 1973. Evaluation of an after-care service for parasuicide (attempted suicide) patients. *Social Psychiatry* 8: 67–81.

Chun, K. T., Cobb, S., and French, J. 1975. *Measures for Psychological Assessment*. Ann Arbor, MI: Institute for Social Research.

Ciminero, A. R., Calhoun, K. S., and Adams, H. E. 1986. Self-monitoring Procedures. In A. R. Ciminero, K. S. Calhoun, and H. E. Adams (eds.), *Handbook of Behavioral Assessment*. New York: Wiley.

Ciompi, L. 1983. How to Improve the Treatment of Schizophrenics: A Multi-Causal Illness Concept and Its Therapeutic Consequences. In H. Stierlin, L. Wynne, and M. Wirsching (eds.), *Psychosocial Intervention in Schizophrenia: An International View*. New York: Springer-Verlag.

Clum, G. A. 1989. Psychological interventions vs. drugs in the treatment of panic. *Behavior Therapy* 20: 429–57.

Clum, G. A., Patsiokas, A. T., and Luscomb, R. L. 1979. Empirically based comprehensive treatment program for parasuicide. *Journal of Consulting and Clinical Psychology* 47(5): 937–45.

Cohen, R. E. 1970. Preventive mental health programs for ethnic minority populations: A case in point. Paper presented at the Congresso Internacional de Americanistas, Lima, Peru.

Colletti, G., and Brownell, K. D. 1982. The Physical and Emotional Benefits of Social Support: Application to Obesity, Smoking and Alcoholism. In M. Hersen et al. (eds.), *Progress in Behavior Modification*, vol. 13, 109–78. New York: Academic Press.

Comery, A. L., et al. 1973. *A Sourcebook for Mental Health Measures*. Los Angeles: Human Interaction Research Institute.

Communication Technologies and Research and Decisions Corporation. 1986. Reaching Ethnic Communities in the Fight Against AIDS. August 1. Xerox.

Compton, B. R., and Galaway, B. (eds.). 1989. *Social Work Processes*. Belmont, CA: Wadsworth.

Congdon, D. C., and Holland, T. P. 1989. Measuring the effectiveness of substance abuse treatment: Toward a theory-based index. *Journal of Social Service Research* 12: 23–48.

Conte, H. R., Plutchik, R., Karasu, T. B., and Jarrett, I. 1980. A self-report borderline scale: Discrimination validity and preliminary norms. *Journal of Nervous and Mental Disease* 168: 428–35.

Cook, T. D., and Leviton, L. C. 1980. Reviewing the literature: A comparison of traditional methods with meta-analysis. *Journal of Personality* 48: 449–72.

Coombs, D., and Miller, H. 1975. The Scandinavian suicide phenomenon: Fact or artifact? Another look. *Psychology Reports* 37: 1075–78.

Cooper, H. M., and Rosenthal, R. 1980. Statistical versus traditional procedures for summarizing research findings. *Psychological Bulletin* 87: 442–49.

Cooper, N. A., and Clum, G. A. 1989. Imaginal flooding as a supplementary treatment for PTSD in combat veterans: A controlled study. *Behavior Therapy* 20: 381–91.

Corcoran, K. J. 1982. Behavioral and non-behavioral methods of developing two types of empathy: A comparative study. *Journal of Education for Social Work* 18: 85–93.

_____. 1985. Clinical practice with non-behavioral methods: Strategies for evaluation. *Clinical Social Work Journal* 13(3): 78–86.

_____. 1988. Selecting a Measurement Tool. In R. M. Grinnell, Jr. (ed.), *Social Work Research and Evaluation*, 3rd ed. Itasca, IL: Peacock.

_____. 1990. Doing Family Therapy With an Acting-Out Adolescent: Applying the Empirical Clinical Practice Model. In C. W. LeCroy (ed.), *A Casebook for Social Work Practice*. Belmont, CA: Wadsworth.

Corcoran, K., and Fischer, J. 1987. *Measures for Clinical Practice*. New York: Free Press.

Cordon, J., and Preston-Shoot, M. 1987. *Contracts in Social Work*. Hants, England: Gower.

Cormier, W. H., and Cormier, L. S. 1985. *Interviewing Strategies for Helpers,* 2nd ed. Belmont, CA: Brooks/Cole.

Coulton, C. J., and Solomon, P. L. 1977. Measuring outcomes intervention. *Social Work Research and Abstracts* 13: 3–9.

Council on Ethical and Judicial Affairs. 1988. Ethical issues involved in the growing AIDS crisis. *Journal of the American Medical Association* 259(9): 1360–61.

Council on Social Work Education. 1988. *Handbook of Accreditation Standards and Procedures.* Washington, DC: Council on Social Work Education.

Cox, W. M. (ed.). 1987. *Treatment and Prevention of Alcohol Problems: A Resource Manual.* New York: Academic Press.

Cunningham, M. 1978. Assertion training: an essential part of the undergraduate social work field program. Paper presented at the Council on Social Work Education Annual Program Meeting, New Orleans, LA.

Curran, J. P., and Monti, P. M. 1982. *Social Skills Training: A Practical Handbook for Assessment and Treatment.* New York: Guilford Press.

Curtis, G. C., and Thyer, B. A. 1983. Fainting on exposure to phobic stimuli. *American Journal of Psychiatry* 140: 771–74.

Curtis, J. D., and Detert, R. A. 1981. *How to Relax: A Holistic Approach to Stress Management.* Palo Alto, CA: Mayfield.

Daley, D. C. 1986. *Relapse Prevention Workbook.* Holmes Beach, FL: Learning Publications, Inc.

Dardick, L. and Grady, K. E. 1980. Openness between gay persons and health professionals. *Annals of Internal Medicine* 93(part I): 115–19.

Davidson, J. 1978. *Effective Time Management: A Practical Workbook.* New York: Human Sciences Press.

Davis, R. 1979. Black suicide in the seventies: Current trends. *Suicide and Life Threatening Behaviors* 9: 131–40.

DeLange, J. 1982. Depression in Women: Explanations and Prevention. In A. Weick and S. Vandiver (eds.), *Women, Power and Change.* Washington, DC: NASW Publications.

deShazer, S. 1988. *Clues: Investigating Solutions in Brief Therapy.* New York: W. W. Norton.

Deschner, J. (1984a). *The Hitting Habit.* New York: Free Press.

————. (1984b). *How to End the Hitting Habit: Anger Control for Battering Couples.* New York: Macmillan.

Detmer, W. M., and Lu, F. G. 1986. Neuropsychiatric complications of AIDS: A literature review. *International Journal of Psychiatry in Medicine* 16(1): 21–29.

Diekstra, R. 1973. A social learning theory approach to the prediction of suicidal behavior. Paper presented at the Seventh Annual International Congress on Suicide Prevention, Amsterdam, the Netherlands.

Donovan, B. M., and Marlatt, G. A. 1988. Assessment of Addictive Behaviors: Implications of an Emerging Biopsychosocial Model. In B. M. Donovan and G. A. Marlatt (eds.), *Assessment of Addictive Behaviors: Behavioral, Cognitive, and Physiological Procedures.* New York: Guilford Press.

Douglas, J. D. 1967. *The Social Meanings of Suicide.* Princeton, NJ: Princeton University Press.

Duehn, W. 1985. The Problem-Solving Process. In R. M. Grinnell, Jr., (ed.), *Social Work Research and Evaluation,* 2nd Ed. Itasca, IL: Peacock.

Dune, E., McIntosh, J., and Dunne-Maxim, K. (eds.). 1987. *Suicide and Its Aftermath*. New York: W. W. Norton.

Dunn, G., Dunn, K., and Price, G. 1975. *Learning Style Inventory*. Lawrence, KS: Price Systems, Inc.

Dunnette, M., Campbell, J., and Joasted, K. 1963. The effect of group participation on brainstorming effectiveness for two industrial samples. *Journal of Applied Psychology* 47: 30–37.

Durkheim, E. 1952. *Le Suicide [Suicide]*. New York: Free Press. (Original work published in 1897).

Dusek, J. B. 1987. *Adolescent Development and Behavior*. Englewood Cliffs, NJ: Prentice-Hall.

Eckblad, M., and Chapman, L. J. 1983. Magical ideation as an indicator of schizotypy. *Journal of Consulting and Clinical Psychology* 51: 215–25.

Eckrich, S. 1985. Identification and treatment of borderline personality disorder. *Social Work* 30: 166–71.

Ellis, A. 1962. *Reason and Emotion in Psychotherapy*. New York: Stuart.

Epstein, L. H., and Wing, R. R. 1984. Behavioral Contracting: Health Behaviors. In C. M. Franks (eds.), *New Developments in Behavior Therapy*. New York: Haworth Press.

Ettinger, R. W. 1975. Evaluation of suicide prevention after attempted suicide. *Acta Psychiatrica Scandinavia* (suppl. 260).

Evarts, W., Greenstone, J., Kirkpatrick, G., and Leviton, S. 1983. *Winning Through Accommodation: The Mediator's Handbook*. Dubuque, IA: Kendall/Hunt.

Ewart, C. K., Taylor, C. B., Kraemer, H. C., and Agras, W. S. 1984. Reducing blood pressure reactivity during interpersonal conflict: Effects on marital communication training. *Behavior Therapy* 15(5): 473–84.

Fairweather, G., and Tornatzky, L. 1977. *Experimental Methods for Social Policy Research*. New York: Pergamon.

Falloon, I. 1988. How to Improve the Treatment of Schizophrenics: A Multicausal Illness Concept and Its Therapeutic Consequences, In H. Stierlin, L. Wynne, and M. Wirsching (eds.), *Psychosocial Interventions in Schizophrenia: An International View*. New York: Springer-Verlag.

Farberow, N. L., and MacKinnon, D. 1974. Prediction of Suicidal in Neuropsychiatric Hospital Patients. In C. Neuringer (ed.), *Psychological Assessment of Suicidal Risk*. Springfield, IL: Charles C. Thomas.

Ferner, J. 1980. *Successful Time Management*. New York: Wiley.

Fingarett, H. 1988. Alcoholism: The mythical disease. *Utne Reader* 30: 64–68.

Fisch, R., Weakland, J., and Segal, L. 1982. *The Tactics of Change*. San Francisco: Jossey-Bass.

Fischer, J. 1973a. Is casework effective? A review. *Social Work* 18: 5–20.

―――――. 1973b. Has mighty casework struck out? *Social Work* 18: 104–10.

―――――. 1976. *The Effectiveness of Social Casework*. Springfield, IL: Charles C. Thomas.

―――――. 1978. *Effective Casework Practice: An Eclectic Approach*. New York: McGraw-Hill.

―――――. 1981. The social work revolution. *Social Work* 26: 199–207.

―――――. 1983. Evaluations of social work effectiveness: Is positive evidence always good evidence? *Social Work* 28: 74–77.

_____. 1986. Eclectic Casework. In J. C. Norcross (ed.), *Handbook of Eclectic Psychotherapy*. New York: Brunner/Mazel.

_____. 1990. Meta-Analysis: The Premise, the Problems. In W. J. Reid and L. Videka-Sherman (eds.), *Advances in Clinical Social Work Research*. Silver Spring, MD: National Association of Social Workers.

Flowers, J. V., and Booraem, C. D. 1980. Simluation and Role Playing Methods. In F. H. Kanfer and A. P. Goldstein (eds.), *Helping People Change*, 2nd ed. New York: Pergamon.

Fogg, R. 1985. Dealing with conflict: A repertoire of creative, peaceful approaches. *Journal of Conflict Resolution* 29: 330–58.

Foreyt, J. P. 1987. The Addictive Disorders. In G. T. Wilson et al. (eds.), *Review of Behavior Therapy*, vol. 10. New York: Guilford Press.

Fox, K., and Weissman, M. 1975. Sucicide attempts and drugs: Contradiction between method and intent. *Social Psychiatry* 10:31–38.

Foy, D. W., Cline, K. A., and Laasi, N. 1987. Assessment of Alcohol and Drug Abuse. In T. D. Nirenberg and S. A. Maisto (eds.), *Developments in the Assessment and Treatment of Addicitive Behaviors*. Norwood, NJ: Ablex.

Franklin, J. L., Solovitz, B., Mason, M. Clemons, J. R., and Miller, G. E. 1987. An evaluation of case management. *American Journal of Public Health* 77: 674–78.

Fraser, M., and Kohlert, N. 1988. Substance abuse and public policy. *Social Service Review* 62: 103–26.

Fredman, N., and Sherman, R. 1987. *Handbook of Measurements for Marriage and Family Therapy*. New York: Brunner/Mazel.

Freed, A. O. 1980. The borderline personality. *Social Casework* 61: 548–58.

_____. 1984. Differentiating between borderline and narcissistic personalities. *Social Casework* 65: 395–404.

Freedman, B. J., Rosenthal, C., Donahoe, C. P., Schlundt, D. G., and McFall, R. M. 1978. A social-behavioral analysis of skill deficits in delinquent and nondelinquent adolescent boys. *Journal of Consulting and Clinical Psychology* 48: 1448–62.

Freud, S. 1926. Inhibitions, symptoms, and anxiety. *Standard Edition*, 20. London: Hogarth Press.

Friedman, R., and Dermit, S. 1988. Popular stress management: A selected review. *Behavioral Medicine* 14(4): 186–89.

Galatner, M. 1983. *Recent Developments in Alcoholism*, vols. I and II. New York: Plenum.

Gallassi, J. P., and Gallassi, M. P. 1978. Modification of Heterosocial Skill Deficits. In A. S. Bellak and M. Hersen (eds.), *Research and Practice in Social Skills Training*. New York: Plenum.

Gambrill, E. D., and Richey, C. A. 1975. An assertion inventory for use in assessment and research. *Behavior Therapy* 6: 550–61.

Gambrill, E. and Richey, C. 1988. *Taking Charge of Your Social Life*. Belmont, CA: Behavioral Options.

Gendlin, E. T. 1973. Experiential Psychotherapy. In R. Corsini (ed.), *Current Psychotherapies*. Itasca, IL: Peacock.

_____. 1978. *Focusing*. New York: Bantam.

Gerber, R. 1988. *Vibrational Medicine: New Choices for Healing Ourselves*. Santa Fe, NM: Bear and Company.

Gerson, M. J. 1984. Splitting: The development of a measure. *Journal of Clinical Psychology* 40: 157–62.

Ghosh, A., and Marks, I. M. 1987. Self-treatment of agoraphobia by exposure. *Behavior Therapy* 18: 3–16.

Gibbons, J. S., Bow, I., Butler, J., and Powell, J. 1979. Client's reactions to task-centered casework: A follow-up study. *British Journal of Social Work* 9: 203–15.

Gibbons, J. S., Butler, P. U., and Gibbons, J. L. 1978. Evaluation of a social work service for self-poisoning patients. *British Journal of Psychiatry* 133: 111–18.

Gibbs, J. P., and Martin, W. L. 1964. *Status Integration and Suicide: A Sociological Study*. Eugene: University of Oregon Press.

Gilbert, L. 1980. Feminist Therapy. In A. Brodsky and R. Hare-Mustin (eds.), *Women and Psychotherapy*. New York: Guilford Press.

Gilchrist, L. D., and Schinke, S. P. 1983. Coping with contraception: Cognitive and behavioral methods with adolescents. *Cognitive Therapy and Research* 7: 379–88.

Gilchrist, L. D., Schinke, S. P., and Blythe, B. J. 1985. Preventing Unwanted Adolescent Pregnancies. In L. D. Gilchrist and S. P. Schinke (eds.), *Preventing Social and Health Problems Through Life Skills Training*. Seattle, WA: Center for Social Welfare.

Gingerich, W. J. 1983. Significance Testing in Single-Case Research. In A. Rosenblatt and D. Waldfogel (eds.), *Handbook of Clinical Social Work*. San Francisco: Jossey-Bass.

Girdano, D., and Everly, G. S. 1986. *Controlling Stress and Tension: A Holistic Approach*. Englewood Cliffs, NJ: Prentice-Hall.

Girodo, M. 1974. Yoga meditation and flooding in the treatment of anxiety neurosis. *Journal of Behavior Therapy and Experimental Psychiatry* 5: 157–60.

Gochros, H. 1988. Risks of abstinence: Sexual decision-making in the era of AIDS. *Social Work* 33(3, May–June): 254–56.

Gochros, H. L., Gochros, J. S., and Fischer, J. 1986. *Helping the Sexually Oppressed*. Englewood Cliffs, N.J.: Prentice-Hall.

Goering, P. N., Wasylenki, D. A., Farkas, M., Lancee, W. J., and Ballantyne, R. 1988. What difference does case management make? *Hospital and Community Psychiatry* 39: 272–76.

Goffman, E. 1961. On the Characteristics of Total Institutions. In E. Goffman, *Asylums*, 1–124. Garden City, NY: Anchor Books.

Golan, N. 1979. Crisis Theory. In F. J. Turner (ed.), *Social Work Treatment*. New York: Free Press.

Goldberg, K. S. C., Schooler, N. R., Hogarty, G. E., and Roper, M. 1977. Prediction of relapse in schizophrenic outpatients treated by drug and socio-therapy. *Archives of General Psychiatry* 34: 171–84.

Goldfried, M. R., and D'Zurilla, T. J. 1969. A Behavioral-Analytic Model for Assessing Competence. In C. D. Spielberger (ed.), *Current Topics in Clinical and Community Psychology*. New York: Academic Press.

Goldfried, M. R., and Goldstein, A. P. 1980. Cognitive change methods. In F. H. Kanfer and A. P. Goldstein (eds.), *Helping People Change*, 2nd ed. New York: Pergamon.

Goldman, B., and Sanders, J. 1974. *Directory of Unpublished Experimental Mental Measures, Vol. 1*. New York: Behavioral Publications.

Goldman, B., and Busch, J. 1978. *Directory of Unpublished Experimental Mental Measures, Vol. II*. New York: Human Sciences Press.

Goldman, B., and Busch, J. 1982. *Directory of Unpublished Experimental Mental Measures, Vol. III*. New York: Human Sciences Press.

Goldstein, A. P., and Kanfer, F. H. 1979. *Maximizing Treatment Gains*. New York: Academic Press.

Goldstein, A. P., Sprafkin, R. P., Gershaw, N. J., and Klein, P. 1978. Training aggressive adolescents in pro-social behavior. *Journal of Youth and Adolescents* 7: 735–92.

_____. 1983. *Skill-Streaming the Adolescent*. Champaign, IL: Research Press.

Goldstein, M. J., Rodnick, E. H., Evans, J. R., May, P. R. A., and Steinberg, M. R. 1978. Drug and family therapy in the aftercare of acute schizophrenia. *Archives of General Psychiatry* 35: 1169–77.

Goldstein, W. M. 1988. Beginning psychotherapy with the borderline patient. *American Journal of Psychotherapy* 42: 561–73.

Gordon, T. 1970. *P.E.T. Parent Effectiveness Training: The Tested New Way to Raise Responsible Children*. New York: Wyden.

Gordon, W. E. 1983. Social work revolution or evaluation? *Social Work* 28: 181–85.

Gottman, J. M. 1979. *Marital Interaction: Experimental Investigations*. New York: Academic Press.

Gottman, J. M., and Leiblum, S. R. 1974. *How to Do Psychotherapy and How to Evaluate It*. New York: Holt, Rinehart and Winston.

Gottman, J., Notarius, C., Gonso, J., and Markman, H. 1976. *A Couple's Guide to Communication*. Champaign, IL: Research Press.

Granvold, D. 1988. Treating Marital Couples in Conflict and Transition. In J. McNeil and S. Weinstein (eds.), *Innovations in Health Care Practice*. Papers from the Health/Mental Conference, New Orleans, LA, National Association of Social Workers.

Greenburg, L., Fine, S., Cohen, C., Larson, K., Michaelson-Baily, A., Rubinton, P., and Glick, I. 1988. An interdisciplinary psychoeducation program for schizo-phrenic patients and their families in an acute care setting. *Hospital and Community Psychiatry* 39: 277–81.

Greer, S., and Bagley, C. 1971. Effect of psychiatric intervention in attempted suicide: A controlled study. *British Medical Journal* 1 (February): 210–312.

Grinnell, R. M., Jr. (ed.). 1991. *Social Work Research and Evaluation*, 4th ed. Itasca, IL: Peacock.

Grinnell, R. M., and Williams, M. 1990. *Research in Social Work: A Primer*. Itasca, IL: Peacock.

Grove, J. B. 1981. *Unobtrusive Measures: Non-Reactive Research in the Social Sciences*. Boston: Houghton Mifflin.

Guay, P. 1989. Psychotherapy and HIV disease. Paper presented at the Seventh National AIDS Forum, San Francisco, April.

Guerney, B. G., Jr. 1977. *Relationship-Enhancement Methods*. San Francisco: Jossey-Bass.

Guerney, B. G., Jr., Stollak, G., and Guerney, L. 1971. The professional psychologist as educator: An alternative to the medical practitioner model. *Professional Psychology* 2: 276–82.

Gunderson, J. G., Franks, A. F., Runningstam, E. F., Wachter, S., Lynch, V. J., and Wolf, P. J. 1989. Early discontinuance of borderline patients from psychotherapy. *The Journal of Nervous and Mental Disease* 177: 38–42.

Gunderson, J. G., and Kolb, J. 1978. Discriminating features of borderline patients. *American Journal of Psychiatry* 135: 792–96.

Gunderson, J. G., Kolb, J. E., and Austin, V. 1981. The diagnostic interview for borderline patients. *American Journal of Psychiatry* 138: 896–903.

Gurman, A., and Kniskern, O. 1981. The Research on Marital and Family Therapy: Progress, Perspective, and Prospect. In S. L. Garfield and A. E. Bergin (eds.), *Handbook of Psychotherapy and Behavior Change*, 2nd ed. New York: Wiley.

Hafner, H., and van der Heiden, W. 1989. Effectiveness and cost of community care for schizophrenic patients. *Hospital and Community Psychiatry* 40: 59–63.

Haley, J. 1973. *Uncommon Therapy*. New York: W. W. Norton.

Hamilton, J., Siwolop, S., et al. 1987. The AIDS epidemic and business. *Business Week*, March, 122–32.

Hansell, N. 1978. *The Person-in-Distress*. New York: Behavioral Publications.

Hansen, D., St. Lawrence, J., and Christoff, K. 1985. Effects of interpersonal program solving component skills and effectiveness of solutions. *Journal of Consulting and Clinical Psychology* 53: 167–74.

Hargreaves, W. A., Shaw, R. E., Shadoan, R., Walker, E., Surber, R., and Gaynor, J. 1984. Measuring case management activity. *Journal of Nervous and Mental Disease* 172: 296–300.

Harris, H. 1987. Psychoanalytic Therapy and Depression. In R. Formanek and A. Gurian (eds.), *Women and Depression*. New York: Springer.

Harris, M., and Bergman, H. C. 1988. Capitation financing for the chronic mentally ill: A case management approach. *Hospital and Community Psychiatry* 39: 68–72.

Harrod, J. 1986. Defining case management in community support systems. *Journal of Psychosocial Rehabilitation* 9(3): 57–61.

Harwood, R. L., and Weissberg, R. P. 1987. The potential of video in the promotion of social competence in children and adolescents. *Journal of Early Adolescence* 7: 345–63.

Haussman, M., and Holseth, J. (1987). Rexamining Women's Roles: a Feminist Approach to Decreasing Depression in Women. In C. M. Brody (ed.), *Women's Therapy Groups; Paradigms of Feminist Treatment*. New York: Springer.

Hawton, K. 1980. Domiciliary and Outpatient Treatment Following Deliberate Self-Poisoning. In R. Farmer and S. Hirsch (eds.), *The Suicide Syndrome*. London: Croom Helm.

Hawton, K., and Catalan, J. 1987. *Attempted Suicide: A Practical Guide to Its Nature and Management*, 2nd Ed. New York: Oxford University Press.

Hayes, S. C., Nelson, R. O., and Jarrett, R. B. 1987. The treatment utility of assessment. *American Psychologist* 42: 63–71.

Hazel, J. S., Schumaker, J. B., Sherman, J. A., and Sheldon-Wilder, J. 1981. The Development and Evaluation of a Group Skill Training Program for Court-Adjudicated Youths. In D. Upper and S. M. Ross (eds.), *Behavioral Group Therapy, 1981: An Annual Review*. Champaign, IL: Research Press.

Hazelrigg, M. D., Cooper, H. M., and Borduin, C. M. 1987. Evaluating the effectiveness of family therapies: An integrative review and analysis. *Psychological Bulletin* 101: 428–42.

Heath, D. B. 1987. "Addictive Behaviors" and "Minority Populations" in the United States: American Indian Drug Use as a Case Study. In T. D. Nirenberg and S. A. Maisto (eds.), *Developments in the Assessment and Treatment of Addictive Behaviors.* Norwood, NJ: Ablex.

Heiby, E. M. 1983. Assessment of frequency of self-reinforcement. *Journal of Personality and Social Psychology* 44: 1304–07.

Heinrich, D., and Buchanana, R. 1988. Significance and meaning of neurological signs in schizophrenia. *American Journal of Psychiatry* 145: 11–18.

Helzer, J. E. 1987. Epidemiology of alcoholism. *Journal of Consulting and Clinical Psychology* 55: 248–92.

Henry, A. F., and Short, J. F. 1954. *Suicide and Homicide.* London: Free Press, Glencoe, Collier-Macmillan.

Hepworth, D., and Larsen, J. 1986. *Direct Social Work Practice: Theory and Skills.* Chicago: Dorsey Press.

Herbert, M. 1986. Social Skills Training with Children. In C. R. Hollin and P. Trower (eds.), *Handbook of Social Skills Training,* vol. I. Oxford, England: Pergamon.

Herman, E. 1988. The twelve-step program: Cure or cover. *Utne Reader* 30: 52–63.

Hersen, M., and Barlow, D. H. 1986. *Single Case Experimental Designs.* New York: Pergamon.

Hersen, M., and Bellack, A. S. (eds.) 1988. *Dictionary of Behavioral Assessment Techniques.* New York: Pergamon.

Hersen, M., Bellack, A. S., Himmeloch, J. M., and Thase, M. E. 1984. Effects of social skills training, amitriptyline, and psychotherapy in unipolar depressed women. *Behavior Therapy* 15: 21–40.

Herzbreg, A. 1941. Short-term treatment of neuroses by graduated tasks. *British Journal of Medical Psychology* 19: 22–36.

Hester, R. K., and Miller, W. R. 1989. *Handbook of Alcoholism Treatment Approaches.* New York: Pergamon.

Hiew, C. C., and MacDonald, G. 1986. Delinquency prevention through promoting social competence in adolescents. *Canadian Journal of Criminology* 28: 291–302.

Hilton, M. R., and LoKare, V. G. 1978. The evaluation of a questionnaire measuring severity of alcohol dependence. *British Journal of Psychiatry* 132: 42–48.

Himle, J., and Thyer, B. A. (1989). Clinical social work and obsessive compulsive disorder: A single-subject investigation. *Behavior Modification* 13: 459–70.

Hirsch, S. R., Walsh, C., and Draper, R. 1982. Parasuicide: A review of treatment interventions. *Journal of Affective Disorders* 4(4): 299–311.

Hofferth, S. L., Kahn, J. R., and Baldwin, W. 1987. Premarital sexual activity among U.S. teenage women over the past three decades. *Family Planning Perspectives* 19: 46–53.

Hoffman, A. 1987. *Steal This Urine Test.* New York: Penguin.

Hogarty, G. E. 1989. Social Work Research on Severe Mental Illness: Charting a Future. NIMH Task Force on Social Work Research Workshop: Social Work Research and Community-Based Mental Health Services, November 1–2, Rockville, MD.

Hogarty, G. E. and Ulrich, R. F. 1977. Temporal effects of drug and placebo in delaying relapse in schizophrenic outpatients. *Archives of General Psychiatry* 34: 297–301.

Hollin, C. R., and Trower, P. (eds.). 1986. *Handbook of Social Skills Training*, vols. I and II. Oxford, England: Pergamon.

Howard, G. S. 1980. Response-shift bias: A problem in evaluating interventions with pre/post self-reports. *Evaluation Review* 4: 93–106.

Howe, M. W. 1974. Casework self-evaluation: A single-subject approach. *Social Service Review* 48: 1–23.

Hoyt, M. F. 1989. On Time in Brief Therapy. In R. A. Wells and V. Giannetti (eds.), *Handbook of the Brief Psychotherapies*. New York: Plenum.

Hudson, W. 1982. *The Clinical Measurement Package: A Field Manual*. Chicago: Dorsey Press.

Hudson, W. W. 1987. Future Directions in Clinical Evaluation. In N. Gottlieb, H. A. Ishisaka, J. Kropp, C. A. Richey, and E. R. Tolson (eds.), *Perspectives on Direct Practice Evaluation*, Monograph #5. Seattle, WA: School of Social Work, University of Washington.

Hudson, W. W. 1990. *Computer Assisted Social Services*. Tempe, AZ: Walmyr Publishing Company.

Hudson, W. W., and Thyer, B. A. 1987. Research Measures and Indices in Direct Practice. In A. Minahan (ed.), *Encyclopedia of Social Work*, 487–98. Washington, DC: National Association of Social Workers.

Hunt, S. W., Hyles, S. E., Frances, A., Clarkin, J. F., and Brent, R. 1984. Assessing borderline personality disorder with self-report, clinical interview, or semistructural interview. *American Journal of Psychiatry* 141: 1228–31.

Ingram, J. A., and Salzberg, H. C. 1988. Cognitive-Behavioral Approaches to the Treatment of Alcoholic Behavior. In M. Hersen et al. (eds.), *Progress in Behavior Modification*. New York: Academic Press.

Institute for Juvenile Research. 1972. *Juvenile Delinquency in Illinois: Highlight of the 1972 Adolescent Survey*. Chicago: Institute for Juvenile Research.

Intagliata, J. 1982. Improving the quality of community care for the chronically mentally disabled: The role of case management. *Schizophrenia Bulletin* 8(4): 655–74.

Ito, J. K., and Donovan, D. 1986. Aftercare in Alcoholism Treatment: A Review. In W. R. Miller and N. Heather (eds.), *Treating Addictive Behaviors*. New York: Plenum.

Ivanoff, A. 1984. *In-Patient treatment for suicide attempters*. Doctoral diss., University of Washington.

Ivanoff, A., and Jung, S. J. 1989. Hopelessness, suicidality and social desirability in a prison population. Unpublished manuscript. Columbia University.

Jack, D. 1987. Self-in-Relation Theory. In R. Formanek and A. Gurian (eds.), *Women and Depression*. New York: Springer.

Jackel, M. M. 1975. Borderline Personality Disorders. In G. H. Wiedeman (ed.), *Personality Development and Deviation: A Textbook for Social Work*. New York: International Universities Press.

Jackson, A. W., and Hornbeck, D. W. 1989. Educating young adolescents: Why we must structure middle grade schools. *American Psychologist* 44: 837–40.

Jacobson, N. S. 1977. Problem-solving and contingency contracting in the treatment of marital discord. *Journal of Consulting and Clinical Psychology* 45: 92–100.

————. 1978. A stimulus control model of change in behavioral couples' therapy: Implications for contingency contracting. *The Journal of Marriage and Family Counseling*: 4: 29–35.

_____. 1984. The Modification of Cognitive Processes in Behavioral Marital Therapy: Integrating Cognitive and Behavioral Intervention Strategies. In K. Hahlweg and N. S. Jacobson (eds.), *Marital Interaction.* New York: Guilford Press.

Jacobson, N. S., and Dallas, M. 1981. Helping Married Couples Improve Their Relationships. In W. E. Craighead, A. E. Kazdin, and M. J. Mahoney (eds.), *Behavior Modification.* Boston: Houghton Mifflin.

Jacobson, N. S., and Holtzworth-Munroe, A. 1986. Marital Therapy: A Social Learning-Cognitive Perspective. In N. S. Jacobson and A. D. Gurman (eds.), *Clinical Handbook of Marital Therapy.* New York: Guilford Press.

Jacobson, N. S., and Margolin, G. 1979. *Marital Therapy.* New York: Brunner/Mazel.

Jacobson, N. S., and Martin, B. 1976. Behavioral marriage therapy: Current status. *Psychological Bulletin* 83: 540–56.

Jacobson, N. S., and Moore, D. 1981. Behavior Exchange Theory of Marriage: Reconnaissance and Reconsideration. In J. P. Vincent (ed.), *Advances in Family Intervention, Assessment, and Theory,* vol. II. Greenwich, CT: JAI.

Jacobson, N. S., Waldron, H., and Moore, D. 1980. Toward a behavioral profile of marital distress. *Journal of Consulting and Clinical Psychology* 48: 696–703.

Janis, I. L., and Mann, L. 1977. *Decision-Making.* New York: Free Press.

Jayaratne, S. 1978. Analytic procedures for single-subject designs. *Social Work Research and Abstracts* 14(4): 30–40.

Jayaratne, S., and Levy, R. L. 1979. *Empirical Clinical Practice.* New York: Columbia Unversity Press.

Jessor, R. 1982. Problem behavior and developmental transition in adolescence. *The Journal of School Health* 53: 295–300.

Johnston, L. D., O'Malley, P. M., and Bachman, J. G. 1986. *Drug Use among American High School Students, College Students, and Other Young Adults.* Rockville, MD: National Institute on Drug Abuse.

_____. 1987. National Trends in Drug Use and Related Factors among American High Schools Students and Young Adults, 1975–1986, (DHHS Publication No. ADM 87-1535). Washington, DC: U.S. Government Printing Office.

Jordan, C., Cobb, N., and McCully, R. 1989. Clinical issues of the dual-career couple. *Social Work,* January, 29–32.

Joseph, S. 1987. Cognitive Theory. In R. Formanek and A. Gurian (eds.), *Women and Depression.* New York: Springer.

Kanfer, F. H. 1986. Implications of a Self-Regulation Model of Therapy for Treatment of Addictive Behaviors. In W. R. Miller and N. Heather, (eds.) *Treating Addictive Behavior.* New York: Plenum.

Kantor, S., and Zimring, F. M. 1976. The effects of focusing on a problem. *Psychotherapy: Theory, Research and Practice* 13(3): 255–58.

Karoly, P., and Steffen, J. J. (eds.). 1980. *Improving the Long-Term Effects of Psychotherapy.* New York: Gardner.

Kaschak, E. 1981. Feminist Psychotherapy: The First Decade. In S. P. Cox (ed.), *Female Psychology: The Emerging Self.* New York: St. Martin's Press.

Kazdin, A. E. 1979. Unobtrusive measures in behavioral assessment. *Journal of Applied Behavior Analysis* 12: 713–24.

_____. 1982. *Single-Case Research Designs.* New York: Oxford University Press.

Kelly, J. 1982. *Social Skills Training*. New York: Springer.

Kendall, P. C., and Hollon, S. D. 1980. Cognitive self-statements in depression: Development of an automatic thought questionnaire. *Cognitive Therapy and Research* 4: 383–95.

Kenmore, T. 1987. Negotiating with clients: A study of clinical practice experience. *Social Services Review* 61: 132–44.

Kennedy, P. 1972. Efficacy of a regional poisoning treatment center in preventing further suicidal behavior. *British Medical Journal* 4 (November): 255–357.

Kernberg, O. F. 1975. *Borderline Conditions and Pathological Narcissism*. New York: Jason Aronson.

_____. 1976. *Object-Relations Theory and Clinical Psychoanalysis*. New York: Jason Aronson.

Kernberg, O. F., Burstein, E. D., Coyne, L., Applebaum, A., Horwitz, L., and Voth, H. 1972. Psychotherapy and psychoanalysis: Final report of the Menninger foundation's psychoherapy research project. *Bulletin of the Menninger Clinic* 36: 1–277.

Kernberg, O. F., Goldstein, E. G., Carr, A. C., Hunt, H. F., Bauer, S. F., and Blumenthal, R. 1981. Diagnosing borderline personality: A pilot study using multiple diagnosis methods. *Journal of Nervous and Mental Disease*, 169: 225–31.

King, N. J. 1980. The Therapeutic Utility of Abbreviated Progressive Relaxation: A Critical Review with Implications for Clinical Practice. In M. Hersen, R. Eisler, and P. Miller (eds.), *Progress in Behavior Modification*, vol. 10. New York: Academic Press.

Kiresak, T. J., and Sherman, R. 1968. Good attainment scaling: A general method for evaluating comprehensive mental health programs. *Community Mental Health Journal* 4: 443–53.

Knox, D. 1973. Behavioral contracts. *Journals of Family Counseling* 1: 22–28.

Koehn, H. E. 1988. Living and dying with AIDS: One futurist's struggle. *The Futurist* 22(2): 21–22 (March–April).

Kohut, H. 1977. *The Restoration of the Self*. New York: International Universities Press.

Kohut, H., and Wolff, E. S. 1978. The disorders of the self and their treatment: An outline. *International Journal of Psychoanalysis* 59: 413.

Kolb, D. 1983. *The Mediators*. Cambridge, MA: MIT Press.

Kolb, J. E., and Gunderson, J. G. 1980. Diagnosing bordering patients with a semi-structural interview. *Archives of General Psychiatry* 37: 37–41.

Kovacs, M., Beck, A. T., and Weissman, A. 1975a. Hopelessness: An indicator of suicidal risk. *Suicide* 29(5): 363–68.

_____. 1975b. Hopelessness and suicide behavior: An overview. *Journal of the American Medical Association* 234: 1146–49.

Kravetz, D. 1986. Women and Mental Health. In N. Van Den Bergh and L. Cooper (eds.), *Feminist Visions for Social Work*. Silver Spring, MD: NASW Publications.

Kreitman, N. 1977. *Parasuicide*. London: Wiley.

Kreitman, N., Smith, P., and Tan, E. 1970. Attempted suicide as a language: An empirical study. *British Journal of Psychiatry* 116(534): 465–73.

Krieger, I. 1988. An approach to coping with anxiety about AIDS. *Social Work* 33(3): 263–64.

Kroll, J., Pyle, R., Zander, J., Martin, K., Lari, S., and Sines, L. 1981. Borderline personality disorder: Reliability of the Gunderson diagnostic interview for borderliners (DIB). *Schizophrenia Bulletin* 7: 269–72.

Lakein, A. 1973. *How to Get Control of Your Time and Your Life*. New York: New American Library.

Lamb, R. 1980. *Treating the Long-Term Mentally Ill*. San Francisco: Jossey-Bass.

Lange, A., and Jakubowski, P. 1976. *Responsible Assertive Behavior: A Cognitive-Behavioral Approach*. Champaign, IL: Research Press.

Lankton, S., and Lankton, C. 1983. *The Answer Within*. New York: Brunner/Mazel.

Larson, D. 1989. Unpublished speech given at Castle Medical Center, Honolulu, Hawaii, August 17.

LeCroy, C. W. 1983a. Social Skills Training with Adolescents: A Review. In C. LeCroy (ed.), *Social Skills Training for Children and Youth*, 91–116. New York: Haworth Press.

_____. 1983b. Promoting social competence in early adolescents: An experimental evaluation. Doctoral diss., University of Wisconsin-Madison.

LeCroy, C. W., and Rose, S. D. 1986. Evaluation of preventive interventions for promoting social competence in adolescents. *Social Work Research and Abstracts* 22: 8–17.

Leff, J., and Vaughn, C. E. 1985. *Expressed Emotion in Families*. New York: Guilford Press.

Lettieri, D. J. 1974a. Research Issues in Developing Prediction Scales. In C. Neuringer (ed.), *Psychological Assessment of Suicidal Risk*. Springfield, IL: Charles C. Thomas.

_____. 1974b. Suicidal Death Prediction Scales. In A. T. Beck, H. C. P. Resnick, and D. J. Lettieri (eds.) *The Prediction of Suicide*. Bowie, MD: Charles Press.

Levenson, M., and Neuringer, C. 1971. Problem-solving behavior in suicidal adolescents. *Journal of Consulting and Clinical Psychology* 37(3): 433–36.

Levi, A., and Benjamin, A. 1977. Focus and flexibility in a model of conflict resolution. *Journal of Conflict Resolution* 21: 405–25.

Levi, D., Fales, C., Skin, M., and Sharp, V. 1966. Separation and attempted suicide. *Archives of General Psychiatry* 15: 158–64.

Levitt, J. L., and Reid, W. J. 1981. Rapid-assessment instrument for practice. *Social Work Research and Abstract* 17: 13–20.

Levy, R. L. 1981. On the nature of the clinical research gap: The problems with some solutions. *Behavioral Assessment* 3: 235–42.

Levy, R. L., and Shelton, J. L. 1989. Tasks in Brief Therapy. In R. A. Wells and V. Giannetti (eds.) *Handbook of the Brief Psychotherapies*. New York: Plenum.

Levy, R. M., Bredsen, D. E., et al. 1985. Neurological manifestations of AIDS. *Journal of Neurosurgery* 62 (April): 475–95.

Lewis, J. A., Dana, R. O., and Blevins, G. A. 1988. *Substance Abuse Counseling: An Individualized Approach*. Pacific Grove, CA: Brooks/Cole.

Liberman, R. 1988. Psychosocial management fo schizophrenia: Overcoming disability and handicap. *The Harvard Medical School Mental Health Letter* 5(5): 4–6 (November).

Liberman, R., and Eckman, T. 1981. Behavior therapy vs. insight-oriented therapy for repeated suicide attempters. *Archives of General Psychiatry* 38: 1126–30.

Light, R. J., and Pillemer, D. B. 1984. *Summing Up: The Science of Reviewing Research*. Cambridge, MA: Harvard University Press.

Linehan, M. M. 1984. *Dialectical Behavior Therapy for Treatment of Parasuicidal Women: Treatment Manual*. Seattle, WA: University of Washington.

_____. 1986. A Social-Behavioral Analysis of Suicide and Parasuicide: Implications for Clinical Assessment and Treatment. In H. Glazer and J. F. Clarkin (eds.) *Intervention Strategies*. New York: Garland.

_____. 1987. Dialectical Behavior Theory in Groups: Treating Borderline Personality Disorders and Suicidal Behavior. In C. M. Brody (ed.), *Women's Therapy Groups: Paradigms of Feminist Treatment*. New York: Springer.

_____. 1988. Dialectical behavior therapy: A treatment for the chronic parasuicidal client. *Journal of Personality Disorders* 1(4): 328–33.

Linehan, M. M., Camper, P., Chiles, J. A., Strosahl, K., and Sheann, E. 1987. Interpersonal problem-solving and parasuicide. *Cognitive Therapy and Research and Therapy* 11 (1): 1–12.

Linehan, M. M., Chiles, J. A., Devine, R. H., Laffaw, J. A., and Egan, K. J. 1986. Presenting problems of parasuicides versus suicide ideators and nonsuicidal psychaitric patients. *Journal of Consulting and Clinical Psychology* 54: 880–81.

Linehan, M. M., Goodstein, J. L., Neilsen, S. L., and Chiles, J. A. 1983. Reasons for staying alive when you are thinking of killing yourself: The reasons for living inventory. *Journal of Consulting and Clinical Psychology* 51: 276–86.

Litman, G. K. 1986. Alcoholism Survival: The Prevention of Relapse. In W. R. Miller and N. Heather (eds.), *Treating Addictive Behaviors*. New York: Plenum.

Locke, E. A., Sarri, L. M., Shaw, K. N., and Latham, G. P. 1981. *Psychological Bulletin* 90: 125–52.

Lockhart, L. L., and Wodarski, J. S. 1989. Facing the unknown: Children and adolescents with AIDS. *Social Work* 34 (3): 215–22.

London, P. 1986. *The Modes and Morals of Psychotherapy*, 2nd ed. Washington, DC: Hemisphere Publishing.

Lourie, N. V. 1978. Case Management. In J. Talbot (ed.), *The Chronic Mental Patient*, 159–60. Washington, DC: American Psychiatric Association.

Lum, D. 1986. *Social Work Practice and People of Color*. Pacific Grove, CA: Brooks/Cole.

MacKenzie, A., and Waldo, K. C. 1981. *About Time! A Woman's Guide to Time Management*. New York: McGraw-Hill.

Mager, R. F. 1972. *Goal Analysis*. Belmont, CA: Fearon.

Mahler, M. S., Pine, F., and Bergman, A. 1975. *The Psychological Birth of the Human Infant*. New York: Basic Books.

Maisto, S. A., and Carey, K. B. 1987. Treatment of Alcohol Abuse. In T. D. Nirenberg and S. A. Maisto (eds.), *Developments in the Assessment and Treatment of Addictive Behaviors*. Norwood, NJ.: Ablex.

Maisto, S. A. and Cooper, A. M. 1980. A Historical Perspective on Alcohol and Drug Treatment Outcome Research. In M. B. Sobell et al. (eds.), *Evaluating Alcohol and Drug Abuse Treatment Effectiveness*. New York: Pergamon.

Malloy, P., and Levis, D. J. 1988. A laboratory demonstration of persistent human avoidance. *Behavior Therapy* 19: 229–41.

Maloney, D. M., Harper, T. M., Braukmann, C. J., Fixesen, D. L., Phillips, E. L., and Wolf, M. M. 1976. Teaching conversation-related skills in predelinquent girls. *Journal of Applied Behavior Analysis* 9: 371.

Maltsberger, J. T. 1986. *Suicide Risk: The Formulation of Clinical Judgment.* New York: New York University Press.

Maluccio, A., and Marlow, W. 1974. The case for the contract. *Social Work* 19: 28–36.

Mander, A., and Rush, A. 1974. *Feminism as Therapy.* New York: Random House.

Mantell, M. R. 1988. *Don't Sweat the Small Stuff: P. S., It's All Small Stuff.* San Luis Obispo, CA: Impact Press.

Marcus, B. 1987. Object Relations Theory. In R. Formanek and A. Gurian (eds.) *Women and Depression.* New York: Springer.

Margolin, G., and Weiss, R. L. 1978. Communication training and assessment: A case of behavioral marital enrichment. *Behavior Therapy* 9: 508–20.

Maris, R. W. 1981. Deviance as therapy: The paradox of the self-destructive female. *Journal of Health and Social Behavior* 12: 113–24.

Markman, H. J. 1979. Application of a behavioral model of marriage in predicting relationship satisfaction of couples planning marriage. *Journal of Consulting and Clinical Psychology* 47: 743–49.

Marks, I. M. 1978. *Living with Fear.* New York: McGraw-Hill.

————— 1987. *Fears, Phobias, and Rituals.* New York: Oxford University Press.

Marks, I. M., and Mathews, A. M. 1979. Brief standard self-rating for phobic patients. *Behavioral Research and Therapy* 17: 263–67.

Marlatt, G. A. 1976. The Drinking Profile: A Questionnaire for the Behavioral Assessment of Alcoholism. In E. J. Mash and L. G. Terdal (eds.), *Behavioral Therapy Assessment: Diagnosis, Design, and Evaluation.* New York: Springer.

—————. 1979. Alcohol Use and Problem Drinking: A Cognitive-Behavioral Analysis. In P. C. Kendall and S. D. Hollon (eds.), *Cognitive-Behavioral Interventions.* New York: Academic Press.

—————. 1985. Relapse Prevention: Theoretical Rationale and Overview of the Model. In G. A. Marlatt and J. R. Gordon (eds.), *Relapse Prevention: Maintenance Strategies in the Treatment of Addictive Behaviors.* New York: Guilford Press.

Marlatt, G. A., and Gordon, J. R. 1985. Determinants of Relapse: Implications of the Maintenance of Behavior Change. In P. O. Davidson and S. M. Davidson (eds.), *Behavioral Medicine: Changing Health Lifestyles.* New York: Brunner/Mazel.

Marlatt, G. A., and Marques, J. K. 1977. Mediation, Self-Control and Alcohol Use. In R. B. Stuart (ed), *Behavioral Self-Management: Strategies, Techniques and Outcomes.* New York: Brunner/Mazel.

Marshall, J. J., and Peck, D. F. 1986. Facial expression training in blind adolescents using EMG feedback: A multiple-baseline study. *Behavior Research and Therapy* 24: 429–35.

Masterson, J. F. 1972. *Treatment of the Borderline Adolescent: A Developmental Approach.* New York: Wiley.

—————.1976. *Psychotherapy of the Borderline Adult: A Developmental Approach.* New York: Brunner/Mazel.

Matson, J. L. 1981. A controlled outcome study of phobias in mentally retarded adults. *Behavior Research and Therapy* 19: 101–7.

Matson, J. L., Manikam, R., Coe, D., and Raymond, K. 1988. Training social skills to severely mentally retarded multiple handicapped adolescents. *Research in Developmental Disabilities* 9: 195–208.

Matuscha, P. R. 1985. The Psychopharmacology of Addiction. In T. E. Bratter and G. G. Forrest (eds.), *Alcoholism and Substance Abuse*. New York: Free Press.

Mawson, D., Marks, I. M., Ramm, L., and Stern, R. S. 1981. Guided mourning for morbid grief: A controlled study. *British Journal of Psychiatry* 138: 185–93.

Maxman, J. S. 1986. *Essential Psychopathology*. New York: W. W. Norton.

McClellan, A. T. 1988. Addiction Severity Index. In M. Hersen and A. S. Bellack (eds.), *Dictionary of Behavioral Assessment Techniques*. New York: Pergamon.

McClellan, A. T., et al. 1980. An improved evaluation instrument for substance abuse patients: The addiction severity index. *Journal of Nervous and Mental Disorders:* 168: 26–33.

McCormick, I. A. 1984. A simple version of the Rathus assertiveness schedule. *Behavioral Assessment* 7: 95–99.

McCrady, B. S. 1985. Alcoholism. In D. H. Barlow (ed.), *Clinical Handbook of Psychological Disorders*, 245–98. New York: Guilford Press.

_____. 1986. The Family in the Change Process. In W. R. Miller and N. Heather (eds.), *Treating Addictive Behaviors*. New York: Plenum.

McCrady, B. S., and Sher, K. 1985. Treatment Variables. In B. S. McCrady, N. E. Noel, and T. D. Nirenberg (eds.), *Future Directions in Alcohol Abuse Treatment Research*. Washington, DC: U.S. Department of Health and Human Services.

McFall, R. M. 1982. A review and reformulation of the concept of social skills. *Behavioral Assessment* 9: 1–33.

McGlashon, T. H. 1983. The borderline syndrome: I. Testing three diagnostic systems. *Archives of General Psychiatry* 40: 1311–18.

McGlynn, F. D. 1985. Cue-Controlled Relaxation. In A. S. Bellack and M. Hersen (eds.), *Dictionary of Behavior Therapy Techniques*. New York: Pergamon.

McLaughlin, M., Cormier, L. S., and Cormier, W. H. 1988. Relation between coping strategies and distress, stress and marital adjustment of multiple-role women. *Journal of Counseling Psychology* 35(2): 187–93.

McNesse, R. M., Curtis, G. C., Thyer, B. A., McCann, D., Huber-Smith, M., and Knopf, R. 1985. Endocrine and cardiovascular responses during public anxiety. *Psychosomatic Medicine* 47: 320–32.

Meichenbaum, D. H. 1975. Self-Instructional Methods. In F. H. Kanfer and A. P. Goldstein (eds.), *Helping People Change*, 1st ed. New York: Pergamon.

Meichenbaum, D. 1983. *Coping with Stress*. New York: Wiley.

Meichenbaum, D., and Turk, D. C. 1987. *Facilitating Treatment Adherence*. New York: Plenum.

Merbaum, M., and Rosenbaum, M. 1984. Self-Control Theory and Technique in the Modification of Smoking, Obesity, and Alcohol Abuse. In C. M. Franks (ed.), *New Developments in Behavior Therapy*. New York: Haworth Press.

Miers, T. C., and Raulin, M. L. 1985. The development of a scale to measure cognitive slippage. Unpublished manuscript. Available from M. Raulin, SUNY-Buffalo, Department of Psychology, Buffalo, NY 14260.

Milgram, G. G. 1987. Alcohol and drug education programs. *Journal of Drug Education* 17: 43–57.

Miller, P. M. 1981. Assessment of Alcohol Abuse. In D. H. Barlow (ed.), *Behavioral Assessment of Adult Disorders*, 271–300. New York: Guilford Press.

_____. 1987. Commonalities of Addictive Behaviors. In T. D. Nirenberg and S. A. Maisto (eds.), *Developments in the Assessment and Treatment of Addictive Behaviors*. Norwood, NJ: Ablex.

Miller, W. R. 1985. Motivation for treatment: A review with special emphasis on alcoholism. *Psychological Bulletin* 98: 84–107.

Miller, W. R., and Heather, N. (eds.), 1986. *Treating Addictive Behaviors*. New York: Plenum.

Miller, W. R., and Hester, R. K. 1986. The Effectiveness of Alcoholism Treatment: What Research Reveals. In W. R. Miller and N. Heather (eds.), *Treating Addictive Behaviors*. New York: Plenum.

Minkin, N., Braukmann, C. J., Minkin, B. L., Timbers, G. K., Timbers, B. J., Fixen, D. L., Phillips, E. L., and Wolf, M. M. 1976. The social validation and training of conversational skills. *Journal of Applied Behavior Analysis* 9: 127–39.

Mintz, R. S. 1968. Psychotherapy of the Suicide Patient. In H. L. P. Resnik (ed.), *Suicidal Behaviors: Diagnosis and Management*. Boston: Little, Brown.

Mintz, J., and Kiesler, D. J. 1982. Individualized Measures of Psychotherapy Outcome. In P. C. Kendall and J. N. Butcher (eds.), *Handbook of Research Methods in Clinical Psychology*. New York: Wiley.

Minuchin, S. 1974. *Families and Family Therapy*. Cambridge, MA: Harvard University Press.

Modrcin, M., Rapp, C. A., and Poertner, J. (No date). The evaluation of case management services with the chronically mentally ill. Unpublished manuscript.

Montgomery, S. A., and Montgomery, D. 1982. Pharmacological prevention of suicide behavior. *Journal of Affective Disorders* 4: 291–98.

Monti, P. M., Abrams, D. B., Kadden, R. M., and Cooney, N. L. 1989. *Treating Alcohol Dependence: A Coping Skills Guide*. New York: Guilford Press.

Morris, R., and Lescohier, I. H. 1978. Service Integration: Real Versus Illusory Solutions to Welfare Dilemmas. In R. Sarri and Y. Hasenfeld (eds.), *The Management of Human Services*. New York: Columbia University Press.

Morrow-Bradley, C., and Elliott, R., 1986. Utilization of psychotherapy research by practicing psychotherapists. *American Psychologist* 41(2): 188–97.

Mosher, L., and Keith, S. 1980. Psychosocial treatment: Individual, group, family and community support approaches. *Schizophrenia Bulletin* 6: 10–41.

Motto, J. A. 1986. Clinical considerations of biological correlates of suicide. *Suicide and Life Threatening Behavior* 16(2): 83–102.

Moxley, D. P. 1989. *The Practice of Case Management*. Newbury Park, CA: Sage.

Mullen, E. J., 1985. Methodological dilemmas in social work research. *Social Work Research and Abstracts* 21: 12–20.

Mullen, E. J., Dumpson, J. R., and Associates. 1972. *Evaluation of Social Interventions*. San Francisco, Jossey-Bass.

Nathan, R. G., Staats, T. E., and Rosch, P. J. 1987. *The Doctor's Guide to Instant Stress Relief: A Psychological and Medical System*. New York: Putnam.

National Center for Health Statistics. 1988a. Annual Summary of Births, Marriages, Divorces, and Deaths: United States, 1987. *Monthly Vital Statistics Report* 36(13). [DHHS Pub. # (PHS) 88–1120]. Hyattsville, MD: U.S. Public Health Service.

_____. 1988b. Vital Statistics of the United States, 1986, Vol. II. Mortality Part A. [DHSS Pub. # (PHS) 88–1122]. Washington, DC: U.S. Government Printing Office.

National Institute of Drug Abuse. 1986. *Highlights: 1985: National Household Survey on Drug Abuse*, 7–9. Washington, DC: National Institute of Drug Abuse.

Navran, L. 1967. Communication and adjustment in marriage. *Family Process* 6: 173–84.

Nelson, C. H., and Rieman, M. J. 1987. Confronting the AIDS dilemma in nursing homes. *Contemporary Long-Term Care*, November, 44–122.

Nelson, H. F., Tennen, H., Tasman, A., Borton, M., Kubeck, M., and Stone, M. 1985. Comparison of three systems for diagnosing borderline personality disorder. *American Journal of Psychiatry* 142: 855–58.

Nelsen, J. C. 1981. Issues in single-subject research for nonbehaviorist. *Social Work Research and Abstracts* 17(2): 31–37.

————. 1984. Intermediate treatment goals as variables in single-case research. *Social Work Research and Abstracts* 20(3): 3–10.

————. 1988. Single-subject Designs. In R. M. Grinnell, Jr. (ed.), *Social Work Research and Evaluation*, 3rd ed. Itasca, IL: Peacock.

Nerabian, A. 1972. *Nonverbal Communication*. Chicago: Aldine Publishing Company.

Nirenberg, G. I. 1968. *The Art of Negotiations: Psychological Strategies for Gaining Advantageous Bargains*. New York: Hawthorn Press.

Nirenberg, T. D., and Maisto, S. A. 1987. *Developments in the Assessment and Treatment of Addictive Behavior*. Norwood, NJ: Ablex.

Nugent, W. 1989. An Experiment and Qualitative Analysis of a Cognitive-Behavioral Intervention for Anger. Unpublished manuscript.

Nugent, W. (In press). Psychometric characteristics of self-anchored rating scales in clinical application. *Journal of Social Science Research*.

O'Farrell, T. J. 1987. Marital and Family Therapy for Alcohol Problems. In W. M. Cox (ed.), *Treatment and Prevention of Alcohol Problems*. New York: Academic Press.

Okin, R. 1987. The case of deinstitutionalization. *Harvard Medical School Mental Health Letter* 4: 5–7.

Olsen, L. 1978. Focusing and self-healing. Audio cassette. Continuum Tape Montage, 8970 Ellis Avenue, Los Angeles, California.

Omer, H. 1985. Fulfillment of therapeutic tasks as a precondition for acceptance in therapy. *American Journal of Psychotherapy* 39: 175–86.

Ornstein, A. 1986. Supportive psychotherapy: A contemporary view. *Clinical Social Work Journal* 14: 14–30.

Ost, L. G., and Hugdahl, H. (1981). Acquisition of phobias and anxiety response patterns in clinical patients. *Behavior Research and Therapy* 19: 439–47.

Ostensen, K. W. 1981. The runaway crisis: Is family therapy the answer? *American Journal of Family Therapy* 9: 3–12.

Parad, H. J., and Parad, L. J. 1968a. A study of crisis-oriented planned short-term casework, part I. *Social Casework* 49: 346–55.

————. 1968b. A study of crisis-oriented planned short-term casework, part II. *Social Casework* 49: 418–26.

Parson, B. S., and Baer, D. M. 1978. The Analysis and Presentation of Graphic Data. In T. R. Kratochwill (ed.), *Single-Subject Research: Strategies for Evaluating Change*. New York: Academic Press.

Patsiokas, A., Clum, G., and Luscomb, R. 1979. Cognitive characteristics of suicide attempters. *Journal of Consulting and Clinical Psychology* 47(2): 478–84.

Patterson, G. R., and Reid, J. B. 1970. Reciprocity and Coercion: Two Facets of Social Systems. In C. Neuringer and J. C. Michael (eds.), *Behavior Modification in Clinical Psychology*. New York: Appleton-Century-Crofts.

Paykel, E. S. 1979. Life Stress. In L. D. Hankoff and B. Einsidler (eds.), *Suicide: Theory and Clinical Aspects*. Littleton, MA: P.S.G. Publishing.

Paykel, E. S., and Dienelt, M. N. 1971. Suicide attempts following acute depression. *Journal of Nervous and Mental Disease* 153: 234–43.

Peck, B. B. 1975. Psychotherapy with disrupted families. *Journal of Contemporary Psychotherapy* 7.

Peele, S. 1989. *The Diseasing of America: How the Addiction Industry Captured Our Soul*. Cambridge, MA: Lexington.

Pendleton, B. F., Poloma, M. M., and Garland, T. N. 1980. Scales for the investigation of the dual-career family. *Journal of Marriage and the Family* 42: 269–75.

Pentz, M. A. 1985. Social Competence Skills and Self-Efficacy as Determinants of Substance Use in Adolescence. In S. Shiffman and T. A. Wills (eds.), *Coping and Substance Use*. New York: Pergamon.

Perlman, B., Melnick, G., and Kentera, A. 1985. Assessing the effectiveness of a case management program. *Hospital and Community Psychiatry* 36: 405–7.

Perr, I. N. 1979. Legal Aspects of Suicide. In L. D. Hankoff and B. Einsidler (eds.), *Suicide: Theory and Clinical Aspects*. Littleton, MA: P.S.G. Publishing.

————. 1985. Suicide litigation and risk management: A review of 32 cases. *Bulletin of the American Academy of Psychiatry and Law* 13(3): 209–19.

Perry, J. C., and Klerman, G. 1980. Clinical features of the borderline personality disorder. *American Journal of Psychiatry* 137: 165–73.

Perry, M. A., and Furukawa, M. J. 1986. Modeling Methods. In F. H. Kanfer and A. P. Goldstein (eds.), *Helping People Change*, 3rd ed. New York: Pergamon.

Piaget, J. 1953. *The Psychology of Intelligence*. New Haven, CT: Yale University Press.

Pierce, R., and Drasgow, J. 1969. Teaching facilitative interpersonal functioning to psychiatric inpatients. *Journal of Counseling Psychology* 16: 295–98.

Piot, P., Plummer, F., et al. 1988. AIDS: An international perspective. *Science* 239 (February): 573–622.

Pleck, J. 1982. *Husbands and Wives: Family Work, Paid Work, and Adjustment*. Working paper no. 95. Wellesley, MA: Wellesley College.

Polich, J. M., Armor, D. M., and Braiker, H. B. 1981. *The Course of Alcoholism: Four Years After Treatment*. New York: Wiley.

Pomeranz, D. M., and Goldfried, M. R. 1970. An intake report outline for modification. *Psychological Report* 26: 447–50.

President's Commission on Mental Health. 1978. *Report to the President from the President's Commission on Mental Health*, vol. II. Washington, DC: U.S. Government Printing Office.

Quayle, J., D. 1983. American productivity: The devastating effect of alcoholism and drug abuse. *American Psychologist* 38: 454–58.

Radloff, L. S. 1977. The CES-D Scale: A self-report depression scale for research in the general population. *Applied Psychological Measurement* 1: 385–401.

Raine, 1989. Black American Faces AIDS. *San Francisco Examiner*, April 1.

Rapp, C. 1983. Community Mental Health Case Management Project: Final Report. University of Kansas School of Social Welfare.

Rapp, C. A., and Chamberlain, R. 1985. Case management services for the chronically mentally ill. *Social Work* 30: 417–22.

Rapp, C. A., and Wintersteen, R. 1986. Case Management with the Chronically Mentally Ill: The Results of Seven Replications. Unpublished manuscript. University of Kansas School of Social Welfare.

Raulin, M. L. 1984. Development of a scale to measure intense ambivalence. *Journal of Consulting and Clinical Psychology* 52: 63–72.

Rawlings, E., and Carter, D. 1977. Feminist and Nonsexist Psychotherapy. In E. Rawlings and D. Carter (eds.), *Psychotherapy for Women*. Springfield, IL: Charles C. Thomas.

Reid, W. J., and Epstein L. (1972). *Task-centered casework*. New York: Columbia University Press.

Reid, W. J., and Hanrahan, P. 1982. Recent evaluations of social work: Grounds for optimism. *Social Work* 27: 328–341.

Reiger, D. A., Boyd, J. H., Burke, J. D., Rae, D. S., Myers, J. K., Kramer, M., Robins, L. N., George, L. K., Karno, M., and Locke, B. Z. 1988. One-month prevalence of mental disorders in the United States: Based on five epidemiological catchment area sites. *Archives of General Psychiatry* 45: 977–86.

Relman, A. S. 1985. AIDS: The emerging ethical dilemmas. *Hastings Center Reports: Special Supplement*, August.

Rhodes, J. E., and Jason, L. A. 1988. *Preventing Substance Abuse Among Children and Adolescents*. New York: Pergamon.

Richmond, M. 1917. *Social Diagnosis*. New York: Russell Sage Foundation (reprinted in 1935).

Ridley, T. D., and Kordinak, S. T. 1988. Reliability and validity of the quantitative inventory of alcohol disorders (QIAD) and the veracity of self-report by alcoholics. *American Journal of Drug and Alcohol Abuse* 14: 263–92.

Rinsley, D. B. 1971. The adolescent inpatient: Patterns of depersonification. *Psychoanalytic Quarterly* 45: 3–22.

Roberts-DeGennaro, M. 1987. Developing case management as a practice model. *Social Casework*, October, 466–70.

Robin, A. L. 1982. A controlled evaluation of problem-solving communication training with parent-adolescent conflict. *Behavior Therapy* 12: 593–609.

Robins, L. N., et al. 1984. Lifetime prevalence of specific psychiatric disorders in three sites. *Archives of General Psychiatry* 41: 949–58.

Robinson, J. P., and Shaver, P. R. 1973. *Measures of Social Psychological Attitudes*, rev. ed. Ann Arbor, MI: Institute for Social Research.

Rose, S. D., and Edelson J. L. 1987. *Working With Children and Adolescents in Groups*. San Francisco: Jossey-Bass.

Rosen, A., and Proctor, E. K. 1978. Specifying the treatment process: The basis for effectiveness. *Journal of Social Service Research* 2: 25–26.

Rosenbaum, M., and Richman, J. 1970. Suicide: The role of hostility and death wishes from the family and significant others. *American Journal of Psychiatry* 126: 1652–55.

Rosewater, L., and Walker, L. 1985. Introduction: Feminist Therapy, A Coming of Age. In L. Rosewater and L. Walker (eds.), *Handbook of Feminist Therapy*. New York: Springer.

Rotheram-Borus, M. J., and Troutman, P. D. 1988. Hopelessness, depression, and suicidal intent among adolescent suicide attempters. *Journal of the American Academy of Child and Adolescent Psychiatry* 27(6): 700–4.

Rothery, M. A. 1980. Contracts and contracting. *Clinical Social Work Journal* 8: 179–87.

Rothman, J. 1980. *Using Research in Organizations: A Guide to the Successful Application*. Newbury Park, CA: Sage.

Roy, A., and Linnoila, M. 1986. Alcoholism and suicide. *Suicide and Life Threatening Behavior* 16(2): 244–73.

Rubenstein, R., Moses, R., and Lidz, T. 1958. On attempted suicide. *American Medical Association Archives of Neurology and Psychiatry* 79: 103–12.

Rubin, A. 1987. Case Management. In the *Encyclopedia of Social Work*. Silver Spring, MD: NASW Publications.

Saenz, J. 1978. The Value of a Humanistic Model in Serving Families. In M. Monteil (ed.), *Hispanic Families*. Washington, DC: COSSMHO.

Sarason, I. G., and Ganzer, V. J. 1973. Modeling and group discussion in the rehabilitation of delinquents. *Journal of Counseling Psychology* 20: 442–49.

Saxton, W. 1979. Behavioral contracting. *Child Welfare* 63: 523–29.

Schafer, W. 1987. *Stress Management for Wellness*. New York: Holt, Rinehart and Winston.

Schinke, S. P., Blythe, B. J., and Gilchrist, L. D. 1981. Cognitive-behavioral prevention of adolescent pregnancy. *Journal of Counseling Psychology* 28: 451–54.

Schinke, S. P., Schilling, R. F., Gilchrist, L. D., Barth, R., Bobo, J. K., Trimble, J. E., and Cvetkovich. G. T. 1985. Preventing substance abuse with American-Indian youth. *Social Casework* 66: 213–17.

Schlesinger, S. E. 1988. Cognitive-Behavioral Approaches to Family Treatment of Addictions. In N. Epstein, S. E. Schlesinger, and W. Dryden (eds.), *Cognitive Behavioral Therapy With Families*. New York: Brunner/Mazel.

Schooler, N. R., and Hogarty, G. E. 1987. Medication and Psychosocial Strategies in the Treatment of Schizophrenia. In H. Y. Meltzler (ed.), *Psychopharmacology: The Third Generation of Progress*. New York: Raven Press.

Schwartz, E. B., and Waetjen, W. B. 1976. Improving the self-concept of women managers. *Business Quarterly* 41(4): 20–27.

Scopetta, M. A., and Alegre, C. 1975. Clinical issues in psychotherapy research with Latins. Paper presented at the Third National Drug Abuse Conference, New Orleans, LA.

Scott, W. O., Baer, G., Kristoff, K. A., and Kelly, J. 1984. The use of skills training procedures in the treatment of a child-abusive parent. *Journal of Behavior Therapy and Experimental Psychiatry* 15: 329–36.

Seabury, B. A. 1989. Negotiating Sound Contracts With Clients. In B. R. Compton and B. Galaway (eds.), *Social Work Processes*. Belmont, CA: Wadsworth.

Segal, R., and Sisson, B. V. 1985. Medical Complications Associated With Alcohol Use and the Assessment of Risk of Physical Damage. In T. E. Bratter and G. G. Forrest (eds.), *Alcoholism and Substance Abuse*, 137–175. New York: Free Press.

Sekaran, U. 1986. *Dual-Career Families*. San Francisco: Jossey-Bass.

Seligman, M. E. P. 1981. A Learned Helplessness Point of View. In L. P. Rehm (ed.), *Behavior Therapy for Depression*. New York: Academic Press.

Selzer, M. L. 1971. The Michigan alcoholism screening test: The quest for a new diagnostic instrument. *American Journal of Psychiatry* 127: 89–94.

Shaffer, D., Garland, A., Gould, M. Fisher, P., and Trautman, P. 1988. Preventing teenage suicide: A critical review. *Journal of the American Academy of Child and Adolescent Psychiatry* 27(6): 675–87.

Shaffer, D., and Gould, M. 1987. Study of Completed and Attempted Suicides in Adolescents. Progress report. Rockville, MD: National Institute of Mental Health.

Shaffer, H., and Kauffan, J. 1985. The Clinical Assessment and Diagnosis of Addiction: Hypothesis Testing. In T. E. Bratter and G. G. Forrest (eds.), *Alcoholism and Substance Abuse*, 225–58. New York: Free Press.

Shapiro, D. A., and Shapiro, D. 1982. Meta-analysis of comparative therapy outcome studies: A replication and refinement. *Psychological Bulletin* 42: 581–604.

Shapiro, M. B., and Zifferblatt, S. M. 1976. Zen mediation and behavioral self-control: Similarities, differences, and clinical applications. *American Psychologist* 31: 519–32.

Shapiro, T. 1989. Psychoanalytic classification and empiricism with borderline personality disorder as a model. *Journal of Consulting and Clinical Psychology* 57: 187–94.

Sheafor, B., Horejsi, C., and Horejsi, G. 1988. *Techniques and Guidelines for Social Work Practice*. Boston: Allyn and Bacon.

Sheehy, M., Goldsmith, L., and Charles, E. 1980. A comparative study of borderline patients in a psychiatric out-patient clinic. *American Journal of Psychiatry* 137: 1374–79.

Shelton, J. L., and Levy, R. L. 1981. *Behavioral Assignments and Treatment Compliance*. Champaign, IL: Research Press.

Shelton, R., Karson, C., Doran, A., Pickar, D. Bigelow, L., and Weinberger, D. 1988. Cerebral structural pathology in schizophrenia: Evidence for a selective prefrontal cortical defect. *American Journal of Psychiatry* 145: 154–63.

Shneidman, E. S. 1976. The components of suicide. *Psychiatric Annals* 6: 51–66.

Shneidman, E. S., Farberow, N. L., and Litman, R. E. (eds.). 1970. *The Psychology of Suicide*. New York: Science House.

Siegel, S., and Fouraker, L. E. 1960. *Bargaining and Group Decision-Making*. New York: McGraw-Hill.

Silver, D. 1985. Psychodynamics and psychotherapeutic management of self-destructive character disordered patients. *Psychiatric Clinics of North America* 8: 357–75.

Simkin, J. S., and Yontef, G. M. 1984. Gestalt Therapy. In R. Corsini (ed.), *Current Psychotherapies*. Itasca, IL: Peacock.

Simons, R. L., and Aigner, S. M. 1985. *Practice Principles: A Problem-Solving Approach to Social Work*. New York: Macmillan.

Siporin, M. 1975. *Introduction to Social Work Practice*. New York: Macmillan.

Skinner, H. A. 1982. The drug abuse screening test. *Addictive Behaviors* 7: 363–71.

Smith, A., and Siegel, R. 1985. Feminist Therapy: Redefining Power for the Powerless. In L. Rosewater and L. Walker (eds.), *Handbook of Feminist Therapy*. New York: Springer.

Smith, A., and Reid, W. 1986. *Role-Sharing Marriage*. New York: Columbia University Press.

Smith, M. L., and Glass, G. V. 1977. Meta-analysis of psychotherapy outcome studies. *American Psychologist* 32: 752–60.

Smith, M. L. Glass, G. V., and Miller, T. I. 1980. *The Benefits of Psychotherapy*. Baltimore: Johns Hopkins University Press.

Sobell, L. C., Sobell, M. B., and Nirenberg, T. D. 1988. Behavioral assessment and treatment planning with alcohol and drug abusers: A review with an emphasis on clinical application. *Clinical Psychology Review* 8: 19–54.

Social Casework. 1989. 70(6). Entire issue.

Soloff, T. H. 1981. Concurrent validation of a diagnostic interview for borderline patients. *American Journal of Psychiatry* 138: 691–93.

Spence, A. J., and Spence, S. H. 1980. Cognitive changes associated with social skills training. *Behavior Research and Therapy* 18: 265–72.

Spielberger, C. D., Jacobs, A., Russell, S., and Crane, R. S. 1983. Assessment of Anger: The State Trait Anger-Scale. In J. N. Butcher and C. D. Spielberger (eds.), *Advances in Personality Assessment*, vol. 2. Hillsdale, NJ: Lawrence Erlbaum.

Spitzer, R., Endicott, J., and Robins, E. 1978. Research diagnostic criteria: Rationale and reliability. *Archives of General Psychiatry* 35: 773–85.

Staab, S., and Lodish, D. 1985. Reducing Joblessness among Disadvantaged Youth. In L. D. Gilchrist and S. P. Schinke (eds.), *Preventing Social and Health Problems Through Life Skills Training*. Seattle, WA: Center for Social Welfare Research, University of Washington.

Stangl, D., Pfhol, B., Zimmerman, M., Bowers, W., and Corenthal, C. 1985. A structural interview for the DSM-III personality disorders. *Archives of General Psychiatry* 42: 591–96.

Stein, L. I. (ed.). 1979. *Community Support Systems for the Long-Term Patient*. San Francisco: Jossey-Bass.

Stein, L. I., and Test, M. A. 1980. An alternative to mental hospital treatment; Conceptual model, treatment program, and clinical evaluation. *Archives of General Psychiatry* 37: 392–97.

Stein, T. J. 1981. Macro and Micro level Issues in Case Management. In *Case Management: State of the Art*, Washington, DC: NASW Publications.

Steketee, G. S. 1987. Behavioral social work with obsessive compulsive disorders. *Journal of Social Service Research* 10 (2,3,4): 53–72.

Stengel, E. 1964. *Suicide and Attempted Suicide*. Baltimore: Penguin.

Stitzer, M. L., Bigelow, G. E., and McCaul, M. E. 1983. Behavioral Approaches to Drug Abuse. In M. Hersen et al. (eds.), *Progress in Behavior Modification*, vol. 14. New York: Academic Press.

Strayhorn, J., Jr., 1977. *Talking It Out: A Guide to Effective Communication and Problem-Solving*. Champaign, IL: Research Press.

Stuart, R. B. 1980. *Helping Couples Change: A Social Learning Approach to Marital Therapy*. New York: Guilford Press.

Sullivan, H. S. 1954. *The Psychiatric Interview*. New York: W. W. Norton.

Svec, H., and Bechard, J. 1988. An introduction to a metabehavioral model with implication for social skills training for aggressive adolescents. *Psychological Reports* 62: 19–22.

Sweetland, R. C., and Keyser, D. J. 1983. *Tests: A Comprehensive Reference*. Kansas City, MO: Test Corporation of America.

Szabo, E. A. 1986. The Reduction of Symptomatology of High Risk Antepartum Obstetrical Patients: Case Studies. Unpublished raw data.

————. 1988. Treatment of Post Traumatic Stress Disorders with War Veterans; Case Studies. Unpublished raw data.

Szapocznik, J., and Kurtines, W. 1980. Acculturation, Biculturalism, and Adjustment Among Cuban Americans. In A. Padilla (ed.), *Psychological Dimensions on the Acculturation Process: Theories, Models, and Some New Findings*. Boulder, CO: Westview Press.

Szapocznik, J., Kurtines, W., Hervis, O., and Spencer, F. 1983. One Person Family Therapy. In B. Lubin and W. A. O'Connor (eds.), *Ecological Models; Applications to Clinical and Community Mental Health*. New York: Wiley.

Szapocznik, J., Santiesteban, D., Kurtines, W., Perez-Vidal, A., and Hervis, O. 1984. Bicultural effectiveness training: A treatment intervention for enhancing intercultural adjustment in Cuban American families. *Hispanic Journal of Behavioral Sciences* 6(4): 317–44.

Szapocznik, J., and Truss, C. 1978. Intergenerational Sources of Conflict in Cuban Mothers. In M. Montiel (ed.), *Hispanic Families*. Washington, DC: COSSMHO.

Szasz, T. (1986). The case against suicide prevention. *American Psychologist* 41(7): 806–12.

Talbot, J. 1979. Deinstitutionalization: Avoiding the disasters of the past. *Hospital and Community Psychiatry* 30: 621–24.

Tarnopolsky, A., and Berelowitz, M. 1987. Borderline personality: A review of recent research. *British Journal of Psychiatry* 151: 724–34.

Taylor, D., Barry, P., and Block, C. 1958. Does group participation when using brainstorming facilitate or inhibit creative thinking? *Administrative Science Quarterly* 3: 23–47.

Termansen, P. E., and Bywater, C. 1975. S.A.F.E.R.: A follow-up service for attempted suicide in Vancouver. *Canadian Psychiatric Association Journal* 20(1): 29–34.

Tetenbaum, T. J., Lighter, J., and Travis, M. 1981. Educator's attitudes toward working mothers. *Journal of Educational Psychology* 73: 369–75.

Thibaut, J. W., and Kelly, H. H. 1959. *The Social Psychology of Groups*. New York: Wiley.

Thomas, E. J., and Yoshioka, M. R. 1989. Spouse interventive confrontations in unilateral family therapy for alcohol abuse. *Social Casework* 70: 340–47.

Thomlinson, R. J. 1984. Something works: Evidence from practice effectiveness studies. *Social Work* 29: 51–57.

Thyer, B. A. 1981. Prolonged *in-vivo* exposure therapy with a 70-year-old woman. *Journal of Behavior Therapy and Experimental Psychiatry* 12: 69–71.

————. 1983. Treating anxiety disorders with exposure therapy. *Social Casework* 64: 77–82.

————. 1987. *Treating Anxiety Disorders: Guidelines for Human Service Professionals*. Newbury Park, CA: Sage.

————. 1990. Should All Social Workers Be Required to Be Well Trained in Behavioral Principles? In E. Gambrill and R. Pruger (eds.), *Controversial Issues in Social Work*. Boston: Allyn and Bacon.

_____. 1991. Single-subject Designs. In R. M. Grinnell, Jr., (ed.), *Social Work Research and Evaluation*, 4th ed. Itasca, IL: Peacock.

Thyer, B. A., Baum, M., and Reid, L. D. 1988. Exposure techniques in the reduction of fear; A comparative review of the procedure in animals and humans. *Advances in Behavior Research and Therapy* 10: 105–27.

Thyer, B. A., and Curtis, G. C. 1983. The repeated pretest–Post-test single subject experiment: A new design for empirical clinical practice. *Journal of Behavior Therapy and Experimental Psychiatry* 14: 311–15.

Thyer, B. A., Papsdorf, J. D., Davis, R., and Vallecorsa, S. 1984. Autonomic correlates of the clinical anxiety scale. *Journal of Behavior Therapy and Experimental Psychiatry* 15: 3–7.

Thyer, B. A., Parris, R. T., Himle, J., Cameron, O. G., Curtis, G. C., and Nesse, R. M. 1986. Alcohol abuse among clinically anxious patients. *Behavior Research and Therapy* 24: 357–59.

Thyer, B. A., and Stocks, J. T. 1986. Exposure therapy in the treatment of phobic blind persons. *Journal of Visual Impairment and Blindness* 80: 1001–03.

Tisdelle, D. A., and St. Lawrence, J. S. 1986. Interpersonal problem-solving competency: Review and critique of the literature. *Clinical Psychology Review* 6: 337–56.

Tobler, N. S. 1986. Meta-Analysis of 143 adolescent drug prevention programs: Quantitative outcome results of program participants compared to a control or comparison group. *The Journal of Drug Issues* 4: 537–67.

Tranchia, P., and Serra, P. 1983. Community Work and Participation in the New Italian Psychiatric Legislation. In H. Stierlin, L. Wynne, and M. Wirsching (eds.), *Psychosocial Intervention in Schizophrenia—An International View*. New York: Springer-Verlag.

Tuckman, J., and Youngman, W. F. 1968. Assessment of suicide risk in attempted suicides. In H. L. Pflesnik (ed.), *Suicidal Behaviors: Diagnosis and Management*. Boston: Little, Brown.

Turner, J. E., and Shifren, I. 1979. Community Support System: How Comprehensive? In L. I. Stein (ed.), *Community Support Systems for the Long-Term Patient*. San Francisco: Jossey-Bass.

Turner, R. M. 1989. Case study evaluation of a bio-cognitive behavioral approach for the treatment of borderline personality disorder. *Behavior Therapy* 20(4) 477–89.

U.S. Department of Health, Education, and Welfare. 1979. *Background Papers for Health People: The Surgeon General's Report on Health Promotion and Disease Prevention*. DHEW Publication No. 79-55072. Washington, DC: Government Printing Office.

Van Den Bergh, N., and Cooper, L. B. 1988. *Feminist Visions for Social Work*. Silver Spring, MD: NASW Publications.

Vattano, A. J. 1978. Self-management procedures for coping with stress. *Social Work* 23: 113–20.

Videka-Sherman, L. 1985. *Harriet M. Bartlett Practice Effectiveness Project*. Silver Spring MD: NASW Publications.

_____. 1988. Meta-analysis of research for social work practice in mental health. *Social Work* 33: 325–38.

_____. 1989. The Effects of Intervention for Child Abuse and Neglect: A Meta-Analysis. Final project report. Albany, NY: School of Social Work, State University of New York.

_____. 1990. A User's Perspective on Meta-Analysis. In L. Videka-Sherman and W. J. Reid (eds.), *Advances in Clinical Social Work Research*. Silver Spring, MD: NASW Publications.

Vinogradoov, S. Thornton, J. E., et al. 1984. If I Have AIDS, Then Let Me Die Now! *A Hastings Center Report*, February, 24–26.

Waldinger, R. J. 1987. Intensive psychodynamic therapy with borderline patients: An overview. *American Journal of Psychiatry* 144: 267–74.

Walters, L. 1988. Ethical issues in the prevention and treatment of HIV infection and AIDS. *Science* 239 (February): 597–603.

Wandrei, K. E. 1985. Identifying potential suicides among high-risk women. *Social Work* 30 (6) 511–17.

Wartenberg, A. A., and Liepman, M. R. 1987. Medical Consequences of Addictive Behaviors. In T. D. Nirenberg and S. A. Maisto (eds.), *Developments in the Assessment and Treatment of Addictive Behaviors*. Norwood, N.J.: Ablex.

Watzlawick, P. 1978. *The Language of Change*. New York: Basic Books.

Watzlawick, P., Beavin, J. H., and Jackson, D. D. 1967. *Pragmatics of Human Communication: A Study of Interactional Patterns, Pathologies, and Paradoxes*. New York: W. W. Norton.

Watzlawick, P., Weakland, J. and Fisch, R. 1974. *Change: Principles of Problem Formation and Problem Resolution*. New York: W. W. Norton.

Webb, E. J., Campbell, D. T., Schwartz, R. D., Sechrest, L., and Grove, J. B. 1981. *Unobtrusive Measures: Non-reactive Research in Social Sciences*. Boston: Houghton Mifflin.

Weeks, G. 1977. Toward a dialectical approach to intervention. *Human Development* 20: 277–92.

Weeks, G., and L'Abate, L. 1982. *Paradoxical Psychotherapy*. New York: Brunner/Mazel.

Weiss, R. L., Hops, H., and Patterson, G. R. 1973. A Framework for Conceptualizing Marital Conflict, A Technology for Altering It, Some Data For Evaluating It. In L. S. Hamerlynck, L. C. Handy, and E. J. Mash (eds.), *Behavior Change: Methodology, Concepts, and Practice*. Champaign, IL: Research Press.

Weissman, M. 1980. Depression. In A. Brodsky and R. Hare-Mustin (eds), *Women in Psychotherapy*. New York: Guilford Press.

Weissman, M., and Klerman, G. 1987. Gender and Depression. In R. Formanek and A. Gurian (eds.), *Women and Depression: A Lifespan Approach*. New York: Springer.

Wells, E. A., Hawkins, J. D., and Catalano, R. F. 1988a. Choosing drug use measures for treatment outcome studies, I: The influence of measurement approach on treatment results. *The International Journal of the Addictions* 23: 851–73.

_____. 1988b. Choosing drug use measures for treatment outcome studies, II: Timing baseline and follow-up measurement. *The International Journal of the Addictions* 23: 875–85.

Wells, R. A. 1982. *Planned Short-Term Treatment*. New York: Free Press.

Wells, R. A., Figurel, J. A., and McNamee, P. 1975. Group Facilitative Training With Conflicted Marital Couples. In A. S. Gurman and D. G. Rice (eds), *Couples in Conflict*. New York: Jason Aronson.

Wells, R. A., and Giannetti, V. (eds.). 1989. *Handbook of the Brief Psychotherapies*. New York: Plenum.

Wells, R. A., and Phelps, P. A. 1989. The Brief Psychotherapies: A Selective Overview. In R. A. Wells and V. Gianetti (eds.), *Handbook of the Brief Psychotherapies*. New York: Plenum.

Welton, G., Pruitt, D., and McGillicudy, N. 1988. The role of caucusing in community mediation. *Journal of Conflict Resolution* 32: 181–202.

Welu, T. C. 1977. A follow-up program for suicide attempters: Evaluation of effectiveness. *Suicide and Life Threatening Behavior* 7: 17–30.

Westhuis, D., and Thyer, B. A. 1989. Development and validation of the clinical anxiety scale: A rapid assessment instrument for empirical practice. *Educational and Psychological Measurement* 49: 153–63.

Wetzel, H. 1987. *American Youth: A Statistical Snapshot*. Washington, DC: William T. Grant Foundation Commission on Youth and America's Future.

Wetzel, J. 1982. Redefining Concepts of Mental Health. In A. Weick and S. Vandiver (eds.), *Women, Power, and Change*. Washington, DC: NASW Publications.

Wetzel, R. D. 1976. Semantic differential ratings of concepts and suicide intent. *Journal of Clinical Psychology* 32: 11–12.

Wexler, L., Weissman, M. M., and Kasl, S. V. 1978. Suicide attempts 1970–75: Updating a United States study and comparisons with international trends. *British Journal of Psychiatry* 132: 180–85.

William T. Grant Foundation 1988. *The Forgotten Half: Pathways to Success for America's Youth and Young Families*. Washington, DC: William T. Grant Foundation Commission on Work, Family, and Citizenship.

Williams, J. 1984. *The Psychological Treatment of Depression*. New York: Free Press.

Wills, T. A., Weiss, R. L., and Patterson, G. R. 1974. A behavioral analysis of the determinants of marital satisfaction. *Journal of Consulting and Clinical Psychology* 42: 802–11.

Wine, J. D. 1981. From Defects to Competence Models. In J. D. Wine and M. D. Smye (eds.), *Social Competence*. New York: Guilford Press.

Wing, J. 1985. The Management of Schizophrenia in the Community. In R. Cancro and S. Dean (eds.), *Research in the Schizophrenic Disorders*. New York: Spectrum Publications.

Winnicott, D. W. 1969. The use of an object. *International Journal of Psychoanalysis* 41: 594–95.

Witheridge, T. F. 1985. The assertive outreach work: An emerging role and its implications for professional training. Paper presented at Wingspread, Racine, Wisconsin, May.

Witheridge, T. F., and Dincin, J. 1985. The Bridge: An Assertive Outreach Program in an Urban Setting. In L. I. Stein and M. A. Test (eds.), *The Training in Community Living Model: A Decade of Experience*. San Francisco: Jossey-Bass.

Witty, C. 1980. *Mediation and Society: Conflict Management in Lebanon*. New York: Academic Press.

Wolkin, A., Angrist, B., Wolf, A., Brodies, J., Wolkin, B., Jaeger, J., Cancro, R., and Rotrosen, J. 1988. Low frontal glucose utilization in chronic schizophrenia: A replication study. *American Journal of Psychiatry* 145: 251–53.

Wolpe, J. 1958. *Psychotherapy by Reciprocal Inhibition*. Stanford, CA: Stanford University Press.

Wood, K. M. 1978. Casework effectiveness: A new look at the research evidence. *Social Work* 23: 437–59.

Wool, R. L., Car-Kaffashan, L., McNulty, T. F., and Lehrer, P. M. 1976. Meditation training as a treatment for insomnia. *Behavior Therapy* 7: 359–65.

Wyatt, R. 1986. Scienceless to homeless: Editorial. *Science* 234: 1309.

Yamaguchi, K., and Kandel, D. B. 1984. Patterns of drug use from adolescence to young adulthood, III: Prediction of progression. *American Journal of Public Health* 74: 673–81.

Zetzel, E. R. 1971. A developmental approach to the borderline patient. *American Journal of Psychiatry* 127: 867–71.

Zung, W. W., 1971. A rating instrument for anxiety disorders. *Psychosomatics* 12: 371–79.